D0023169

ESSENTIALS OF FORESTRY PRACTICE

ESSENTIALS OF FORESTRY PRACTICE

4th Edition

Charles H. Stoddard
Resource Consultant
Formerly Director of the Bureau of Land Management

Glenn M. Stoddard
Executive Director of the Wisconsin Land Conservation Association

JOHN WILEY & SONS
New York • Chichester • Brisbane • Toronto • Singapore

Library of Congress Cataloging in Publication Data:

Stoddard, Charles Hatch, 1912-
Essentials of forestry practice.

Bibliography: p. 375
Includes index.
1. Forests and forestry. 2. Forests and forestry—
United States. I. Stoddard, Glenn M. II. Title.

SD373.S79 1987 634.9′0973 86-22408
ISBN 0-471-84237-0

Printed in the United States of America

10 9 8 7 6 5 4 3 2 1

ABOUT THE AUTHORS

Charles H. Stoddard, the senior author, is a natural resource consultant and tree farmer. During his professional career he has held positions of Director of the Secretary of Interior's planning staff and of the Bureau of Land Management. A graduate of the University of Michigan, Mr. Stoddard has also served as a research associate with the U.S. Forest Service and on the staff of Resources For the Future, the U.S. Senate Committee on Small Business and with the Minnesota Legislature's Interim Committee on Forestry. He is a long time member of the Society of American Foresters and has managed his own forest property in northern Wisconsin throughout much of his career.

Glenn M. Stoddard is the son of Charles H. Stoddard. He is a natural resources policy specialist and a northern Wisconsin tree farmer. Mr. Stoddard is the executive director of the Wisconsin Land Conservation Association. He has served as a forest policy analyst with the Wisconsin Legislature, as assistant director of the 1985 Wisconsin Governor's Commission on Agriculture and in various other natural resource positions. Mr. Stoddard is a graduate of the University of Wisconsin and a member of the Society of American Foresters.

To those unsung, stout-hearted idealists who have given unselfishly of their time, talents, and treasure to conserve America's unique natural environment for generations unborn.

PREFACE

The United States has entered an era of forest culture in which humans must assist nature to produce the abundance of timber crops required to meet the demands of a mounting population. American forestry now has a solid foundation of research. Since the first edition of this book, applied forestry has been practiced on a majority of our forest lands, private and public. This achievement has required increasing amounts of technical expertise. Professional foresters are finding that their efforts are most effective when they are carried out with the assistance of well-trained forest technicians and forestry aides capable of assuming responsibility for technical field work.

This book presents an expanded coverage of the basic and practical methods of forestry. The discussion of field practices and operations in timber growing, logging, protection, harvesting, and processing is designed to meet the needs of both those seeking an overview of the whole forestry field and of those needing a knowledge of principal forestry techniques used in woodland management. The results of recent research and future research problems are succinctly covered.

In recent years, a "knowledge explosion" has taken place in forestry as in nearly all other technical fields. The new developments run the gamut from measurements used in timber cruising, logging techniques, and methods for the control of forest fires and insect depredations to the impact of the use of forest lands for recreation. A wide variety of source material was reviewed, and the significant new developments were incorporated.

This book has proved to be well adapted to introductory college courses in forestry at the professional level as well as to the growing number of resource conservation courses requiring a comprehensive textbook in the forest resource sector. It has been widely used in forestry technician training programs and in vocational school courses. This textbook has also been used in farm forestry courses given in agricultural colleges and as a home study text for students and field employees unable to attend resident schools. It has proved suitable for in-service training classes such as those given by federal and state resource management agencies and private companies for nonprofessional field employees. Also, individual forest owners who seek a better technical grasp of their own private forestry management problems have found the book useful.

ACKNOWLEDGMENTS

In previous editions, Charles Stoddard acknowledged the assistance and help of the following friends and professional associates: M. W. Bryan, Dan Bulfer, the late S. R. Gevorkiantz, R. W. Harris, J. C. Kern, Elbert M. Little, Jr., Merle Lowden, C. W. Mattison, M. M. Nelson, William Parke, G. R. Salmond, Fred Simmons, Herbert Storey, and Lloyd Swift, all of the U. S. Forest Service. The assistance of C. W. Mattison has been extremely helpful at every stage. Source material from several Forest Service publications has been used with the permission of the Forest Service.

Also helpful were George B. Amidon, Boise-Cascade Corporation; Kenneth B. Pomeroy and William E. Towell, American Forestry Association; Solon Barraclough; F. H. Eyre, The Society of American Foresters; Frank H. Fixmer, Mosinee Paper Mills Co.; James McClellan and John Witherspoon, American Forest Products Industries; Clarence Prout and Edward Lawson, Minnesota Department of Conservation; E. W. Littlefield, New York State Department of Conservation; Charles G. Geltz, Professor Emeritus, University of Florida, and Carl J. Holcomb, Virginia Polytechnic Institute. Jay H. Cravens, who was especially helpful in reviewing and commenting on the whole manuscript, made a number of valuable suggestions for improving the use of the text in teaching forestry students.

The authors are also indebted to the following men, who have brought to their attention a large number of new techniques: Archie Craft, U. S. Department of the Interior, Bureau of Land Management; H. R. Josephson, U. S. Department of Agriculture, U. S. Forest Service; Arthur B. Meyer, editor, *Journal of Forestry*, Society of American Foresters; U. S. St. Arnold, U. S. Department of the Interior; Edwin Zaidlicz, U. S. Bureau of Land Management; and Donald H. Graves, superintendent, and Robert L. Howard, instructor, Department of Forestry, University of Kentucky.

This edition has benefited especially from suggestions of the faculty of the College of Natural Resources, University of Wisconsin–Stevens Point; particularly helpful have been the following: the late Professor

James G. Newman, and Professors Robert J. Engelhard, Carl Lee, Robert W. Miller, Hans G. Schabel, William A. Sylvester, and Joseph Roggenbuck. Other most helpful reviewers include John Carow, Stephen Spurr, James Kennedy, and Charles Widmark. Their contributions have been particularly noteworthy in the many new and important additions that have been made in this edition to include the most recent developments in forest policy, national timber supplies, forest protection, methods of measuring forest lands and timber, processing forest products, multiple-use technology, forest recreation management, and administrative changes among the forestry organizations. Throughout the text, material is clarified wherever improvements seemed to aid class instruction.

Wolf Springs Forest
Minong, Wisconsin

CHARLES H. STODDARD
GLENN M. STODDARD

CONTENTS

APPENDIXES

Essentials of Forestry Practice

ONE

THE FORESTRY CHALLENGE

When the early explorers penetrated the American continent more than four centuries ago in search of yellow gold, they considered the vast forests covering hundreds of millions of acres an enormous obstacle to their ambitions. But this pessimistic view was promptly reversed by pioneer settlers who viewed the forests as green gold—source of timber for homes and shipbuilding, of wild game for food, and furs for trade—all for their use in an abundance they could never have imagined in their old world homelands.

From the very beginning of settlement, our forest lands have been a mainstay of American civilization. Land with rich soil was cleared for farming, while wood for building our cities, for export, for industrial raw materials, and for fuel to heat homes and drive steam engines was harvested from the abundant wild forests. The storehouse of timber seemed limitless for centuries as civilization pushed West. Today the last virgin stands of mature, marketable timber are being harvested in the western states and Alaska right to the limit—the shore of the Pacific Ocean.

The enormous abundance of American forests did not encourage prudence and care in their use. In fact, the opposite was the case. While logging over vast areas, much waste was left to rot, or worse, to fuel huge forest fires that set back regrowth many decades. Only during the present century has a deliberate effort been made to reverse the past three centuries of forest abuse. Substantial and encouraging progress is evident in the newly planted forests that cover the cutover lands. Given a chance and a helping human hand, nature's regenerative capacity is capable of restoring the productivity of American forests so that new crops of timber and other resources can be grown and sustained for future generations.

The role that forests play today in industrialized and urbanized America has, if anything, become even more important than ever before. In addition to supplying wood products for our economy, they perform a variety of vital environmental functions that have been largely taken for granted until recent decades. Regulation of stream flow essential to pure water supplies, prevention of soil erosion, opportunities for outdoor recreation by our urbanbound populace, a balanced habitat for fish and wildlife resources and a source of livestock forage are some of the auxiliary benefits from the multiple uses of forest lands. And our concern over air pollution has made us especially aware of the critical role of the forest as a producer of oxygen through its photosynthesis process.

It is also useful to remind ourselves, as the world enters a new age of diminishing fossil fuel supplies, that our forest lands will be called upon, once again, to supply fuel wood for home heating and for industrial power. Trees, in the final analysis, are nature's way of storing solar energy.

The practice of multiple use forest management makes possible the production of timber crops and other benefits by applying scientific principles of ecology. Over many scores of years foresters have developed a variety of techniques applicable to the several forest types and regions that can unite the production of timber crops with wildlife, watershed, recreational, and livestock uses.

WHAT IS FOREST CONSERVATION?

Conservation of all natural resources has come to mean wise use and management. Gifford Pinchot, a pioneer American forester, described conservation as meaning "the foresighted utilization, preservation and/or renewal of forests, waters, lands, and minerals, for the greatest good of the greatest number for the longest time." On forest lands this means growing and managing timber crops so as to obtain the maximum yields of timber, wildlife, and watershed protection and other values without destruction of the forest or its soil. Because trees

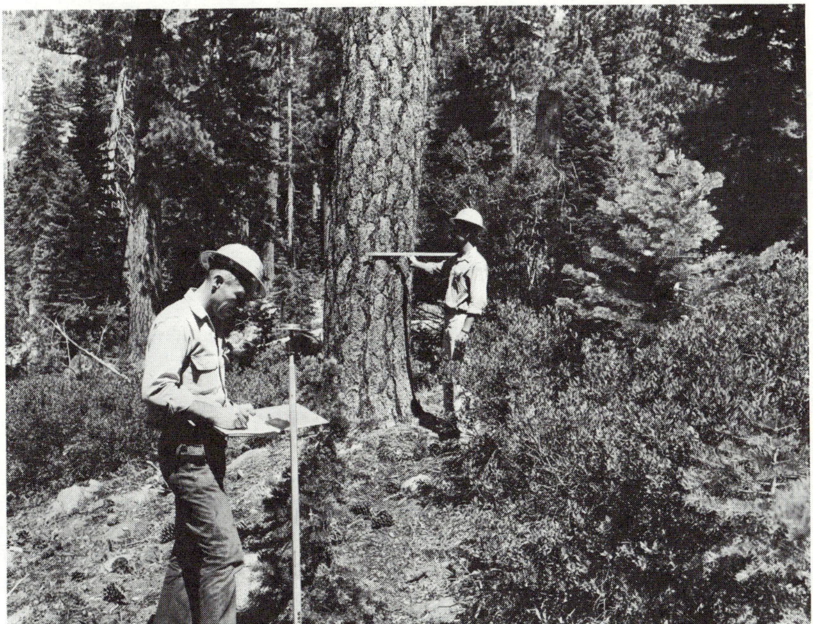

FIGURE 1–1. Foresters cruising (estimating volumes and mapping area) ponderosa pine timber. The man on the left is mapping forest cover type as well as tallying trees measured by the man on the right. (U. S. Forest Service)

may take two decades or more to produce marketable timber products, forestry requires special knowledge of: their growth habits; the methods for their protection from fire, insects, and disease; measuring and mapping them; tree planting; and methods for harvesting the crop. In some ways forestry is similar to agriculture, but the length of growing time and the size of the final crop, coupled with difficult social and ecological factors create important differences. That is one reason why a forestry career appeals to young people of vision and foresight.

Forestry programs require trained people who have skills in the many aspects of forestry and conservation. While more professional foresters will continue to graduate from the forestry colleges in the country, there are opportunities for forestry technicians possessing the necessary training and experience for important field jobs.

In Germany, where forestry has reached a high degree of development, one person trained in forestry techniques is responsible for the supervision of each 1200 acres. One in six of these people is a

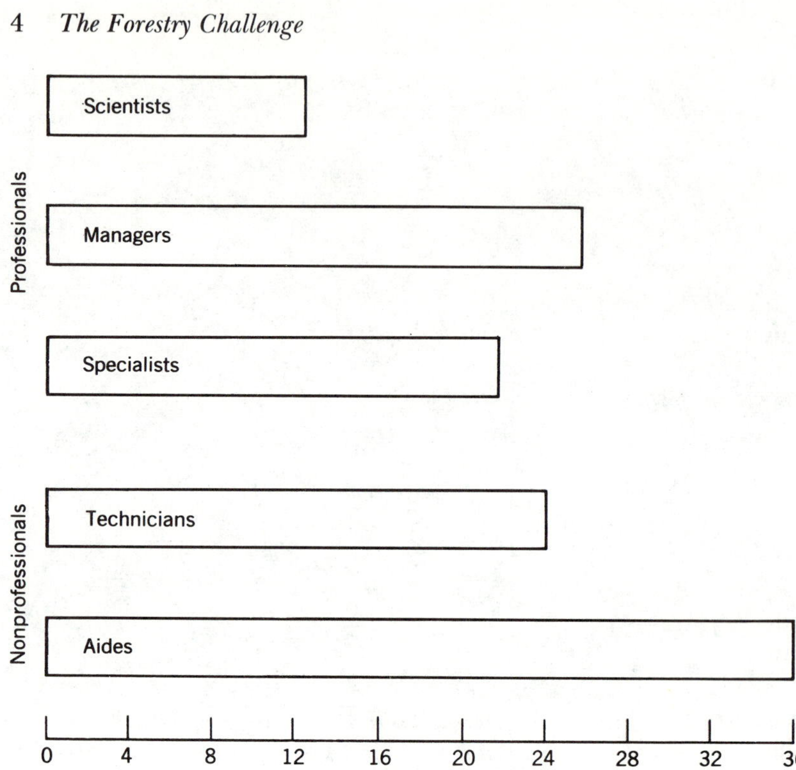

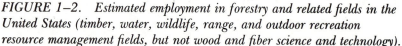

FIGURE 1–2. Estimated employment in forestry and related fields in the United States (timber, water, wildlife, range, and outdoor recreation resource management fields, but not wood and fiber science and technology).

graduate of a professional forestry college. The other five have technical or vocational school training.

Professional foresters and technicians will be needed to carry out reforestation programs for the millions of acres of forest land that lie unproductive. Other millions of acres of young trees require intensive stand improvement efforts—thinning and sanitation cuttings. Protection programs against fire, disease, and insects will be needed with increasing intensity as these young forests increase in acreage and size. For the person willing and able to obtain the education needed, forestry opportunities will continue to be abundant (Figure 1–2).

EDUCATION IN FORESTRY

Training in forestry is available at several levels: professional programs of forestry located at universities and colleges offer courses of study leading to various degrees in forestry, and a number of technical schools offer training in field techniques for the forestry technician. In addition, home study, in-service training, and special short courses are available for people on the job and for forest landowners and managers seeking a working knowledge of practical forestry. The Society of American Foresters in Washington, D.C., can furnish information on institutions that offer forestry related educational opportunities.

The student who is seeking a professional forestry career will find this book a source of information concerning the major aspects of American forestry. It will serve as an introduction to the important specialized details with which a professional forester must be familiar and as a general survey of the forest situation in the United States. Each of the chapters treats one or more topics which are subjects of separate college courses and which are covered separately in special textbooks. Professional foresters will be concerned in their careers with overall management, planning, and supervision of forestry programs, forest research, or with the execution of policies. And, in addition, they must be intimately familiar with all technical details and be able to integrate them toward a unified management program.

Another large group of people interested in acquiring a working knowledge of forestry are the owners of small private forests—more than 4 million in all. Small private forest owners and farmers are an important segment of forest products producers. Currently, commercial timberlands held by farmers and other private owners total 278 million acres, some 58 percent of the commercial forestland area in the United States. There is a tremendous need for these private forest owners to manage their land more intensively in order to realize their potential contribution to the timber demands of society and to the income of the owners. As farmers or woodland owners, they are occupied with other activities most of the time, but when a forestry problem comes up—such as when logging is to be done or replanting is to be carried out—they must turn to a reliable source for help. The advice of a professional forester is the first step, and the next step is to put the forester's recommendations into practice. Many of the chapters of this book will be helpful in giving specific directions on how to conduct various forestry measures in the field. The book may also be used as a source of reference for many of the details of these practices.

Professional foresters, forestry technicians, and landowners will find it easier to visualize many of the technical field practices after they obtain an understanding of the agencies and organization of forestry programs. A review of the job descriptions will be helpful in understanding how forestry work is conducted in the field and how responsibilities are divided.

PERSONAL REQUIREMENTS FOR A FORESTRY CAREER

A genuine preference for outdoor work and a feeling of being "at home in the woods" are essential characteristics of a career forester. But merely liking the outdoors is not enough. One must spend some time in the open, learn some of the trees, and acquire an interest in the plant and animal life of the forest. Forestry does offer many inspiring experiences and challenges, but it is also hard work requiring many public contacts.

The qualities needed on most other jobs of responsibility are needed in forestry. These need not be listed here, but it should be pointed out that the forester and forest technician are on their own a good deal more than is the case with most jobs. The boss cannot always be looking over their shoulders. They will need to take responsibility willingly, use initiative, and go about their work in a business-like manner. Forestry work will be rewarding in many more ways than most routine desk jobs. And opportunities for advancement will develop with work done well.

The field of forestry has developed to the point where there are many subdisciplines that may be entered during a person's career. These include public relations, silviculture, research, administration, data management and computer programming, economics, planning, policy, and other disciplines; all carried out as important parts of modern forestry in both the public and private sectors. For this reason, many foresters and forestry students are obtaining education in these specific disciplines to augment their traditional forestry training. And many colleges and technical schools offering forestry education are now requiring students of forestry to enroll in a broad array of classes covering many of these disciplines.

The field forester or technician, however, is still the person who in many ways must carry out things in the forest. For this reason, good field personnel will always be necessary.

FIELDS OF WORK

Up to the end of the first decade of this century, the U.S. government was the principal employer of American foresters. Since then, the states, municipalities, educational institutions, and private corporations have absorbed large numbers of forestry-trained individuals. However, even with the expansion of private industrial forestry activities in recent years, public agencies still remain the largest employers of trained foresters.

Federal Forestry Activities

Although a majority of foresters now employed by the federal government are in the Forest Service of the Department of Agriculture, many are employed in the management of forest lands on Indian reservations under the Bureau of Indian Affairs, by the National Park Service, the Bureau of Land Management, and by the Fish and Wildlife Service of the Department of Interior; by the Tennessee Valley Authority, and by the Soil Conservation Service of the Department of Agriculture, and by other federal agencies.

In addition to its permanent force of professional foresters, the Forest Service also employs forestry technicians and aides, soil and water scientists, wildlife biologists, landscape architects, and clerical, administrative, custodial, protection, and construction personnel. About two-thirds of this staff is employed in the national forests as supervisors, assistant supervisors, rangers, and so forth. The remainder is engaged in administrative, scientific, and clerical work at the Washington, D.C. and regional headquarters, the Forest Products Labo-

FIGURE 1–3. This forest, located in the state of Washington, was named for this country's pioneer forester. It is 1 of 155 national forests managed by the U. S. Forest Service. (U. S. Forest Service)

ratory, the forest and range experiment stations, or in state and private cooperative work in various parts of the country. In addition, lookouts, patrollers, fire fighters, scalers, tree markers, and other forestry workers are employed seasonally in the national forests. Foresters are also assigned to wildlife management, recreation area supervision, management, fire control, and a variety of other land-use–related responsibilities.

Some forestry activities are open to people trained in forestry in the Department of Interior's National Park Service, the Bureau of Land Management, the Bureau of Indian Affairs, or in the Fish and Wildlife Service. The Office of Personnel Management, which has long provided opportunities for college-trained foresters, is finding the demand for forestry technicians and aides by these agencies to be increasing and is making more and more openings available as federal forestry work expands.

The national forests, which are the responsibility of the Forest Service, are shown on the map in Figure 12–2. (See Chapter 12 for a discussion of federal forestry programs.) Industrial and state forests are not shown, but they include much of the area between and some within the public forests in the forested areas. Farm and other small forests are scattered over most forest regions but are located mainly in the eastern half of the country.

State Forestry Programs

Forestry work in the states has made notable progress in recent years, and all states now employ foresters in various capacities. The state forester usually assumes heavy responsibilities as the director of a large organization responsible for the annual disbursement of large appropriations. About 27 million acres of land in state and municipal forests are managed intensively, along lines similar to national forest management. Some state forests and parks are devoted primarily to public recreational use.

State activity in protecting forests from fire, with the cooperation and financial aid of the federal government, has opened a field for the employment of many foresters. Trained individuals are also used in the propagation and distribution of planting stock. In those states where an active state forestry program has been developed, a number of trained foresters are employed. The state forester's staff may include technical assistants in immediate charge of the various lines of activity carried on by the state organization. District foresters or state forest rangers may be assigned responsibility for the development and maintenance of the fire-control organization and other state forestry work in a designated part of the state. The work of the state district forester corresponds generally with that of a federal district ranger except that usually he or she deals cooperatively with private forest landowners in addition to supervising work on the state forests under his or her direct charge. Extension and intensification of cooperative technical assistance to landowners on a scale commensurate with the needs would call for employment of many additional foresters and forestry technicians in state forestry work.

Forest Products Industries

Although federal and state agencies, educational institutions, and semipublic associations will doubtless continue to lead in research and extension, an increasingly important field for foresters and forestry technicians will be in private work. Three-fourths of the 347 million acres of commercial forest land is in private ownership. This fact alone clearly indicates a large and fruitful field in private work for the trained forester.

Private owners may be classified in a general way as industrial, including lumber, pulp, and paper manufacturing companies, and other large manufacturers of wood products; public service companies, such as railroads and water companies; recreation and hunting clubs; mining companies; owners of large private estates; and farmers and other small woodland owners. Many of these owners are included in the private Tree Farm System and practice good forestry (Figure 1–4).

The person who enters the lumber, pulp, paper, or other forest products industries may be assigned to estimating standing timber (*cruising*), appraising stumpage, determining the best methods of cutting, making growth studies, surveying for logging roads, and many types of duties on logging and milling operations. Many forestry-trained people find opportunities in this field, with possibilities of advancement to important managerial positions.

Other Private Forestry Work

A growing field for forestry is among public service corporations owning timberlands. Some railroads and public utilities own extensive tracts in need of management. Mining companies frequently hold considerable areas for mineral development that can be managed for timber, wildlife, and other uses.

Another kind of private owner consists of clubs or individuals who have acquired forest property for hunting, fishing, and other recre-

FIGURE 1–4. This well-managed private forest, located in California, is a part of the Tree Farm System sponsored by the American Forest Institute, Inc.

ational purposes. On such properties, work on the ground is usually supervised by a resident woods manager under the direction of a consulting forester who visits the tract at intervals and works closely with the land manager or owner. There are now many private consulting foresters who also employ field assistants for field work on the tracts of forest owner-clients.

Forest Owner Management

One important purpose of this book is to provide owners of woodlands with the essential information for the management of their properties. Although they may obtain the assistance of professional foresters in making plans, the foresters' recommendations can be executed more effectively with an understanding of technical details. The forest owner may select from the material presented here the information needed for each special situation.

DESCRIPTIONS OF FORESTRY POSITIONS

Young people trained in forestry generally start at the forestry technician level, from where new opportunities for advancement will develop. They may start at any one of a number of positions (e.g. compassperson on a timber survey crew, fire-control aide, forest fire dispatcher, insect and disease control, marking timber for sale, scaling logs, or maintaining forest roads and trails, to mention only a few). Their training courses will have prepared them to take on most such assignments, and these courses will give them the opportunity to show their supervisors that they have sound technical training. One good way to get started is on a summer job with one of the forestry agencies or companies. This can then lead to a permanent assignment.

Federal Agencies

The minimum of a high school education is usually required to acquire introductory work at a federal agency. Experience is counted heavily and forestry training is given credit in federal Civil Service examinations. Qualifying by starting as a seasonal employee is often the route to permanent employment. Beginning employees are usually assigned to positions that include the principal titles and duties listed below.

Fire-Control Aide

Under direction of the forester, the fire control aide detects, locates, and reports fires; patrols fire lines; occupies forest fire towers, assists in organizing and works with fire-fighting crews; maintains and repairs fire-fighting equipment and tools; works on fire prevention, slash disposal, forest insect and disease control programs, and other work related to the above; makes inventories and surveys; and keeps records and makes reports.

Forestry Aide

A technician who has been made a forestry aide assists in timber cruising and mapping forest areas; marks timber for timber sales; directs forest planting crews; marks forest boundaries; scales (measures) logs on timber sales; does tree and log grading; assists in maintenance work on recreational areas; handles range management work and wildlife habitat improvement under the direction of the forester in charge; and assists in research investigations.

Forest Engineering Aide

Under the supervision of a forest engineer, this technician assists in surveying roads and trails; in the construction of roads, dams, and watershed improvements; and in the establishment and maintenance of recreational facilities.

State Forestry Agencies

Jobs in the state conservation departments are quite similar to those in the federal service but also include general forest fire prevention and control as well as technical aid services to private owners. Entrance requirements for many state forestry jobs emphasize field experience and offer many opportunities for promotion within the organization to those with less formal education, but with initiative and ability. The following list summarizes some of the titles and duties of forestry technicians employed in state forestry jobs:

Forest ranger or district forester	In charge of forest fire control activities in district, under supervision of the district forester.
District fire warden	In charge of fire control crews; issues burning permits.
Forest fire patrolman	Patrols forest fires after they have been brought under control.
Timber scaler	Measures logs and pulpwood on state timber sales.
Timber sales marker	Marks timber prior to sale.
Fire dispatcher	Handles central coordination of fire detection and control in the district forestry office.

Salaries in state forestry work compare well with other types of state employment. As a rule, they have retirement provisions, sick leave, and annual leave. Generally speaking, state forestry technicians will live in a town near the area where they work, but not necessarily in the forest. Occasionally, the state furnishes living quarters in state forests.

Private and Industrial Forestry

Working with one of the large paper companies or lumber companies with huge tracts of forest land offers one of the most challenging jobs in forestry. The forester will not specialize in one job or another but (usually) will shift from one job to another as the season progresses. For example, in the spring the forester may supervise a planting crew reforesting idle land, but the planting crew will have to be ready for a fire call at any time. In the summer, the crew will be out thinning overcrowded young forests, marking timber for stand improvement, or controlling disease or insect outbreaks. By fall they may shift over to marking timber for a winter logging job or help the forester in charge cruise timber on a tract of land that the company is purchasing. When winter comes, foresters are busy checking loggers to see that they are cutting the right trees, scaling logs on the decks, and dispatching truckers to the mill with loads of logs.

Generally, the descriptions of industrial forest job duties are not given in the same detail as in the public agencies. This is partly due to the wide range of activities involved.

Types of Duties for Forestry-Trained People

The following responsibilities are frequently assigned to those skilled in forestry practice. In many cases a forester will be doing several of the jobs that may develop during the course of the year because of seasonal variation in work requirements: tree planting in the early spring, forest fire protection in the dry seasons, marking timber for cutting any time, and so forth. Some of the beginning jobs to which the newly trained people would be assigned when they arrive at their first assignment are the following.

Timber Cruising Appraisal and Inventory

These highly skilled functions are usually undertaken by the professional forester with the assistance of forestry technicians or aides. They require considerable experience and additional training to handle well. All of these functions require knowledge of the several methods of estimating volumes of standing timber, and methods of financial evaluation.

General Engineering

The forestry aide or technician assists civil engineers in road location, surveying, and topographic mapping in advance of logging, as well as supervision of road, bridge, and other heavy construction.

Compassperson

Compasspersons on a timber survey party must be able to read and use the compass to run the line for the estimators who determine the tree volume and sketch the map as the party progresses. They must also be able to run out boundaries, read maps, and pace distances.

Planting Crew Supervision

The reforestation crew supervisors are assigned the task of training and supervising unskilled labor in tree planting—both machine and hand operations. They must call for seedlings at the nursery, know how to care for them until time for planting, show the crew how tree planting is properly done, and inspect their work as they proceed to make sure that the seedlings are properly set in the ground.

Marking Timber

Tree markers must be able to determine the proper trees to be marked for thinning, stand improvement cuttings, and harvesting, and to instruct untrained markers in the methods of selection. Knowledge is essential to defend the choices of marked trees to a superior.

Scaling Pulpwood and Logs

Log scalers measure the logs cut during logging operations and record them in a tally book. They must learn to use the log scale stick, learn the elements of volume tables, and know how to deduct for defective material in logs as well as be able to identify the species. A knowledge of pulpwood volumes, log grades, and other forest products is required. Much of this same work is done in sawmill and paper mill yards, at veneer mills, and at other industries where logs are purchased from independent loggers.

Forest Fire Detection and Control

Forest fire dispatchers are usually assigned to the central ranger station, where they operate as the nerve center of the forest fire protection system. After the towerperson calls in the bearings of a fire, the dispatcher must be able to use these bearings and distances to locate the fire on the map, before sending the suppression crew out to the job. Accurate records of the time fires are reported, their location, the length of time needed to control and put them out, must be kept.

Checking Timber Sales

Timber sale checkers are assigned to see that the requirements of a timber sale contract are lived up to—that the loggers cut low stumps, that they only cut designated trees, that good utilization is practiced, that slash is properly disposed of, and other requirements met.

Controlling Insects and Diseases

Insect or disease control crew supervisors are assigned to such work as the supervision of white pine blister rust control or bark beetle control. Some previous knowledge of these activities is essential, but those with training and a little experience will have no difficulty in assuming such responsibility.

Inspecting Forest Practices

Many states have minimum forest practice cutting laws requiring forest owners to harvest their forests in such a way as to leave adequate growing stock for another crop of timber. In order to enforce such laws, these states have forest practice inspectors who are familiar with logging methods, principal species, and other aspects of this assignment.

Multiple Use Supervision

In addition to technical forestry functions, the forest land manager must give attention to recreation use and development, to the effect of logging and road building on watershed conservation, sometimes to livestock grazing and mineral development, and always to wildlife. While specialists in these fields are available to help on more difficult problems, multiple use decisions often fall to the forest manager.

Public Relations

To convey the idea that forest land should be producing timber crops, much educational work is done by foresters at various times of year. Exhibits at fairs, talks before sportsmen's clubs, 4-H groups, scouts, and garden clubs often fall to the local foresters because they are considered the authority on the subject in their locality. Supervision of group tree-planting programs, fire prevention crusades, and similar activities will occasionally draw on the forester's time.

QUESTIONS

1. What has the term "conservation of resources" come to mean?
2. What must America's forests produce in the future, besides wood?
3. Name four important kinds of forestry work.
4. What are the two main classifications of forestry-trained people?
5. Give three major kinds of organizations employing professional foresters and forestry technicians.
6. Where do forestry personnel find more employment: in public agencies or private forestry programs?

7. Do you think that an interest in the outdoors is important in a forestry career? Why?
8. What value does a knowledge of forestry have for the forest owner?
9. Why does competence in forestry require both study and field work?
10. Why are more trained forestry technicians needed now (and in the future) than in the past?

EXERCISES

1. Find out what private and public forestry programs are being carried on in your locality.
2. Discuss different types of forestry jobs with one or more professional foresters or forestry technicians in your area and find out what qualifications are expected.

TWO

Forestry—Yesterday, Today, and Tomorrow

The field of forestry has a long and rich history that was as much a part of folklore as it was a developing practical science. Forestry as a distinct discipline began in Europe but was brought to the United States in the latter part of the eighteenth century by foresters who had received their training overseas.

A BRIEF HISTORY OF FORESTRY IN THE UNITED STATES

When the North American continent was first settled by European immigrants, a vast area of forests stretched from the Atlantic Coast to the Great Plains, broken only by middle western prairies (Figure 2–1). Farther west, forests covered much of the Rocky Mountains and other ranges and the northern portion of the Pacific Coast region. It is estimated that the forests of the continental United States, excluding Alaska, once covered 820 million acres—more than 40 percent of the total land area.

In contrast to Europe, which has less than a dozen commercial tree species, the new settlers found well over 100 conifers and broadleaved trees in the East alone. Western forests, which are mainly coniferous, contained additional species—many larger than any found elsewhere in the world.

Early settlers viewed the forests as a mixed blessing. A source of building material and fuelwood as well as game for food, the forests could be cleared for cultivation only with backbreaking labor. For nearly 200 years (1620–1800), settlement was limited mainly to the coastal plain and piedmont between the Atlantic and the Appalachians. But timber—white pine lumber and oak for shipbuilding—made an important contribution to the Colonial trade because it was abundant and easily obtained.

The greatest onslaught on our forests took place during the century following the Revolutionary War. Lands were cleared for farms throughout the South, Middle West, and mountainous portions of the East; many of these lands proved to be too poor for agriculture. Commercial lumbering, which was begun in New England by the colonists, was extended into New York and Pennsylvania prior to the Civil War. Following the war and during the remainder of the nineteenth century, the great pine forests of the Great Lake states were the main source for the nation's lumber market. From 1900 and continuing for nearly 40 years, the southern pine forests became the major source of forest products for the nation. In recent years, the Douglas-fir forests of the Pacific Northwest have become the nation's chief source of timber supplies.

In the process of supplying a growing nation with lumber, vast areas of timber were cut over with little thought of regrowth. In the United States, forestry as a method of growing a timber crop was unknown. It was believed by all but a few doubters that all the cleared land would be needed for farms, and what was a cheaper way of doing it than by logging and uncontrolled forest fires? The main difficulty was that the lands with the most marketable timber were frequently too sandy or rocky for profitable agriculture. Too often new communities sprang up around sawmills and lumber camps, flourished for a time, and then became stranded ghost towns in a desert of stumps. Long before there was serious danger of our national timber supplies becoming exhausted, thoughtful people became concerned with the manner in which the forests were being exploited. As might be expected, there was resistance to many of the conservation proposals, but public opinion ultimately demanded that action be taken.

The earliest laws passed by Congress between 1799 and 1831 regarding the nation's forests were intended to ensure supplies of live oak for shipbuilding. During the nineteenth century, several states inquired into the possibilities of action to protect their forest resources

FIGURE 2–1. This stand of old-growth northern hardwood in Wisconsin is a remnant of the vast virgin forest that once extended from the Eastern seaboard to the prairies. (U. S. Forest Service)

and laws to encourage tree planting were passed in some states. In 1875 the American Forestry Association was founded to educate people on the need for conservation measures. Not until 1891, however, when the national forest system was started, did the conservation movement get under way on a nationwide scale. An act of Congress in 1891 authorized the establishment of the Forest Reserves and marked the real beginning of a national forest conservation policy. And the Forest Service Organic Act of 1897 gave the authority to manage these lands according to forestry principles.

1905 The act of February 1, 1905, provided for the transfer of the forest reserves from the Department of the Interior to the Forest Service in the Department of Agriculture. Gifford Pinchot was appointed the first chief forester. The present Forest Service dates from this act. When the Forest Service took charge, there were 60 forest reserves with a net area of some 62 million acres of land. During his administration, from 1901 to 1909, President Theodore Roosevelt added a total of 128 million acres to the established reserves. The name "Forest Reserves" was changed in 1907 to "National Forests" because "reserve" implies that the area is withdrawn from use.

President Theodore Roosevelt held the famous White House conference of governors, May 13–15, 1907, to consider the fact that our natural resources were being consumed, wasted, and destroyed at a rate that threatened them with exhaustion. As a result, an inventory of our natural resources was published in 1909.

1911 New national policy was established by the Weeks law, which authorized the purchase by the federal government of forest lands necessary to the protection of the headwaters of navigable streams.

1916 The National Park Service was organized in the Department of the Interior.

1924 The Clarke–McNary law extended the federal land purchase policy under the Weeks law of 1911. Lands necessary for the production of timber, as well as for the protection of navigation, within the watersheds of navigable streams could be purchased. This law also authorized the Secretary of Agriculture to enter into cooperative agreements with the states for the protection of state and private forests against fire. State and private owners were to contribute not less than half the total cost. Other sections of the law provided for studies of forest taxation, cooperation with the states for the establishment of shelterbelts, management of farm woodlands, and cooperative work in farm forestry extension.

1927 One of the first private sustained-yield management programs was adopted by the Goodman Lumber Company in Wisconsin. The same year, the Wisconsin Legislature enacted the landmark Forest Crop Law to encourage the reforestation of cutover lands through property tax deferral.

1928 The Woodruff–McNary Act, approved April 30, authorized a series of yearly appropriations up to a total of $8,000,000 to protect watersheds of navigable rivers. The McSweeney–McNary Act of May 22 authorized a program of forest research to "insure adequate supplies of timber and other forest products, to promote the full use of timber growing and other purposes of forest lands in the United

States, including farm wood lots and those abandoned areas not suitable for agricultural production, and to secure the correlation and the most economical conduct of forest research in the Department of Agriculture. . . ." For the first time a forest inventory was authorized to establish basic facts on the forest resources.

1930 The Knutson–Vandenberg Act of June 9 authorized the Secretary of Agriculture to expand tree-planting operations on the national forests and pay for them out of receipts from timber sales.

1933 On March 21, President Franklin D. Roosevelt sent to Congress his message urging legislation to relieve unemployment, to train men, and to build up the nation's forest resources by the establishment of the Civilian Conservation Corps (CCC). During the life of the CCC program, more than 2 million young men participated, and a vast amount of forest protection, tree planting, watershed restoration, erosion control, and other resource improvement work was accomplished. The first major industrial effort to establish large-scale forestry on logging operations came about during the New Deal's National Recovery Act in 1933, when Article X of the National Recovery Act (NRA) Lumber Code included requirements for minimum forestry practices.

The Forest Service prepared and sent to the Congress "A National Plan for American Forestry," popularly known as the Copeland Report. The main recommendations for a satisfactory solution of the nation's forest problem were (1) a large extension of public ownership of forest lands, (2) more intensive management on all forest lands, and (3) public control over private forest cutting practices. The Tennessee Valley Authority (TVA), which was established in 1933, also developed an active forestry and watershed management program.

The Soil Erosion Service (which later became the Soil Conservation Service) and the Agricultural Adjustment Administration were also established in the middle 1930s. These agencies developed large-scale programs for the conservation of land and soil resources and helped many farmers improve their management of soil. The Taylor Grazing Act of 1934 established a permanent system of conservational management of the federal grazing lands in West that were still held as Public Domain.

1937 The Norris–Doxey Cooperative Farm Forestry Act provided for increased technical forestry aid to forest owners.

1937 Oregon and California Act of 1937. The Nation's first public sustained yield forestry law was passed by the Congress to apply to western Oregon forest lands under the Bureau of Land Management (BLM).

1940 President Franklin D. Roosevelt combined the Bureau of Fisheries and the Biological Survey into a Fish and Wildlife Service in the Department of Interior, under Ira N. Gabrielson, its first chief. All wildlife programs (migratory waterfowl, fish hatcheries, and research) were brought under this bureau.

1941 The forest industry Tree Farm movement was born in the state of Washington. Currently owners of nearly 80 million acres of private forests (30,000 Tree Farms) will be cooperating in this program.

1941–45 World War II caused heavy inroads on the nation's forests, as wood became a critical war material. Although winning the war was the most important thing, more forestry legislation was passed by the 78th Congress (1943–45). The Clarke–McNary Act was amended to authorize increased appropriations for cooperative fire protection, and appropriations were made to keep forest surveys up to date.

Private industry, which had only begun to practice forestry on a portion of its own lands prior to World War II, began an extensive program of management. In addition, the paper industry was active in purchasing very extensive holdings in both the South and Pacific Northwest.

1944–46 An international organization for forestry was started under the auspices of the United Nations Food and Agriculture Organization (FAO).

A special amendment to the federal income tax favored private forestry and encouraged many landowners to begin a sustained yield program.

1946 The American Forestry Association called a postwar forestry conference to develop a program to meet the changing forestry problem.

1945–47 The Forest Service completed an appraisal of the forest situation, which showed that there had been a marked deterioration in quality as well as quantity of timber during the war. Cutting practices were poorest on small private forest lands and best on large private forests and public forests.

The forest industry responded to the growing need for more intensive forestry by establishing large acreages of well-managed company forests in every region of the country, and by developing an educational program through its American Forest Products Industries organization. Marked progress in better forestry on larger ownerships took place.

1947 Congress passed a Forest Pest Control Act which provided for federal cooperation with the states and private owners to control outbreaks of forest insects and diseases. Private consulting foresters became active in large numbers during the postwar period.

1952–57 The Forest Service undertook a new appraisal of the forest situation under the title *Timber Resource Review*. The details of subsequent studies findings are set forth in a following section.

At the same time the strength of several forest conservation programs was tested by proposals in Congress designed to provide certain groups with special rights in the public forests. These measures met defeat partly because of organized resistance from the citizens' conservation movement.

In 1953 the American Forestry Association called an American Forestry Congress, which recommended a series of policy proposals, and Resources for the Future, sponsored by The Ford Foundation, called a "Mid-Century Conference on Natural Resources" which provided a forum for all proposals and suggestions on needed resource programs.

In 1956 the National Park Service embarked upon "Mission 66," a program designed to improve many of the park facilities needed for increasingly intensive uses. The Forest Service undertook "Operation Outdoors," a similar program for the national forests.

1958 The Outdoor Recreation Resources Review Commission, appointed by President Eisenhower and headed by Laurance S. Rockefeller, made very comprehensive surveys of the nation's future demands and needs for outdoor recreation facilities. Its work culminated in a large number of reports and recommendations including the establishment of a Bureau of Outdoor Recreation (BOR) in the U.S. Department of the Interior in 1962. (The BOR changed to the Heritage Conservation and Recreation Service in 1977.)

1960 The Multiple Use Act and the Sustained Yield Act (P.L. 86–517) for National Forests broadened the authority of the Forest Service to manage National Forests for all consistent uses including timber, wildlife, grazing, watershed, minerals, wilderness, and recreation.

1964 The Land and Water Conservation Fund Act provided for new sources of revenue for the acquisition of national parks, national forest recreation lands, national recreation areas, and grants to states for state recreation lands and facilities.

1964 The Multiple Use and Classification Act authorized multiple use management on public domain lands under the Bureau of Land Management for a five-year period until the Public Land Law Review Commission recommendations determine the future of public domain lands.

The Wilderness Act provided for preservation of a few million acres in National Forests and Parks and Wildlife Refuges as a remnant of the original frontier wilderness.

1968 National Trails Systems Act created a national system of recreation and scenic trails.

Wild and Scenic Rivers Act preserved selected rivers or sections thereof in free-flowing condition to maintain water quality.

1969 National Environmental Policy Act provides for appraisal of federal programs in terms of their environmental impact.

1970 Youth Conservation Corps Act provided employment and training of youths for the purpose of developing, preserving, and maintaining the lands and waters of the United States.

1974 The Forest and Rangeland Renewable Resources Planning Act called for an assessment of 1.6 billion acres of the nation's forest and rangeland and broadened the integrated planning approach to National Forests.

1976 The National Forest Management Act, a long and involved piece of legislation enacted after the clearcutting controversy, essentially requires interdisciplinary planning of national forest operations including timber harvesting *before* logging takes place to prevent environmental damage and to assure prompt regeneration of new forests.

1976 The BLM Organic Act finally established resource management authority for the Bureau of Land Management over the residual public domain by repealing disposal laws and permitting classification of administrative units (National Resource Lands) similar to National Forests and Parks.

1980 The Alaska National Interest Lands Conservation Act established federal land use and management authority over millions of acres of remaining federal land in Alaska. It is widely regarded as one of the most sweeping conservation laws in history.

All of these great steps forward in building our conservation programs were brought about by the hard, patient efforts of a few far-sighted persons, often opposed by powerful forces who viewed them as radical visionaries. But for their persistent efforts and intelligent idealism, few of these programs would have developed.

OUR PRESENT FOREST SITUATION

Forest Area

A recent analysis by the U. S. Forest Service indicates that the United States has a very large forest resource. Approximately 737 million acres, or one-third of the nation's land area, is forested. Nearly two-thirds of this, or 483 million acres, is classified as commercial timberland capable of producing at least 20 cu. ft of industrial wood per acre per year and not reserved for uses incompatible with timber production.

About three-fourths of the forested area of the United States lies east of the Great Plains, and most of it is in second-growth or young timber. The other fourth, still with a considerable area of virgin sawtimber, is located in the Rocky Mountain and Pacific Coast regions.

The commercial forest area is divided almost equally between softwoods (conifers) and hardwoods (broadleaved trees). The western forests are nearly all in softwoods, while slightly more than half of the southern forests, and about five-sixths of the northern forests, are in hardwoods.

Timber Volumes

The commercial timberlands of the United States contain approximately 792 billion cu. ft of sound wood, with about 64 percent of the total in sawtimber trees and about 26 percent in poletimber trees—collectively defined as growing stock (Table 2–1).

Softwoods constitute about 61 percent of the total volume of all classes of timber and about two-thirds of growing stock. Almost half of the softwood growing stock and 59 percent of the sawtimber inventories are in the Pacific Coast region of the country. This is a significant contrast to the distribution of commercial timberland, which is predominantly in the East. It reflects the concentration of the softwood sawtimber inventory in the West, most of which is in the Pacific Coast states of Oregon and Washington. In terms of volume, the most important species in the West are Douglas-fir, ponderosa pine, and the spruces.

Eastern softwoods, mainly southern pine species, constitute about 20 percent of the nation's growing stock, and about 17 percent of softwood sawtimber volumes. Most southern pine timber is relatively small (normally less than 15 in. in diameter), whereas softwood timber in the Pacific Coast region is much larger (generally 19 in. or more in diameter).

Hardwood species make up about 39 percent of all classes of standing timber and about 27 percent of all sawtimber. Just over half of all hardwood growing stock is in the northcentral and northeastern parts of the country, and about 41 percent is in the South. The remainder of hardwood growing stock is in the West, primarily in the Pacific Coast region. Of the total hardwood sawtimber volume, about two-fifths, or 232 billion board feet (b.f.), is in select species including red and white oaks, hard maple, yellow birch, sweetgum, yellow pop-

TABLE 2–1 LAND AREA OF THE UNITED STATES, BY SECTION AND TYPE OF LAND

Type of land	*Total United States*		North (million acres)	South (million acres)	Rocky Mountain (million acres)	Pacific Coast (million acres)
	Area (million acres)	Proportion (percent)				
Commercial timberland	482.5	21.4	166.1	188.0	57.8	70.5
Other forest land						
Productive reserved	20.7	.9	6.1	2.1	8.4	4.1
Productive deferred	4.6	.2	.2	.1	3.2	1.2
Other	228.8	10.1	5.3	16.7	68.4	138.4
Total	254.1	11.3	11.5	18.8	80.0	143.7
Total forest land	736.6	32.7	177.7	206.9	137.7	214.3
Other land[a]	1,518.2	67.3	445.9	300.3	416.1	356.0
Total land area	2,254.8	100.0	623.6	507.1	553.8	570.3

Source: U. S. Forest Service.

[a]Includes rangeland, cropland, pasture, swampland, industrial and urban areas, and other nonforest land.

Note: Data may not add to totals because of rounding.

lar, ash, black walnut, and black cherry. These are preferred species for furniture, paneling, and other uses that demand high quality and surface appearance considerations. The remaining hardwood sawtimber, about 361 billion b.f., is composed of upland oaks, hickory, beech, cottonwood, and other species that have somewhat limited potential for high quality products. However, most of this timber is well suited for the manufacture of railroad ties, pallet lumber, construction timber, and other such uses.

Quality of Timber Stands

By and large, American forests are far below their productive potential for wood products. About one fourth of all forest land is understocked, and about four-fifths of the hardwood forests contain growing stock that is low quality, defective, and unsalable. The Forest Service has estimated that most of these hardwood forests will require cultural treatments such as cull removals, thinnings, and improvement cuttings to achieve the production of high-quality timber. Under- and interplanting with more desirable tree species would improve productivity even further.

Timber Growth and Cut

On the brighter side, total growth has been increasing more rapidly than the volume removed in recent years. But much of this growth has been in hardwood growing stock, whereas most of the cut has been in softwood sawtimber. However, currently about as much sawtimber is being grown as is being cut (for the first time in recent history) and more growth is being laid on poletimber than is being cut. Better forestry on the same forest area could increase our present growth even further.

Mortality Losses

Vegetative competition, insects, diseases, fire, storms, pollution, and other destructive agents cause the annual mortality of about 4 billion cu. ft of growing stock and about 12 billion b.f. of sawtimber volume in the United States. Most sawtimber mortality has been in the softwood species of the Pacific Coast region because of the area's high proportion, and volume of old-growth timber.

Though the uses are somewhat limited, part of the annual mortality is salvaged. The Forest Service estimates that in a recent year about 22.5 million cu. ft of dead softwood timber and 55 million cu. ft of dead hardwood timber was salvaged. This represented only 10 percent of the mortality of softwood and only 3 percent of hardwood mortality.

TABLE 2–2 NET VOLUME OF GROWING STOCK AND SAWTIMBER ON COMMERCIAL TIMBERLAND IN THE UNITED STATES, BY SOFTWOODS AND HARDWOODS AND SECTION

Growing Stock	*All Species*		*Softwoods*		*Hardwoods*	
Section	Volume (million cu. feet)	Proportion (percent)	Volume (million cu. feet)	Proportion (percent)	Volume (million cu. feet)	Proportion (percent)
North	173,145	24.4	44,574	9.8	128,571	50.4
South	202,009	28.4	97,136	21.3	104,873	41.1
Rocky Mountain	99,814	14.0	94,935	20.8	4,879	1.9
Pacific Coast	236,000	33.2	219,134	48.1	16,866	6.6
United States	710,968	100.0	455,779	100.0	255,189	100.0
Sawtimber						
	(million b.f.[a])	(percent)	(million b.f.[a])	(percent)	(million b.f[a])	(percent)
North	359,021	13.9	96,504	4.9	262,517	44.2
South	614,709	23.9	341,023	17.1	273,686	46.1
Rocky Mountain	390,169	15.1	380,380	19.2	9,790	1.7
Pacific Coast	1,215,042	47.1	1,167,503	58.8	47,539	8.0
United States	2,578,940	100.0	1,985,408	100.0	593,532	100.0

Source: U. S. Forest Service.

[a]International ¼-in. log rule.

Note: Data may not add to totals because of rounding.

In the past, most salvaged timber has come from major catastrophes such as storms or fires when the large timber volumes have made salvage operations economically advantageous. Most other scattered mortality can only be harvested economically during normally scheduled harvesting or commercial thinning operations.

Acid rain and other precipitation resulting from atmospheric pollutants is now widely recognized as a cause of forest mortality in some regions of the United States. It is not clear whether salvage operations will be economically feasible in areas affected by acid rain, or whether future losses will be prevented by pollution controls.

Forest Ownership

Forested lands owned by farmers and other individual private land owners—a diverse group that includes an economic and cultural cross section of the population exclusive of forest industries—total some 278 million acres, or about 58 percent of the commercial timberland in the United States. Another 69 million acres, or 14 percent, is owned by forest industries. The remaining area, some 136 million acres, or 28 percent of the total, is in public ownership; and of this, the largest part is in the National Forest System, which contains 89 million acres (Table 2–2).

Generally, the best managed and most productive forests are owned by large industry and the government, whereas the poorest and least intensive management is found on farms and other small private forests. The difference in productivity between these ownership classes is due to a number of factors including widely divergent ownership objectives, tenure of ownership, knowledge of forest management principles, and the availability of forestry expertise and assistance.

It is widely accepted that the greatest opportunity for increasing forest productivity is in improving the management of small private forests held by farmers and other individual landowners. The challenge lies in providing adequate assistance and in convincing these owners of the multiple benefits that can be realized by the owner, the forest ecosystem, and society as a whole from good forest management.

STEPS TOWARD MORE INTENSIVE MANAGEMENT

It is generally accepted that the Forest Service figures on the present forest situation are accurate and that they faithfully reflect the status of our timber resources as far as it is humanly possible to measure them. Differences have cropped up over the interpretation of some of these figures, particularly over the amount of timber we will need in the future. Some people believe that the United States will need less wood per person than the Forest Service estimates if wood declines in importance or increases in price. Others believe that more wood will be needed as other nonrenewable resources become more scarce.

Regardless of whether the United States has a high or low per capita rate of wood consumption, considerably more wood will be required to meet the needs of an expanding population. As a provident nation we will need to undertake the following measures to meet future wood supply demands: a more effective job of protecting our commercial forests from fire; a more intensive and integrated program of pest, insect, and disease control; an all-out effort to prevent forest mortality from pollution, including acid rain; increased tree planting on bare, understocked, and harvested lands; a vigorous program of thinning, stand improvement, and other forest cultural measures on millions of acres of public and private forests; a still better job of managing our forest harvest so as to protect watersheds, wildlife habitat, and aesthetics, and at the same time produce an ample supply of wood products; increased salvage logging operations to utilize dying trees before they decay; improving tree growth through selective breeding, fertilization, and nutrient recycling; and more effective land-use planning by all government and private owners to prevent the conversion of forest land to other uses. These and other intensive forestry measures will make it possible to grow more and better timber on our present forest acreage, both public and private. Jay H. Cravens, former regional forester and associate deputy chief of the U. S. Forest Service and professor of forestry at the University of Wisconsin at Stevens Point, has noted that "the greatest enemy of the forest is neglect."

QUESTIONS

1. When were the Forest Reserves set aside from the public domain?
2. In what year did President Theodore Roosevelt change the name of the Forest Reserves to National Forests?
3. Who was the first chief forester of the United States?
4. What president started the Civilian Conservation Corps (CCC), and in what year was it begun?

5. When did the forest industries' Tree Farm Program begin?
6. What is the present acreage of commercial forest land in the United States?
7. In what part of the United States is most of the sawtimber found today?
8. Which part of the country has the largest area of forest land?
9. Are American forests growing about as much, more, or less sawtimber than we are cutting?
10. How does the acreage of forest land owned by public agencies and private owners compare?

EXERCISES

1. What is the principal kind of forest ownership in your locality? What is next in importance?
2. Are most forest lands in your locality held in large or small tracts?
3. Do the forest lands appear to be well managed or neglected?

THREE

Characteristics and Growth Requirements of Forest Trees

The study of requirements and processes of tree growth and the environment under which it takes place is called *silvics.* Intelligent management of the forest must rest upon a solid foundation of knowledge of silvical processes. Identification of trees according to species has been termed *dendrology* and includes a study of all the significant identifying characteristics. Both of these topics are the subject of this chapter.

A knowledge of tree names, tree identification, and growth habits of trees are the fundamentals of the practicing forester. It is absolutely essential that the technician be able to identify the most important commercial trees in the part of the country where he or she lives or works, and to know the names of most other important timber trees in the United States. A few of the distinguishing characteristics must be memorized for each tree species.

It is one thing to learn to identify the tree as it stands in the forest or park and quite another to learn to identify the wood. Just as there are key characteristics of leaves, bark, fruit, and twigs to indicate the tree species, in the wood there are certain indicators that tell the expert how to find the name. Because wood identification is a special technical study that this book does not treat, it is suggested that this subject be made a topic for future consideration. Close observation of different woods, in the meantime, will be helpful in making important distinctions.

IDENTIFICATION CHARACTERISTICS

A tree is usually defined as a perennial woody plant with a single main stem (bole or trunk) attaining a height of 20 ft or more and a diameter of over 4 in. at maturity. Trees have three main parts: roots, trunk (or bole), and crown. Every tree has one or several common names, but only one scientific name in Latin. Latin is used universally because it is a "dead" language and no longer subject to change by usage.

Tree Parts

Positive identification of plants is ordinarily made by distinguishing tiny differences in the flowers, but leaves, bark, twigs, buds, and fruit (including nuts) are adequate for the practical forester. In summer one can identify a tree by the leaves or needles alone (in the great majority of species), but in winter, when the leaves of broadleaved trees have fallen, the other characteristics must be relied on. Figure 3–1 shows principal types of leaf forms for both hardwoods and conifers, which should be used as one important guide in identification. The identifying features of many important forest trees in the United States are set forth in Appendix B.

The twigs of a tree may be helpful as a means of tree identification when the leaves are off. Distinctive features of the twig are the bud, the bark, and the leaf scars formed after the leaf has fallen. Most of these features are sufficiently different in each species to be noted by close observation.

Bark is also one of the most important means of determining tree species, especially of mature trees when the leaves are off. As the new wood is made in the cambium layer, inner bark is pushed outward; the dead outer bark cracks into plates (or scales) and ridges in different ways for different species. In identifying both the bark and twigs there is no substitute for actual observation.

One of the best ways to learn to identify trees is to go on field trips

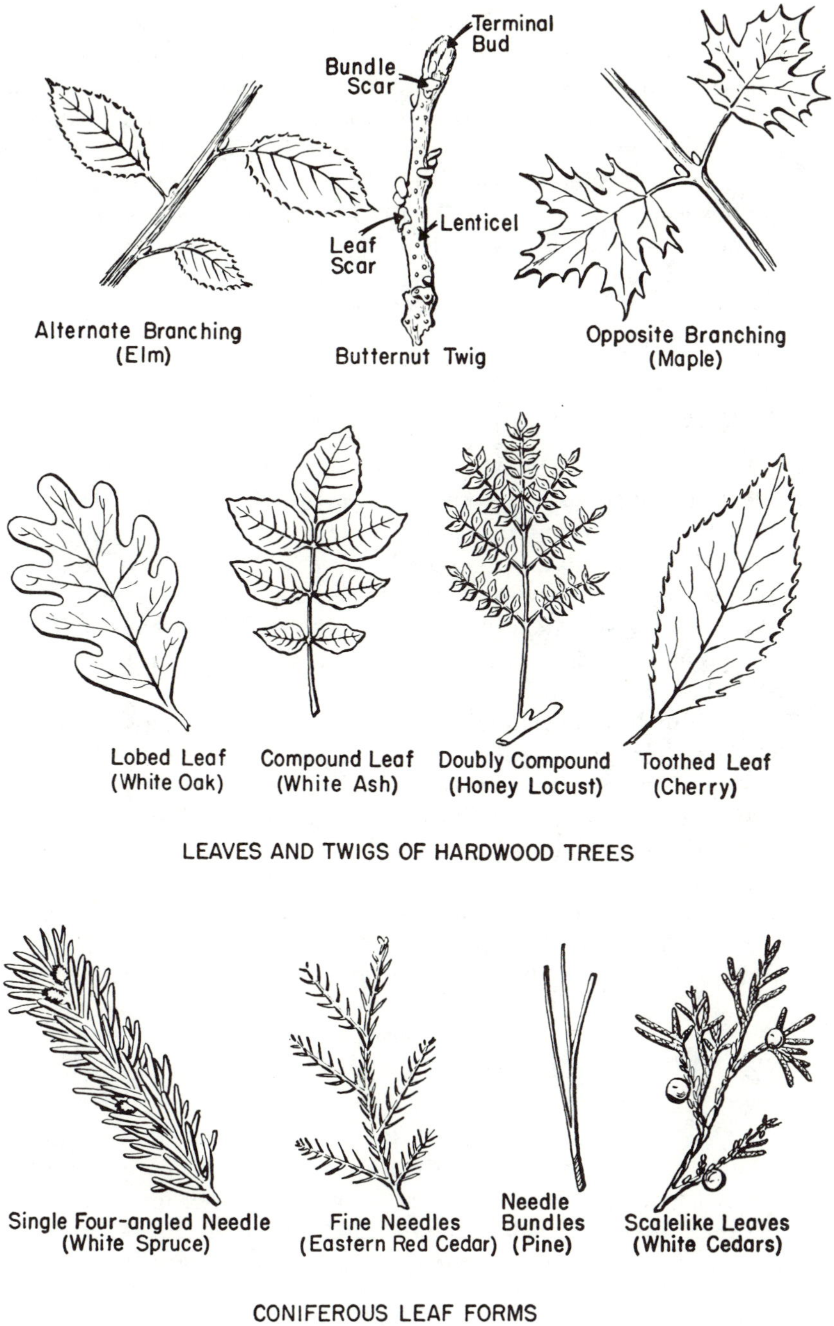

Terminal Bud
Bundle Scar
Lenticel
Leaf Scar
Alternate Branching (Elm)
Butternut Twig
Opposite Branching (Maple)
Lobed Leaf (White Oak)
Compound Leaf (White Ash)
Doubly Compound (Honey Locust)
Toothed Leaf (Cherry)
LEAVES AND TWIGS OF HARDWOOD TREES
Single Four-angled Needle (White Spruce)
Fine Needles (Eastern Red Cedar)
Needle Bundles (Pine)
Scalelike Leaves (White Cedars)
CONIFEROUS LEAF FORMS

FIGURE 3–1. Leaf and twig forms.

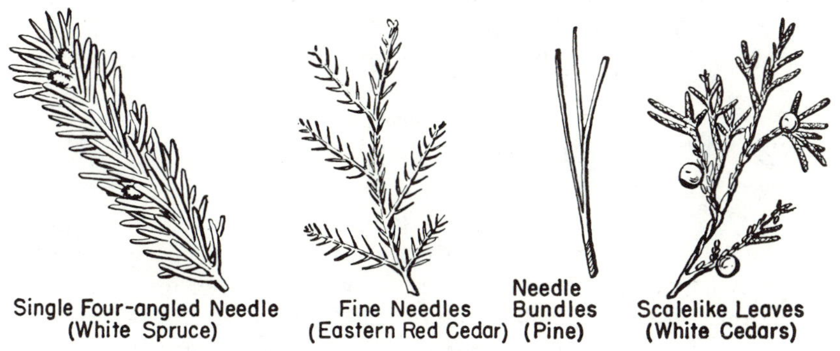

with someone familiar with each species of tree. One can then keep a record of the characteristics in a notebook for future reference. There are many books on tree identification that give the tree features, its range, and other pertinent information. Most states publish booklets describing the trees growing within their boundaries. It is suggested that students write their state foresters for one of these publications in order to develop their knowledge of trees in their part of the country. Appendix B briefly describes many of the most important commercial trees and is primarily for reference and not field use. This will be helpful in familiarizing oneself with the terms and descriptions used.

Tree Names

All timber trees are divided into two main groups: the conifers, which are the needle trees with cones, and the broadleaved trees. Deciduous trees drop their leaves in winter and are dormant, whereas evergreens do not. Most deciduous trees are broadleaved hardwoods; coniferous softwoods are evergreen with the exception of the larches and bald cypress. Although the terms *softwood* and *hardwood* are commonly used in the timber trade, some hardwoods such as yellow poplar and basswood have *soft* wood.

Botanists have developed a systematic method of classifying plants by classes, orders, families, genera, and species. The conifers are in the class Gymnosperms, and the broadleaved trees are in the class Angiosperms. Individual kinds of trees are called species,* and their scientific names always include both the *genus* and *species*. As an example, all oaks belong to the genus *Quercus*; white oak is called *Quercus alba* and northern red oak is called *Quercus rubra*. The pines are easy because they belong to the genus *Pinus*; white pine is *Pinus strobus* and Virginia pine is *Pinus virginiana*.

FUNCTIONS OF TREE PARTS

Tree roots serve a double purpose: to anchor the tree to the ground against winds and to supply the tree with water and chemical nutrients. Some species of trees have deep roots going well into the subsoil, whereas others are shallow rooted. Shallow-rooted species are usually found on moist sites where they do not have to reach far down for

*The term "species" is both singular and plural when used with plants and animals. The letter *s* is never dropped in the singular.

moisture. They are more subject to windthrow, especially when other trees are cut from around them and they are left to stand against the full force of the wind. Species that grow in swamps and bottomlands where surface moisture is usually present are generally shallow rooted. Deep-rooted trees found on higher sites are more resistant to windthrow. Some species with *tap roots* are very well anchored and stand up well against wind even when other trees are cut away. Open-grown trees are generally more windfirm than forest-grown specimens. Conifers may be either shallow or deep rooted, whereas broadleaved trees often combine both root systems.

The root system of a tree consists of the large main roots, root branches that bear smaller rootlets, and in some species additional fine root hairs. The root hairs and rootlets absorb water and dissolve soil nutrients that are carried up through the roots into the rest of the tree. Unlike most plants, some conifers and beech lack root hairs. This function is taken care of by mycorrhiza, associated organisms that attach themselves to the rootlets.

The trunk or bole of the tree contains layers of cells (see Appendix A for definition) that conduct chemical nutrients dissolved in water (sap) to the branches and leaves. It also acts as a storage area for some plant foods manufactured by photosynthesis and supports the whole crown. It is of course the most valuable part of the tree and the object of most foresters' attention.

The tree trunk consists of heartwood and sapwood, which are made up of a series of concentric growth rings, one for each year of the tree's life. The sapwood often shows as the outer, light-colored or white layer nearest the bark while the heartwood is the darker center of the tree. Sapwood (xylem) is made up of live growing cellular tissues that carry the sap up the tree. The heartwood of a tree is made of dead sapwood cells that have ceased to function, but continue to provide mechanical support. It frequently contains mineral or chemical deposits that give greater durability. Between the inner layer of bark (phloem) and outer layer of sapwood is the cambium layer, a thin layer of cells that does the growing for the trunk and lays on the diameter growth. On the outside of the cambium, the inner layer of bark (the phloem) conducts the food made in the leaves down to the branches, trunk, and roots for growth processes. Just outside the inner bark may be found a special cambium layer that makes bark tissue alone.

The crown of the tree is made up of branches, twigs, and broad leaves or coniferous needles. Larger twigs and branches have a wood structure similar to that found in the tree trunk. The smaller twigs contain conduction cells that carry the dissolved nutrients brought up from the roots to the leaves. With the aid of sunlight, the green-colored chemical in the leaves (called *chlorophyll*) absorbs carbon dioxide (CO_2) from the air and combines this with the water and nutrients to make carbohydrates in the form of sugars and starches. This process is called *photosynthesis*. Carbohydrates, often with nitrates and minerals, may be converted into proteins, fats, and other substances such as oils, resins, latex, pigments, tannins and other acids, vitamins, and alkaloids. The wood itself is a carbohydrate in the form of cellulose plus a chemical complex called lignin that binds the wood cells together.

One major use for the water carried up from the roots is for the manufacture of foods. Water also serves for the upward transportation of minerals and the downward transportation of the manufactured sugar and other chemicals for storage in the trunk and roots. Another function of water is to maintain an even temperature for the tree through transpiration and evaporation of moisture from the pores (stomata) of the leaves. The leaves, which break down carbon dioxide through photosynthesis, also return oxygen to the air in excess of that used in the manufacture of carbohydrates.

FALL COLOR

The colored substances in plants are known as pigments. In summer the bright green of plant life is caused by the pigment chlorophyll. During summer nights the sugars pass through the leaf veins into other parts of the plant.

There are pigments other than chlorophyll in green plants. If you place an object through which light cannot pass, such as a board, on your lawn for two or three days, the covered grass will become yellow. Chlorophyll is destroyed by the prolonged absence of light. Yellow pigment, *xanthophyll*, and orange-yellow pigment, *carotene*, become apparent. These yellow pigments are present in the green leaves, but chlorophyll is more conspicuous. In Indian summer, when night temperatures are in the 40s, and length of day decreases, photosynthetic activities in leaves cease. The plants lose much or all of the chlorophyll and yellow pigments become dominant, as in the autumn foliage of the cottonwood, aspen, birch, hickory, tulip poplar, oak, maple, and others.

Leaves of maples, especially the red maple, also develop a red pigment, *anthocyanin*, and may retain a little chlorophyll. In Indian summer anthocyanin pigments also develop in the leaves of scarlet oak, sourwood, dogwood, and certain other trees, shrubs and vines. Brown color in the leaves of beech and some oaks is caused by *tannin* in the leaves.

Our deciduous or broadleaf forests are found in the region southward from southeastern Canada through our eastern states to Georgia and Alabama. In this region there are many different kinds of trees, shrubs, and vines, and this is where you will find the most colorful array during Indian summer.

In New England the maples are especially colorful. From New England southward, especially along the mountains and foothills where there are numerous kinds of woody plants, the autumn coloring is unequaled anywhere in the world. In the central and western states, south of the Great Lakes, the yellow of cottonwoods and birches, and red of the oaks dominate. These, mixed with evergreen conifers, are very attractive.

HOW TREES START

Seed

Most people know how farm crops grow and produce seed. Trees, which go through exactly the same sort of process, have many ways of producing seeds. Some grow inside of fleshy fruits (the persimmon, plum, apple, and pawpaw), some have wings (the elms, pines, and maples), some occur in cones (pines, hemlocks, firs, and spruces), and others have the form of nuts (walnuts, hickory, basswood, and butternuts), some produce male and female organs in the same flower (apples, black cherry, elms, and basswood), some produce the male organs and female organs in separate flowers (walnuts, hickories, and maples), some have male and female trees (ashes and holly). Our pioneer forebears knew when good and bad seed years came for the oaks, hickories, walnuts, and beeches because the hogs that ran in the woods depended on the tree seeds or *mast* for sustenance. The factors that determine a good or poor seed year vary according to the species of the tree, and they often occur in fairly regular cycles.

Birds and rodents help a great deal in spreading the larger-seeded species. Squirrels often bury quantities of acorns and nuts in various places. Seeds from some light seeded species, such as maples, elms, ash, yellow poplar, sycamore, and cottonwood, catch the wind, which spreads them far beyond the limits possible for heavier-seeded species. Seeds from oaks, walnuts, hickories, basswood, pines, beech, maples, and black cherry are food for wildlife, which carry them considerable distances from the parent tree, thus spreading the species. However, distribution of seeds is not enough. They must have proper conditions to begin germination, and only a very, very small percentage of the seeds that are produced ever develop into seedlings.

Just as with any other seed that goes into the ground, tree seeds are specific in their requirements for germination. Most of them for example pine, elm, ash, yellow poplar, and birch, do much better if they lie next to the mineral soil and are covered up a little. Many seeds do not germinate unless they go through a very cold winter, as for example, thornapples, dogwood, and some pines. Some of the small, harder-shelled species, if passed through the digestive tracts of birds or animals, are in better condition for germination than before they were eaten. Thus, the fruits of honey locust and Osage orange are eaten by cows; red cedar, hackberry, and black cherry are eaten by birds, and the germinating quality of the seeds is improved.

Each species has definite requirements that must be met before the seed will germinate and become established. A proper supply of moisture is essential to good germination.

Sprouting

Most hardwoods reproduce not only from seed but also from sprouts. Examples are all species of oak and black locust. Redwood, bald cypress, pond, and shortleaf pine are the only important conifers in this hemisphere that sprout new growth from stumps. The stumps of young trees sprout much more vigorously than those of mature trees, and old stumps of many species do not sprout at all. Sprouts may come from both the stumps or the roots, but the highest yields come from the stumps. Black locust and aspen are the exceptions to this rule.

THE BATTLE FOR SURVIVAL

After seeds have once germinated, they are influenced by all the variations in conditions around them. Some species, such as cottonwood, willow, ash, white elm, sycamore, and hemlock, thrive in moist sites; other species, such as black walnut, southern yellow pines, and black locust, grow in full light and warm temperatures; still others, the hard pines* and many oaks, do well in dry situations. Species characteristic of moist shady sites and moderate temperatures are

*Hard pines include practically all pines not of the five-needle white pine groups: eastern and western white pines and sugar pine.

beech, sugar maple, dogwood, and hemlock. All sorts of combinations of these factors are found as requirements of different species.

Only a small proportion of the seedlings that germinate and get above the ground continue to grow. Many seedlings are apparently able to grow in competition with other types of vegetation such as weeds and shrubs. But they require light, moisture, and fertile soil to survive and develop. In the heavy competition of nature, only those plants best fitted to compete will survive. Seedlings that come through and finally outgrow the competing vegetation are usually in good condition and grow to maturity.

Ecology is defined as the study of all forms of life in relation to environment. Nut trees that depend on squirrels to plant their seeds and squirrels that eat some of the nuts have an ecological relationship. Hemlocks are dependent in their early years on shade-giving species for protection. The world of nature is full of ecological relationships. Birds feed on insects for food and nest in trees; birds often help in controlling outbreaks of damaging insects. Ecology is a highly complex subject but one that the forester must be aware of in managing a community of trees, plants, and animals.

HOW GROWTH TAKES PLACE

All new tree growth each spring comes from the *buds, cambium,* and *root tips* (see Figure 3–2). From the buds come leaves, flowers, and new twig growth. A good observer who is out in the woods frequently during early spring has seen the buds open slowly and new leaves appear. The new terminal growth on pines is often called a *candle* and is a lighter green color than the old growth of previous years.

Growth in tree diameter is due to the division and growth of the cambium cells which, as we have learned, occur just inside the bark and form a sheath around the tree. The initiation of growth is caused by hormones or *auxins* formed in the youngest cells. As these cells divide, new cells are formed and increased diameter results. Cells formed in the spring, when growth is rapid, are larger than those formed in the summer. In the *diffuse porous* group of hardwoods (birch, maple, beech, and red gum), however, the vessels (pores) are usually of uniform size. It is the difference between spring wood (lighter and wider) and summer wood that shows up as annual rings so clearly on the stump of a tree. *Ring porous* hardwoods, such as elms, oaks, and ashes, have distinct rows of tiny vessels at the edge of the spring wood.

The variations in the annual ring widths tell the story of a tree's growth. Thin rings can mean that the tree has been crowded, if it is

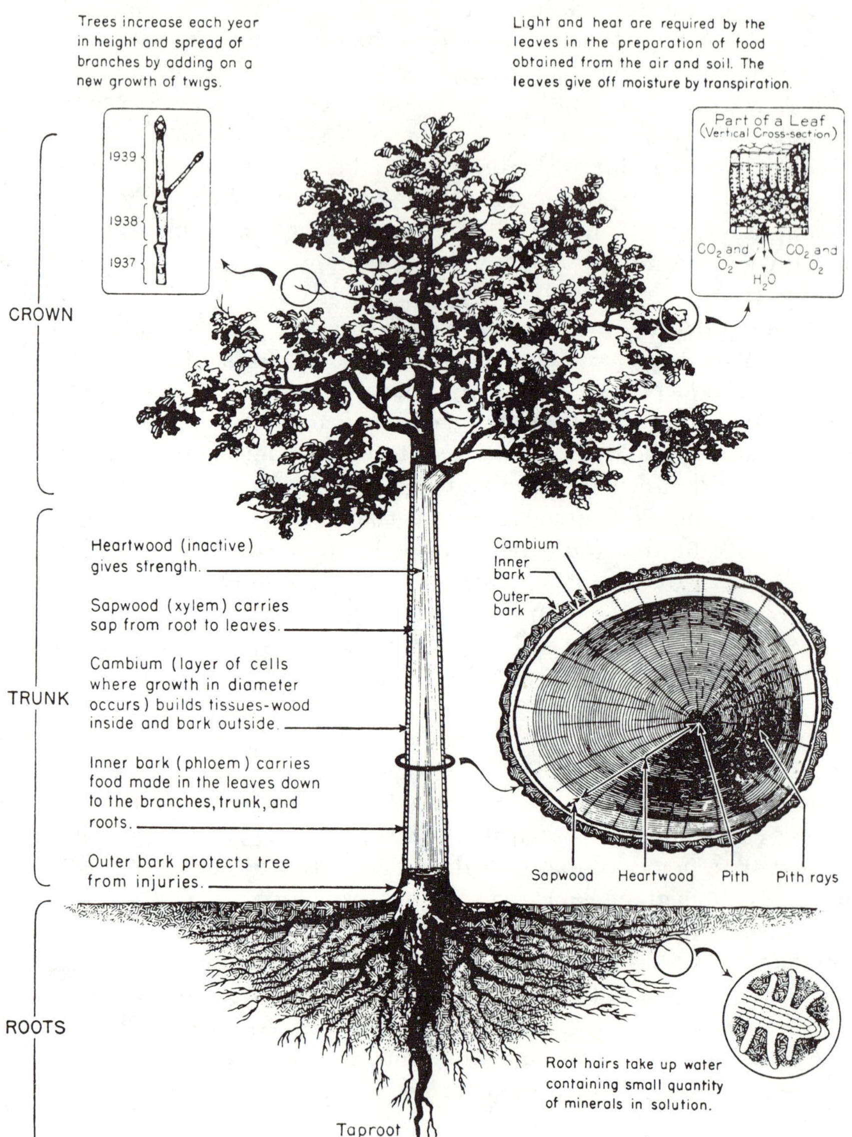

Trees increase each year in height and spread of branches by adding on a new growth of twigs.
1939
1938
1937
Light and heat are required by the leaves in the preparation of food obtained from the air and soil. The leaves give off moisture by transpiration.
Part of a Leaf
(Vertical Cross-section)
CO_2 and O_2
CO_2 and O_2
H_2O
CROWN
TRUNK
ROOTS
Heartwood (inactive) gives strength.
Sapwood (xylem) carries sap from root to leaves.
Cambium (layer of cells where growth in diameter occurs) builds tissues-wood inside and bark outside.
Inner bark (phloem) carries food made in the leaves down to the branches, trunk, and roots.
Outer bark protects tree from injuries.
Cambium
Inner bark
Outer bark
Sapwood
Heartwood
Pith
Pith rays
Root hairs take up water containing small quantity of minerals in solution.
Taproot
The buds, root tips, and cambium layer are the growing parts. The tree takes in oxygen over its entire surface through breathing pores on leaves, twigs, branches, trunk, and roots.

FIGURE 3–2. How a tree grows. (U. S. Forest Service)

in a dense forest, or that there has been a dry year, if it is in the open (see Figure 3–3). Wider rings show that plenty of sunlight and moisture are available to the tree. Well-spaced trees generally grow faster and produce wider rings than those under crowded conditions. When a tree is released from overtopping by another tree, its rings begin to widen within a year or two as it responds to the better growing conditions.

Young trees are vigorous and fast-growing. Old trees slow down in growth, eventually become overmature, and die if not cut. Overmature trees are less resistant to disease and insects and are therefore a poor risk. Rot frequently increases in old trees more rapidly than volume growth. The rate of growth of trees varies with species, with conditions of soil and moisture, and with the way in which the forest is managed and cutting is done.

Because photosynthesis takes place in the leaves, the number of leaves and the amount of light that they get determines, to a large extent, the rate at which trees grow. Therefore, the size of the top of a tree is important. It must also have plenty of room in which to expand and have a good chance at the available sunlight if it is to reach optimum size at maturity for the site.

FIGURE 3–3. Variation in tree growth rings. These trees were 10 years old when cut. (U. S. Soil Conservation Service)

Tree Age

The age of a cut tree can be determined by a careful count of annual rings from the middle of the stump to the outside bark. Several years should be added to the number of rings to account for the growth of the tree from ground level to stump height. To find the age or rate of growth of a tree without cutting it, foresters use a thin hollow auger (increment borer). It is drilled into the tree to the pith and the count of rings on the extracted cylindrical core shows the age.

Many conifers, such as red (Norway) pine, white pine, spruces, and firs produce one whorl of new branches each year near the top. The age of such trees, especially if they are not very old, can be found simply by counting whorls. This does not hold true with southern pines, however, which may form two or more whorls of new branches each year. Two periods of growth are not uncommon in the South, especially when growth is interrupted by a drought. As a result, two growth rings are occasionally produced in one year.

FACTORS OF SITE

The rate at which trees grow and the kinds of trees that grow on a given area depend upon the factors of *site*, which is defined as the combination of soil, moisture, and climatic factors present. Foresters have classified sites for tree growth based on the heights that trees will grow in a given time. Site quality is measured by the height to which each species grows in a given period of years, usually 50. Trees grow taller on good sites than on poor ones. *Site index* tables have been constructed so that it is possible to determine what the site quality may be for trees at any age beyond sapling stage.

Light Requirements

In managing a forest and applying forestry measures, one of the most important considerations is the degree of tolerance of each tree species to shade. Some trees require bright open sunlight and even a little shade will prevent them from growing. Others require much shade, especially in their early years, or they soon die. In deciding what species to plant, which trees to favor in thinning, and what trees to harvest and what to leave, tolerance is the primary factor to be considered. The classification of important timber trees according to a scale of tolerance is given in Table 3–1, at the end of this chapter.

Air

Trees growing in the open obtain sufficient oxygen, nitrogen, and carbon dioxide from the air. However, in cities and near some types of industrial plants, air pollutants and acid rain can adversely affect tree growth. Where there is too much pollution, as there is around some nickel and copper smelters, all vegetation may be killed. Air movement, especially high winds, often affects tree form. Timberline trees are bent and twisted by the constant winds found on high mountains. Windstorms may blow down large stands of trees. The amount of moisture held in the air (humidity) affects the rate of moisture loss from the leaves and often proves to be a limiting factor for some species. Oxygen can become a limiting factor for root system growth and vitality when they are smothered by flood waters or filling of soil around trees.

Temperature

Air temperature is especially important for tree growth. Some species can stand cold winters; others will die rapidly in prolonged cold spells. Likewise, some trees can grow in hot dry climates and others must grow in climates with more humidity. Some need cool fog belts to survive. Cool north slopes favor certain species, whereas on exposed southern slopes only species that can live in the hot, direct rays of the sun will survive.

Growing Season

Long growing seasons (as in the South) make for more tree growth than in the shorter seasons of the North. The volume of growth in any season is directly related to the amount of rainfall. Plenty of rainfall during the spring and summer results in better tree growth and wood production. Tree growth stops when annual rainfall is less than 20 in., as is the case in the Great Plains of the West. In the Tropics, where there are balmy temperatures and adequate rain all year, trees grow the year around. No annual rings are to be found.

Site Indicator Plants

Because a forest is a community of plants (trees, shrubs, and ground cover plants) it follows that certain combinations of species will be found in association with each forest type. For example, blueberry, wintergreen, and scrub oaks are usually present together on jack pine sites, whereas dogwoods, jack-in-the-pulpit and ironwood are present on northern hardwood sites. The redwoods of California are often found with a species of oxalis, or wood sorrel. These low growing plants are helpful to foresters and landowners in indicating which tree species will grow well on various sites. A thorough knowledge of plant indicators is best acquired through field observation and experience, but once gained such knowledge is very useful in forestry as well as other natural resources disciplines. In fact, for many years the use of plant indicators was the primary method of developing soil maps.

Soil Requirements

The soils on which forests grow vary greatly in texture, fertility, and water-holding capacity. Because the most fertile soils have been largely taken over for agriculture, forests now occupy more of the sandy, heavy, poorly drained, clay, rocky, swampy, and other kinds of soils unsuitable for farming. Silty soils are usually found in river bottoms; rocky and gravelly soils in glaciated areas of the northern states. Most other soils are derived from parent rock material that has been deteriorated by water, weather, and other natural actions.

Forest soils consist of several distinct layers or horizons, which are classified in the following manner.

1. Surface undecomposed and partly decomposed organic material, such as leaves, twigs, decaying wood and bark, unmixed with mineral subsoil.
2. Decomposed humus mixed with mineral particles of the subsoil.
3. An intermediate horizon of organic material and soluble salts carried down by water from the above layers and largely composed of mineral matter.
4. Several deeper layers that shade from those containing small quantities of dissolved organic chemicals on down to the basic subsoil derived from the parent rock material.

The surface soil acts like a sponge that absorbs water from rains or melting snow, stores some for future plant use, and permits the balance to filter down through to the subsoil where it eventually penetrates the ground water table. In open soils, where cover is absent and the soil particles are compacted, water tends to run off more

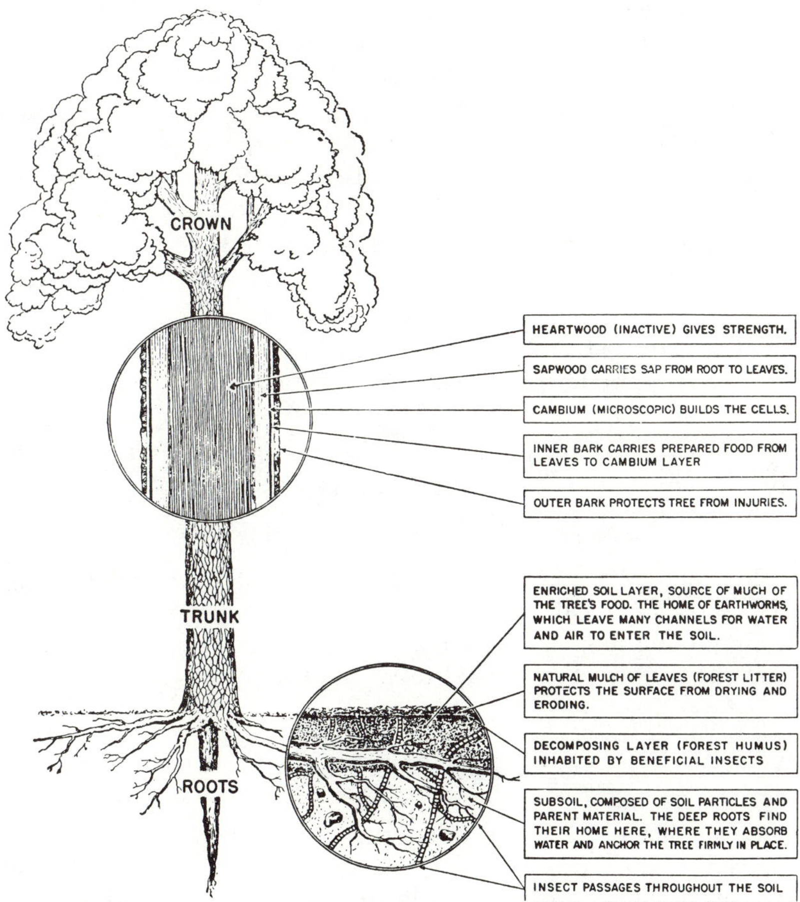
CROWN
TRUNK
ROOTS
HEARTWOOD (INACTIVE) GIVES STRENGTH.
SAPWOOD CARRIES SAP FROM ROOT TO LEAVES.
CAMBIUM (MICROSCOPIC) BUILDS THE CELLS.
INNER BARK CARRIES PREPARED FOOD FROM LEAVES TO CAMBIUM LAYER
OUTER BARK PROTECTS TREE FROM INJURIES.
ENRICHED SOIL LAYER, SOURCE OF MUCH OF THE TREE'S FOOD. THE HOME OF EARTHWORMS, WHICH LEAVE MANY CHANNELS FOR WATER AND AIR TO ENTER THE SOIL.
NATURAL MULCH OF LEAVES (FOREST LITTER) PROTECTS THE SURFACE FROM DRYING AND ERODING.
DECOMPOSING LAYER (FOREST HUMUS) INHABITED BY BENEFICIAL INSECTS
SUBSOIL, COMPOSED OF SOIL PARTICLES AND PARENT MATERIAL. THE DEEP ROOTS FIND THEIR HOME HERE, WHERE THEY ABSORB WATER AND ANCHOR THE TREE FIRMLY IN PLACE.
INSECT PASSAGES THROUGHOUT THE SOIL

FIGURE 3–4. The tree and the soil. (U. S. Forest Service and Soil Conservation Service)

rapidly, much less of it infiltrating to the subsoil. Soil erosion, siltation, and floods are more common on bare soil than where forests protect the surface. Soil characteristics strongly influence the rate of growth and distribution of different tree species. Fertility, composition, texture, and water-holding capacity, all strongly influence forest yields.

Different tree species have varying soil requirements. Pines, for example, are best suited to light sandy or gravelly soils whereas hardwoods require heavier and richer soils. There are exceptions to both generalizations. The following data describes the soil requirements of many important commercial species that should be kept in mind, particularly on reforestation plans.

1. *Light upland soils* (sandy, gravelly, or other well-drained soils). Jack, Virginia, red (Norway), lodgepole, loblolly, shortleaf, longleaf, and ponderosa pines. Oaks often occur on these sites also.
2. *Slightly more moist but well-drained poor upland soils* (mixed with clay or loam). Eastern and western white pines, sugar pine, eastern and western hemlocks, Douglas-fir, balsam and other true firs (oaks also found here), red and white spruce.
3. *Upland moist, well-drained better soils* (clays and loams). Birch, beech, cherry, elm, hickory, maple, aspen, sweet gum, Sitka spruce, western larch.
4. *Bottomland and cool rich silty moist soils.* Cottonwood, yellow poplar, sycamore, western red-cedar, Port-Orford-cedar, coast redwood, walnut.
5. *Swampy mucks and peats* (the better the drainage the better the site for growth). Black spruce, bald cypress, eastern and southern white-cedars, tamarack.

Slope or aspect is an important determining factor in tree location. Dry south- and west-facing slopes may support species that can only live in the full sunlight. Cool moist north and east slopes are favored by shade and moisture-loving trees.

OTHER SILVICAL FEATURES

Some characteristics of individual species have been discussed—tolerance for shade, root systems, preferred soil conditions, and locality of growth. These are inherent in the nature of the species just as some birds, such as quail, prefer fence rows whereas others, such as the ruffed grouse, like the deep woods. Some species of trees live longer than others. Some reproduce quickly and easily; others are very demanding in the seedbed requirements for young seedlings. Certain species are quite temporary, giving way to species that are relatively permanent. A forest composed mostly of permanent species is referred to as a *climax* forest.

Some species have a long life span; for others, it is quite short. Aspen, paper birch, jack and Virginia pine, for example, seldom live much more than 50 years. This is generally true of species found in *temporary* forest types. Climax species such as oak, maple, white pine, and hemlock, which grow to larger sizes, live much longer. This aspect of ecology, of great importance to the forester, is called *ecological succession.* Table 3–1 shows the relative position of many important species in the scale of succession.

TABLE 3–1 SOME SILVICAL CHARACTERISTICS OF IMPORTANT FOREST TREES

Species	Rate of Growth	Repro-duction	Succession Place	Longevity	Tolerance
		Pines (eastern)			
Jack	R	E–M	P–S	M–S	I
White	R	E–M	S–C	L	M
Red (Norway)	R	D	S–C	M–L	I
Shortleaf	R	M	P–S	M–L	I
Slash	R	E	P–S	M	M
Longleaf	R	D	P–S	L	I
Loblolly	R	M	P–S	M–L	I
Virginia	M	E	P	S	I
		Pines (western)			
Ponderosa	M	M	P–C	L	I
White	R	E	S	L	M
Lodgepole	M	E	P	M–S	I
		Other Conifers (eastern)			
Balsam fir					
Black spruce	R	E	S–C	S	T
White spruce	S–M	E	S–C	M–L	T
Red spruce	M–R	M	S–C	L	T
Hemlock	R	M	S–C	L	T
Tamarack (larch)	S	M	C	L	T
Northern	R	M	P–S	M	I
white-cedar	S	M–E	S–C	L	T
Bald cypress	S	M	C	L	M
		Other Conifers (western)			
Larch	R	E	P–S	L	I
Engelmann spruce	S	D	C	M–L	T
Douglas-fir	R	M	S	L	I
Western red-cedar	M–R	E	C	L	T
Western hemlock	M	E	C	L	T
White fir	R	E	S–C	M	T
Coast redwood	R	D	C	L	T

TABLE 3–1 CONTINUED

Species	Rate of Growth	Repro-duction	Succession Place	Longevity	Tolerance
			Hardwoods (eastern)		
Sugar maple	M–R	E	C	M–L	T
Beech	M	E	S–C	M	T
Black cherry	S	D	S	M	I
Northern red oak	R	D	S–C	M	M
Basswood	R	M–D	S	M	T
American elm	R	M	S	M–L	M
Yellow birch	M–S	M	S–C	L	M
Black walnut	M–R	D	S	M–L	I
Shagbark hickory	S	M	S	M	I
Tulip (yellow) poplar	R	M	S	L	I
White oak	S	M	C	L	M
Red gum	R	E	P–S	M	I
All aspens	R	E	P	S	I
All ashes	M–R	M–E	S	M	M

Source: Adapted from Forbes and Meyer (1955, Section 6, Table 2) and Wenger (1984, Section 1, Table 1).

Note: Rate of growth: R (rapid), M (medium), S (slow).

Rate of reproduction: E (easy), M (medium), D (difficult).

Place in succession: P (pioneer or temporary), S (subclimax or transition), C (climax).

Longevity: S (short, up to 50 years), M (medium, 50 to 100 years), L (long, over 100 years).

Tolerance of shade: I (intolerant), M (intermediate), T (tolerant). Tolerance applies largely to trees in early growth stages. Even the most tolerant species in youth require full sunlight to attain optimum growth during maturity.

The growth habits of trees are important in shaping their development. Black cherry, for instance, will bend and twist toward open sunlight in the forest canopy, often developing a crooked trunk. Some species grow much more rapidly than others on the same site. White pine will grow 2 to 4 ft a year, whereas hemlock may add only 4 to 6 in. to its height. Black walnut seldom grows in groups, more often with other species.

In Table 3–1, five important silvical characteristics are set forth for a number of commercial species as a guide to the forestry manager and forest owner. This information applies entirely to those parts of the tree's range and those sites where it makes its best growth.

QUESTIONS

1. What is the definition of a tree?
2. Name the three main parts of a tree and give the functions of each.
3. Why do trees have scientific (Latin) names?
4. What does the process of photosynthesis do for plants?
5. What parts of the tree are used to distinguish one species of tree from another?
6. How can one tell the age of a tree from the stump?
7. Give the definition of *site* as used by foresters.
8. What function does the cambium layer have in a tree?
9. What do wide annual rings show about a tree's growth? What do narrow rings show?
10. Name one species of tree with a compound alternate leaf. Name one with a simple opposite leaf.
11. What is meant by *tolerance* in a tree?
12. Why do shade-tolerant species form all-aged forests and intolerant species even-aged forests?

EXERCISES

1. Collect and identify the leaves or needles of 12 trees growing in your locality.
2. Name three tolerant and three intolerant local species.
3. Identify three species growing on moist soils (river bottoms or swamps) and three growing on light upland soils.

FOUR

THE COMPOSITION AND DISTRIBUTION OF FORESTS

The forest is more than a group of individual trees—it is a complex plant community. Because the community includes not only trees, but shrubs, annual plants, soils, and animal life of many kinds as well, it might be compared with human community relationships in a city or town. The individual trees in a forest are as interdependent with other living things as are the people in a community.

To be classed as a forest, a group of trees must have crowns close enough to encourage natural pruning by shading the lower limbs and an accumulation of undecomposed and decomposed material overlying mineral soil. Other associated elements usually include smaller plants and many forms of animal life. A new plantation of small pines cannot meet these standards, nor can trees in a city park, nor scattered remnant trees after heavy logging.

CLASSIFICATION OF TREES WITHIN A FOREST

Within the forest it has been helpful to classify individual trees in a number of ways as an aid to forest management. The most important are shown in the following groupings.

Classification by Size

Beginning with the smallest and youngest size classes, the following groupings are based upon dbh. (diameter breast high) and height of the tree.

Seedlings, up to 4.5 ft high

Saplings, 4.5 to 10 ft high and up to 5 in. in diameter

Poles, 5 to 11 in. in diameter

Small saw timber, 11 to 15 in. in diameter

Saw timber, 15+ in. in diameter

Classification by Position in the Stand

Another basis for classification of trees is by the relative position of their crowns in the general level of the forest canopy (the covering formed by the interlacing of tree crowns). This crown classification is more useful in even-aged forests. (See Figure 4–1.)

Dominant Trees with wide crowns above the level of the forest canopy, that receive sunlight from above and also from the sides.

Codominant Large-crowned trees at the general level of the forest canopy, that receive direct sunlight from above and partly from the sides. Crowns somewhat smaller than dominants but healthy and vigorous.

Intermediate Trees with much of the crown below general level or pinched at general canopy level, that receive some sunlight from above with little or none from the sides.

Suppressed Trees overtopped by large trees that receive no full, direct sunlight from above or the sides.

In addition to the above classifications there are these that consider tree quality:

Wolf Trees Trees with widespread crowns that hinder the growth of thrifty trees and are of little value themselves.

FIGURE 4–1. Tree crown classes: D, dominant; CD, codominant; I, intermediate; and S, suppressed.

Crooked and Forked trees The forms of which render them poor merchantable material.

Fire-scarred, hollow, or rotten trees Also of little value.

CLASSIFICATION OF FORESTS

For purposes of mapping forests for forest management, forests may be grouped according to composition of species, density of stand, age composition, and forest type. Each of these classifications is set forth in the following paragraphs, followed by a discussion of the distribution of the several forest types and where they are to be found.

By Species Composition

A *pure forest* is one in which all or nearly all the trees are of the same species. A *mixed forest* is one consisting of trees of two or more species. Pure or mixed forests may be either even-aged, uneven-aged, or all-aged.

Intolerant species such as pines, tamarack, yellow poplar, basswood, or yellow birch often begin in pure, even-aged stands. Later on, the hardwoods tend to evolve toward an all-aged, mixed condition. Trees in dense, young, even-aged forests compete so fiercely that their growth is slow and mortality is very heavy. In dense forests on poor sites most trees tend to stagnate; on good sites dominant trees will develop and crowd out competitors. Shade-tolerant species, such as hemlocks, beech, and the true firs, usually grow well in either pure, preferably uneven-aged forests, or with other species. Intolerant species cannot withstand competition from tolerant trees and cannot successfully reproduce under their cover.

By Stand Density

Because forests vary considerably in numbers of trees, volume per acre, basal area, and other criteria, it is important that we find a means of expressing differences. The difference between a dense stand and an open one is obvious to the eye when it is expressed on the basis of the amount of crown opening. The density as expressed in other ways (volume, basal area, number of stems per acre) must be measured in order to detect the actual differences. But for purposes of convenience, three classes of crown density have been recognized.

Dense or well stocked, over 70 percent of crown closure.

Thin or medium stocked, 40–70 percent of crown closure.

Poorly stocked, under 40 percent of crown closure.

One way to determine crown density rapidly is by measuring the amount of shade and open sunlight in a stand at midday. There is often so much variation within a stand that occular judgment is accurate enough for most purposes.

It is apparent that any forest that has less than a dense crown is functioning below the most efficient level *unless* there are young trees coming up to fill the openings. If a stand is too dense, it may become stagnant, and growth will slow down because the competition for light, water, and soil nutrients is too great. Extremely slow growth is the result. But a forest does not usually stay this way very long. Competition among trees will result in the elimination of the weaker ones and the dominance of the stronger.

Likewise, a stand that is too open (understocked) will produce large-crowned, limby trees with tapering trunks. A well-managed forest is one in which the density is kept at the optimum level so that the trees can make full use of water, sunlight, and soil chemicals. In some forests underbrush occupies much good growing space and only through its elimination will trees develop and grow.

By Age Composition

When practically all the trees are of the same age, even though they may vary in size because of their different rates of growth, a forest is *even-aged*. An *all-aged* forest is one in which the trees range from seedlings to large merchantable timber, with all age and size classes represented. This condition rarely occurs in nature (Figure 4–2 *a,b*).

In some stands there may only be two size classes, seedlings and sawtimber, without pole-sized trees; or there may be overmature, defective trees along with saplings and nothing in between. Forests that may have only two or three distinct age or size groups are commonly referred to as being *uneven aged*.

Uneven-aged forests have a more uniform distribution of sizes and generally include more of the shade-tolerant species (usually hardwoods), while even-aged stands are most often made up of intolerant conifers. There are exceptions such as ponderosa pine, which grows in both uneven-aged and even-aged stands, and sugar maple, which starts off on cutover lands in even-aged stands and gradually develops into uneven-age distribution. Windstorms, overcutting, fire, and other losses create openings in the forest and create uneven-age groupings. The endless variety of situations found in every forest makes it difficult to standardize or classify each one, and this complicates the practice of silviculture.

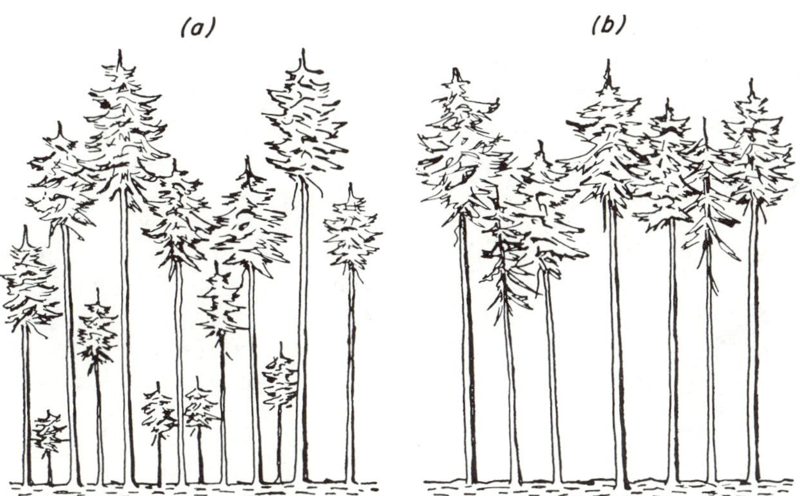

FIGURE 4–2. All-aged and even-aged forest profiles. In the all-aged forest (a), *the trees range from small seedlings to mature and overmature veterans. In an even-aged forest* (b), *the trees are all about the same age. Some are dominant, some are codominant, and the remainder are intermediate or suppressed.*

By Forest Types

Natural groups or associations of different species of trees that commonly occur together over large areas are called forest types. Forest types are defined and named after the one or more dominant species of trees, such as the spruce–fir and the birch–beech–maple (northern hardwood) types within the Northern forest region. Other examples are the Douglas-fir–western hemlock types of the Pacific Coast forest region, and the longleaf pine type in the Southern region.

Many of the forest types are only *temporary* types that in time will give way to another completely different group of transition (or subclimax) species and finally the climax type. For example, white pine on old fields of heavy soils in New England will be replaced by climax northern hardwoods. Aspen–birch on the Lake States cutovers is being replaced in some soils by white pine or by northern hardwoods, which are climax species for these soils. Thus, types that are strongly influenced by underlying soils change, over time, both by humanity's disturbance and nature's evolutionary development.

Common Forest Types of the Continental United States

It is possible to describe a wide number of combinations of species that occur in nature and call each one a forest type. In fact, the Society of American Foresters recognizes 106 different types in the eastern United States and 50 in the western. Most forest types are mixtures of species, although some are in pure stands, for example, lodgepole pine, redwood, Engelmann spruce, or white pine. In general, eastern types are more complex than western, and coniferous types less complex than hardwood forests. The number of species appears to increase as one proceeds from north to south.

Because of the large numbers of forest types that are found with greater or lesser proportions of different species, an effort has been made to set forth a few of the more common forest types found over each of the major regions. Most of the other forest types contain various combinations of these species in addition to others less commonly found.

AMERICAN FOREST REGIONS

Different combinations of species of trees are found in natural associations or mixtures in various parts of the United States. Varying conditions of temperature, precipitation, and of soil are the major

Eastern United States

Northern
Eastern white pine
Red (Norway) pine
Jack pine
Hemlock–yellow birch
Spruce–fir
Aspen–birch
Birch–beech–maple (Northern hardwoods)
Black spruce–tamarack–white-cedar (swamp conifers)

Central
Oak–hickory (also in South)
Oak–pine–silver maple
Elm–ash–cottonwood (bottomland hardwoods)

Southern
Loblolly–shortleaf pine
Longleaf–slash pine
Bald cypress–southern hardwoods
Oaks–pine
Oak–gum–yellow poplar

Western United States

Rocky Mountain
Ponderosa pine
Western white pine
Lodgepole pine
Spruce–fir
Western larch

Pacific Coast
Douglas-fir–western hemlock
Ponderosa pine
Sugar pine–ponderosa pine
Western white pine–western larch
Spruce–fir
Redwood
Western red-cedar

determinants of the six major forest regions in the continental United States and the two in Alaska. Most of the trees in a forest region differ from those in the others, yet a few overlap in two or three regions, especially in the eastern part of the United States.

The four forest regions of the eastern half of the United States are the *northern, central hardwood, southern,* and *subtropical* and the three western regions are the *Rocky Mountain, Pacific Coast,* and *Alaska* as shown in the map (Figure 4–3). The forests of Alaska are divided into the *coast* and *interior* forest regions. There are many local variations, as, for example, along the central portion of the East Coast where northern, central, and southern species often intermingle.

The Northern Region

Covering most of New England and New York, this region extends southward over the Appalachian Mountain highlands to northern Georgia, and westward into the Lake States, including most of Michigan, Wisconsin, and Minnesota.

The northern forest region is characterized by the predominance

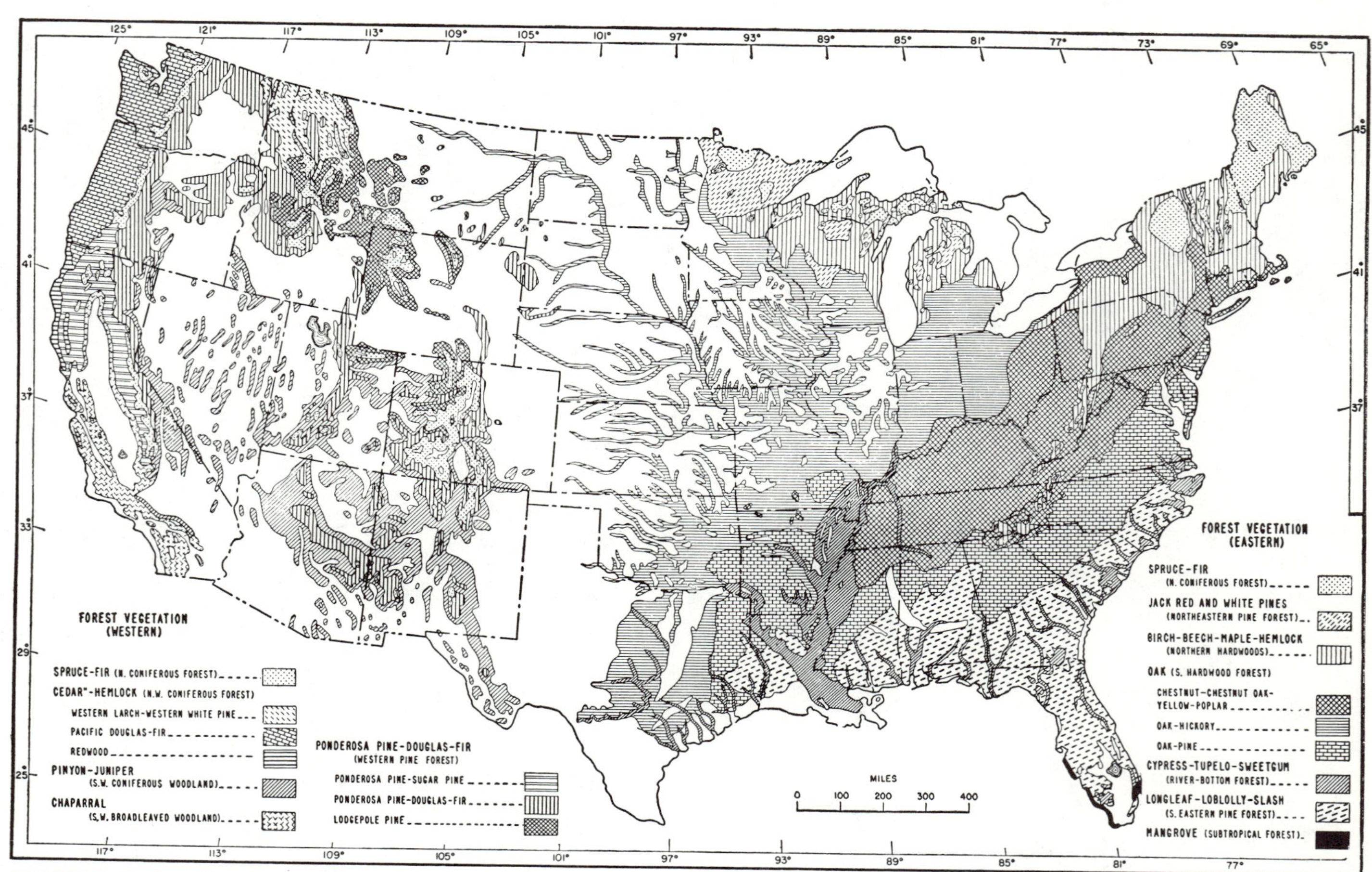

FIGURE 4–3. *Forest vegetation of the United States. (Adapted from Shantz and Zon, 1900; U. S. Forest Service)*

of northern white pine, red or Norway pine, eastern hemlock, balsam-fir, red and white spruces, gray, paper (white), sweet, and yellow birches, elm, beech, sugar maple, basswood, and northern red oaks. Each of these species varies in abundance in different parts of the region, and many of them are absent in other parts.

The more abundant or valuable trees composing the two divisions of the northern forest region are as follows.

Northern Portion (Northeast and Lake States)

Red, black, and white spruces
Balsam fir
White, red (Norway), and jack pines
Hemlock (eastern)
Sugar and red maples
Beech
Northern red, white, black and scarlet oaks
Yellow, paper, and gray birches
Aspen, quaking and largetooth
Basswood
Black cherry
American, rock, and red elms
White, green, and black ashes
Shagbark and pignut hickories
Butternut
Northerm white-cedar
Tamarack

Southern Portion (Appalachian region; includes most species in northern portion and in addition)

Chestnut oak
Chestnut (nearly extinct)
White, shortleaf, pitch and Virginia pines
River birch
Beech, white, bur and pin oaks
Red spruce
Yellow poplar (tulip poplar)
Black walnut
Pignut, mockernut, and red hickories
Black locust
Tupelo
American, red, and rock elms
Fraser fir

The Central Region

This region covers a large amount of the central portion of the eastern half of the United States, almost to the Atlantic Coast. It extends from southern Minnesota eastward to Connecticut and, excluding the southern Appalachian Mountain country, south through the Piedmont area and the Cumberland Plateau to the northern parts of the southern states. The region includes an abundance of different oaks and hickories and, on the better soils, yellow or tulip poplar and black walnut.

The principal species of commercial trees that make up the central forest region are the following.

White, black, northern red, scarlet, bur, chestnut, and post oaks
Shagbark, mockernut, pignut, and bitternut hickories
White, blue, and green ashes
American and red elms
Red, sugar and silver maples
Black cherry
Basswood
Dogwood
Eastern red-cedar
Beech
Pitch, shortleaf, and Virginia pines
Yellow poplar (tulip poplar)
Sycamore
Chestnut
Black walnut
Cottonwood
Black locust
Willows (many species)
Sassafras

The Southern Region

The yellow pine forests of the southeastern states provide the most important source of sawtimber in the eastern United States. Mixed stands of hardwoods and cypress are found on river and creek bottom lands and in swamps. The region extends along the Atlantic and Gulf Coastal Plains from eastern Maryland to eastern Texas, and includes portions of Missouri, Arkansas, and Oklahoma. The natural conditions are a soil of relatively low agricultural value, abundant rainfall, and a long growing season. The region contains about 30 percent of all our forest lands, consisting largely of southern pines and with smaller acreages of lowland hardwoods and cypress. The four most important species of pines (shortleaf, loblolly, longleaf, and slash) are found from north to south across the region.

The principal trees that compose the forest of the southern region are the following.

Longleaf, shortleaf, loblolly, and slash pines
Southern red, black, post, laurel, and willow oaks
Winged, American, and cedar elms
Eastern red-cedar
Pond and sand pines
Red, tupelo, and swamp black gums
Water, laurel, live, overcup, and swamp chestnut oaks
Water and black tupelos
Red gum
Bald cypress
Pecan, water, and pignut hickories
Beech
River birch
Green and white ashes
Red and silver maples
Cottonwood and willows
Sycamore
Magnolia
Atlantic white-cedar

The Rocky Mountain Region

Spread over a vast extent of mountains and high plateaus in the central-western part of the United States, the Rocky Mountain forest region reaches from Canada to Mexico, a length of about 1300 miles, and from the Great Plains west to the great basin of Nevada and eastern parts of Oregon and Washington, a breadth of 800 miles.

The total area of the many separate divisions or blocks of the Rocky Mountain region amounts to about one-eighth of the total forest land in the United States. The most extensive forest type is the ponderosa (western yellow) pine, followed by lodgepole pine, western white pine, western larch, and finally Douglas-fir and Engelmann spruce.

The principal species of the region are the following.

Lodgepole pine
Douglas-fir
Western larch
Engelmann spruce
Western white pine
Limber pine
Aspen and cottonwood
Ponderosa pine
Western red-cedar
White and alpine firs
Mountain hemlock
Junipers

The Pacific Region

Stands of very large firs, pines, hemlock, and cedars characterize this westernmost area. The dense coastal forests of Washington, Oregon, and the Sierra Nevada mountains of eastern California are dominant features of the landscape.

The California big trees, or Sierra redwoods, and the redwood of central and northern California coasts reach over 300 ft in height with diameters up to 40 ft. The western red-cedar, Douglas-fir, and sugar pine of California all grow to heights of over 200 ft with diameters up to 15 ft.

The Pacific Coast forest region contains about one-eighth of the commercial forest area in the country. The Douglas-fir–western hemlock types contain the largest acreage, followed closely by ponderosa pine. Other important types are the sugar pine, western white pine, western larch, spruce–fir, the coast redwood, and the giant sequoias. The principal species are the following.

Douglas-fir
Western hemlock
White, noble, red, silver and grand firs
Western red-cedar
Ponderosa and Jeffrey pines
Sugar pine
Redwood and giant sequoias
Incense-cedar
Sitka and Englemann spruces
Western white pine
Port-Orford-and Alaska-cedars
Oaks, ash, maples, birches, alders, cottonwood, madrone
Knobcone and digger pines
Monterey pine
Western larch
Lodgepole pine
Coulter pine

The Forests of Alaska

Along the southeastern coast of Alaska, stretching for more than 1000 miles, is a gradually narrowing belt of dense forest (about 5 million acres) made up of large trees. This is the most northern extension of the coniferous forest found in Oregon, Washington, and British Columbia. About three-fourths of the total stand of timber consists of western hemlock and the remainder is mostly Sitka spruce, with small amounts of western red-cedar and Alaska-cedar. In the interior there are more than 100 million acres of spruce–birch forest land—much of it small in size and subject to recurring forest fires.

QUESTIONS

1. (a) Give the term used to describe a forest with many sizes and ages of trees.
   (b) Give the term used for forests in which the trees are nearly of the same size and age.
2. What is the difference between a *pure* and a *mixed* forest?
3. Name the four classes used to classify trees according to their crowns.
4. Give the three classes used to describe stand density.
5. What is the definition of a forest type?
6. Name two important forest types in the South.
7. Name two important forest types in the northern states.
8. Name two important western forest types.
9. In which of the six major forest regions of the United States do you live?

EXERCISES

1. Visit a nearby forest area and locate an *even-aged* and an *uneven-aged* stand.
2. In each of the above stands determine in which *stand density class* they fall.
3. Identify the forest type of each of the above stands.

FIVE

APPLYING SILVICULTURAL SYSTEMS

Silviculture may be defined as the science and art of continuously reproducing and managing forests to obtain sustained yields of forest crops and other benefits through the application of silvics. (See also the definition in Appendix A.) A forest can grow naturally without interference by humans and still produce timber, but by applying what we have learned about forest growth we can create the desired kinds of forests in shorter periods. This is the heart of the practice of forestry. It is a conscious, intelligent use of human abilities to assist nature, in contrast to careless cutting and lack of foresight. The techniques used by foresters in managing forests are governed both by a knowledge of silvics and an understanding of the forest as a plant community. Most of this knowledge has been obtained by scientific observation, research, and experimentation.

The several stages of forest development require different treatments to obtain the desired results. The economic objectives of forest owners in obtaining certain kinds of forest products (sawlogs, pulpwood, Christmas trees, etc.) and services strongly govern the silvicultural treatment to be followed. Forest types, size, species composition, and silvical characteristics are the basic determining factors, however. Taken together, the silvical characteristics that govern the handling of a particular forest type or species are

1. Degree of tolerance to shade.
2. Windfirmness of root system.
3. Ability to grow in pure or mixed stands.
4. Growth in even-aged, all-aged, or uneven-aged stands.
5. Relative ease or difficulty of obtaining reproduction.

Silvicultural measures can be separated into two major groups: those that are applied to young growing stands, and those that are followed in harvesting mature stands.

INTERMEDIATE CUTTINGS IN IMMATURE STANDS

The term *intermediate cuttings* refers to those cuttings made in a stand of timber from the time of its formation until it is ready for harvesting. This group of measures includes a number of practices designed to improve the quality of the stand by removing the poorer trees and to increase the rate of growth of the residual trees in the stand. Silvicultural practices classified as intermediate cuttings include timber stand improvement (TSI), weeding or cleanings, release or liberation cuttings, sanitation cuttings, thinnings, and pruning. Essentially, the purpose of intermediate cuttings is to achieve the proper growing space for the best trees in the forest by favoring them and limiting competition. Salvage of trees that might otherwise be lost through mortality is another important result of TSI work.

The spread of the roots of a forest tree is often approximately the same as that of its branches, so that when the crowns of adjoining trees are too crowded, their roots are also in conflict; tree growth greatly suffers for both these reasons. Trees should not be too close together nor should there be too much space between them if growth and vitality are to be optimized.

As the forest grows, the number of trees decreases. In a seedling stand 20,000 or more small seedlings may be found on an acre. Usually from 1000 to 1600 seedlings per acre properly spaced will produce a well-stocked stand. After 20 to 30 years only 400 to 800 trees will remain. A well-stocked, mature, even-aged forest may contain 150 to 200 large and evenly distributed trees an acre. The amount of space needed between trees increases with their age and size. Shade intolerant trees need more room than those that are tolerant of shade.

Forests in the eastern part of the country are largely second- and third-growth woodlands that have sprung up from cutover land or land that has been both cut and burned. Fortunately, fire protection has been extended over wide areas during the past quarter century so that nature's recuperative powers have restored trees to much land that was nearly barren not too many years ago. Forest plantings begun on a wide scale by the Civilian Conservation Corps in the 1930s have developed to the point where they need attention just as much as the millions of acres of natural forests. At each stage in the development of the young forest during its life cycle, silvicultural measures will be required (Figures 5–1 and 5–2). Those described in the following pages would be applied at various stages of growth and to the several forest types as indicated.

FIGURE 5–1. A white pine stand marked for thinning. The trees marked are those that are to be left standing. (Champion Paper & Fibre Co.)

Weedings or Cleanings

A new forest just starting from the seedling stage may include a variety of undesirable species that may overtake and crowd out the more

FIGURE 5–2. The same stand, after thinning. The heavy volume removed (about 41 cords per acre) can be seen in the cut timber. Note the good spacing in the residual stand. These trees will accelerate rapidly in growth for nearly a decade. (Champion Paper & Fibre Co.)

valuable trees. Young pines can exist for a short time in shade but undesirable weed-tree sprouts and reproduction will soon gain the upper hand. Cleanings can be accomplished easily through the use of brush-killing chemicals in mixed hardwood–pine stands, but is more difficult in mixed hardwood stands where elimination of poor hardwoods is desired.*

Release or Liberation Cuttings

Young sapling stands often start under weed or wolf trees, which cause suppression and stagnation of the new growth at its most rapid stage of development. Much cutover land now growing into new forests has such overtopping trees, which can easily take over the site unless removed. In many areas where wildlife management is prac-

*See especially "Caring for the Young Forest Plantation" near the end of this chapter for information on some of the newer techniques used for weedings and release cuttings.

ticed, however, these wolf trees are selected to be left as den trees for wildlife or because they produce needed food, especially nuts. Removal of wolf trees can be done either by cutting where there is a market for the wood or by girdling and poisoning where there is not. Girdling is accomplished by cutting a V-shaped notch into the cambium layer, either with a mechanical girdler or with an axe. Sometimes the notches are filled with a poison to prevent sprouting or to ensure rapid death, because some species will linger for a long time after girdling. A plantation is often planted under an existing canopy for protection during the early years. After attaining vigorous growth the overstory is removed in a liberation cutting. Liberation cuttings are also needed in young forest plantations where undesirable trees are overtopping the smaller planted trees seeking their place in the sun.

Sanitation Cuttings

Trees are sometimes attacked by insects or diseases that may kill infected trees and spread to uninfected ones. Trees with a heavy infestation of bark beetles, for instance, will die and the insects harbored by them will attack other trees. Sanitation cuttings remove the source of trouble from the stand and leave the healthy trees to grow. Sanitation cuttings to control diseases are usually carried out as part of the regular improvement cutting program. If diseased trees are not removed in the regular commercial operations, they may be removed as soon as possible thereafter in order to free the ground for new growth.

Sanitation cuttings to control infestations of bark beetles are emergency measures to be undertaken as needed. Infested trees are often felled and removed from the stand. In case the outbreak is severe, it may be necessary to spray unremoved tops and stumps with approved chemicals to prevent further spread and damage by the insects.*

Salvage Cuttings

Forest stands are sometimes so severely injured by fire, insect attack, or by windstorm or sleet that it is necessary to salvage the damaged timber. Occasionally a single tree of value and quality is killed by lightning. Salvage operations remove the merchantable dead and damaged trees, leaving the uninjured trees to grow. In the case of fire-injured trees, salvage cuttings remove the weakened trees that

*See Chapter 9 for detailed discussion of techniques used.

will not recover and if left, might be an invitation to attack by insects or disease.

Thinnings

Because trees cannot be moved to provide proper spacing as they grow, some of the trees must be cut to *thin* the forest where crowding becomes too great. Thinnings are mainly made in even-aged stands of young timber. Good trees that die naturally mean that much wood volume is lost. Thinnings anticipate this loss and provide usable posts, pulpwood, fuel, or mine props. A first thinning is usually needed when the trees are between 15 and 25 years old. By then the crowns of the grown trees are closed in and lower branches have begun to die. The need for thinning is obvious when there is severe overcrowding of tree crowns, spindly stems, narrow growth rings, and frequent dead and dying trees. Although foresters have developed several methods of thinning for intensive forestry, the two most commonly used are low thinning (or thinning from below) and high or crown thinning.

Crown Thinning

Thinning from above is a cutting of the larger (dominant) trees in young stands with rapid recuperative powers. By removing some of the larger trees, more space is made available to the smaller trees for additional growth. This method is used extensively in jack, Virginia, and lodgepole pines, balsam fir, and aspen (and other short-lived species in temporary forest types). Pulpwood can often be harvested by this method, but care must be taken to leave enough residual trees to form a closed stand and to permit the smaller residual trees to continue growing (Figure 5–3). This kind of thinning removes dominant, suppressed, and some intermediate crown classes, and leaves codominants to grow for a time.

Low Thinning (Thinning from Below)

When the object of thinning is the maximum future benefit, the practice is to *thin from below,* that is, provide for proper spacing by cutting the inferior, smaller, or defective trees, and leaving the best and most vigorous ones to grow. Such thinnings will help the best trees develop into sawlogs much sooner than without this treatment. Low thinnings are best applied to older stands and to species with a long growing life, usually 75 years or more.

When marking trees for thinning from below, dominant and codominant trees are the most desirable to save. All the suppressed,

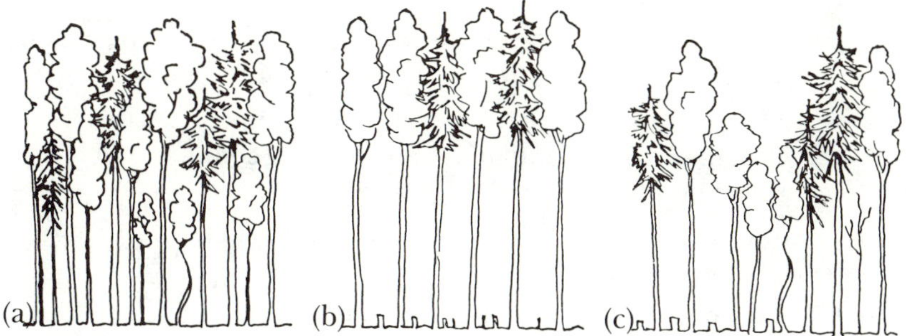

FIGURE 5–3. Thinning from above and below. The stand before thinning (a) *has many intermediate and suppressed trees. Thinning from below* (b) *removes most of the poorer trees and leaves the best for future growth. Thinning from above* (c) *removes the larger trees and only the poorer small ones.*

poor intermediates, and some of the limby or crooked dominant trees are cut.

Low thinnings are most commonly practiced today. It is best not to thin too heavily, but to do it often. Not more than one-third of the trees should be cut at one time, unless overcrowding is serious. Cutting should be repeated at 5 to 10-year intervals, when the crowns become crowded again. Properly done in a dense young forest, thinnings will greatly increase the growth rate of residual trees and yield higher quality material on shorter rotations. Larger volumes can be harvested, in total, because of the salvage of much wood that would otherwise be lost through mortality.

One way to check on a stand to determine whether it needs thinning is to take increment borings in a number of the best trees (dominants). If the annual rings indicate that growth has slowed down in the past 5 years compared with the previous 5 years, thinning is needed. Where the stand has been thinned previously, the borings will show that the annual rings become much wider a year or two after the thinning and then become gradually narrower as the stand closed in again. Another means of determining the need for thinning is by comparing basal area, stocking density, and volume distribution of the stand in question with data from yield and other data tables for normal stands. (See Chapter 6.)

Nine rules to keep in mind when thinning from below are

1. Mark the stand carefully *before* cutting. Do not make marking and cutting one job.
2. Mark all trees to be cut on one side only. Marks should be clear so they can be easily seen by the loggers.

3. Plan the marking to secure the best development of the most promising trees rather than the removal of the poor trees.
4. Look up and down when marking. Remember that it is the size, shape, and spacing of the crowns that count as much as the spacing of the stems.
5. Do not mark trees if there is no definite beneficial purpose in their removal.
6. Always mark whips, but do not always mark butt-scarred or wolf trees. Removing them may sometimes cause more harm than good to the stand. Removing den trees may reduce wildlife value.
7. Concentrate the thinnings on areas to which one can easily return for another cut. Frequent and light thinnings are far better than heavy thinnings with long intervals.
8. Do not let the best trees develop into wolf trees. Keep sufficient crown density to prevent this.
9. Know the silvicultural properties of the species and the quality of the site before marking is started.

Spacing Determinations in Improvement Cuttings

Foresters have devised some simple rule-of-thumb spacing guides that are fairly accurate and easy to apply in thinnings. These rules, which have come to be known as the *D plus* rules, are simple guides for determining the spacing between trees left standing after a thinning operation in a young stand. Here is what they are and how they work.

We define *D* as the average diameter of the trees to be left, and for trees 6 in. and over, dbh., the rule is *D* plus 6. This gives the average spacing in feet. For instance, if the diameters of the trees to be left average 10 in., then 10 plus 6 equals 16. So the average spacing between the trees left is 16 ft.

This rule is useful for most tree types in the eastern United States. For the West, the principle of *D plus* is the same, but the "6" is reduced. The spacing requirements for some of the western types for trees left after thinning are:

Pure ponderosa pine	*D* plus 4
Mixed conifers (white pine, larch, Douglas-fir, ponderosa pine)	*D* plus 3
West Coast Douglas-fir and redwood	*D* plus 2

For stands under a 6-in. diameter, use *D* plus 4 in the East, and *D* plus 2 in the West.

These rules are no substitute for common sense. Rules of thumb should be used only as a guide that needs to be well seasoned with judgment. Proper marking cannot be done entirely mechanically. For example, a clump of eight or ten good trees with room on the outside, but crowded in the center, might be thinned to two or three according to the rule. Actually, wise selection and cutting of three trees might give the whole group enough room. In short, each tree should be sized up individually for its chances of growing into profitable timber. Generally, not more than one quarter of the wood volume is taken out at any one thinning so as to avoid producing too great a shock to the remaining trees.

Pruning

High-grade logs with wood largely free of knots are an important forestry objective. In its early life, a stand must be kept sufficiently dark under the crowns so that shade will kill off branches on the lower trunks of the trees. The small branches decay and fall off, and the trees grow clear wood. If the forest is not sufficiently dense when it is young, large branches develop and, even though they are later killed by shading, persist for years, thus forming knotty logs and lumber.

To produce high-grade lumber or veneer logs when natural pruning has been unsatisfactory, the best trees should be selected and pruned by cutting the lower branches. Pruning should be started when the trees are about 4 in. dbh.; and only about 200 crop trees per acre that are straight, sound, and fast growing, and that will develop into high-quality sawlogs, should be pruned. Pruning trees that are crooked, or that have very thick branches, does not pay if they are over 8 or 10 in. in diameter. Pruning usually pays only on the better conifers —white pine, Douglas fir, red pine, longleaf pine—and on hardwoods of value for veneer.

Pruning live branches should be done during the dormant period in the winter (Figure 5–4). The first pruning should remove branches up to one-half log above stump height on the bole. As growth continues, pruning should be extended to 12 ft above the ground. After another interval, the pruning may be extended to a height about 17 ft if a 16-ft clear log is desired. No more than one-third of the height of young trees should be pruned at any time.

An axe is not suitable for pruning because it leaves spikes and pitch hollows. The best tool is a sharp saw with from 6 to 8 teeth per in., mounted on a pole, when pruning above the hand's reach. Cut the

FIGURE 5–4. Pruning a thinned ponderosa pine stand to improve lumber quality. (U. S. Bureau of Land Management)

branches cleanly, flush with the trunk so that no stubs are left, to provide good healing and to prevent decay. Live branches over 1½ in. thick should not be pruned.

SILVICULTURAL SYSTEMS USED IN HARVEST CUTTINGS

Applied forestry differs from unplanned logging in that specific systematic methods are followed in choosing the trees to be cut. A number of silvicultural systems originally developed in Europe are being adapted to the requirements of our own forests as they are put under management programs. Properly managed forests yield much greater volumes of better quality wood over the long run than do lands on which unplanned logging is done. But destructive cutting usually yields a heavier immediate volume, and that is why so much of it is still done, especially on small forest holdings. Many years elapse before such timber lands may be harvested again.

The objective of a silvicultural system is to permit the harvesting of the mature timber crop while providing for the regeneration of the forest. Basically, silvicultural techniques fall into two broad groups: the *area management system*, which removes all merchantable trees by clearcutting, and the *individual tree management system*, which selects only marked trees for removal.

If clearcutting is done too extensively the whole forest ecosystem is drastically changed for several decades until new growth restores the forest environment. Small patch cuts surrounded by larger timber, not clearings of large acreages, are preferred in intolerant forest types.

While nature has created many even-aged forests, the individual tree management methods are more in harmony with the forest ecosystem in that they tend to be similar in effect to natural processes of tree mortality. Small tract owners tend to prefer tree selection whereas large operators generally favor area management systems.

Under the area management system, clearcutting is done in strips or blocks and is followed by natural sprouting in hardwoods or by planting conifers. It is mainly useful in even-aged stands made up of intolerant forest types.

Individual tree management systems include the *seed tree method* and the *shelterwood system* for even-aged forests and the *selection system* for uneven- and all-age forests.

These silvicultural systems are intended for forests that have a volume of mature timber ready for harvesting. Because so many American forests have been carelessly handled in the past, the systems that are described may not always fit every situation to be found. Variations using several systems are frequently employed to fit timber type and species combinations, topography, and local market conditions. Each system must be considered a theoretically ideal procedure, needing modification in actual practice on the ground. Natural reproduction, if inadequate, is often supplemented by planting young trees in open spaces.

The choice of the proper harvesting method depends upon a number of factors, of which the following are of major importance.

1. It must fit the peculiar characteristics and silvical requirements of the forest type and species.
2. It must supply a sufficient volume of forest products to permit efficient logging and favorable marketing.

3. It should result in prompt restocking of desirable species and have a beneficial result on all valuable residual trees on the land, so far as possible. (An exception to this last factor is the several clearcutting systems that do not leave any residual trees of value.)

Some species reproduce themselves quite easily from seeds or from sprouts; others are slow and difficult and often require supplemental forest planting if the right proportions of desirable species are to be obtained. As a practical matter, the kind of silvicultural system to be followed on any tract should be chosen to obtain restocking at the earliest possible time after cutting, or to do the least damage and give the greatest stimulus to residual trees; but if the area does not restock naturally, supplemental planting may be required. The following description of each method sets forth the types and species to which it is best suited, its advantages and disadvantages, and other pertinent information.

Clearcutting Systems

When clearcutting is used in the management of a forest, it may be done in a variety of ways, each one of which is designed to bring about a new growth of reproduction following cutting. The variations of this method described below are usually applied to forest situations that meet one or more of the following conditions.

1. Intolerant trees that need full sunlight for germination of the seed and development of the seedlings.
2. Shallow-rooted species or those growing in exposed places where there is danger of the whole stand being thrown by the wind.
3. Even-aged stands of species that must develop uniformly in order to provide merchantable growing stock.
4. Success can be achieved only where there are light-seeded species easily windborne into the cutover areas.
5. Where whole stands are overmature, clearcutting is needed to utilize the merchantable material without wasting it.
6. Where opening up the site does not encourage a growth of shrubs before valuable tree seedlings become established.

Clearcutting of any type has the disadvantages (1) of overexposing some sensitive sites to drying out by the sun and wind, (2) of gravely impairing natural reproduction (often resulting in planting costs), (3) of leaving large areas of slash that are a fire hazard, and (4) of leaving the soil susceptible to erosion. In spite of these disadvantages, which at first appear quite serious, the method can be useful when it is properly applied and modified in the following ways.

Clearcutting in Strips or Blocks

In order to avoid some of the disadvantages resulting from clearcutting large areas, some forest types may be handled by cutting alternate strips or blocks and patches. Areas of uncut timber on the side of the prevailing winds are left standing for a long enough time to reseed the cutover areas, after which they are cut. For species that reproduce easily, such as jack and lodgepole pine, Douglas-fir, western larch and black spruce, the clearcutting method in strips or blocks that are not too large to allow for the quick salvage of blowdown, is an acceptable forestry practice (Figure 5–5).

Southern pines have been successfully regenerated by clearing and disking strips 200 to 300 ft wide and leaving intervening seed source strips of standing timber about 66 ft in width. Livestock must be kept out of young seedling areas for 8 to 10 years to avoid serious losses.

The Seed-Tree Method

This variation of the clearcutting system leaves scattered windfirm trees at intervals close enough to provide adequate seeding for establishment of the new crop of trees. It has the disadvantage of loss of seed trees by blowdown and difficulty of salvage of the seed trees after the new growth has started because of the damage caused in logging. In some of the northern pine types the seed-tree method has been tried without much success because of heavy invasion of brush. Longleaf pine in the South has been managed with good results by this system.

It is essential that sound, large-crowned windfirm trees be left standing if maximum seeding is to be obtained. Seed trees may be left singly or in small groups in order to have the advantages of mutual protection. The required number of seed trees depends upon the species and its ability to produce seed. In most cases 5 or 10 trees per acre are the minimum needed. They should be left for at least 5 years, or until adequate reproduction is established.

Clearcutting and Planting

Some species, such as red (Norway) pine, do not reproduce very quickly and are soon prevented from doing so by the invasion of brush. If clearcutting is practiced, the only sure way of obtaining reproduction with this situation is to follow immediately with planting. In some forest types it is more satisfactory and economical to plant

FIGURE 5–5. Block clearcutting in Douglas-fir in the Pacific Northwest. Block cutting is necessary because Douglas-fir reproduces poorly in the shade of larger trees. (American Forests Products Industries, Inc.)

immediately after cutting because of the time saved in establishing the new forest and the assurance of the proper density of stocking. This method is widely practiced with Douglas-fir in the Pacific Northwest.

The Coppice System

This system of silviculture is applicable only to species that sprout easily from both the stumps and roots. Essentially, it is a variation of the clearcutting method except that sprout reproduction is relied upon entirely to bring about the next stand.

The coppice method is successful in the aspen type of the Lake States because this species begins to put up root sprouts (suckers) the first year after cutting. It has been found that better sprouting takes place on winter-logged areas than on those where summer logging has been followed.

The Selection System (Selective Cutting)

Cutting is called selective when each tree cut is chosen with regard to its present position in the stand and future possibilities for growth. This system is naturally suited to all-aged and uneven-aged woodlands, especially the hardwoods. Clearcutting, high-grading (removing the best and leaving the poorest trees), and diameter-limit cutting* are usually a drastic shock to the forest, whereas properly conducted selective cutting merely works with nature by removing the older trees to make room for the younger ones.

The selection system has many silvicultural advantages. It affords good site protection, windfall is kept to a minimum, reproduction is easy and certain, fire hazard is kept low and slash is scattered, and cutting can be adjusted to fit market conditions. Its main disadvantages are economic: logging costs may increase because light volumes are removed at frequent intervals and heavy investments in growing stock are required. Furthermore, damage to residual trees may be severe at times.

Selective cutting is very simple in a well-stocked, all-aged forest. The older and larger trees are marked and cut as they reach maturity. The growth of younger adjacent trees is accelerated while the seedlings readily develop in the small openings made by cutting. Frequent light cuttings at 5 or 10-year intervals tend to keep up to the quality of the growing stock.

Unmanaged and neglected woodlands often contain some trees of inferior species, as well as deformed, diseased, and partly decayed trees. Trees may be too scattered or be so crowded that their growth has almost stopped. Selective cutting in such cases offers excellent opportunities for harvesting wood while at the same time improving the spacing and increasing the rate of growth (Figure 5–6).

Under careless cutting, which removes the best trees and leaves the worst, the forest would cease to be an efficient wood producer. The aim of selective cutting is just the opposite; such poor material as can be used should be taken along with "the cream." How far this should be carried depends on the kind of forest, on the availability of markets, and on the need for improving the forest in order to improve future yields in both quality and quantity.

Proper cutting in an overcrowded forest releases the best trees and improves their growth. Cutting too heavily so as to leave only a few trees exposed has just the opposite effect. They receive a shock from which they may not recover. Trees need the protection of one another. Trees suddenly released from the protection of other trees removed

*Cutting all trees above a certain diameter and leaving all others below, regardless of quality, condition, or position in the stand.

FIGURE 5–6. All-aged northern hardwood–hemlock stand. Above, *before selective cutting. The trees to be felled are those with a line drawn through the trunk.* Below, *residual stand 10 years after selective cutting.*

by heavy cuttings may be blown over by the wind or injured by frost or sun scald. A high wind can uproot shallow-rooted species or trees growing on shallow or wet soil; prolonged exposure to wind may weaken or kill them gradually by weakening their roots and increasing evaporation from their foliage. Slender tall trees with brittle wood (such as spruce or fir), break off easily. All of these reasons dictate the desirability of partial cuttings.

The following rules will be helpful in choosing the right trees in selection cuttings.

1. Mark for harvest all overmature trees that are making little growth.
2. Immature, thrifty, fast-growing trees of better species should be left standing.
3. In clumps of trees growing too thickly, remove the poorer specimens and inferior species.
4. Aim for proper spacing even if it means leaving a few trees that should ordinarily be cut. This will assure continuation of proper forest conditions.
5. Remove defective, poorly formed trees of valuable species for which there is a market. Leave one per two acres (or girdle but leave standing) for den, nesting, or wildlife food.

6. Try to release the maximum number of thrifty young saplings and poles without too sudden an overexposure to sun and wind.
7. Make light cuts at frequent intervals (5 or 10 years). This will encourage regular growth acceleration and greater growth rate. Heavier cuts at long intervals disturb a forest more severely.

The Shelterwood System

This method combines some of the features of clearcutting with those of selective cutting and is applied to even-aged stands or uneven-aged stands with large trees in the majority. Some of the more shade tolerant species such as white pine, sugar pine, or redwood need to have some shade during their first years, and a partial cover can supply this. Under the shelterwood method, the stand is removed in two, three, or more cuts several years apart, with the poorest timber being taken first. The best trees that are left may put on some fast growth for a period but, more important, they continue to supply seed so as to assure an adequate growth of seedlings on the ground. The system is used mainly in ponderosa and white pine, and in the southern pine and upland oak forest types. It is also being tried in even-aged northern hardwoods.

The series of shelterwood cuttings is divided into three phases: *preparatory cutting, seed cutting,* and *removal cutting.* The preparatory cutting removes only the most mature, defective, and other trees whose absence will benefit the residual stand. Openings are created that are not so large as to encourage undesirable brush, but large enough to allow enough light to stimulate seedling growth. Usually not more than one-third to one-fourth of the volume in the largest trees is removed in the preparatory cut. The residual trees serve as continual sources of new seed to assure adequate restocking.

The seed cutting is the heaviest harvest cutting and is usually timed right after a good seed year so as to encourage the most abundant reproduction in the additional open space made available. The trees marked in a seed cutting include all of the remaining slower growing and intermediate trees, while the very best windfirm dominants are left to stand. About 30 to 60 percent of the remaining volume is taken in this cutting (Figure 5.–7). Natural regeneration can often be greatly stimulated by mechanical scarification of the soil that improves the seed bed and reduces brush invasions.

The final or removal cutting takes place after reproduction is well established. All merchantable timber is cut from the area.

The shelterwood system has several advantages. Brush and unde-

FIGURE 5–7. Shelterwood cutting in southern pine in which 15 to 20 of the best trees are reserved per acre for seed production, shelter, and long rotation quality growth. After seedlings are established, the overstory will be removed. (U. S. Forest Service)

sirable hardwoods can be kept fairly well under control while seedlings start up; reforestation is accomplished by nature; seedlings develop from the choicest seed trees, thereby giving some control over the quality of the new forest; the change in forest conditions is gradual, not sudden, so the seedlings and the soil can adapt themselves more readily to the change in the forest environment; and finally, the trees left standing after the first and second cuts will accelerate in growth and produce wood more rapidly as a result of increased light and lessened competition for moisture and soil nutrients.

The shelterwood system's disadvantages are that it takes considerable skill, reproduction may be damaged in the second and third cuts, prices and markets may not fit silvicultural timing, and logging may be more expensive.

OTHER ASPECTS OF HARVEST CUTTING

Marking Mature Timber for Harvest

Proper selection of the trees to be cut and those to be left under any partial cutting system is one of the most critical forest jobs. It should be done with care, well in advance of cutting, and by experienced personnel. The importance of proper marking is so great that the time it requires certainly should be considered well invested. It takes the forest many years to replace wasted timber. The trees to be cut are marked by axe blazes or spotted with paint on the trunk *and* on the butt (to serve as a check on loggers). Although axes are still used for marking timber, paint guns make it possible for a good marker to cover a larger forest area in a day. Most paint guns are simply quart cans equipped with a nozzle and a handle. The paint (usually yellow) is diluted 50 percent with kerosene to make a freer flowing liquid (Figure 5–8).

Blazes or paint spots should all face one direction, preferably toward the nearest logging road. Ordinarily only trees to be cut are marked, but in dense stands those that are to be left standing are marked. Under this system, blazes should not go into the wood because injury to the tree may result.

The external evidences of trees to be marked are

1. Dead limbs on the top of the tree.
2. Sparse and yellowish foliage.
3. Abnormally rough bark.
4. Large size (growth rate should be checked).
5. Crown of tree thinning out noticeably.

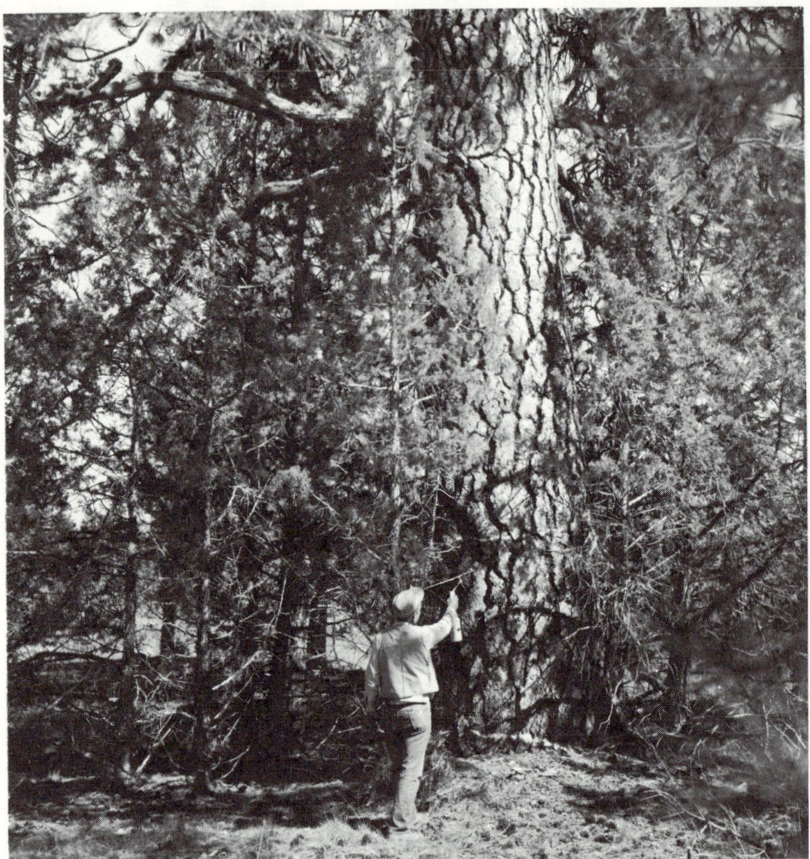

FIGURE 5–8. Cruising and marking a mature 64 ft ponderosa pine for timber sale south of Bly, Oregon. (U. S. Bureau of Land Management.)

The other trees that must be considered in timber cutting operations are the damaged or defective trees. These are trees that have been damaged by grazing, fire, insects, disease, or injured by some other cause such as lightning or previous logging.

Some of the things to look for are

1. The presence of shelf fungus (conks) or decay on the trunk.
2. Rotten spots, or hollows, at the base of the tree trunk.
3. Many dead limbs near the top.
4. Swollen areas on the trunk of the tree indicating internal defect.

5. Holes in the trunk.
6. Hollow trunk (can be determined by pounding on the trunk).
7. Loose bark or other indications of injury.
8. Frost cracks and fire-scarred butts.

Defective or damaged trees should be given first consideration in timber harvesting so that they can be removed while there is still a chance to obtain sound logs above or below the point of damage. Also, the removal of defective or damaged trees makes more room for sound, vigorous trees that will produce high returns in future growth.

Keep the following factors in mind when selecting trees to be harvested under partial cutting systems.

1. Leave the forest borders as dense as possible. This reduces wind damage to trees in the woods and provides cover for wildlife.
2. Remember that cutting too heavily will open the woods to drying sun and wind and which may cause mortality.
3. Remember that the *condition* of the tree, and not its *size*, should be the first consideration as to whether to cut it or leave it.
4. If the stand is understocked, the volume of timber cut in any one period should be slightly less than the net growth for the same period. This method of cutting will ensure continuous timber crops.

Except for stands with undergrowth, it is preferable to mark while the trees are leafed out, so that dead and dying trees can be easily recognized. But be sure to leave occasional nesting and den trees to maintain a good ecological balance between trees and wildlife.

To control the volume and species of wood to be marked for cutting from an area, the trees should be tallied, according to their size and species, as they are marked. This is explained in the next chapter.

Preparation of the Soil for Natural Reproduction

Skidding logs (mechanically dragging cut logs) in many types of forest with an open soil free of brush before cutting will make a perfect seedbed for germination of seeds. But in many areas underbrush of various kinds such as hazel brush in the Lake States and inferior oak sprouts in the South soon invade after cutting and take over good growing soil. A number of measures have been developed to eliminate brush and open up the soil for reception of tree seeds.

Just prior to or immediately following logging (if slash is not too abundant), it has been found that disking the cutover areas with a large bull disk pulled by a crawler tractor will turn up subsoil essential for a good seedbed while setting brush back quite effectively. This is called *mechanical scarification.* From here on it is a race between the regrowth of the inferior tree sprouts and brush and the development of the new seedlings.

Clearcutting–When, Where, How Large?

Clearcutting is the simplest (and crudest) harvesting method. It requires no special skill in selecting trees for future growth, seed source, nor careful planning of roads to protect the watershed and the natural environment. Clearcutting in large areas is the most destructive logging method because it completely disrupts the delicately balanced forest ecosystem through severe soil disturbance and drastic change in plant–animal relationships and habitat. It is usually followed by even-aged stands of a single species as all new growth begins at the same time and is much more susceptible to attack by insects and diseases.

A very vehement controversy has raged over the use of clearcutting for several decades that gives little sign of abating. Yet this method is appropriate for shade-intolerant types as pointed out earlier. Granted its appropriate use in aspen, jack and lodgepole pine, and even Douglas fir, the question still unsettled is how large should the clearcut be? Generally speaking, the smaller the clearcut area, the less likely it will disturb the forest ecosystem, wildlife relationships, and watershed quality.

How small is small? Scientific studies are not available on optimum size of clearcut areas except regarding California redwood—20 acres or less. Yet a 20-acre rectangle is 1320 ft long (¼ mile) and 660 ft wide (⅛ mile)—a relatively large hole in the forest.

The great advantage claimed for large clearcuts is that they are less costly to administer, allow the use of highly mechanized (and energy consumptive) logging equipment, and produce wood at low unit costs. No one claims silvicultural or environmental benefits from large clearcuts, and not much forestry expertise is needed. Small clearcuts however have these advantages.

1. Slash and logging debris are less likely to become fire hazards because more rapid decay will result in protection against drying wind and sunshine.

2. Seed from the adjacent uncut forest is more abundantly spread over smaller areas and results in natural reproduction—thus making replanting unnecessary.
3. More total *edge* effect is created, which is valuable to wildlife.
4. Instead of recreating extensive even-aged new forests as with large clearcuts, small patch cuts carried out over the same area over the same period of years will result in a series of age class stages of greater diversity for wildlife, and a more pleasing landscape.
5. Small clearcuts can be handled by self-employed loggers with less total investment in heavy machinery and less damage to the surviving understory of young trees.
6. Small clearcuts can be blended more effectively into the landscape and are less offensive to recreational viewers.

Thus when there is a choice between large area clearcuts and smaller ones, the latter should be preferred unless salvage of fire killed, diseased, or windthrown timber becomes necessary. This preference should not limit large timber sales but rather restrict the size of patches to be cut each year so that the timber is harvested in stages over several years to avoid the disadvantages of extensive clearings as indicated above.

But clearcutting is also the most inexpensive way to cut forests and so it is still commonly practiced. To clearcut large areas requires no knowledge of silviculture and minimal professional forestry expertise.

ARTIFICIAL REFORESTATION

When nature has failed to seed in a new crop of trees on cutover land, where forest lands are too thinly stocked or where it is desired to reforest open lands such as old fields, artificial planting is needed. More than 10 million acres are presently in need of planting if they are to become productive. Some of this acreage may not be needed for future timber crops and some of it may be too poor to yield profitably, but much of it will eventually be restored to tree growth by planting. Prior to World War II, federal and state forestry agencies did most of the planting, but today small owners and big companies are engaged in extensive planting of hundreds of thousands of acres annually. Reforestation is an expensive operation and is undertaken to speed up restocking more rapidly than under natural conditions.

In addition, artificial reforestation is a way of introducing genetically superior species of strains to an area. Many new strains of forest trees are being developed by forest geneticists both for resistance to disease and improved growth characteristics using superior tree seed selection and cross fertilization.

Choice of Species for the Planting Site

Before starting out on a reforestation program, a good deal of advance planning is essential. Proper choice of tree species depends upon location of the area and the kind of soil available. Generally speaking, coniferous seedlings or transplant stock are favored because most hardwoods reproduce well naturally. Figure 5–9 shows the species

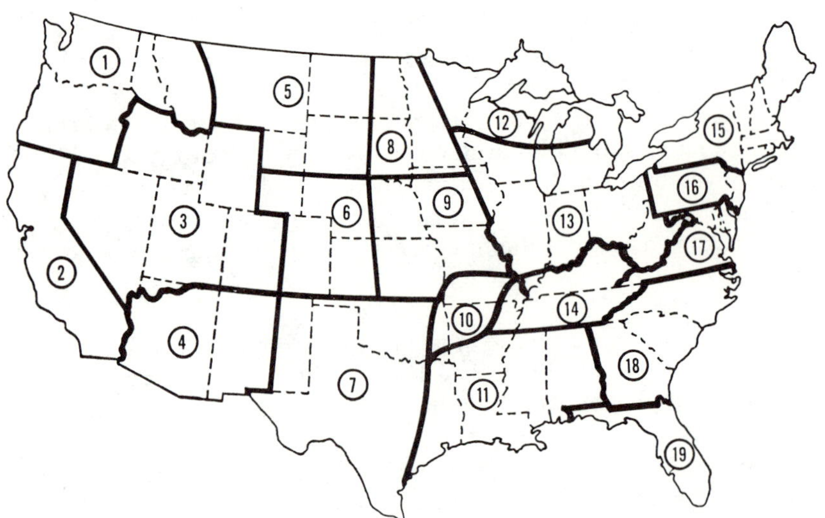

FIGURE 5–9. Recommended species for forest planting, by climatic zones. Where exotic species are listed, planting stock should come from seed collected from locally proven trees.

1. Douglas-fir, western white pine, ponderosa pine.
2. Redwood, ponderosa pine, Douglas-fir, white fir, Sitka spruce, Monterey pine, Monterey cypress, sequoia.
3. Ponderosa pine, Douglas-fir, blue spruce, white fir.
4. Ponderosa pine, blue spruce, Arizona cypress, Rocky Mountain red-cedar, Austrian pine, Chinese arborvitae.
5. Jack pine, white spruce, eastern red-cedar, ponderosa pine.
6. Jack pine, ponderosa pine, eastern red-cedar, western white spruce.

7. Eastern red-cedar, ponderosa pine, Arizona cypress, Chinese arborvitae, one-seed juniper.
8. Ponderosa pine, white spruce, jack pine, European larch, northern white-cedar.
9. Norway spruce, white spruce, blue spruce, eastern white pine, western white spruce, European larch, northern white-cedar, eastern red-cedar.
10. Shortleaf pine, eastern red-cedar.
11. Loblolly pine, shortleaf pine, slash pine, longleaf pine, eastern red-cedar, southern cypress.
12. Eastern white pine, red pine, jack pine, white spruce, balsam fir.
13. Eastern white pine, jack pine, Norway spruce, white spruce, blue spruce, northern white-cedar, European larch, Douglas-fir.
14. Shortleaf pine, eastern white pine.
15. White spruce, Norway spruce, eastern white pine, red pine, jack pine, European larch, northern white-cedar.
16. Eastern white pine, red pine, pitch pine, northern white-cedar, Norway spruce, European larch, white spruce.
17. Shortleaf pine, loblolly pine, eastern white pine, southern cypress, Norway spruce.
18. Loblolly pine, shortleaf pine, longleaf pine, slash pine, eastern white pine, Norway spruce, eastern red-cedar, southern cypress.
19. Slash pine, longleaf pine, loblolly pine, southern red-cedar, southern cypress.

that are generally adapted to planting in the several climatic areas in the United States. However, the planting of species native (indigenous) to the area, grown from seed collected from nearby stands, offers the surest road to success in forest planting. If nonnative, exotic species are planted, they should be only those that have already been demonstrated to be successful on other nearby forest plantations.

The soil preferences of the different species are given in Chapter 3, which may serve as a guide in selecting proper species at each location. Failure to fit the appropriate species to the site may result in losses, therefore advance soil tests should be carried out if any doubt exists. Another test is to investigate which species grew on the area previously even though the site may now be too exposed to replant the same species. In such cases it may be possible to use a species found in temporary or transition types for planting on open lands. And climax species often do well for underplanting in poorly stocked stands.

Seasons for Tree Planting

Seedlings should be ordered weeks, months, or even a full year ahead of the date desired; they should be lifted and distributed from the nursery during the dormant period for tree growth. Late winter (in the South) or spring planting (in the North) is usually preferable to fall planting because the small trees have more opportunity to develop their root systems during the ensuing growing season.

The seedlings should be planted promptly after they are received from the nursery. If planting cannot be done within a day or two, the seedlings should be *heeled in* temporarily and lifted again as needed. Early planting is desirable because the small trees can become established, ready for growth when warm weather starts. Late plantings may suffer loss of advance root growth.

Reforestation Methods

The two methods most commonly used in artificial reforestation are (1) direct seeding (sowing the area to be reforested with seeds) and (2) planting nursery-grown seedlings. The choice of the method depends on several important factors such as expense, time required, availability of seedlings, and chances of success. The two methods are described as follows.

Direct Seeding

Until recently, direct seeding of pine and Douglas-fir has been considered quite risky with heavy losses of seedlings. However, with proper ground preparation and the use of chemical repellents, which discourage birds and rodents from eating the seed, survival is more successful. This is especially true on recently logged or thoroughly scarified land where mineral soil or churned-up humus provides a favorable seed bed. Tractors with bull discs are used in heavy brush on recently cut areas to prepare the seed bed particularly in the southern pine and West Coast Douglas-fir areas. On extensive areas, seed is distributed by special attachments to helicopters, airplanes, or tractors. Hand seeding is commonly used in smaller patches where thorough ground scarification has been done in advance.

The direct seeding method lends itself to use of machinery and reduction of hand labor. In addition to high machinery costs, seed must be distributed abundantly in order to obtain desirable stocking of seedlings. This method can be considered most economical on large private or public forest tracts. Smaller tract owners are better advised to use seedling trees for planting success—especially where brush and predators interfere with seedling germination. Spot planting of oak, walnut, or other hardwoods is frequently used by small owners in the central hardwood regions.

Optimum conditions for seeding occur either in late autumn or early spring for previously disked sites. Moisture will have thoroughly penetrated the soil and new seedlings are thus able to resist drought should dry weather follow. A sowing rate of 3 lb of dewinged and chemically treated coniferous seed per acre has been found to give full stocking of seedlings on undisked lands; whereas 1½ lb will suffice on scarified areas.

Field Planting

Planting of nursery-grown stock gives the best results. Seedlings can be grown to the proper size and with proper root development in nursery beds. The whole process of gathering seed, preparing soil, seeding, protecting the seedlings from insects and diseases, and lifting and packaging can be efficiently organized so as to produce seedlings in abundance and at a reasonable cost. Nursery-grown seedlings have been used with very little failure, due to their developed root systems. The forest manager can decide on the number of seedlings to be grown per acre and act accordingly. This measure of control may save the cost of the early thinning of young natural stands or direct-seeded stands, as well as the loss of growth due to overcrowding.

By obtaining stock from a forest nursery, many problems involved in obtaining seed and growing seedlings are eliminated. Large state, federal, or company nurseries produce high quality stock, relatively free of injury and disease, and of the proper size and development for planting. Consideration is given to selection of tree seed from quality parent trees adapted to local conditions. The large nurseries produce many million seedlings at a lower cost than most owners can grow them. Nursery stock comes properly wrapped and in excellent condition for planting and gives results that are simpler and surer, on the average, than from home-grown seedlings.

Preparatory Considerations

Proper Spacing

The spacing to be followed in planting tree seedlings depends on the cost of planting, the rate of growth of the trees, and the nature of the products for which the trees are to be used. Close spacing gives

*The term *seedlings* as used here also includes transplanted nursery stock. A seedling which has been in the seedbed 2 years is called 2–0 stock. Stock that has been in the seedbed 2 years and in the transplant bed 2 years is called 2–2 transplants, and so on.

a quicker cover of the soil. Therefore, spacings such as 4ft by 4ft, 4ft by 5ft, and 5ft by 5ft are used for Christmas trees and soil erosion control plantings. Close spacing up to 6ft by 6ft results in early killing of the side branches and hence permits the development of trees with a greater percentage of clear wood free of knots.

Close spacing utilizes the available soil, water, air, and sunlight more fully, thus producing a greater volume of wood in a shorter period. If a close-spaced stand is kept properly thinned, it will produce a greater volume of usable wood products. If such a stand is not thinned, it will become crowded early and will require more years to reach merchantable size in either pulpwood or sawlogs than a more open or thinned stand. By planning the spacing so that an early thinning will be required, the trees to be removed can be used or sold. Close spacing, such as 4ft by 4ft and 5ft by 5ft, will usually benefit from early thinnings for Christmas trees before the trees can be sold for pulpwood. A 6ft by 6ft spacing is often used when no early thinnings are planned. The optimum number of seedlings for different spacing, per acre, is as follows.

Spacing	*Number of Seedlings*	*Formula*
4 ft × 4 ft	2722 per acre	$\frac{43{,}560 \text{ ft/acre}}{\text{Spacing ft}^2} = \text{No. of seedlings}$
5 ft × 5 ft	1742 per acre	
6 ft × 6 ft	1210 per acre	
8 ft × 8 ft	680 per acre	

Wide spacing allows each tree more room to grow, but the tree does not shed its lower branches as early or as thoroughly. As a result, the trunk has more and larger limbs, and the forest products, such as lumber, have more knots. Products from limby trees are of lower quality and value.

Preparing the Land

Seedlings grow faster in old fields than in land not previously cultivated because there is usually less competition from grass and brush. Where heavy sod or brush is encountered, the land is usually furrowed with a plow in advance of hand planting. If this is not possible, the tree planter usually *scalps* off sod with a mattock to lessen competition. Areas with very heavy growths of such undesirable species as scrub oak may have to be killed by chemicals or partially cleared prior to planting. When there is no use for the wood, killing by girdling or felling is often done.

Caring for Nursery Planting Stock
Seedlings from private and state nurseries come properly packaged with the roots moistened and protected against drying. The tree roots must be kept cool and moist. Purchased seedlings represent an expenditure that should be safeguarded. This can best be done by the proper care of planting stock, as follows.

1. Be on the lookout for the shipment of seedlings and accept them promptly.
2. Do not let seedlings freeze or heat up while in bales, or dry out as they are opened.
3. Carry seedlings to the planting site without delay, or *heel in* in a cool, moist place protected from the sun and wind. They will keep well for several weeks.
4. Use the following practices when *heeling in*:
   a. Dig a V-shaped trench in a moist, shady place.
   b. Break bundles and spread roots out evenly.
   c. Cover roots with loose soil at the same level as they grew (do not bury tops) and dampen with water.
   d. Complete filling in soil and tramp firmly with feet to pack soil on roots.

Handling Seedlings at Planting Time

1. When ready to plant be sure to have sufficient tools, water, and buckets for handling and planting.
2. Keep the seedling roots moist until planted.
3. Do not unnecessarily delay or prolong planting.
4. Read the planting instructions carefully and follow them closely.

Field Planting Methods

Tree seedlings may be planted with the use of hand tools such as a dibble, shovel, mattock, or post-hole auger. They may also be planted with a tractor and planting machine. In addition, containerized stock (individual peat pots for each seedling) is being increasingly used. For small areas, and where labor is available, hand planting will serve. It can be hastened if the ground is furrowed with a plow ahead of the planting. For large areas, machine planting may prove less expensive and equally successful. Whatever the planting method, use precautions to obtain the correct depth of planting. A safe rule is to put the tree in the ground with the roots at the same depth as they grew in the nursery. Most trees will die if planted too high or too low.

Mixed plantings of most species of conifers are considered to be more insect- and disease-proof than pure stands. Furthermore a loss of one species—if infestation hits a mixed stand—does not wipe out the years of work and growth that have taken place.

On slopes where trees are often planted to control soil erosion, it is very important to place furrows and plant trees on the contour. Furrows off the contour can lead to serious gullying. Furthermore, contoured furrows will not only prevent erosion but act as water catchments essential to the life of a new, struggling seedling.

Hand Planting

Methods of planting by hand are shown in Figures 5–10 and 5–11. (See Wenger, 1984).

Machine Planting

Several planting machines are now on the market and in some areas such machines are available for hire. In many localities, banks or civic-minded groups will furnish a planting machine at a modest charge. Use of the machine is recommended for a large area where there are not too many obstacles such as standing trees, gulleys, stumps, or rocks. Seedlings may be planted by machinery at the rate of about 1000/hr. The costs are relatively lower than for hand planting. The principles given for hand planting should be followed when using machine planting (Figure 5–12).

Until recently most tree planting was done in old fields, but new machinery using crawler tractors with brush cutters and heavy plows are successfully converting low quality brush and poor tree areas to productive forests. The higher cost of this method is offset by low land costs and thus makes it economically feasible. This one process of brush-clearing tree planting is also useful in recently logged areas where heavy slash would prohibit use of the standard equipment.

Chemical Fertilizers to Stimulate Growth

Because some forest soils (especially sandy plains) are often deficient in certain plant nutrients, growth rates can be slow. Research has found that providing supplemental nourishment through chemical fertilizers will stimulate growth for periods up to 10 or 12 years. Before using fertilizers, forest owners should have their soils tested (collected samples should be taken to the county agricultural agent) to determine what deficiencies exist. Forest soil fertilizers are available

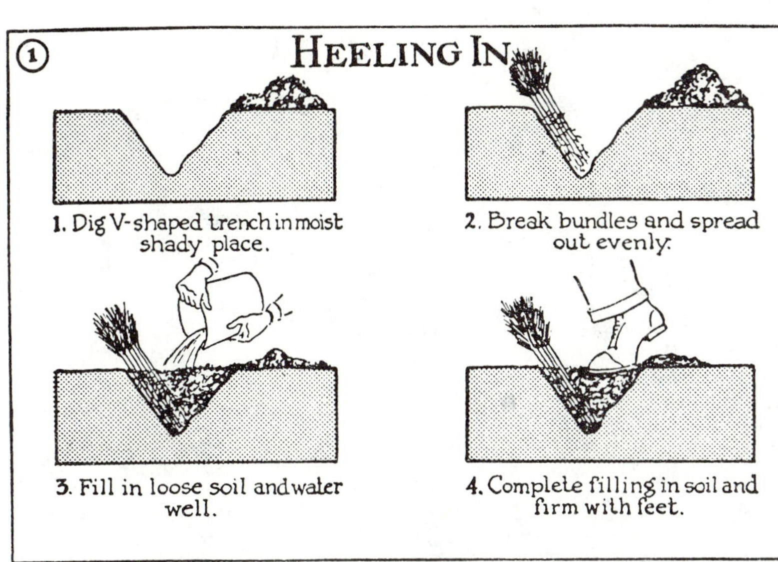

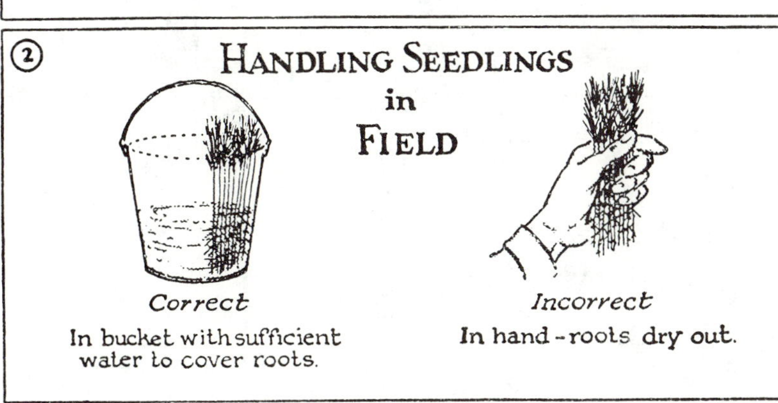

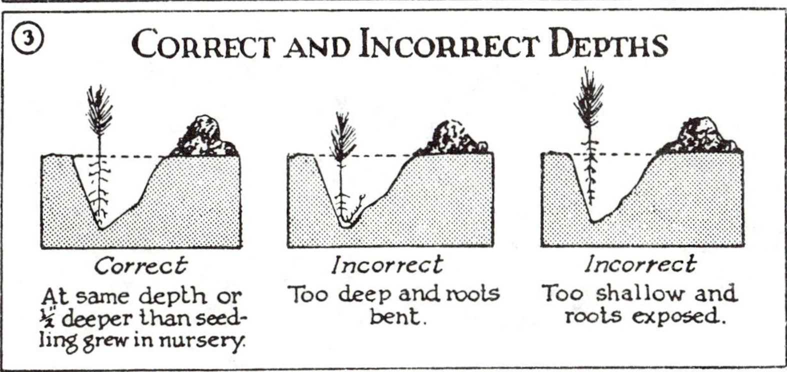

FIGURE 5–10. Hand-planting methods. (From Wenger, 1984)

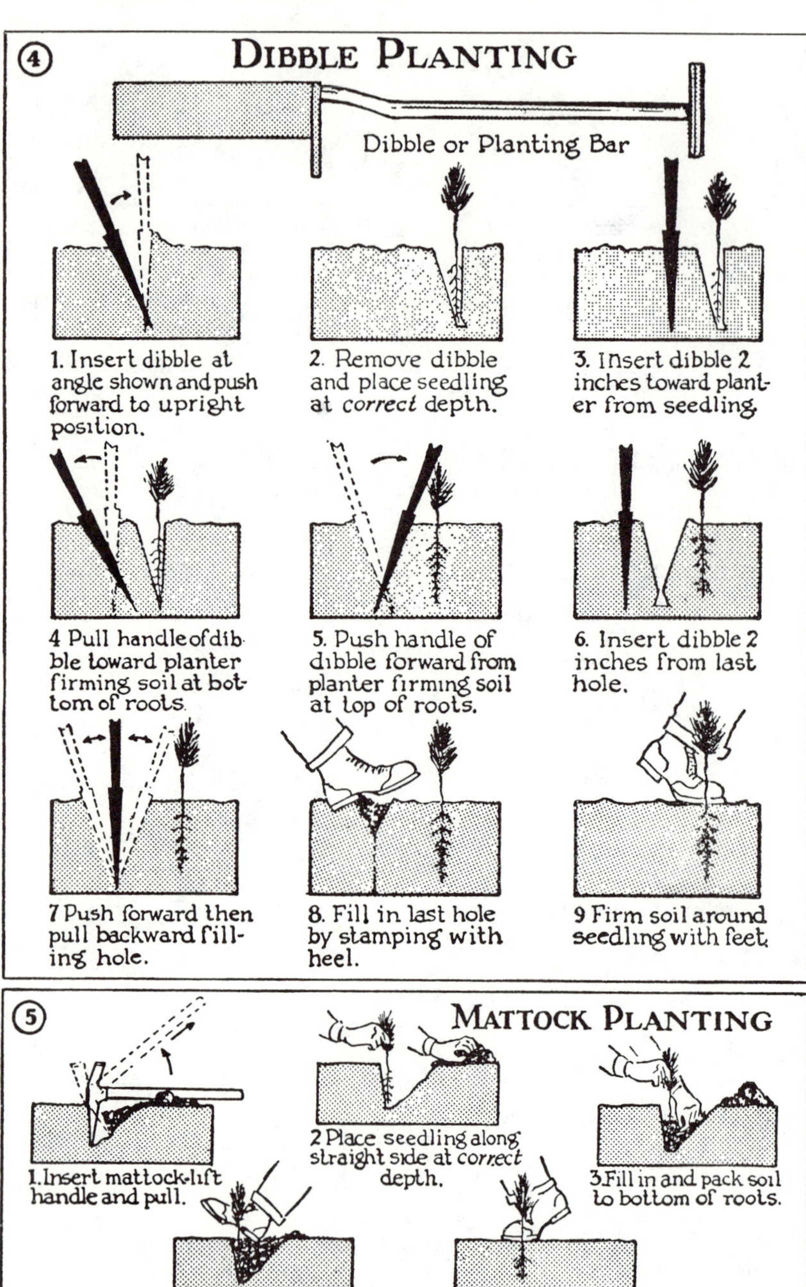

4
DIBBLE PLANTING
Dibble or Planting Bar
1. Insert dibble at angle shown and push forward to upright position.
2. Remove dibble and place seedling at correct depth.
3. Insert dibble 2 inches toward planter from seedling.
4 Pull handle of dibble toward planter firming soil at bottom of roots.
5. Push handle of dibble forward from planter firming soil at top of roots.
6. Insert dibble 2 inches from last hole.
7 Push forward then pull backward filling hole.
8. Fill in last hole by stamping with heel.
9 Firm soil around seedling with feet.
5
MATTOCK PLANTING
1. Insert mattock-lift handle and pull.
2 Place seedling along straight side at correct depth.
3 Fill in and pack soil to bottom of roots.
4. Finish filling in soil and firm with heel.
5. Firm around seedling with feet.

FIGURE 5–10. (continued).

FIGURE 5–11. Southern farmer plants loblolly pine seedlings in a gully on his farm. (U. S. Forest Service)

FIGURE 5–12. Typical tree-planting machine. (1) Rolling coulter; (2) double plow or sod buster; (3) planting shoe (opens trench); (4) packing wheels close trench and firm soil. (From Wenger, 1984)

in pellet or cake form and inserted through a hole punched in the ground near the trunk.

Soil tests may show a lack of trace elements needed for tree growth. These can be easily supplied through the powdered chemical in the form most easily utilized by the tree. It is not yet clear through research whether chemical fertilizers are economical to use—that is, whether their costs are equal to or exceed the value of the growth increase.

Taking Soil Samples

Methods and procedures for taking soil samples vary considerably depending upon the purpose and information desired. However, for routine testing to obtain information regarding lime requirements, organic matter, and the amounts of available nutrients in the plow layer, the following procedure is recommended:

1. Take samples with a soil auger, sampling tube, or a spade to a depth of 6in. or 7in. (see illustration).
2. Collect samples, four to six sites from fields that are relatively uniform as to soil type (color, texture, drainage, and productivity). Thoroughly mix and place portion (about a cupful) in the sampling bag to be sent to the laboratory.
3. Never mix samples from soils of distinctively different color, texture, drainage, or productivity. These samples should be taken and tested separately.
4. Avoid unusual spots, such as dead furrows, near fences and roads, and places that may have received excessive amounts of crop residues, manure, lime, or fertilizer.
5. Clean paper or cloth bags are most convenient containers for soil samples. It is very important to number or mark these

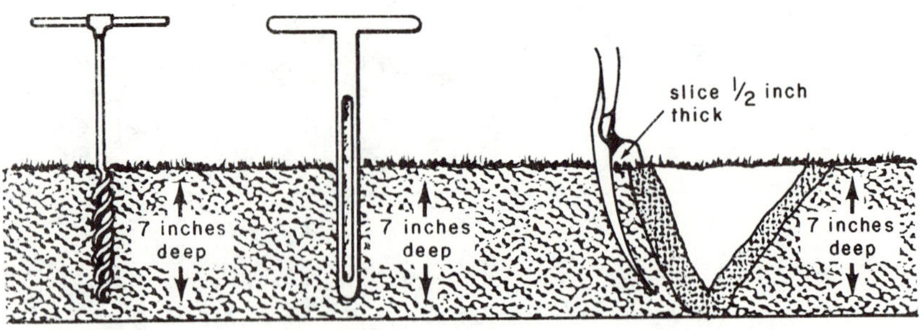

bags or containers so that there will be no question as to the farm, field, and portion of the field from which the sample came. Where forest maps are available, the sampling spots should be indicated by number on the maps.

CARING FOR THE YOUNG FOREST PLANTATION

Young trees, whether they are planted or grown naturally, require special care, such as the following.

1. Young seedlings are easily killed by fire and must be protected. A good road system in and around the plantation assures points from which to backfire.* Firebreaks through the planted area serve to localize possible fires and reduce the chances of complete loss.
2. New plantations usually do not have a 100 percent *catch* of planted seedlings. This may be due to poor planting methods, dry weather, or other causes. In order to assure complete stocking, these *fail* spots should be replanted by hand the following spring.
3. The young trees should be protected from damage by grazing. Light grazing by cattle may do little harm, but grazing by sheep, goats, and hogs can seriously injure the seedlings. Where the damage from grazing could be serious, livestock should be excluded by fencing. Trampling in clay soils will greatly reduce the capacity of the soil to absorb and store water and will adversely affect tree growth.
4. As the trees grow and become crowded, the forest should be thinned and weeded of the poorly formed, diseased, and otherwise undesirable trees.
5. In some instances, it may be necessary to release young seedlings from overtopping by undesirable trees.
6. If early thinnings for Christmas trees are desired, shaping of crop trees by pruning is a highly desirable practice, described later in this chapter.

*A fire purposely set to burn fuel ahead of the wildfire to prevent further spreading.

Forest planting in plantations is becoming an increasingly important aspect of forestry. This is apparent in the large number of Christmas tree plantations that each year supply a large portion of the national production.

Of great importance, especially during planting time and the early years, is the control of weeds that compete for mineral nutrients, water, and growing space. The trees 'fight' for survival if the weeds are uncontrolled greatly lengthens the maturity and rotation age and results in lower stand densities. This may contribute to the failure or success of a plantation venture.

The weeds can be controlled by mechanical means such as disks and cultivators; however, this type of control after planting, can injure the root systems of the tree seedlings.

Many weed control chemicals or herbicides are on the market and the list continues to grow. Some eliminate all vegetation for many years while others are selective and affect only certain groups of plants or certain species within a group. All *must* be used with extreme caution and within the special state and federal laws and manufacturer's directions.

Soil type, climate, species to be controlled, and conditions of growth all affect the rate of application and method used. Recommendations of the manufacturer should be read very carefully and followed. Use for purposes other than that intended by the manufacturer and concentrations other than those recommended can lead to unsatisfactory or even disastrous results.

Many of the new "wonder" chemicals are being found to have serious environmental effects—especially, but not limited to, the chlorinated hydrocarbons such as DDT. Mechanical and biological pest controls (such as insect-eating songbirds) harmonize more beneficially with natural ecosystems.

Christmas Tree Plantation Management

Plantation-grown Christmas trees are competing with such wild trees as balsam fir, white, black, and red spruce, and red-cedar in many large city markets. Scotch, red, and white pine, Douglas fir, Norway spruce, and other species have been planted extensively in old fields for this market. Many people believe that large sums can be made easily in Christmas trees when in 8 to 12 years 1200 trees per acre can be sold from $10 to more than $50 each. Too often forgotten, however, is the cost of production, losses, poor unsalable trees, and the often glutted market for Christmas trees.

In addition to the cost of establishment—often $300 or more per acre—taxes, fire protection, pest and weed control, fertilizers, and, particularly, the hand labor required for pruning and shearing to shape trees should be considered. Shearing to proper shape, which is an annual process between the third or fourth year (24 to 30 in. in height) after planting up to the second year of harvest, provides a full, well-shaped tree.

Pruning or shearing of pines should be done in the spring and early summer when the new growth (*candles*) is still soft and succulent, and before it hardens. This period usually ranges from June 1 to July 15, depending upon the section of the United States. It is recommended that white pine be sheared as early as possible.

One method to determine whether height and lateral growth has slowed down or stopped is to observe the needles on the new growth. If the needles lie close to the stem, growth is still active. When the needles start to stand away from the stem cell enlargement is near completion and there will be no further lengthening of the terminal or lateral branches. Too early pruning will result in few buds, slow growth, and dead stubs. In most pine plantations there will be a period of about 10 to 15 days when conditions are ideal for pruning or shearing. If the trees are pruned too late, the new buds will be small, and new growth the following year will have a bird's nest effect. The pruning or shearing of spruce or fir can be done at any time of the year, but best results are obtained if the work is done while the trees are dormant during late fall and winter.

How to Prune

Pine

Start by cutting the terminal (*leader*) branch to desired length, usually about 12 in.; make the cut at a 45° angle; then clip the laterals of the terminal whorl so that they are 3 to 5 in. shorter than the terminal. Next, proceed around the tree and prune or shear all laterals so as to shape the tree into an inverted cone. Any branches that are too long or irregular may need to be removed back to second-year wood. In most instances, no pruning or shearing should be done during the growing season prior to harvest.

Spruce and Fir

Start pruning by cutting the terminal to proper length, usually 8 to 12 in. Make the cut at a 45° angle at a point just above a good, live single bud. If the cut is made above two or more buds in a cluster, a multiple terminal will develop. To prevent multiple terminals, remove extra buds by pinching or twisting them off. After the terminal is cut, prune the lateral branches so the tree is cone shaped. If there are extra long branches, cut them back.

It must be remembered that the tree needs a base or *handle* (a section of the tree's lower stem cleared to fit the stand) of approximately 1 in. for each foot of tree height, plus a little allowance for a fresh cut for mounting the tree in its holder. Some producers, however, speed and improve their harvesting operations by selecting the tree bases and cleaning handles as a routine part of their pruning or shearing operations.

Pruning or shearing is done to develop quality trees. Its refinements are developed through practice, observation of results, and more practice. The producer must develop and maintain a sense of good tree balance and proportion.

Tree Color and Fertilizers

The color of Christmas trees corresponds to the total nitrogen content of the needle foliage in combination with trace elements of iron and molybdenum. When total needle nitrogen values are in the vicinity of 1 percent, tree color is yellow and needle loss occurs. Trees with dark green foliage have total needle nitrogen values in the vicinity of 1.7 to 1.8 percent.

Consumer acceptance is greatest for trees with dark color. These are the trees with high needle-nitrogen content. The buying public does not care for light colored, yellowish-green trees. Thus many trees that are otherwise acceptable are discarded or never harvested because of inadequate color. With fertilizer treatment, most cases of color deficiency can be overcome, but it should be done experimentally on a few trees to determine the degree of success attainable.

Trees with low needle nitrogen content lose their needles quickly at room temperature. Needle retention is important to the person who dislikes the litter of fallen needles around their Christmas tree. Fertilized trees hold up better during shipment into warm areas than unfertilized trees.

Tree Growth Is Also Related to Nitrogen Supply

Christmas trees can grow from 12 to 14 in. per year without becoming too sparse and losing the desired shape. In many areas, however, the trees fail to grow a foot a year. In some areas, growth is only 3 to 6 in. per year.

The time needed to produce a crop of trees can be greatly reduced by keeping the trees growing as near the allowable maximum of 12 to 14 in. per year as possible. In many cases, this would double the production presently obtained per acre.

For example, if the normal growth rate is 6 in. per year, it will take 12 years to grow a 6 ft tall tree. With the use of fertilizers, a tree of the same height could be ready for market in 7 years. Here soil tests will be needed to assure the proper kind and amount of fertilizers to apply.

QUESTIONS

1. What is the definition of silviculture?
2. What are the two major silvicultural practice groups?
3. Name three kinds of intermediate cuttings in young forests.
4. Select one of the above intermediate cuttings and explain how it will improve the forest.
5. What are some of the benefits of thinning young, even-aged stands?
6. What is the purpose of thinning *from below*?
7. Is clearcutting an accepted forestry practice in some cases? If so, name one species or forest type where it is used.
8. Name three systems of harvesting a forest that leave residual trees on the ground and a forest type in which they are used.
9. What are benefits from pruning young stands?
10. What is meant by *heeling in* nursery seedlings?
11. When planting trees, what is the best depth for setting them?
12. Why should roots of coniferous nursery stock always be kept moist?
13. Give two reasons for close spacing of tree plantations.
14. What benefits come from thinning a dense plantation?

EXERCISES

1. Find an immature forest in need of immediate cuttings, then decide which method is best suited to the situation.
2. On a small part of the tract, using thumb tacks and small squares of white paper, mark those trees that you feel should be removed to improve the stand.

3. Visit a mature stand of timber and decide what silvicultural system is the best method to apply.
4. If it is possible to participate in a reforestation project in your area, spend a day or more planting trees.
5. Examine a recently logged area and determine if the proper cutting method was used.

SIX

MEASURING THE FOREST

Forest measurements include map making, measuring land areas, and determining timber volumes. Prior to carrying out any forestry program, accurate information on timber supplies, boundaries, and location of the important features of the forest tract is essential.

Forest surveying is usually less intensive and exacting than that on lands that have high values such as city lots and farm lands. Because of this it is usually possible to use a hand or staff compass instead of a transit and to pace distances rather than measure them precisely with a tape. However, in the case of disputes over forest property boundaries, road layouts, and condemnations; transit and tape surveys are made. But for most purposes of forest management, including forest-type mapping and timber cruising, the hand compass and pace, or the staff compass and chain tape methods, make it possible to do much more rapid work. Because these methods can give reasonable accuracy as well as speed, they are the ones that forest managers are expected to know.

LAND SURVEYING SYSTEMS

There are two major systems for subdividing lands in the United States: the irregular *metes and bounds* method used in the original 13 colonies, and the *rectangular surveys* that were applied to most of the public lands over the rest of the country. Thomas Jefferson is credited with having been the originator of the rectangular surveys adopted by Congress in 1785.

Metes and bounds survey lines either follow along ridges, streams, roads, and so forth, or they follow lines of a specified angle (*bearing*) and distance from one established corner to the next. Because there is no general system, surveyors must depend on old field notes or titles for guidance. Forest surveys can be made with only a general knowledge of boundaries, which the owner can usually furnish. Boundary lines, such as roads and fences, that have long been accepted by owners on both sides, become legal boundaries if neither party objects. Often owners must agree arbitrarily on a boundary line. (See Figure 6–5.)

The rectangular survey system is laid out into square areas (specific exceptions are noted later), the largest of which is a *township* of 6 square miles (23,040 acres), containing 36 sections of 1 square mile each (640 acres). Sections are in turn divided into four quarter sections, and these into 40-acre tracts one-fourth of a mile square. (See Figure 6–1.) *Forties* were not surveyed out in the early surveys, but as land became subdivided, their lines have been *run out*. There are exceptions to the above definitions that are discussed in detail in Wenger (1984).

The basic system in laying out the public lands includes guide lines or *meridians* running north and south, which are crossed by base lines (*parallels*) running east and west. Between the guide meridian lines, the north–south boundary lines of townships are called township lines; and between the *standard parallels*, the east–west boundary lines are called *range lines*. Townships are described with reference to the *initial point* where the *base line* crosses the *principal meridian*, as Township 3 North, Range 4 West (T3N R4W).

Because the north–south meridian lines converge at the poles, they are not quite parallel (as are the base lines) and thus require corrections in laying out the townships. This is accomplished by reducing the areas of outside forties of the 11 sections on the north and west boundaries of each township.

Boundaries of forest land are marked, at section corners and sometimes at quarter corners, by iron or concrete posts capped with a brass marker indicating their specific location. The earliest surveys were

(a)

6	5	4	3	2	1
7	8	9	10	11	12
18	17	16	15	14	13
19	20	21	22	23	24
30	29	28	27	26	25
31	32	33	34	35	36

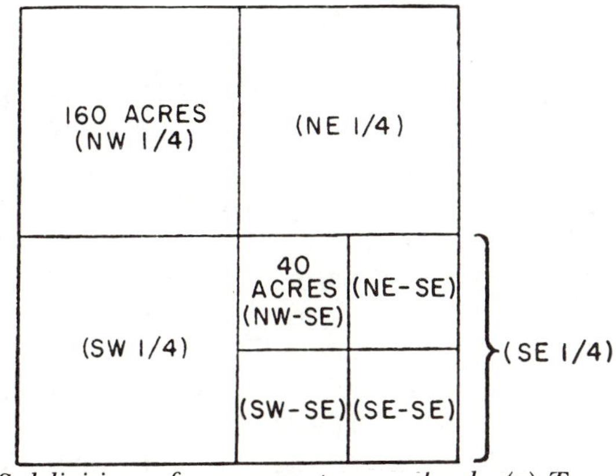

FIGURE 6–1. Subdivisions of government survey lands. (a) *Township divided into sections;* (b) *section divided into quarters and forties.*

marked with wooden posts, blazed trees, or piles of rock, but most of these have disappeared east of the Great Plains, though many remain in the western timber country. Early surveys done with a compass instead of a transit were often inaccurate due to local magnetic attraction or error. Since these incorrect corners are the legal corners, unless corrected by the Bureau of Land Management, many of them still stand today. They can result in greater or lesser acreage in a given forty or section and thus increase or decrease the timber volume present on the description. Blazed trees usually facing the corners were called *witness trees,* and *bearing trees* showed the direction and distance to the established corner.

Obtaining base maps for the general area in which the property is located is a first step. These provide the orientation needed in making a forest-cover-type map. Usually the county surveyor or other county official with this duty can obtain maps of the county showing the subdivisions from records in the county court house.

In map making on forest lands, the primary concern is with sections and forties within sections. It will be recalled that groups of four forties are called quarter sections. Forties are described as NW–SW, SW–NE, SE–NW, and so on. A single forty in a certain section may be described as NE¼ of the SE¼ of Section 9, T2N R1W, with the name of the county often included. These are called *legal descriptions.*

MAPPING FOREST AREAS

Measuring Direction

The first rule in mapping an area is accuracy in direction and distance. Direction is determined with a compass, and distance is measured with a surveyor's tape or by pacing. Since forestry maps are *extensive* and not *intensive,* pinpoint accuracy is not required, but the limit of tolerance in error is only within that attributable to the instruments used—not carelessness! A forester's compass is accurate to the degree but not to minutes, and pacing can be reasonably accurate only if constantly checked. Compass and pacing are the most common methods used in forest mapping.

Accurate surveys can be made only when starting from a known point. Established sections or quarter-corners are the most accurate, in areas where they are available. Elsewhere, known property corners or other permanently located points can be made to serve.

Compasses used in forestry are either hand-held (Figure 6–2) or on a staff, the principal difference being that a staff compass is a little steadier and more accurate, but their operation is identical. Because a compass is used to maintain a specific direction, this is always expressed as a *bearing* or as an *azimuth.* The azimuth may be read clockwise from the compass, which shows north as 0°, east as 90°, south as 180°, and west as 270°. Bearings never exceed 90°, are measured from north or south, and divide the circle into quadrants. (See Figure 6–3.)

To use a hand compass, hold it in both hands with elbows against the body. The needle will usually swing back and forth some time

FIGURE 6–2. Standard forester's hand compass, showing bearings and azimuths in compass circle, with township-section grid on inside of cover.

before coming to rest so that a reading must be taken quickly when an average can be sighted. With a levelled staff compass, one can let the needle come to rest on the exact bearing being sought. In both types, after locating the bearing through the sighting vane, pick out an object (a particular tree, rock, etc.) toward which you proceed for the next compass reading.

The better Silva compasses make use of a sight, similar to that on a gun, and a reflecting mirror. The bearing is translated into azimuth and the azimuth is set on the compass. Sighting is done by lining up the compass needle with the arrow etched in the top glass of the compass. This is done by using the mirror in the hinged cover of the

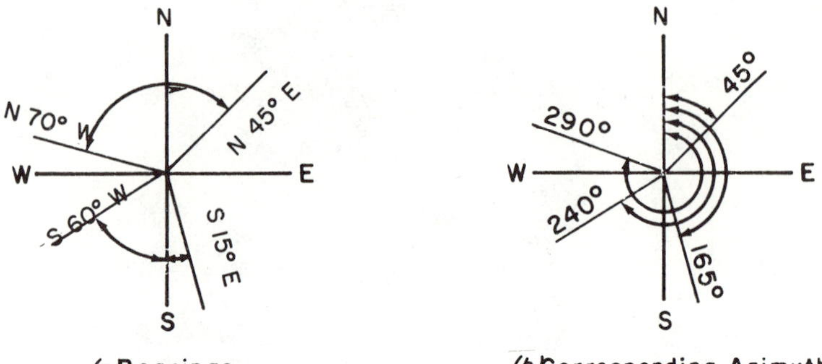

FIGURE 6–3. Bearings and azimuths. (From Wenger, 1984)

compass, then sighting through the *gunsight* notch to a particular object. The compass is held at eye level.

The construction of a forester's compass (Figure 6–4) requires little elaboration here except to draw attention to the 360° shown on the outer circle, to the floating needle that points to magnetic north, and

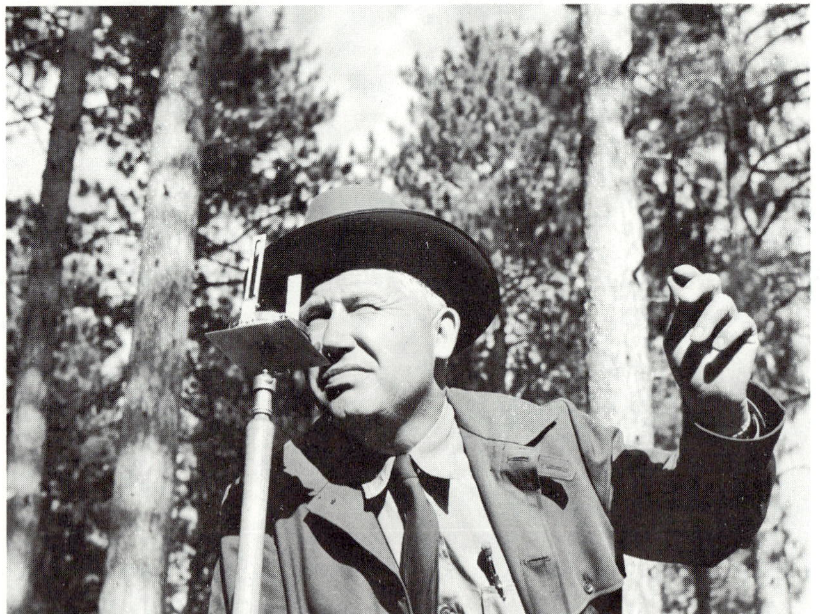

FIGURE 6–4. Forester sighting a staff compass through sighting vanes on a timber survey. (U. S. Forest Service)

to the sighting vane. Three kinds of errors develop in using a compass: inaccurate readings, accidental, and systematic errors. By taking backsights as well as foresights at each station, with intermediate *ties* to corners and other known points wherever available, systematic errors can be checked (Figure 6–4). Accidental errors can only occur through failure to read the correct bearing or failure to follow a correct one. Systematic errors can creep in if a compass is out of adjustment, if it has not been corrected for declination, or if it is too close to metal, such as a knife, which may swing the needle from its course. The student is referred to a text on surveying or the *Forestry Handbook* for such information as the correct bearing for adjusting the compass for declination. The compass needle points to magnetic north, which can differ considerably from true north, so compass correction should be set to the declination of the area being surveyed. Then the sighting will be referenced to true north when the needle is lined up with the arrow. The forester with whom the technician works can usually be helpful in special field problems that develop on the job.

Measurement of Distance

Measurement of distance is taken with either a two-chain tape, or by pacing while the compass is being used to measure direction. Pacing is the least accurate method but is used most often because it is faster and can be done by one person working alone. Here are a few rules for pacing that help to do it accurately.

1. A *pace* in surveying means two steps. Count double steps only—when your left or your right foot hits the ground, not when each hit.
2. Measure your pacing over known distances (checked by a tape), through the type of terrain in which you are apt to be working, and at the speed that you will proceed through the woods. The tendency is to go at a slower, more calculated pace over the measured distance than when pacing in the woods.
3. Keep track of your pacing systematically by counting chains with a tally register, by using your fingers, or by picking up sticks as you progress. Keep track in five chain intervals as one tally. This makes it easier to measure the distance. Four tallies, or 20 chains, to ¼ mile; eight tallies, or 40 chains, to ½ mile; 16 tallies, or 80 chains, to 1 mile.

4. On rough terrain with slopes or in dense cover the number of paces per chain will need to be increased. You can learn the correction needed by practice and experience.

Using a surveyor's tape will give more accuracy, but it takes more time. Most commonly used is the two-chain tape with a trailer for compensating on slopes. A chain is 66 ft in length and graduated into 100 links. Since a *forty* is 20 chains in length (1320 ft), the chain tape is a convenient measure. It always requires a two-person crew because the rear end of the tape must be snubbed each time it is moved a full length.

Units of Measurement Used for Lands and Timber*

Land

1 meter is 3.28 ft in length.

1 link is 7.92 in.; 100 links equal 1 chain.

1 rod equals 16½ ft or about 5 meters.

1 chain equals 66 ft or (4 rods) or about 20 meters.

1 mile equals 5280 ft (80 chains) or 1.609 kilometers.

1 kilometer equals 1000 meters.

1 hectare equals 2.47 acres.

1 acre is 208.7 square ft (10 square chains) or 66.3 square meters.

1 acre contains 43,560 sq. ft or about 13,200 square meters.

A ⅕-acre plot has a radius of 52.7 ft.

A ¼-acre plot has a radius of 58.9 ft.

A section is 1 square mile (80 square chains).

A section is made up of 16 forty-acre square tracts (640 acres).

A township equals 36 sections.

Timber

1 board foot is 12 in. × 12 in. × 1 in.

1 cord is 4ft × 4ft × 8ft or 128 cu. ft or 3.624 cubic meters.

*The United States is gradually converting measurement procedures to the metric system. Since the process has not come about yet in forestry, existing units of measurement are used in this book. To aid the student in making the transition, conversion equivalency can be carried out by using this table and Appendix H.

1 cunit is 100 cu. ft or 2.83 cubic meters.

Diameter breast high (dbh.) 4.5 ft or 1.3 meters.

1 oz. equals 28.3 grams.

1 kilogram (1000 grams) equals 2.204 lb.

The U.S. Metric Conversion Act of 1975 established a gradual, voluntary conversion to the metric system, which is the most widely used system outside of North America. No timetable was scheduled in the law, but inevitably the growing requirement for uniformity in international trade—machinery, commodities, and so forth—will force standardization. There will be a considerable transition period during which we shall have to think in terms of both the old system—miles, feet, acres and board feet, and the new—kilometers, meters, hectares, and cubic meters. The metric system has many advantages besides its nearly universal use: it has one common denominator, the meter, which is directly tied to the decimal system. (See Appendix H.)

It is suggested that students—and their instructors—begin to think in both terms, using conversion factors to understand the new metric system. A bit of mental agility will be needed to be prepared for a future metric system, certain to come.

Drawing the Map

Mapping the forest area in which one is working is usually done at the same time as estimating the volume of standing timber. More often than not, the boundaries of the property are not distinctly marked, so it is necessary to locate corners. In the eastern states, where metes and bounds are used, the boundary lines will be irregular and will be described as bearings and distances. An example of property lines where metes and bounds prevail is shown in Figure 6–5.

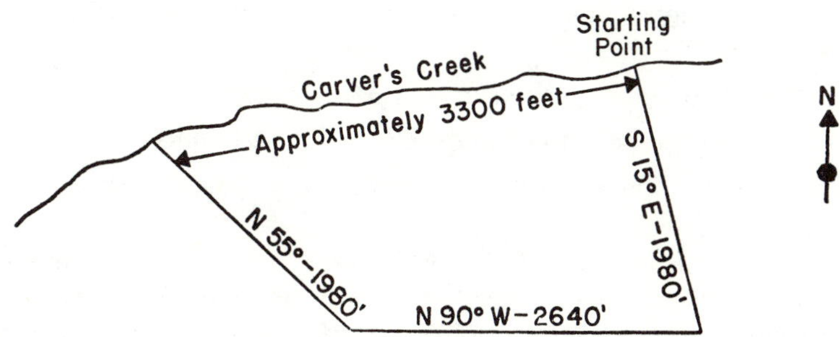

FIGURE 6–5. Traverse of property surveyed with metes and bounds.

Mapping such an area requires that one locate the boundaries by starting at the known corner, sight in each bearing as shown, pace the distance to the next corner and repeat the process until one arrives back at the starting point. Use of previous survey notes is invaluable in locating corners in any survey. Surveyors use a mathematical process for *closing* a *traverse* to make sure of accuracy in legal surveys. However, unless there is some question over the boundaries (and a registered surveyor should handle this), the map should serve its purpose, both as a base map and a means of determining the acreage of the tract.

On lands under the rectangular survey system, the boundaries are run mainly to establish ownership lines for timber sales. The procedure followed in running boundaries is as follows: starting from an established section corner, the technician simply runs a line on the cardinal points of the compass, measuring distance until the corner of the forty being surveyed is found. Then the technician proceeds 20 chains (1320 ft) along each side of the forty until the four sides are *boxed*.

Forestry maps are drawn in the field and are often carried on a clipboard hung from the shoulder with a leather thong. A map sheet such as that shown in Figure 6–6 is one form similar to those used in rectangular surveys. On more intensive surveys, a plane table on a tripod is used for mapping. In addition to determining the area to be covered by the survey, maps serve two other main purposes: they locate and show the extent of the different forest types and they locate important surface features (both artificial and natural) such as roads, power lines, lakes, or streams for future management and logging plans. Maps are always drawn to scale, as for example, 8 in. equal 1 mile. The symbols used in mapping forest land are shown in the cover type map in Figure 6–6. On all forestry maps north is at the top.

All maps should contain the following information.

1. The name or initials of the map maker and the date of the survey.
2. A legend showing the symbols used.
3. The scale used on the map (e.g., 8 in. = 1 mile, etc.)
4. A title such as "Forest Type Map," "Topographic Map," etc.

When sketching in the forest type symbols such as those shown in Figure 6–6, stand density and the range in tree sizes are also shown. Along with the symbol of the pine types *P*, the small letters *r* and *w* are shown to indicate that red and white pine are the principal species.

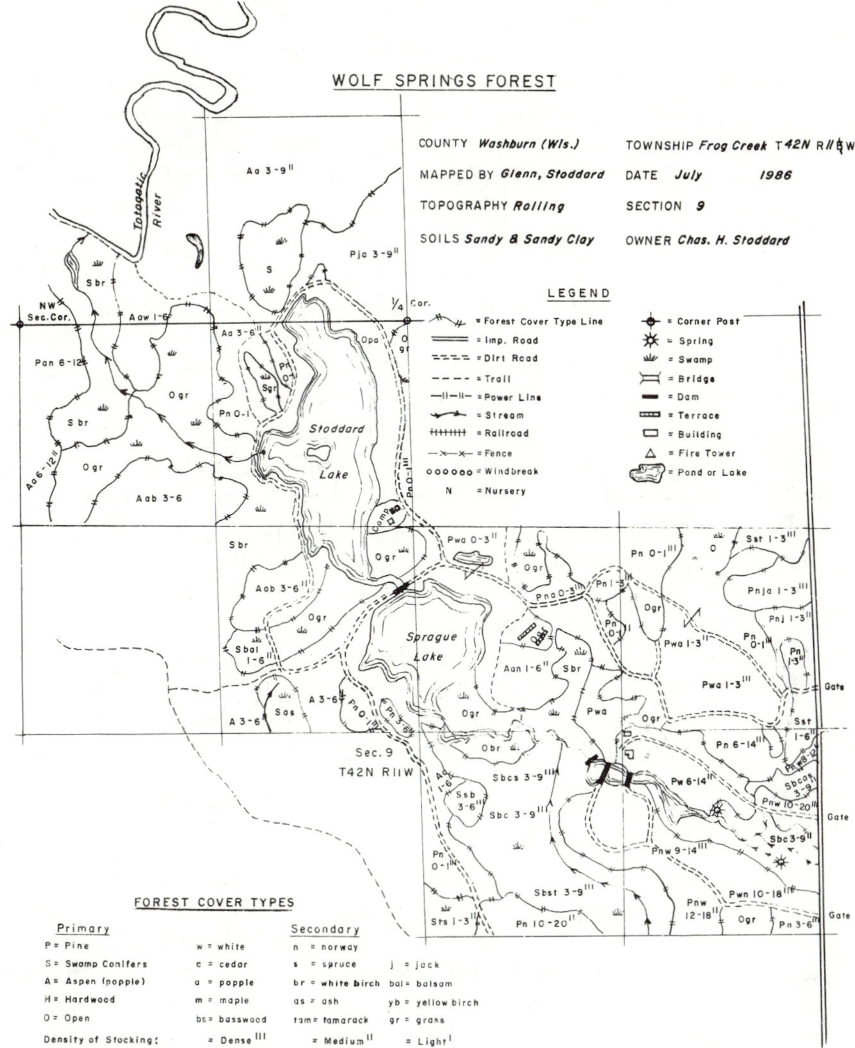

FIGURE 6–6. Map of forest area.

An aspen type *A* accompanied by *w* means an understory of small white pine. The range in diameters is shown simply as 3–9 or 9–12, and so on. Stand density is expressed by underlining with one, two, or three bars under the type lettering to show poor medium or well stocked stands. See Fig 6–6. Thus a completed symbol for a pine type containing red and white pine ranging in dhb. from 9 to 12 in. and well stocked would be Prw 9–12. Medium-stocked long-leaf and slash southern pine ranging from 12 to 16 in. dbh. would be Pls 12–16. Slash marks as in Pls 12–16 are also often used.

One of the important tasks in making forest maps is to keep an accurate check of the distance as one proceeds across forest type boundaries. On the map shown in Figure 6–6, note how type lines are used to denote a change from pine to swamp conifers. Each of these lines must be drawn in and connected on the map.

To determine the area enclosed within an irregularly bounded property or within a forest type, foresters commonly use the *grid* method (small squares). Although a planimeter is more accurate, it is not always available. Knowing the scale of the map drawn, draw a grid on transparent paper, (or take transparent cross-section paper). Each square in the grid represents a known area, such as ½ square in. which in this case is equal to 2½ acres. Place the transparent grid on the map and count all of the grids completely within the area to be determined and add up the acreage. Then, count all the grids that fall partially within the boundary line, estimating the proportion lying inside. If it is half, it will be 1¼ acres, and so on. Other fractions must be estimated proportionately if they are more or less than half of the area. Keep an accurate count on a separate sheet of paper and then add up all the squares and fractions of squares to arrive at the total acreage. A transparent Modified Dot Acreage Grid, which can be used to determine acreage on maps and aerial photos of any scale, may be purchased through firms that handle forestry supplies.

Remote Sensing

There are two methods of recording forest resource information that have opened up whole new dimensions in mapping and in learning where and what is taking place in the forest. These methods are satellite imagery and aerial photography, and they are included under the general heading of *remote sensing*. Satellite imagery is especially useful in detecting insect and disease depredations, acid rain effects and areas where potential forest fire fuels are accumulating. Satellite photography interpretation is an extremely sophisticated art, but its forestry applications are still in their infancy.

Aerial Photographs

Aerial photographs can be of inestimable value in making field maps and in demarcating forest types. Experience with aerial photographs, followed by ground checking, will disclose the relative ease with which different forest types can be delineated. An example is shown on Figure 6–7, with lines added to show compartment boundaries. Roads, waterways, and railroads as well as buildings can be identified on aerial photos. Foresters are developing methods for estimating timber vol-

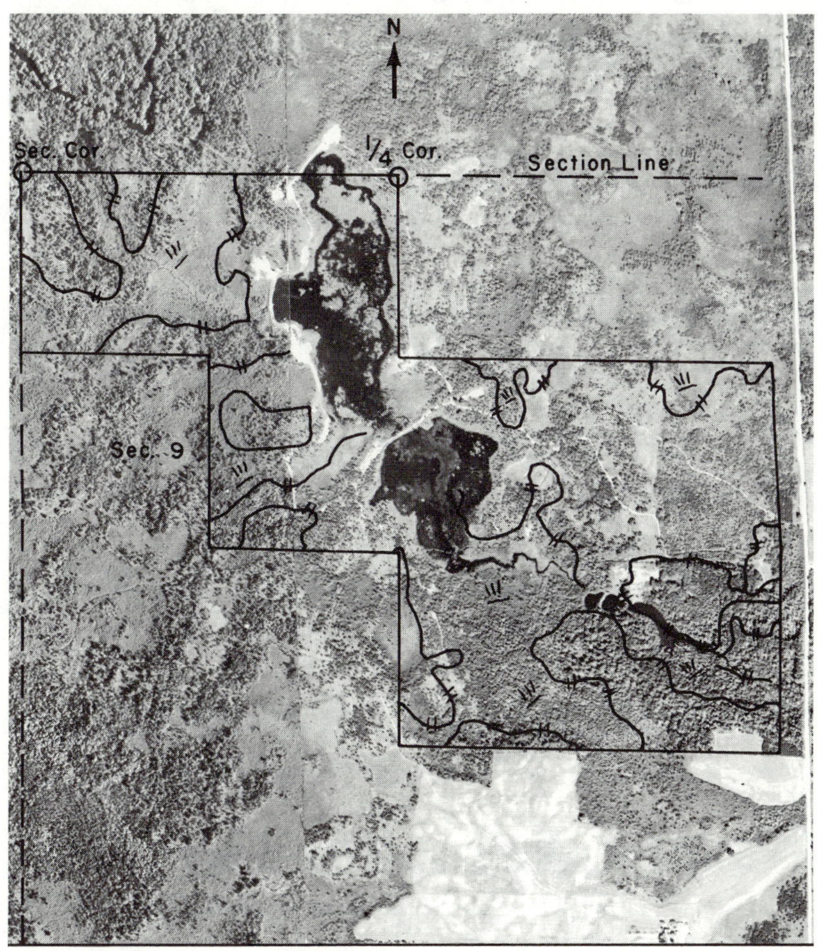

WOLF SPRINGS FOREST
Sec. 9-T42N, R11W
Washburn County, Wisconsin

Scale: 4" = 1 mile —⧺— Forest Type Line

FIGURE 6–7. Aerial photograph of forest area mapped in Fig. 6–6, with compartments delineated.

umes from aerial photos for extensive surveys. Forest types can be determined easily by the use of a stereoscope, and even by the naked eye—especially the type lines between conifers and hardwoods. Small crowned spruce is distinguishable from large crowned pines, for example. Because the use of aerial photos is a highly technical one, detailed study of special texts on this subject is suggested. (See Appendix F.) Aerial photos are usually *read* with the aid of a stereoscope that reveals depth-surface detail through magnification, including hills, valleys, and even tree heights. The stereoscope is made up of two magnifying glasses mounted on an adjustable frame which can be raised or lowered to bring desired parts of the two matching photos into focus. The viewer sees a three-dimensional image with in-depth detail. With proper equipment and training, the viewer can measure tree height and crown width, make timber classifications and even make rough volume estimates. Acreage in aerial photos is also determined by the transparent grid method. The central clearing house for information concerning aerial photographic coverage is the Map Information Office, U.S. Geological Survey, Washington, D. C., 20242. It publishes, at approximately 18-month intervals, a "Status of Aerial Photography," in which a map of the United States is cross-hatched to represent areas that have been photographed, and indicates the agency possessing the photographic negatives.

The procedures for securing aerial photographs are

1. Delineate the area of photographic coverage desired.
2. Locate available photography of the area.
3. Order photo indexes of entire coverage.
4. Determine the area covered by each contact print.
5. Order individual photographs.
6. If necessary, reorder photographs omitted from the first order.

Electronic Surveying

Electronics is another modern science that has revolutionized surveying. Cadastral surveyors are now leapfrogging from mountain to mountain with electronic distance measuring equipment that can measure up to 50 miles and not be off more than a few inches. They do this remarkable feat with lasers.

To clear line and chain distance by hand would take five or six people an entire day to run 1 mile of section line through scrubby timber. The electronic method not only saves time; it also saves thousands of dollars in surveying costs. For instance, it would be virtually impossible to survey much of Alaska by standard methods.

The electronic surveying equipment consists of two units, a master unit that sends out the electronic signal and a remote unit that receives the signal and rebroadcasts it back to the master unit. Both units are portable and can be mounted on tripods. Power is supplied by portable batteries. Both units are equipped with two-way radios so that the operators can talk to each other as they record the measurements, while they are several miles apart.

The laser beam received at the master unit is made visible on a small cathode ray tube (much like the picture tube in a TV set). By measuring electronically to the billionth of a second the time interval between impulses and its radar-like return, the surveyor can calculate the distance between the master unit and the remote unit. The laser beam travels in a straight line and must normally be unobstructed. Ordinarily, it cannot shoot over ridges or through dense timber.

But the flying surveyors have solved this problem, too. They have mounted a master unit in the nose of a helicopter with a built-in hover sight. The hover sight is an arrangement of bubble tubes and prisms developed by the U.S. Geological Survey. It enables the hovering helicopter to sight-in directly over a marked point on the ground. When the vertical position is all right, the operator sends out the signal to the remote unit. This hover sight method works like a giant set of stilts and enables surveyors to "see" over the trees and hills.

Topographic Maps

Occasionally, topographic maps will be needed in rough or mountainous country. These maps differ from land use cover maps by imposing contour lines of known elevations onto a surface base map. Topographic mapping is a complex field operation requiring the use of levels and other refined instruments. Foresters frequently make use of existing local topographic maps for laying out new roads, bridges, or other improvements, but it is not often that they make these maps themselves. Topographic maps have been made for much of the forested area of the United States by the U.S. Geological Survey and may be ordered by sending information on the exact description (i.e., section, township, range, county, state) of the area. Figure 6–8 shows a portion of a topographic map.

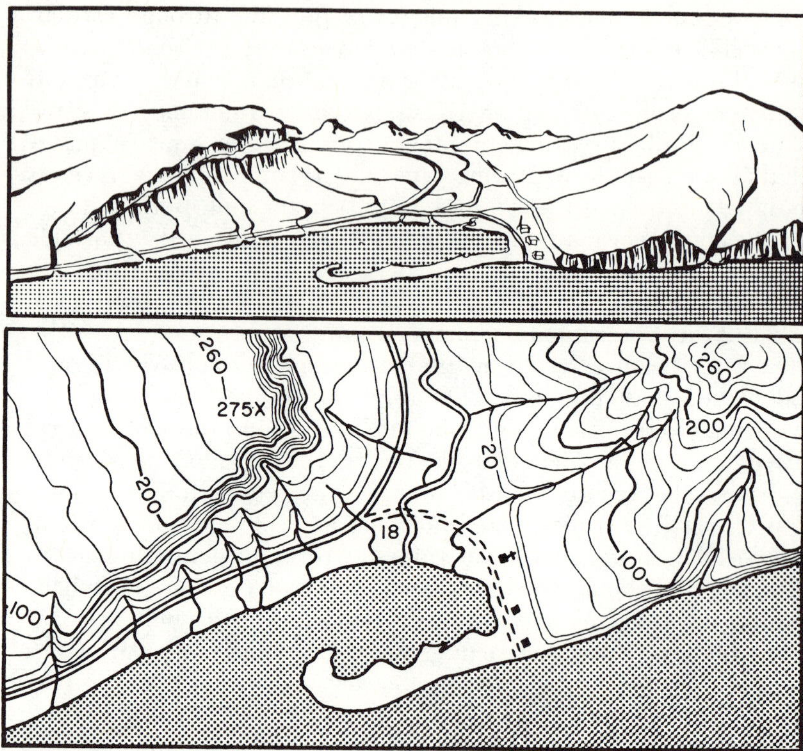

FIGURE 6–8. How relief, hydrographic, and cultural features are shown on a topographic map. Above, *a perspective view of a river valley that lies between two hills. In the foreground is the sea with a bay partly enclosed by a hooked sandbar. On each side of the valley are terraces through which streams have cut gullies. The hill on the right has a gradual slope with rounded forms, while the hill on the left rises abruptly and ends in a sharp precipice from which it slopes gradually away, forming an inclined tableland that is traversed by a few shallow gullies.* Below, *a topographic map of the same area with the ground forms represented by contour lines. The contour interval used here is 20 ft, which means that the vertical distance between one contour and the next is 20 ft (Redrawn from U. S. Geological Survey)*

ESTIMATING STANDING TIMBER VOLUMES

Timber Cruising

Timber cruising is the process by which an estimate of the number of board feet, cords, or pieces (as in the case of posts, poles, piling, etc.) is determined.* On large tracts this determination of the volume of forest products standing in the woods is either by random or systematic sampling of a percentage of the total, multiplying this sample by whatever factor is necessary to determine 100 percent. All the trees in a series of circular plots, usually of ⅕ or ¼ acre in size, are tallied by diameter (and merchantable height). One tally sheet is used for each plot. Ordinarily the decision as to which method (random or systematic sampling) to use will depend on the forester in charge, the agency, or the company's forestry manual, which will have the details spelled out. Random sampling requires considerable judgment and experience; systematic sampling is a mechanical process that can be done by less experienced people.

A simpler method of judging volume, often used on small tracts (less than 10 acres), is to count and keep record of every tenth tree. Trees should be marked after tallying to avoid double counting. Multiplying the total volume of the samples by 10 gives the estimated volume of the entire stand. While this has the advantage of less complexity than the sampling systems, it may actually require more field work.

Most timber cruising is done by a party of two: the *estimator* and the *compassperson*. The estimator makes the map while walking along the line that the compassperson indicates should be followed and notes forest type changes and other symbols at points on the map measured by the compassperson's paces. A beginner on a timber survey party starts as the compassperson; the more experienced person is the estimator. Figure 6–9 shows types of equipment used for timber cruising.

Timber estimators also measure and tally the trees in the strips or sample plots by diameter at breast height (dbh.) 4½ ft above the ground, and the merchantable height by species. They record these facts on tally sheets supplied for this purpose (Figure 6–10). Most tally sheets provide for 2 in. diameter (dbh.) classes—6 in., 8 in., 10

*In addition to these product volumes, measurments often may be in cubic feet, tons of wood, cunits (100 cu. ft of wood) and cubic meters under the metric system.

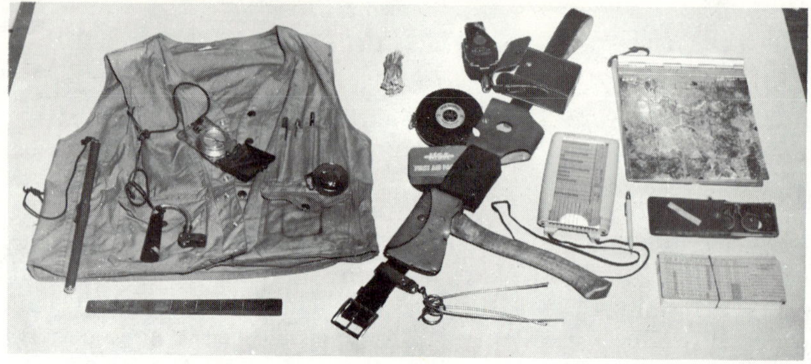

FIGURE 6–9. Instruments and equipment used in forestry practice. On the forester's vest: increment borer, scribe, compass, and diameter tape. Below the vest: a hypsometer stick. Nails. On the forester's belt (from bottom to top): plot pins, hatchet, first aid kit, a 50-ft steel tape, and a spiegelrelaskope (a German device used for determining tree heights and basel area). On the right of the belt are an IBM punch card holder and stylus, a Tatum Board with aerial photo, pocket stereoscope, and punch cards used for IBM data processing. (U. S. Forest Service)

in., 12 in., and so forth. A dot is made for each tree in a box of four, then the four dots are connected with straight lines to make eight trees; and finally, crossed lines are put in the center of the box for the last two trees, giving a total of 10 for each box. The estimator then repeats this process for additional trees, as shown on the tally sheet. Merchantable height is estimated as the number of 16-ft logs and 8-ft half logs, or as the number of pulpwood and sticks in lengths common to the region.

Symbol	·	··	∴	∷	∷	∷	⊐	☐	☒	☒
Number	1	2	3	4	5	6	7	8	9	10

Under mechanical sampling, plots in the property are established at regular intervals so as to cover a predetermined percentage of the area. Let us use forties as an example. Figure 6–11 demonstrates the spacing of 20 fifth-acre plots that are needed to obtain a 10 percent sample (4 acres). A larger percentage would require more sample plots.

The spacing of each plot is shown on the map, and it will be noted that these plots must be taken at these predetermined points wherever they fall. When there are two or more forest types within a forty, there must be a note on each plot tally sheet identifying the forest type in which the plot was located. The forest-type map, which is

TALLY SHEET

STATE *Wisconsin* COUNTY *Washburn* OWNER *Wolf Springs* COVER TYPE *Pnwa*

SECTION *9* T *42N* R *11W* FORTY *NW-SE* ESTIMATOR *C.H. Stoddard* PLOT NO. *8*

D.B.H. IN INCHES	Number of 16-foot logs															NUMBER OF TREES	TOTAL VOLUME 4/ 5/
	PINE 1/					OTHER CONIFERS 2/					HARDWOODS 3/						
	1/2	1	1-1/2	2	2-1/2	1/2	1	1-1/2	2	2-1/2	1/2	1	1-1/2	2	2-1/2		
6																18	.44
8																25	1.22
10																12	524
12																12	746
14																8	909
16																10	1800
18																6	1496
20																3	940
22																2	792
24																–	

TOTAL VOLUME (CORDS–GROSS) *1.66 x 5 = 8.30 cords/acre*

TOTAL VOLUME (BOARD FEET–GROSS) *7207 x 5 = 36,035 B.F./acre*

Field Notes:

1/ Show % in each species: 60% white pine, 30% Norway pine, 10% jack pine.

2/ 80% white spruce, 20% balsam fir.

3/ 20% red maple, 50% aspen, 30% white birch.

4/ Use International Volume Table for board feet (trees 10" and over), cord volume table for those under 10", and multiply number of trees by volume per tree.

5/ Multiply total volume for 1/5 acre plot by 5 to get volume per acre. Deduct from total estimated cull factor.

FIGURE 6–10. Standard tally sheet used to record trees on a sample plot. With regard to Field Note No. 4, see Tables 6–1 and 6–2.

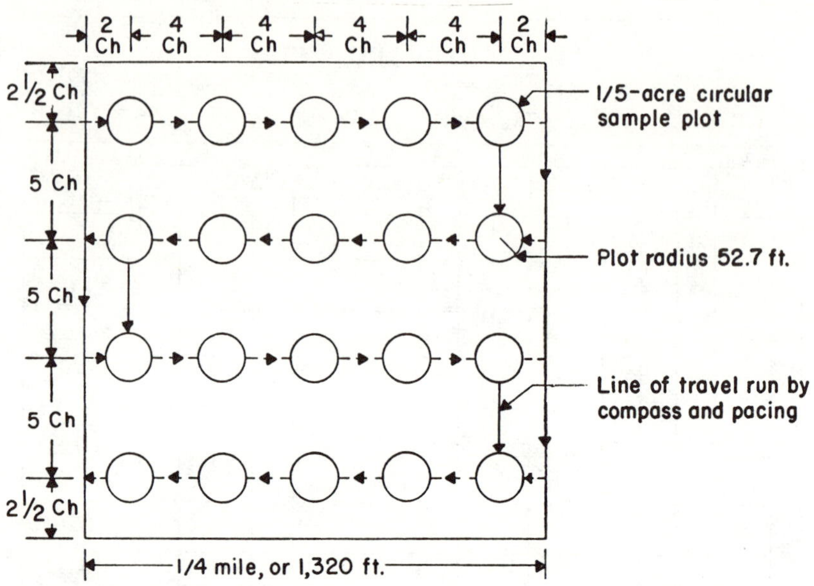

FIGURE 6–11. Plot spacing for a 10 percent sample of a 40-acre tract. (Note: *Ch is abbreviation for chain, 66 ft.)*

prepared as the field work progresses, will show type boundaries so that their areas may be determined later. The volumes present on tally sheets for the same type can thus be brought together and calculated. When the total volume of timber tallied on plots in one type, the total area of the plots, and the area of the forest type within the forty are known, the total volume of timber within the type can be computed. The volumes of timber in each type are then added together to give the total volume on the forty. All tally sheets applying to each description are assembled at the end of the day and separated by type so that the volumes can be calculated.

When estimating timber within an irregularly boundaried property, random sampling is often the most practical method. The number of plots is determined in relation to the percentage sample to be made and the plots are located throughout so as to adequately cover all parts of the area. Where mechanical sampling is used, the procedure just described for irregular types is followed.

In *point sampling* cruising (described in detail later in this chapter) the predetermined number of points are located on the type map or aerial photo to adequately cover and sample all parts of the area to be cruised. Care must be taken to be sure to locate the plots on the ground in the same places they appear on the map or photo, to prevent bias.

Plot lines should be laid out to run perpendicular to the topography. This will ensure a sample of all of the area. If the lines are parallel to the topography, all plots in a line may fall on a ridge or in a valley and one or the other area will be missed.

Equipment Used in Estimating Timber

Several different kinds of tools are used in determining diameter and height of forest trees. Diameters may be measured with *calipers*, with a *diameter tape* (which goes around the circumference), or with a *Biltmore stick*. Heights may be determined with the Biltmore stick or with several other kinds of instruments (hypsometers) designed for this purpose. The *Abney hand level* is also used where accuracy is essential. Both diameter and height are often estimated occularly in the eastern United States. The use of the diameter tape and the calipers to determine dbh are self-explanatory. Figure 6–12 illustrates how the Biltmore stick is used. (See also Figure 1–1.) Tally sheets and base maps are carried in a clip board or aluminum tally-sheet holder that protects them from the weather.

In determining merchantable height, it is important to know how the timber is to be used and the standards used in the volume tables. Sawlogs are usually taken to an 8-in. top (softwoods) and 10-in. top (hardwoods) dib (diameter inside bark) at the small end and pulpwood to 4-in. dib. Measurement of diameters is shown in Figure 6–12. By using the hypsometer scale on the Biltmore stick, one can then determine the merchantable height by counting the number of 16-ft logs and fractional merchantable material in half logs, if they are 8 ft or more in length. A *Pocket Cruiser Stick* is the shortened version of the Biltmore stick hypsometer scale and is often more convenient to handle in the woods. Experienced estimators measure only the occasional *check* trees with instruments because they become quite accurate with occular estimates.

Determining Sawtimber Volumes

Because trees vary according to size, the volume of wood they contain will increase as tree diameter and height increases. Large trees are cut into sawlogs, usually measured in board feet of lumber, whereas small trees used for pulpwood and firewood are figured in cords. A board foot (b.f.) is 12 in. by 12 in. by 1 in. thick, or 144 cu. in. of any dimensions. To determine board feet use the following formula: width in inches times thickness in inches times length in feet divided by 12. Standard cords contain 128 cu. ft and are 4 ft by 4 ft by 8 ft in dimension.

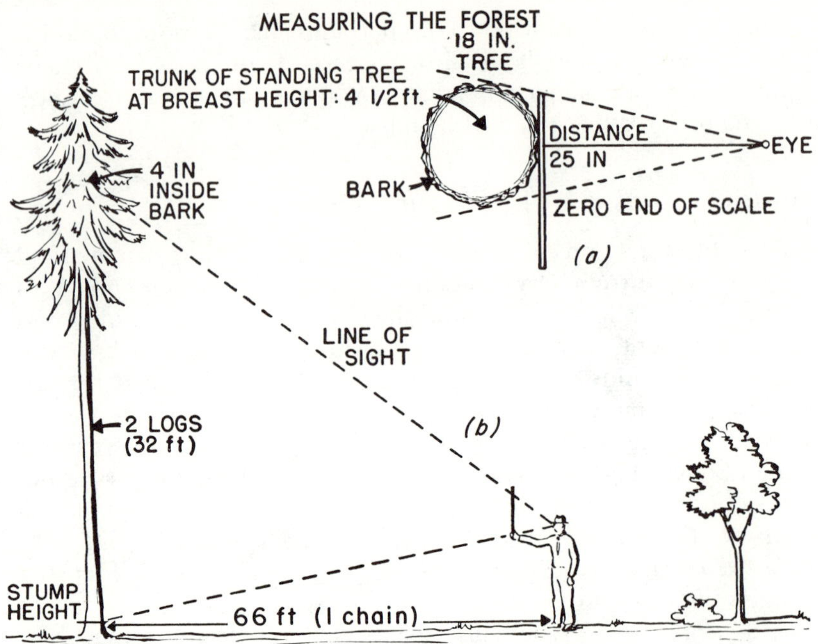

FIGURE 6–12. Using the Biltmore stick. (a) *To measure a diameter, hold the scale horizontally against the tree, 25 in. from the eye, chest high (4½ ft), with the* Biltmore side *of the scale facing the operator. Close one eye and visually line up the zero end of the scale with one side of the tree. Then, holding steady, sight toward the other side of the tree. At the point where the line of vision intersects the scale, read the diameter of the tree.* (b) *To measure merchantable height, stand at a distance of 66 ft from the tree. Hold the Biltmore stick vertically, 25 in. from the eye, with the* hypsometer side *facing the operator. Close one eye and visually line up the zero end of the scale with the stump height. Then, holding steady, sight to the top of the usable trunk length. Where the line of vision intersects with hypsometer scale, the large vertical figure will represent the length, in logs or half logs, of the usable trunk.*

Sawlogs are usually cut into 8-, 10-, 12-, 14-, or 16-ft lengths (up to 32 ft in the West); both hardwood and softwood logs should have 3 to 4 in. additional length for trim allowance to compensate for bottom cuts and crooked end cuts. Poles, posts, and pilings vary according to specification. In determining board foot volume in the East, trees 8- to 10-in. dbh. are considered as sawtimber (depending on local merchantability standards) and hence are measured in board feet. Frequently, those smaller than this are computed in cubic feet or cords.

Volume tables have been constructed (see Chapter 8) that make it possible to determine the number of board feet in standing trees. Trees may vary in form and hence in the volume of board feet or cubic content. Some trees have a relatively large diameter at breast height and become smaller (taper) relatively fast up the stem. Other trees of similar diameter may taper more slowly and consequently have a greater volume of wood. Thus the first log may vary from 80 b.f. in a rapidly tapering tree to 110 b.f. in a slowly tapering tree. Local volume tables have been developed in some areas to account for these differences. Most volume tables specify the conditions and assumptions that went into their construction. A commonly used table is the *composite*, in which variations are averaged out for wide areas (Table 6–1).

Volume tables based on three principal log rules are used in the United States: the International, the Scribner, and the Doyle. In a few localities other log rules are still in use. The International is the most accurate and corresponds closely to the actual amount of lumber a tree will yield. The Scribner is next in accuracy and is based on geometrical construction. When the second digit is dropped from the Scribner and rounded off to the nearest even 10, it is called Scribner Decimal *C*. Although the Doyle is still used mainly in the South, it is least accurate and consistently underestimates volumes of small logs.

TABLE 6–1 COMPOSITE VOLUME TABLES

International 1/4 in. Kerf, Log Scale Volume Table										
dbh	*Number of 16-ft Logs per Tree*									
(in.)	1/2	1	1 1/2	2	2 1/2	3	3 1/2	4	4 1/2	5
	Volume (b.f.)—International Rule									
10	17	39	53	68						
12	30	57	80	100	115					
14	42	79	110	140	163	181	205			
16	59	105	147	180	213	247	278	309		
18	74	135	188	235	278	320	360	400	445	490
20	92	170	236	295	350	402	450	499	552	605
22	112	209	290	362	430	494	555	613	676	704
24	133	252	346	431	512	594	665	742	821	900
26	158	300	409	508	604	698	786	880	980	1080
28	187	348	478	597	705	812	918	1025	1137	1250
30	220	408	552	687	811	934	1061	1180	1315	1450
32	256	471	643	794	935	1077	1216	1358	1519	1680
34	292	534	730	900	1060	1222	1380	1538	1724	1910

TABLE 6–1 *Continued*

International ¼ in. Kerf, Log Scale Volume Table

dbh (in.)	Number of 16-ft Logs per Tree ½	1	1½	2	2½	3	3½	4	4½	5
	Volume (b.f.)—Scribner Rule									
10	14	30	40							
12	28	48	66	78	97					
14	40	70	96	116	141	165	190			
16	54	93	129	158	191	224	252	280		
18	72	122	168	207	248	292	323	355	400	445
20	90	156	212	262	317	366	407	451	502	553
22	111	194	262	328	392	452	505	563	620	678
24	137	236	319	399	472	549	613	687	754	822
26	165	281	381	478	566	653	730	820	901	982
28	195	331	448	559	665	764	857	959	1054	1150
30	227	383	522	648	772	886	995	1112	1228	1345
32	260	439	598	746	888	1019	1140	1278	1424	1570
34	294	500	678	847	1009	1159	1292	1455	1619	1783
	Volume (b.f.)—Doyle Rule									
10	10	16	21							
12	18	29	38	46	52					
14	28	49	66	79	90	104	114			
16	42	71	98	121	142	162	176	189		
18	60	99	134	165	196	224	249	268	296	325
20	80	130	177	220	260	297	330	360	390	420
22	101	170	230	284	336	383	427	464	507	550
24	129	215	292	360	428	486	541	600	655	710
26	160	265	355	436	518	594	667	740	810	880
28	192	320	428	520	620	708	800	888	984	1080
30	228	377	507	626	738	840	949	1040	1170	1300
32	266	440	591	732	862	988	1118	1227	1363	1500
34	305	508	681	849	999	1142	1293	1430	1590	1750

Source: North Central Forest Experiment Station.

Note: Utilization standards: Stump height is 1 ft. Height is the number of usable 10-ft logs to a variable top diameter not smaller than 8 in. inside the bark.

To find the total volume of the trees tallied on a plot tally sheet, multiply the number of trees in each size class by the volume of a single tree of the same class as shown in the appropriate volume table. When this has been repeated for all size classes represented in the tally, sum up the volumes of each to obtain the plot volume.

Estimating or Cruising Pulpwood Timber

The procedure used in estimating standing pulpwood timber is quite similar to that for estimating sawtimber except that the trees are smaller and measured in cords or cubic feet. Plot tallies are obtained in the same fashion. Trees are measured and tallied by (1) dbh classes only (2) by dbh classes and merchantable height classes in terms of 8-ft *bolts* (small logs), or (3) by dbh classes and merchantable height classes in 4-ft bolts. The choice of either the first, second, or third method of measuring or estimating and tallying will depend on whether a local volume table (the one that gives volumes by dbh classes only), or one like Table 6–2 (giving volumes by dbh classes and merchantable height classes in 8-ft lengths), or one which gives volumes by dbh classes and 4-ft lengths is available. If tables of all three methods are at hand, one will have a choice and, other things being equal, should select the local volume table because the work in the field and office will be easier and cheaper.

Table 6–2 gives volumes in terms of cords, but sometimes the only table that can be obtained will give volumes in solid cubic feet. If a table of the latter variety *is* the only one available, the total cubic-foot volume of the trees tallied on a tally form must be divided by the

TABLE 6–2 CORDWOOD COMPOSITE VOLUME TABLE

dbh	*Used Height in Number of 8-ft Bolts*							
(in.)	1	2	3	4	5	6	7	8
	Volume in Cords/Tree							
6	0.02	0.03	0.04	0.06				
8	0.03	0.05	0.07	0.09	0.12	0.14		
10	0.05	0.07	0.10	0.13	0.17	0.20	0.24	0.27
12	0.07	0.10	0.14	0.18	0.22	0.27	0.32	0.36
14	0.10	0.13	0.18	0.23	0.29	0.35	0.42	0.47
16	0.12	0.17	0.22	0.29	0.36	0.44	0.52	0.59
18	0.15	0.20	0.27	0.35	0.44	0.53	0.63	0.72
20	0.18	0.25	0.32	0.42	0.52	0.63	0.76	0.85
22	0.22	0.29	0.38	0.49	0.61	0.74	0.88	1.00

Source: North Central Forest Experiment Station.

Note: Utilization standards: Volume is stem volume above 1-ft stump in standard unpeeled cords. The standard cord is 4 ft × 4 ft × 8 ft. To find the approximate *peeled volume,* subtract 12 percent. Height is number of usable 8-ft bolts to a variable top diameter not less than 4 in. inside the bark.

Cordwood Volume Table (applicable to all species except cedar).

number of solid cubic feet of wood in the average stacked standard cord (4ft × 4ft × 8ft = 128 cu. ft). This will give the plot volumes in terms of standard cords, the common unit of measure of pulpwood. The average standard cord contains about 80 solid cu. ft of wood, and this figure is a safe one to use as a converting factor, (i.e., 128 cu. ft in a stacked cord contains approximately 80 cu. ft of solid wood).

Deductions for Defect and Cull

The tree volumes obtained and recorded by the previously described methods are *gross* volumes, with no allowance for defect. Many trees, especially in old or poorly managed stands, contain some rot or other defective material. If a tree is obviously not sound, it is the usual practice to make arbitrary deductions for the defect. For example, if the first 8 ft in a tree are hollow, this length should be deducted from the total merchantable log length in the tree.

There will also be *hidden* defects that will show up when the logs are sawed even though they are not visible when the trees are marked and measured in the woods. To compensate for these hidden defects, a certain percent of the total gross volume of the trees should be deducted. Usually, the amount of hidden defect varies between 10 and 25 percent. If some timber has been cut and the logs scaled from this or a similar local stand, a close estimate of the defect can be made. (See Chapter 8.) This percentage deduction is subtracted from the total volume and is usually *in addition* to the allowance made for visible defects at the time the tree is measured.

Pulpwood is often cut as either 5 ft 3 in. or 4-ft bolts in the South, 4 ft in the Northeast, and 8-ft (or 100 in.) long in the Lake States.

Cumulative Volume Tally Sheets

Another development that saves time is called the cumulative tree volume tally sheet. Note in the sample shown in Table 6–3 that each tree in the diameter class is crossed off and the last one shows the total volume in that class. Adding the total for all the diameter classes gives the total volume for the plot on a one-per-acre basis. It simplifies the whole process greatly but has some limitations if detail or a high degree of accuracy are desired. Instructions for using the cumulative volume method are shown at the bottom of the tally sheet.

TABLE 6-3

CUMULATIVE-VOLUME TALLY NWSE, SEC. 9 T42N R11W DATE 7/10/85

LINE NO. 2 PLOT NO. 8 BY C.S.

USE 1/5 ACRE PLOTS. VALUES SHOWN IN TABLES ARE PER ACRE VOLUMES

DBH	Number of 16 foot logs per tree: 1	1½	2	2½	3	3½	4	4½	5	TOTALS	ESTIMATED CUT
8	1 2 4 5 6 7 8 10 11 12 13 14 16 17 18 19 20 22 23 24	2 4 5 7 9 11 13 14 16 18 20 22 23 25 27 29	2 4 6 8 10 12 14 16 18 20 23 25 27 29 31 33	2 4 7 9 11 14 16 18 20 22 25 27	LEGEND: X White Pine; Z Norway Pine; X Aspen; ② White Spruce						
10	X X X X X 13 15 16 20 22 24 26 29 31 33 35 37 40 42 44 46 48 51	X X 9 12 15 18 21 24 27 30 32 35 38 41 44 47 50 53	4 8 12 16 20 24 28 32 36 40 43 47 51 55 59 63	4 9 14 18 22 27 32 36 40 45	5 10 15 20 25 30 35	ESTIMATED CULL % 10				3000	
12	X X X X X 20 23 26 30 33 36 40 43 46 50	X X 14 18 23 27 32 36 41 46 50 55	6 12 17 23 29 35 41 46 52 58 64 70	7 14 20 27 34 41 48 54	8 16 23 31 39 46 54 62	9 18 27 35 44	10 19 27 39 48	12 23 35 47 58		4400	
14	4 8 12 17 21 25 29 33 37 42	X X X 23 29 35 41 47	8 16 25 33 41 47	10 19 30 39 48 58	11 22 33 43 54 65	12 25 37 50 62 74	14 27 41 54 68 81	16 33 50 66 82 99	18 35 53 71 88 106	4100	
16	6 11 17 22 28 33 40 44	8 16 24 31 39 47 55 63	X X X 39 49 59 69 79	13 25 38 51 64 76	14 29 43 57 72 86	17 33 50 66 83 99	18 36 54 71 89	23 45 68 90 113	24 48 72 97 121	10,000	
18	7 14 22 29 36 44 51 58	10 21 31 41 52 62 72 82	X X X 52 64	16 ③1 47 63 78 94	19 38 56 75 94	22 43 65 86 108	23 47 70 93 117	30 59 88 118 148	32 63 94 126 158	8300	
20	9 18 27 36 45 54 63 72	13 26 38 51 64 77 90	16 32 48 64 80 97 113	20 39 59 79 118 138	24 47 71 95 118	28 55 83 110 138	30 59 89 118 148	36 72 109 145	38 77 115 154	5200	
22	11 22 33 44 55 66 77 88	16 31 47 62 78	20 39 59 79 98	24 48 72 96 120	29 58 87 115	34 67 101 135 168	36 73 109 145	45 89 134	47 95 142	4400	
24	13 27 40 53 66	19 38 57 75	24 47 71 95	29 58 87 116	35 70 105	41 81 122	44 88 132	51 102 153	54 107 161	BOARD FEET PER ACRE	CUT PER ACRE
26	16 31 47 63 78	22 45 67 89	23 56 84 112	34 68 103	39 78 117	44 89 134	48 97 146	53 107 160	57 114 171	39,400	
28	18 37 55 74	26 53 79	33 66 99	40 80 121	46 92 138	52 105 157	57 114	60 120	63 126		

VOLUME IN HUNDREDS OF BOARD FEET (INTERNATIONAL 1/4)

Instructions for Using Table 6–3

The figures on this volume tally are computed for a ⅕-acre plot (radius 52.7 ft). The figures are cumulative in each block, the first number representing the volume of one tree, the second number the volume of two trees, etc.

Tally trees in each "DBH Merchantable Height" block by crossing out numbers in consecutive order, beginning from the first number in the block. The last number crossed out in each block indicates the combined volume of all trees in that "DBH Merchantable Height" class. For each dbh class add the volume in all blocks and enter this sum as a subtotal in the "Total" column. Total merchantable volume equals the sum of these subtotals.

Sawtimber Tally. Numbers in blocks represent hundreds of board feet (International ¼ in. Rule). They are already multiplied by 5, thus giving volume per acre directly from a ⅕-acre plot.

Legend. Different species or species groups are distinguished by using different symbols or colors in crossing out numbers in each block. Room is reserved in the "Legend" box to record the symbol or color used for each species. (Adapted by Tennessee Valley Authority from S. R. Gevorkiantz, Lake States Forest Experiment Station, St. Paul, Minnesota.)

MISCELLANEOUS FORESTRY MEASUREMENTS

Growth Rates

Quite frequently foresters need to know how fast trees are growing over specific periods of time, either for research data or for planning the allowable cut. The growth rate of individual trees is largely controlled by age, species, site quality, and nearness to surrounding trees. The factors that affect the growth rate of individual trees determine the growth of forest stands. To attain maximum growth of a stand, the stand must approach a fully stocked condition where trees have adequate room to grow and yet where there is a maximum number of trees.

Trees grow in both diameter and height. Repeated measurements of these two variables at 5 or 10-year intervals can provide accurate estimates of growth during the period between measurements. The difference in volume of the tree or stand at the time of the two measurements can be expressed as either annual or periodic growth.

Past growth rates are most often used to evaluate the rapidity of growth in an individual tree and also as a means of predicting future growth of entire stands. Growth of the individual tree may be used to indicate its growth rate as compared to other trees in the stand and indirectly its maturity or desirability as future growing stock. Growth of the entire stand can be used as a rough guide in setting allowable cut.

Growth rate of an individual tree is evaluated on the basis of the width of the annual rings and on changes in its merchantable height. Diameter measurements are made at 4½ ft from the ground (dbh) with the use of an increment borer; or by counting and measuring the annual rings on the stump. Height may be measured directly in the case of a felled tree or estimated in a standing tree.

Growth of a forest stand is expressed in board feet, cords, or any other common forest unit of measure and may be indicated as a percent of the original volume. Growth in a forest stand is often considered to have two basic elements: growth of the merchantable trees and growth of trees that are approaching merchantable size or ingrowth. Only the better trees, trees considered to be desirable growing stock, are used either to predict growth of the stand or as sample trees.

Growth in the forest stand is usually predicted on the basis of sample tree measurements taken in the process of making a timber inventory. It is common practice to measure one or two such trees on each inventory plot.

The diameter of sample trees is measured at dbh with a diameter tape or calipers. The merchantable height is measured or estimated and an increment core is taken and measured. In the sample growth calculation which follows, the number of rings in the last inch of radial growth is used. Other growth prediction systems use measurement of the radial growth during the past 10 or 20 years.

It is very desirable that sample trees be selected in proportion to the acreage and number of trees in various conditions in the forest. This is essential in order to eliminate bias in the sample. When various portions of a forest tract are sampled at different intensity or with recognized variability, the sample trees for each portion thus recognized should be segregated and computed separately. An alternative would be to weigh the sample on the basis of the acreage or number of good growing stock trees found in each tract.

One rough method for calculating the average annual growth of a forest tract is to divide the total timber volume by the average age of the stand. This age can be determined by either counting the annual rings of a sample number of trees of representative sizes on stumps or by the use of an increment borer. For example, a stand with 8000 b.f. per acre that averages 80 years old has grown at the rate of 100 b.f. per acre per year.

Although the most accurate growth estimate would be obtained through the remeasurement of individual trees or stands, only past growth is thus obtained. It is usually desirable to estimate future growth of the stand. A simplified system commonly used for such predictions follows.

Assume that, if in a fully stocked stand, the average for the several sample trees yielded the following information.

Average tree (dbh 12 in. up)—D	13.2 in.
Used height (merchantable)—H	24 ft
Radial growth rate in rings per inch—R	9 rings per in.
Number of near merchantable trees (10 in. dbh)	15 trees
Number of merchantable trees (12 in. up dbh)	50 trees

The growth calculation would then be as follows.

GROWTH ON GOOD GROWING STOCK

1. Average tree (dbh 12 in. up) [dbh 13.2 in. [D] used height 24 [H]→ GROWTH RATE IN RINGS PER INCH 9 [R]

Height Factors
[H] [F]
16 ft–1.20
24 ft–1.07
32 ft–1.00
40 ft– .95

2. Growth per year in average tree $\dfrac{\boxed{D}\,13.2 \times \boxed{H}\,24 \times \boxed{F}\,1.07}{-10 \times \boxed{R}\,9} = 3.8$ b.f. [G]

3. Ingrowth per year from Near merchantable trees (dbh 10 in.) into merchantable stand (dbh 12 in. up)

   Number of trees per acre 10 in. dbh. $15 \times \dfrac{50}{\boxed{R}\,9}$ b.f. $= 83$ b.f. [K]

4. Total growth per year:
   Number of trees per acre (dbh 12 in. up) 50 × [G] 3.8 = 190 plus [K] 83 = 273 b.f. per acre [L]

If there were 20 acres of such forest land then the growth on the entire tract would be:

Number of acres 20 × [L] 273 = [M] 5460 b.f. Total growth

Stand tables show the number of trees in each diameter class on a per-acre basis and are constructed by averaging all plot data on tally sheets. They are mainly used for determining volumes and those trees that might logically be marked for cutting. Stock tables show the corresponding volumes by diameter classes. Growth data obtained from increment borings are added to stand tables to show what sizes and trees may be in the years ahead and so guide the forester in making management plans (Table 6–4).

Basal area, the number of square feet per acre represented in trees measured at dbh, is a useful method for determining proper stocking. By using optimum basal area tables for the species under consideration and comparing them with the stand being managed, a good measure of comparison is obtained. For example, foresters have found that when loblolly, slash, or shortleaf pine reach 120 sq. ft of basal area per acre, they are too dense and are in need of thinning. If the thinning takes the stand down to about 80 ft basal area, it will be in a better situation for new, fast growth.

Yield tables are available for most even-aged forest types. They give the expected volume per acre of timber in fully stocked stands of a given species for a variety of site index classes over a normal range of age classes. The reader should refer to a text on forest mensuration for applications of basal area and yield tables.

Timber Sales Procedures

On both public and private forests, considerable preliminary work is necessary to prepare timber for sale. Most large forest-owning organizations have a manual containing full instructions as to how they proceed with a sale, so the general principles will only be sketched here. Assume that the tract to be sold has already been estimated for volume and that it is part of a forest management plan (see Chapter 7) that shows that a quantity of certain species is ready for cutting. The forest manager assembles a timber marking crew to mark the trees for cutting and the boundaries of the cutting area. The choice of trees to be marked depends upon the size and species composition of the stand and upon the silvicultural system chosen. (See Chapter 5.) Sufficient volume must usually be marked to make it profitable for the logger to operate.

The marked trees are recorded on tally sheets in small tracts, but on large ones the sampling methods used in timber cruising are usually followed. The total volumes for each species are recorded in cords and board feet. The values are determined by methods described in Chapter 7. Timber sale agreement forms are shown in Appendix D.

TABLE 6–4 STAND AND STOCK TABLE FOR NORTHERN HARDWOOD AND HEMLOCK FOREST TYPE (NORTHEASTERN WISCONSIN) AVERAGE ACRE—MERCHANTABLE TIMBER—VOLUMES IN BOARD FEET—SCRIBNER SCALE—NET VOLUME OLD GROWTH STAND

dbh (in.)	*Number of Trees*					
	Hemlock	Sugar Maple	Yellow Birch	Basswood	Miscellaneous Hardwoods	Total
R	15.13	101.74	83.50	3.21	38.21	244.29
2	14.09	64.36	15.75	11.88	9.39	115.47
4	9.61	16.49	8.97	3.54	6.31	44.92
6	8.14	8.11	4.51	1.80	3.49	26.05
8	6.48	5.78	3.04	2.13	2.06	19.49
Total 2 in.+	38.32	93.74	32.27	18.35	23.25	205.93
10	6.08	3.96	1.33	0.88	0.75	13.00
12	4.90	3.77	1.28	0.54	0.83	11.32
14	3.90	3.29	1.44	0.59	0.58	9.80
16	2.86	2.32	1.33	0.50	0.50	7.51
18	2.38	2.33	1.04	0.36	0.30	6.41
20	1.59	1.64	0.90	0.26	0.32	4.71
22	1.27	1.06	0.54	0.15	0.14	3.16
24	0.88	0.86	0.39	0.11	0.03	2.27
26	0.61	0.40	0.12	0.07	0.01	1.21
28	0.32	0.23	0.18	0.03	–	0.76
30+	0.33	0.31	0.20	0.14	—	0.98
Total	25.12	20.17	8.75	3.63	3.46	61.13

dbh (in.)	Net Scribner Volume (b.f.)						Basal Area (sq. ft)
	Hemlock	Sugar Maple	Yellow Birch	Basswood	Miscellaneous Hardwoods	Total	
R							
2							
4				Negligible			
6							
8							
Total 2 in. +							
10	130.9	52.5	16.5	11.7	8.5	220.1	7.08
12	242.6	187.2	59.6	32.0	37.4	558.8	8.90
14	327.4	298.0	116.8	44.6	45.0	831.8	9.86
16	383.7	306.1	168.3	87.4	58.5	1,004.0	10.50
18	460.3	445.1	179.2	77.5	50.8	1,212.9	11.32
20	425.8	435.0	204.8	70.5	74.3	1,210.4	9.58
22	445.8	364.2	153.2	79.8	42.1	1,085.1	8.35
24	386.9	379.0	135.5	75.6	11.3	988.3	7.14
26	331.7	220.2	53.6	59.9	4.6	670.0	4.45
28	210.1	150.4	87.7	45.7	—	493.9	3.24
30 +	299.7	245.2	118.6	144.4	—	807.9	4.80
Total	3,644.9	3,082.9	1,293.8	729.1	332.5	9,083.2	85.22

Source: Adapted from U. S. Forest Service-Forest Survey Stand Tables for Northeastern Wisconsin.

Boundary Marking

Boundary marking is usually done by the compass and pacing method, following the previously prepared map of the area described earlier in this chapter. The compassperson who has developed proficiency can often do this job working alone. Where boundaries may be in dispute, a registered surveyor should be employed.

MORE PROCEDURES FOR TIMBER ESTIMATION

The preceding discussion has described basic methods for determining volumes in timber stands and mapping out areas. There are several additional systems that can speed up the work considerably. One of these methods is called *point sampling*, which uses a glass wedge prism or angle gauge. These are used to determine if a particular tree within the plot should be counted or not.

Other methods for controlling accuracy may be found in the textbooks and government bulletins shown in the references for this chapter. (See Appendix F.) Time will tell how well they stand up in practice. Regarding all methods there is no substitute for practical field application and experience.

Point sampling does not require that the plot diameters and tree diameters be measured. The cruiser counts the number of trees and the heights in bolts or logs whose diameter at breast height appears larger than the cross arm of the angle gauge or that do not appear to be detached from the stem when viewed through the prism wedge.

A simple angle gauge may be constructed by mounting a 1-in. cross arm on the end of a 33-in. stick. A peep sight is mounted on the other end. The end with the peep sight is held up to the eye and the instrument is sighted at the trees. Those trees that appear larger than the cross arm are counted. Those trees that just cover the cross are considered borderline and must be checked carefully, otherwise, a bias can result. To verify whether or not a tree that appears borderline should be counted, the estimator should (1) measure the tree dbh to the nearest 0.1 in. (0.25 cm); (2) tape the horizontal distance from the sampling point to the tree center at dbh, measuring to the nearest 0.1 ft (0.03 m); (3) compute the limiting distance as tree dbh times the PRF (*plot radius factor*, or 10 for a 10-factor prism or angle gauge, etc). If the tree is as close or closer than the limiting distance, it is counted. To save time in the field, tables of limiting distances can be carried.*

*See Wenger (1984) for further details on point sampling.

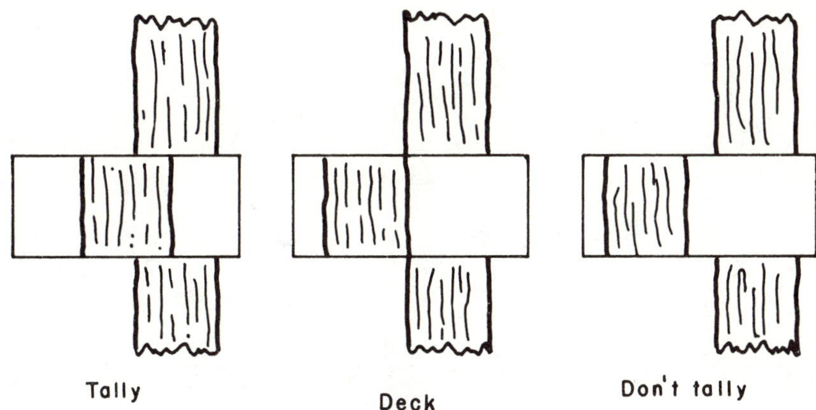

FIGURE 6–13. Use of prism wedge.

When using a wedge prism the sections of the tree covered by the prism appear to be displaced (Figure 6–13). Those sections that do not appear to be completely displaced from the main trunk of the tree are counted. Those in which the opposite edges of the section covered by the prism and the main trunk appear to line up are considered borderline and must be checked. When the section covered by the prism appears to be completely displaced from the main stem the tree is not counted.

Care must be exercised when using either the angle gauge or the prism wedge to eliminate errors that may occur due to improper procedures.

Care must also be taken to assure that the observation on a plot is taken directly over the plot center. When using the *angle gauge*, the eye is the plot or point center. Be certain that the eye is maintained as the center when taking the tree count (Figure 6–14). Trees that lean toward or away from the center are treated as normal trees. Turn the cross arm until it is at right angles to the main stem when sighting on trees that lean to the right or left. Slope correction factors are applied where the slope exceeds 15 percent.

When sighting on trees that are hidden from view from the point center, care must be taken to maintain the same distance when moving off the point center.

When using the prism wedge, the prism is held over the point center. Again care must be taken to assure that observations are made from the point center. As with the angle gauge, precautions should be taken to maintain the same distance when sighting on hidden trees.

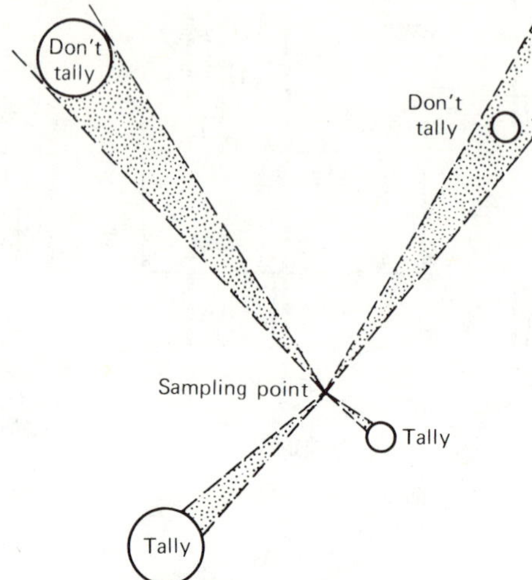

How point-sampling works in the field. Circles represent cross sections of trees at breast height, shaded areas indicate angle-gauge projections from sampling point.

FIGURE 6–14. Use of angle gauge.

Another precaution that applies to the wedge prism is to be sure that it is held in a vertical position and at right angles to the line of sight. Tilting the prism away from or towards the observer can cause a larger displacement and can cause a tree to be omitted from the count. Any rotation of the prism in the vertical position will cause a smaller displacement thereby including trees that should be omitted.

In the *point sampling* method, cruising is commonly done by forest type. Types and acreages are usually determined from aerial photos and type maps.

A reconnaisance of the area is made to determine the variability of the stand and the number of points needed to give the level of accuracy.

Plot lines or point sample lines are laid out on the type map and a predetermined number of preliminary plots taken to obtain the necessary information to determine the variability of the stand between sample points. A count is taken of the *in* trees at each point. Each sample point is tallied separately and the information used in a mathematical formula to determine how representative the samples are of the total forest volume. The student should refer to a standard forest mensuration text for the detailed mathematical methodology needed to calculate the number of sample plots required for any given forest survey.

When the number of sample points needed is determined, cruise lines should be laid out on the type map or aerial photo for each type.

In placing the actual points on the ground, care must be taken to assure that they are on the same place as on the map or photo to ensure against bias.

When the point is established, the cruiser uses the angle gauge (Figure 6–15) or wedge prism and calls out the species and height in bolts or logs. The tally person records the tree on a cumulative volume tally sheet or a tally sheet prepared for a specific basal area factor. The tally person should be careful to tally each plot as it is measured.

The data are summarized into volume per acre and multiplied by number of acres in the tract to obtain the total volume.

In addition to this method of calculating volumes, there are shortcuts that can give good results nearly as good. It so happens that the count of trees, multiplied by 10 gives an estimate of basal area per acre (using a 10 Basal Area Factor prism or angle gauge). Suppose that the cruiser has tallied a total of 240 qualifying trees at 30 sampling points on the area. Then the estimated basal area (b.a.) per acre would be equal to

$$10\,\frac{\text{number of tallied trees } (N)}{\text{number of sampling points}} = 10\,\frac{240}{30} = 80 \text{ sq. ft b.a.}$$

If volume in cords is desired, another shortcut is available:

total number of sticks (not trees) $\times$ 0.6 = cords/acre
total number of sticks plus total number of trees divided by 2

$$\frac{S + T}{2\,N} = \text{cords/acre}$$

To calculate volume in board feet (Scribner) multiply the number of 16-ft logs $\times$ 600 = b.f. for each point per acre.

Continuous Forest Inventory

On large properties a system for keeping current records of timber volumes that is rapidly gaining in favor has been named the *Continuous Forest Inventory*. The *CFI* operates on the principle of regular remeasurement of a representative number of permanently located circular plots. The plot locations are mechanically predetermined to include

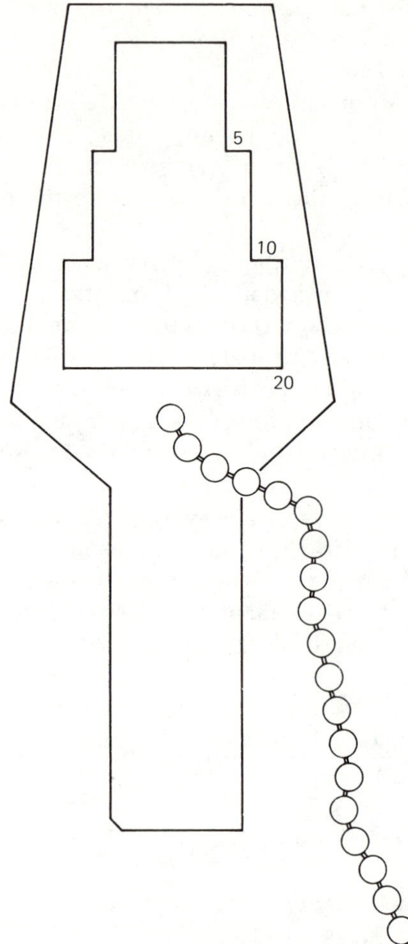

FIGURE 6–15. Fixed type angle gauge. A handy, inexpensive basal area angle gauge with 5, 10, 20, and 40 factors. This die-cut, precision instrument can be used in the same manner as a prism. Hold it exactly 25 in. from the eye with the end of the chain in your teeth; stretch it tight, select the factor you want to use and rotate 360° around a point. Be sure the "Cruise-Angle" is over the point at all times while selecting tally trees. Any tree that more than fills the area designated 5 is a tally tree. The same goes for 10, 20, and 40 factors. Tally all trees around a complete circle and multiply the total number of trees by the factor chosen for basal area per acre. To use the 40-factor gauge, turn the "Cruise-Angle" on its side and use the oblong opening in the same manner. (Ben Meadows Co. Atlanta)

the proper proportions of each type and size class. Tree measurements are made with more than usual care; stand tables are constructed; detailed growth and mortality studies are made; and changes resulting from cutting are recorded. The CFI system also keeps records of changes in size and quality of timber as well as species shifts. While it may not completely replace regular reinventories, the CFI system may reduce the necessity for making them at short intervals.

Computer Programming and Data Processing Systems

Industries and government agencies that use computers put their forest data into a *programmed system* for data recovery. Computers will, for example, take stand table volumes and corresponding growth information and project expected timber yields for 10, 20, or more years into the future. Forest managers can keep a very close watch on each portion of their forest without having to make repetitive field examinations. It is, of course, necessary to make periodic remeasurements, weigh the effects of windstorms, insects, disease, and other causes of mortality. The computerized results are only as good as the data fed into the system itself.

Many other uses for computers have been found by foresters. Land title records, logging cost data analysis, production and sales information, and nearly any part of the forest business that can be measured can be effectively computerized. Computer programmers need to be trained in forestry terms and practices, and foresters need to learn the basics of computer operation if the best results are to be obtained.

Portable data collectors (PDCs) are recent entries into the field of forestry instruments. They are useful where data must be collected at locations remote from data processing equipment. Forestry applications range from timber inventory, log scaling, log and lumber inventory, research monitoring and numerous special field operations. PDCs have the advantage of providing and storing data for later processing and analysis. Less time is required for the collection of data, and the development of final information for decision making, than with traditional manual processes.

Individual project operating costs can also be determined in advance by computer programming. Knowing slopes and topography, earth removal and paving unit costs, the total road cost per unit through a given area can be accurately estimated. Similiar estimates of logging costs and profits can also be calculated from stand volume and logging data.

QUESTIONS

1. How many sections are there in a township?
2. What does T42N R11W mean?
3. Make a sketch of a section showing each forty and locate the NW–SW with the number 1, the SW–NE with number 2 and the SE–SW with number 3.
4. How are distances usually measured in forest surveying?
5. When *sighting* a compass due south, what is the bearing and what is the azimuth reading?
6. How is the acreage of a forest type determined (approximately) from a type map?
7. How does one record seven trees on a standard tally sheet?
8. How many board feet (International Scale) are there in the following trees?
   (a) 14 in. dbh and two logs.
   (b) 18 in. dbh and three logs.
9. Using the composite volume tables for International Rule, what is the total volume of three trees 14 in. dbh with two logs plus two trees 12 in. dbh with 1½ logs?
10. Using the composite cordwood volume table, how much volume (in cords) is there in the following trees?
    (a) 8 in. dbh and four bolts.
    (b) 10 in. dbh and three bolts.
11. What are the tree measurements required to determine growth of a tree?
12. What factors influence rate of tree growth?
13. When using the prism wedge in point sampling, the eye is the sampling point. True or false?
14. When using the angle gauge, the eye is the sampling point. True or false?
15. When border line trees are encountered in point sampling:
    (a) Count all such trees.
    (b) Do not count such trees.
    (c) Count every other tree.
    (d) verify whether or not a tree should be tallied;
    (e) Forget the plot and move on to the next plot.
16. In cruising, all plots should be taken where the density is greater and the trees are larger to assure the greatest volume possible. True or false?
17. A Southern pine forest averages 40 cords per acre in a 25-year growth period. What has been the average annual growth rate?

18. A second-growth Douglas-fir forest in the state of Washington has been growing at the rate of ¾ cord per acre for 60 years. What is its volume per acre?

EXERCISES

1. Locate one of the forest areas in your vicinity by section and township (if this system is used).
2. Check your own pacing and practice using a compass by measuring a known direction and distance through the woods.
3. Make a forest cover map of a small tract showing forest, other natural and artificial features. Use the proper symbols for each.
4. Demonstrate the use of the Biltmore stick, diameter tape, and other forestry instruments to which you may have access.
5. Estimate the volume of timber on a fifth-acre plot by tallying all the trees according to diameter classes and applying the proper volumes to each from the appropriate volume table.
6. Examine an aerial photograph of a forest area with which you are familiar and try to identify the forest types and other features.

SEVEN

FOREST MANAGEMENT AND TIMBER PRODUCTION FINANCE

The late Filbert Roth, the famous teacher of forestry at the University of Michigan, once defined forest management as "setting up, putting in order, and keeping in order a forest business." Order can only be maintained by a well-designed and carefully kept set of records. Forest records mean financial accounting as well as data on timber volumes and growth, plus the necessary maps. Records serve as a tool in management, both to assure profitable operation and continuous yields of timber crops.

The main objective of forestry practice is to obtain a sustained yield of forest products and other benefits without damaging the basic resources—land and growing stock. The methods of managing a forest to produce timber crops according to silvicultural principles have been set forth in earlier chapters. As a means of guiding these management techniques to obtain regular yields, it is necessary to develop plans that bring together all of the information gathered on the forest.

The maps, the volume inventory data from timber cruises, the kinds of silvicultural methods, the products to be grown and marketed, plus the land records, protection plans, and any other data useful to the conduct of a forest business are all brought together into the forest management plan.

Under normal circumstances, forest management plans are drawn up by professional foresters. Forest owners and forest managers often participate in obtaining the basic data and carry out the recommendations called for in the plan. It is well, at this point, to develop the principal elements of a management plan and what items are included in order to gain a better understanding of the recommended practices.

Prior to making the plan itself, several important decisions must be made. A managed forest must be handled so as to have a regular output of timber products, which must come from growth. A forest

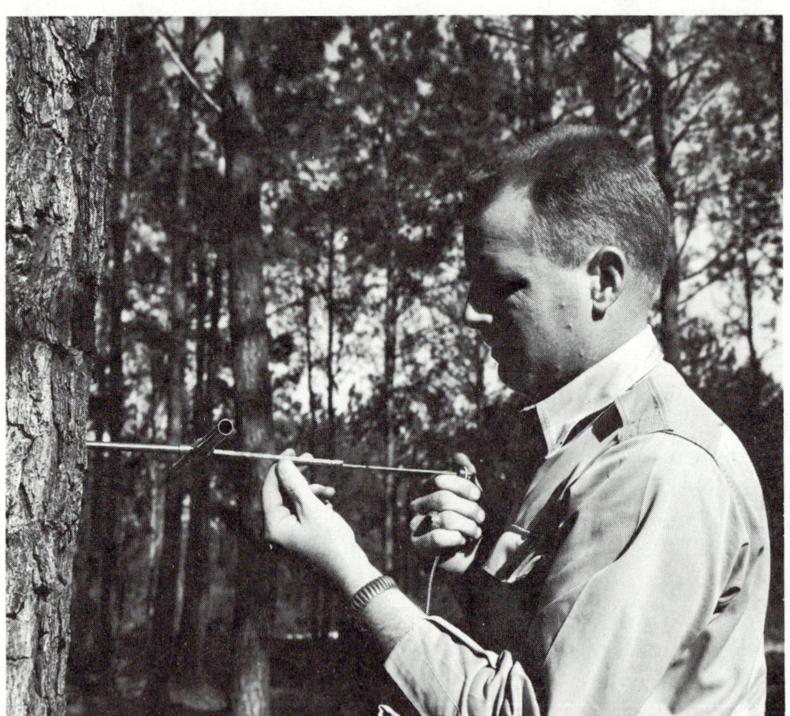

FIGURE 7–1. Measuring tree growth with an increment borer. The hollow borer produces a core that shows the annual rings of the tree. Growth studies are made by this procedure. (American Forest Industries, Inc.)

with regular cuttings governed by its growth is considered to be under *sustained yield management*. Growth studies underlie all sustained yield forestry (Figure 7–1).

MANAGING FOR SUSTAINED YIELD

Sustained yield forest growth should balance the losses in wood volume due to cutting and mortality in the whole forest over a period of time with management at a level high enough to produce optimum yields. This means, of course, that a growing stock of timber advancing on to merchantable age must be maintained at all times. Although a continuous forest business requires a steady output of forest products, the frequency and the amount of the cutting will depend on the market, on the size of the tract and its location, and especially on the rate of growth. These factors are included in the decisions on rotations and cutting cycles.

Forest yields vary greatly with type, site, length of growing season, and the intensity of management practiced. Under intensive management, annual growth may vary from more than 200 b.f. per acre in northern United States to as much as 1000 or 1500 b.f. in the southern pines and on the Pacific Coast. Unfortunately, due to understocking, these high growth rates are seldom achieved on any large areas.

A means of intensifying inputs to secure greater yields from the forest—termed *maximizing sustained yield*—has been developed during the past several decades. By accelerating growth rates through selection of genetically superior seedlings, precommercial thinnings, applying commercial fertilizer and other measures, such as reducing the length of the final rotation, forest yields can be substantially increased. Critics say the assumptions on which this is based are expensive and require investment commitments that may prove difficult to obtain in the future and if the investment inputs are not made, future yields will fall short of expectations.

Scheduling the Harvest Cut

Sustained yield management on even-aged forests differs considerably from that on all aged stands. In both cases it is necessary to decide upon the rotation or the age at which mature timber will be harvested from the property. This decision depends on such specifications for forest products as may be required by the markets.

A forest managed for sustained yield should be able to produce about the same quantity of products every year. This means that growing stock should have what foresters call *normal* distribution. Assuming uniform site, a *normal* forest composed of even-aged stands has an equal number of acres in trees that are one year apart in age for each year of its rotation. For example, an even-aged normal pine forest of 40 acres with a 40-year pulpwood rotation has 1 acre in each age class between 1 and 40 years. (See Figure 7–2.) If this whole forest grows at the rate of 1 cord per acre per year, a volume of 40 cords can be cut each year from the acre that has gone through the full rotation. This would be done under a clearcutting and planting system.

A normal all-aged hardwood forest presents a different situation. Here trees of all sizes would be represented on each acre. (See (Figure 7–2.) Assuming that this forest, too, was growing at the rate of 1 cord per acre per year, it would be necessary to cut 1 cord from each acre under the selection system every year. But as a practical matter this is not done. Instead, a cutting cycle is established, which in this case could be 5 years. Thus, instead of cutting off 40 cords from the whole 40 acres every year, it is possible to cut the 40 cords from 8 acres in each 5 year cutting cycle, or 5 cords per acre every 5 years.

It is more economical to cut a somewhat heavier volume at 5-year intervals from a small area under the cutting cycle plan than to make the cut over the whole property every year. Under this plan a different 8 acres is cut every year during the 5 year cutting cycle. The total cut must not exceed the total growth for the cutting cycle period, nor should the cut result in reducing the growing stock. If an increased cut is made in any year of high prices, it should come from surplus accumulated during years of low prices.

Although the annual cut should equal the annual growth, this applies literally only to normal forests in which trees of all ages—young, middle-aged, and mature—are evenly distributed. Where most trees are mature or overmature, the annual growth is very small; but the annual cut, at first, could be heavy to avoid loss of wood through decay. On a small tract there would be a period during which no cuts could be made in order to allow for the establishment of the regrowth.

Another term used by foresters is *allowable cut.* This is determined both from growth rates and from the amount of growing stock that should either be cut to put the stand in better condition or be withheld in order to build up the stand for the future. The allowable cut is usually calculated for periods of less than 20 years; it may exceed the annual growth of a forest with much over-mature timber and may be below the growth of a young, developing forest.

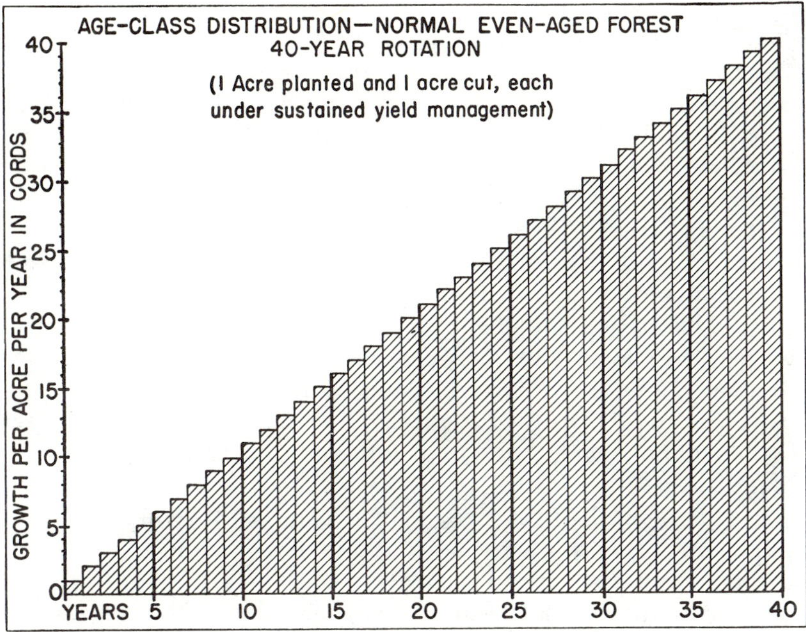

FIGURE 7–2. Age–class distribution in a normal even-aged forest. The actual growth rate would probably follow a curve, flatter for the slower growth at first and steepening toward the end of the rotation.

FOREST MANAGEMENT PLANS

A great deal of planning is required to maintain a sustained yield of timber products. Forest management plans are based on the types of field data obtained from inventorying timber, determining growth, and mapping the forest types and acreages. Protection data, logging methods, marketing, and other information set forth in the preceding chapters are all brought together into a forest management plan that can serve as a guide for some years into the future. A well-prepared plan should indicate which stands and species, amounts, and sizes of timber may be scheduled for cutting in the years ahead; where planting is needed, by number and kinds of trees; and what areas need timber stand improvement on specified dates. A management plan also deals with the forest fire protection system; with provisions for wildlife management by locations and practices; with the numbers of livestock to be permitted to graze in certain areas (if any); and with other important information required in the management of the area, including control of insects and diseases.

For convenience in management, forest properties are often divided into compartments that are frequently areas of similar physical features bounded by roads or other natural boundaries such as lakes or streams. Division into compartments help simplify detailed record keeping.

Systematic record keeping of both finances and physical data is essential in a well-managed forest, just as it is in any other business. Tally sheets and summaries of timber cruises should be filed properly, as should all maps made of the area. Initial records of tree volumes are particularly important in order to make it possible to compare the development of the forest as management continues over a period of time. Forest type maps of the property should be made at 10-year intervals so that changes due to growth and cutting may be kept up to date.

A well-organized forest management plan ties together the specialized details that this book has considered into a unified whole for the operation of the forest business.

The following checklist includes nearly all the essential items to be included in a forest management plan for a timber property. There is no set form to follow, but the following information should be set forth as completely as possible. The plan should be preceded with a brief history of the property that brings out important forestry information and the objectives to be achieved in multiple-use management. For an example of a detailed plan, see Appendix C.

Items to Be Included in a Forest Management Plan

1. Maps of area showing forest types and size classes, tabulation of acreages, and subdivision by compartments.
2. Volume of each species present in each compartment area, and growth rate data showing volumes estimated to be available in a decade or so.
3. On larger forests, an estimate of allowable cut by compartments during specified growth intervals.
4. Forest management operating schedule including the
   a. Harvest cutting areas for the next decade, showing the applicable silvicultural system.
   b. Decisions as to applicable rotations and cutting cycles.

c. Stand improvement cutting areas for the next decade.
d. Slash disposal and site preparation.
e. Forest planting areas showing species and acreages planned, by years.

5. Lists of market outlets, historical price information, products that may be sold, and specifications of products.
6. Logging plans, equipment inventory, labor requirements, facilities needed.
7. Protection program: fire fighting facilities and equipment owned and otherwise available, road and fire-lane system, detection program and system for suppression of fires.
8. Insect and disease problems and methods for their control.
9. Multiple use management programs:
   a. Wildlife—practices and timing with other operations.
   b. Fisheries, water and soil.
   c. Recreational land uses and facilities.
   d. Agricultural and grazing uses.
   e. Other uses.
10. Cost accounting and bookkeeping system.

Computerized Management Planning

The advent of the computer into forestry calculations is especially important in forecasting the consequences of alternative choices and assumptions used in management planning. Now calculations can be carried out in minutes that had previously taken days with slide rules, calculators, and adding machines. The computer does not perform miracles, it performs routine operations in much shorter time. It works well primarily in quantitative calculations (e.g., board feet, cords, acre feet, animal units, etc.) and not so well with qualitative scenic values, recreational uses, wildlife habitat, and so forth.

We can, for example, forecast the probable timber yield from a reforestation project with some degree of accuracy, but not the number of visitors to a wilderness waterfall. As our data collection improves we may do better in assigning numbers to qualitative values. For the time being we must satisfy ourselves with "hard data."

A good management plan should provide for every aspect of forestry and other uses of the land area within the forest property. It should not be considered inflexible and unchangeable but as a useful guiding framework that will need to be adapted to changing conditions and to new information. As new scientific information comes out, markets for new products develop, or nature upsets plans with wind or fires, the plan will need to be brought up to date. A good forest manager adapts planning to changing circumstances while remaining faithful to the principles of sound forest conservation.

Examples of two kinds of forest management plans for small timber tracts are set forth in Appendix C as an aid to the student and forest owner.

Compartment Records

In order to maintain accurate current records of various developments, including work accomplished in each area for the year in which it is done, simple compartment outline sketch maps have been found most practical. A sketch map such as the one shown in Figure 7–3 can be used to record logging information, timber volumes (standing and cut), trees planted, days expended on each kind of job, silvicultural applications, and so forth, carried out during the year. Compartment sketch sheets are made only for the years when work is done, but over a period of time they will represent a continuous forest management and operating record, and form the basis for a case history of the compartment. This system has been successfully used in the Harvard University Forest and elsewhere. The recorded information can provide the basis for revisions in the overall forest management plan from time to time.

Seasonal Work Load Distribution

A managed forest, like a farm crop, goes through a series of seasonal cycles each year, but unlike farmers, foresters have more latitude of choice. They don't have to harvest crops when they are ripe, but they can plant trees, control insects, and do many other operations only in season. Forestry must largely be tuned to the time of year when climatic and growth factors dictate. To illustrate this, Figure 7–4, Forest Management Checklist, shows the way in which forestry operations can be distributed over the year to fit the natural cycle of forest growth. There is an added advantage in a chart such as this; it enables the forest manager to keep the labor force fully occupied the year round.

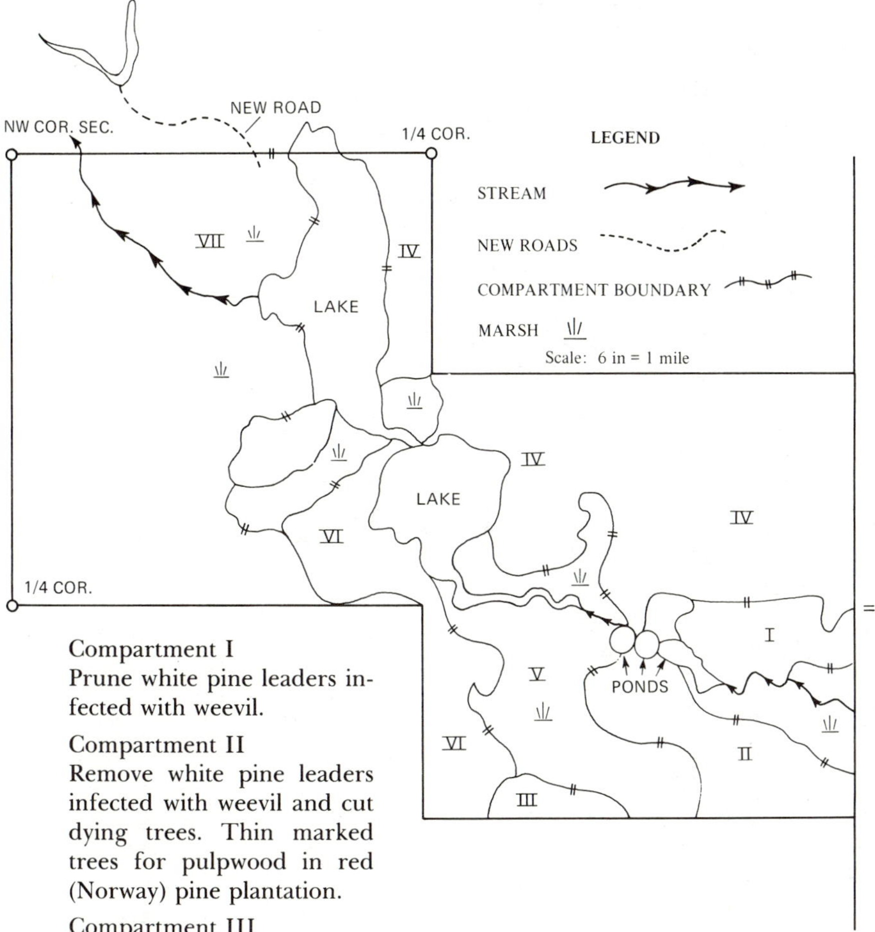

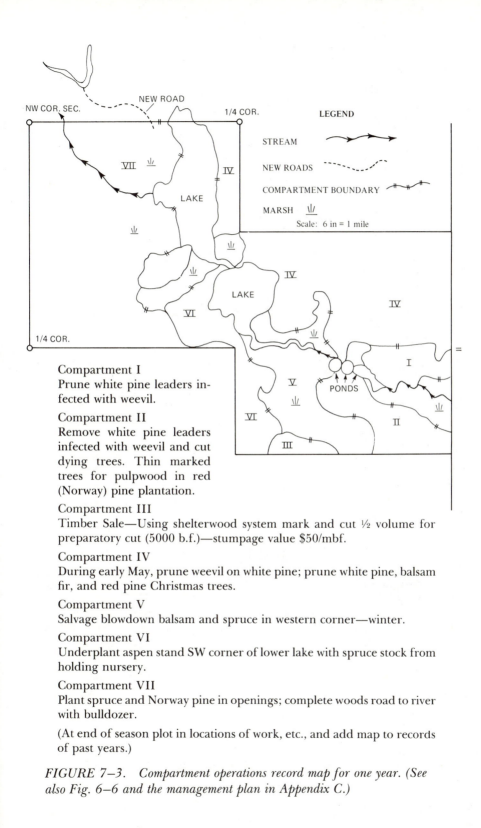

Compartment I
Prune white pine leaders infected with weevil.

Compartment II
Remove white pine leaders infected with weevil and cut dying trees. Thin marked trees for pulpwood in red (Norway) pine plantation.

Compartment III
Timber Sale—Using shelterwood system mark and cut ½ volume for preparatory cut (5000 b.f.)—stumpage value $50/mbf.

Compartment IV
During early May, prune weevil on white pine; prune white pine, balsam fir, and red pine Christmas trees.

Compartment V
Salvage blowdown balsam and spruce in western corner—winter.

Compartment VI
Underplant aspen stand SW corner of lower lake with spruce stock from holding nursery.

Compartment VII
Plant spruce and Norway pine in openings; complete woods road to river with bulldozer.

(At end of season plot in locations of work, etc., and add map to records of past years.)

FIGURE 7–3. Compartment operations record map for one year. (See also Fig. 6–6 and the management plan in Appendix C.)

WHAT TO DO

PLANTING

ORDER SEEDLINGS ____________

PREPARE PLANTING SITE ____________

PLANT SEEDLINGS ____________

PROTECTION

MAINTAIN FIREBREAKS ____________

REPORT INSECTS AND DISEASES ____________

MAINTAIN FENCES ____________

TIMBER STAND IMPROVEMENT

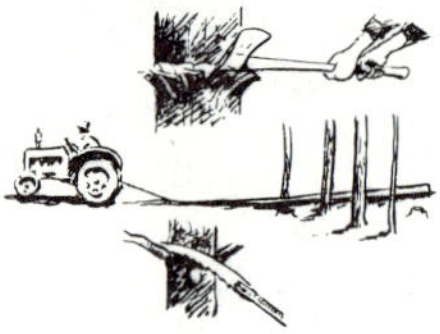

CONTROL WEED TREES ____________

THIN CROWDED STANDS ____________

PRUNE CROP TREES ____________

RECREATION

MAINTAIN PICNIC AREAS ____________

HARVESTING

CUT SAWLOGS, PULPWOOD, VENEER LOGS ____________

CUT POLES, PILING AND OTHER PRODUCTS ____________

FIGURE 7–4. Seasonal forest management checklist and calendar. (American Forest Institute)

WHEN TO DO IT

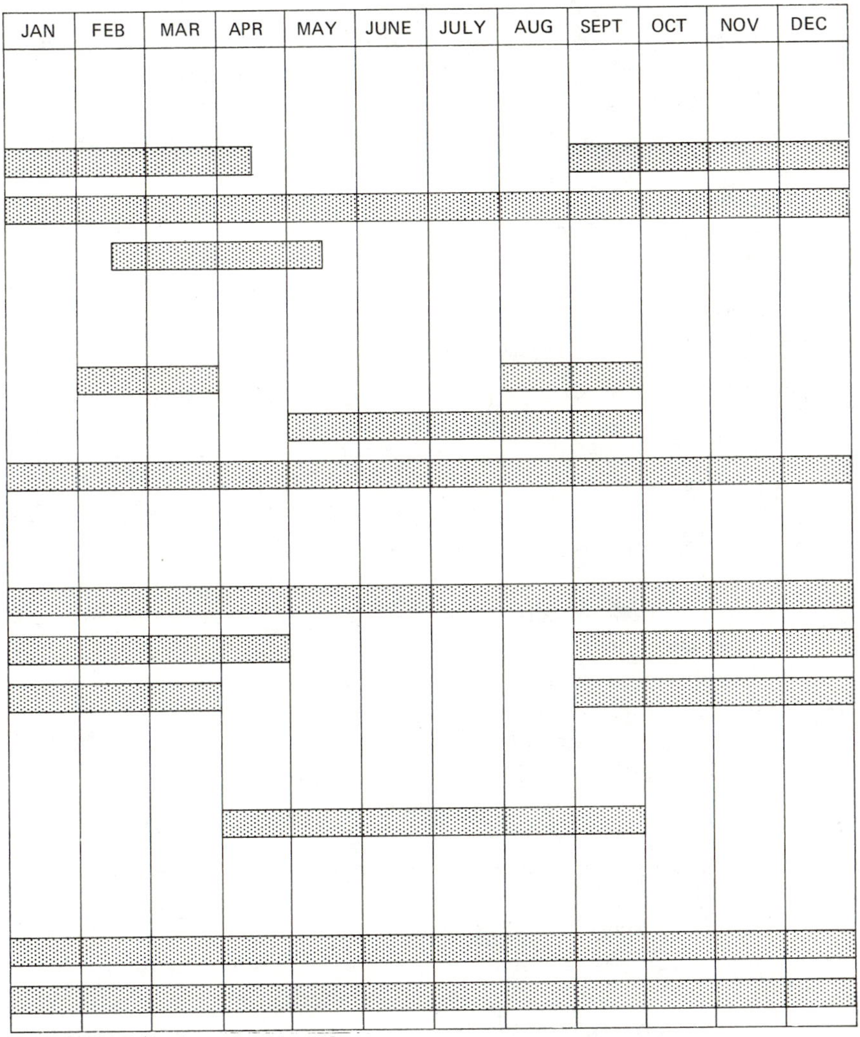

JAN	FEB	MAR	APR	MAY	JUNE	JULY	AUG	SEPT	OCT	NOV	DEC

FIGURE 7–4. (Continued)

MEASURING STUMPAGE VALUES

Determining the value of standing timber (*stumpage*) is a fairly complex process that is usually left to the specialist. Because a knowledge of the principles and the processes followed is useful, it is presented here to introduce the student to the subject. Forest owners seeking information on current prices of their own stumpage usually obtain local sales data from local forest industries, timber buyers, the State Extension foresters, or from local foresters with a knowledge of recent transactions.

Valuation of Stumpage

When land with trees or trees alone are sold, a value is usually determined for the stumpage, which is the only easily measured forest product. Normally no attempt is made to evaluate watershed protection, wildlife habitat or other noncommodity benefits. Traditionally, stumpage values have been derived by arriving at the difference between production costs (logging, transportation, and processing) and the total of the selling prices of the finished products. A margin is also included in the deduction for profit and risk factors. Thus, stumpage value is essentially a residual that bears no relation to the cost of growing timber.

There are two methods for arriving at timber stumpage values. The first, called the *overturn method*, is used for smaller tracts that can be harvested in a relatively short time period—a few months at the most. With this method the estimated cost of production, profit, and risk are subtracted from the expected sale values of the final products.

The other method, called the *investment method*, is used to place a value on large tracts of timber that may require a number of years to harvest. The formula used involves considerable data on manufacturing plant and equipment investment, working capital needed, depreciation, and so forth, to arrive at a realistic cost figure. In addition, income projections for 10 or more years must be made in order to apply a discount interest formula used to arrive at the present value. The investment method process can be a highly complex one requiring professional accountants skilled in data processing and economic analysis.

A common method used by both public agencies and private owners is to establish a minimum price for each species and then to hold an auction either by oral or written bidding.

The following is a simplified illustration of determining timber stumpage values by the overturn method.

Logging Cost/(1000 b.f.)

Cutting	$ 8.00
Skidding	6.00
Hauling	12.00
Road building	2.00
Overhead	2.00
Total logging	$ 30.00

Milling

Sawing	$ 30.00
Handling	5.00
Piling	5.00
Overhead	3.00
Total milling	$ 43.00
Margin for risk	$ 4.00
Margin for profit	$ 8.00
Total cost and margins	$ 85.00
Value of lumber per mbf	$140.00
Value of stumpage per mbf ($140.00 minus $85.00) =	$ 55.00

The overturn and investment methods were developed during an era of abundant old growth-timber that did not cost anything to grow. Reforestation, fire protection, taxes and administrative costs were not part of nature's bounty. Now, however, people are raising questions and criticisms of these old methods and there is some pressure for reform. For example, the Natural Resources Defense Council charged that the Superior and Chippewa National Forests in Minnesota lost $11.3 million during the period from 1978 to 1982 on timber sales constituting unfair competition to private timber growers.

FOREST BUSINESS RECORDS

Systematic financial records are an essential part of any successful forest business. Although it is beyond the scope of this book to develop forest accounting in detail, an overall review of the main features will be outlined briefly. Good accounting serves several important purposes: control over costs and income and hence profits, and for tax records. On smaller forests a *single-entry* accounting system may suffice, but on larger tracts under continuous management a *double-entry* system must be used. In using either system, the advice of a professional accountant is recommended.

Single-Entry System (Small Forests)

The single-entry system is mainly used on smaller forest tracts or operations that have only seasonal production; limited accounts are set up on separate sheets with the following suggested headings.

INCOME ACCOUNTS
Forest Products Income (Sales)
(Logs, lumber, pulpwood, other products)

Date	To Whom Sold	Quantity, Kind, and Price (unit)	Amount Received
12/18	Art Nelson	24 mbf rough pine lumber @$200	$4,800.00

Other Income

Date	Source	Kind	Amount Received
11/25	Wagner Scrap Co.	3 tons steel scrap @ $75	$ 225.00

Accounts Receivable

EXPENSE ACCOUNTS
Labor Hired (Logging, Decking, etc.)

Date	To Whom Paid	Hours Worked	Rate	Kind of Work	Amount Paid	Check no.
12/28	Ole Nordberg	40	$5.00/hr	Skidding logs	$250.00	211

A separate sheet should be set up for each of the following.

Machine, Mill, and Truck Hire
Gasoline, Oil, and Fuel for Business
Water, Rent, Utilities for Business
Supplies Purchased
Cost of Repairs and Maintenance
Freight, Yardage, etc.
Taxes, Interest (including Social Security, Licenses, etc.)
Insurance Premiums
Other Expenses (Bad Debts, Losses, etc.)

The above should be set up with columns showing.

Date	To Whom Paid	For	Amount	Check No.
12/6	Superior Machinery Co.	Tractor Repair Parts	$243.70	162

Accounts payable should be provided for on separate sheets with appropriate headings.

In addition, a simple set of permanent accounts for the tract ownership should include

1. Forest protection, management, planting, and improvements.
2. Depreciation of equipment, machinery, and buildings.
3. Capital account of initial land and timber investment, with provisions for additions through growth and subtraction through cutting.
4. Depletion account to show reduction in timber capital.
5. Inventory account showing logs and other forest products at the beginning and end of the year and interim changes.

Double-Entry System (Medium and Large Forests)

The double-entry system is a more detailed and, therefore, more precise method of keeping business records. For large forest tracts and operations, the double-entry method is recommended. It is suggested that the forest owner obtain the services of an accountant before setting up a double-entry accounting system.

The two basic records in a simple double entry bookkeeping system are the *cash journal* and the *ledger*. The cash journal is usually in two parts, one for listing cash received and one for listing cash disbursed. Each day's cash receipts are listed, showing date, from whom received, the total received, and finally the nature of the receipt (e.g., sale of logs, sale of pulpwood and other forest products). The first amount column (the total received) represents the increase in the bank account and is a *debit* item. The remaining columns describing the nature of the income are known as *credit* items. The cash disbursements are handled in a similar manner. Each check is listed by date, payee, number, the total amount, and the nature of the disbursement. The first amount column (the total amount of the check) represents the decrease in the bank account and is a credit item. The remaining columns, which describe the nature of the disbursement—which is either an expense or an increase in permanent additions to fixed capital—are known as debit items. Each month the cash journal is totaled and posted to the ledger.

The ledger consists of a separate sheet for each account, with a column for debit and credit postings. The accounts are usually grouped in the ledger in three sections: assets, liabilities, and net worth; income; and expense accounts. The net worth represents the initial investment plus or minus each year's profit or loss. The income and expense accounts are totaled each year and the totals transferred to the net worth account. Some of the major headings in the asset accounts include the following but can be expanded in detail as the enterprise grows.

Cash account

Capital accounts
- Initial land and timber cost
- Permanent improvements
  - Roads
  - Buildings
  - Dams
  - Other
- Forest development
  - Planting
  - Protection improvement (fire lanes, towers, etc.)
- Other
  - Mechanical equipment
  - Hand tools
- Reserve for depreciation and depletion
  - (There is usually a separate reserve account for each category above, except land. These accounts have a credit balance representing a decrease in the value of the asset.)

Some of the more important headings in the current expense accounts will include logging, tree planting, machinery repair, building maintenance, road maintenance, utilities, insurance, taxes, wages paid (usually entered under the above items), depreciation and depletion, fire protection, and insect and disease control. Income accounts will include sale of logs, pulpwood, and other forest products, nursery stock sold (if any), and any other cash income received during the operating (fiscal) year. Two expense items that do not involve the outgo of cash are depreciation and depletion. An entry should be made in the ledger accounts each year debiting the expense account and crediting the reserve account for this expense. These two items should be handled with the assistance and advice of an accountant.

Forest Property Taxation

For many years forest economists have contemplated the fairness of applying the ad valorem property tax to private land and timber and over the resultant effect on forestry enterprises. The argument in favor of the ad valorem property tax applied to forestry is that the tax is based on capital and that both land and timber represent accumulated capital. The argument against the ad valorem property tax applied to forestry is that only the bare land should be considered capital and that timber is a growing crop, or "goods-in process."

In spite of the various theories, there has been little empirical research done on this subject, and most states have accepted, in one way or another, the argument against the tax by enacting special private forest tax laws. These laws range from exempting timber from taxation, to land *productivity taxes*, to *yield taxes* that defer the tax until timber is harvested. State forestry agencies are able to provide full information on the laws for each state—most of which differ considerably from one another. (See Appendix E)

Income Taxes and Forests

The relationship of forest lands and forest production to federal income tax laws is a highly complex one that cannot be adequately treated in a paragraph. Forest owners who are keeping accurate records and accounts of expenditures and income by the accounting categories suggested previously, will be in the best position to deal with their income tax filing. The principal issues involved are whether expenditures made in the forest are production expeditures or capital expenditures related to long-term investment. Because federal income tax laws change frequently, forest owners are advised to write to the Division of Forest Economics, Forest Service, U.S. Department of Agriculture, Washington, D.C., 20013, for the most recent bulletin dealing with this subject.

QUESTIONS

1. What is meant by sustained yield in forestry?
2. What is a cutting cycle?

3. What is a rotation?
4. Name five important items to be included in a forest management plan.
5. How does a sketch map aid in recording current forest operations?
6. Describe the method for determining stumpage values.
7. Describe the items included in production costs.
8. Name the two systems of accounting.
9. Name values that must be considered other than timber. How are they valued?
10. What are the two main account headings?
11. Give the two basic divisions used in the double-entry method of accounting.
12. Pine lumber is selling for $150 per mbf rough, logging costs $40 per m delivered at the mill, sawing and piling costs $50, overhead $6. What is the stumpage value of a pine stand with 40 mbf?

EXERCISES

1. Visit a large forest—national, industrial, or state—or an experimental research forest and examine the record system, maps, and forest management plan.
2. If you can locate a timber sale area in your locality, find out how stumpage values were determined.
3. Ask the owner of the stumpage what sort of contract was made with the buyer.

EIGHT

Logging and Measuring Forest Products

LOGGING TIMBER PRODUCTS

Logging has been described as the process of harvesting and hauling rough forest products from stump to the point of processing or sale. Felling trees, dividing them into the desired lengths, skidding, loading, and hauling them to market are all parts of the logging process. But before any logging is begun, many decisions must be made with regard to the layout of the logging operation, the equipment to be used, and the kinds of rough forest products that are to be cut. These decisions are dictated partly by the sizes and species of timber in the forest to be logged, partly by topography, and partly by the markets that are to be supplied.

Most forest products are sold as sawlogs, veneer logs, pulpwood, tie cuts (small sawlogs), bolts for a variety of uses (staves, shingles, excelsior, turnings, etc.), poles, posts, piling, and other products of more local importance (round mine timbers, charcoal wood, furnace poles, etc.). Sawlogs and pulpwood are our principal timber products. Specifications of some of the more important of these timber products are set forth at the end of this chapter.

Logging Methods and Equipment

Logging methods differ considerably between the western mountain states and the states east of the Great Plains. Such factors as timber size, topography, climate, type and skills of the labor force, and transportation systems, all influence equipment and systems to be used. Until World War I, logging was largely accomplished by human and animal labor with few mechanical devices to increase productivity. Trees were cut down with axe and crosscut saw, skidded with horses, mules, and oxen; loaded on wagons or sleighs by cross haul or gin poles; and finally put on railroad cars with animal-powered jammers (loaders). In the western big timber regions, donkey engines with winches and steel cables were used to skid logs too large for animals.

Trucks for hauling and crawler tractors for skidding and road building were the major factors in improving logging efficiency during the years before World War II. Since then there has been a technological revolution in logging methods and equipment. Old time lumberjacks would find nothing familiar but the trees in modern logging operations.

Powered chain saws for small and large timber, crawler tractors for skidding, rubber-tired skidders, and loading winches are examples of the new equipment that has increased productivity in the woods so significantly in the southern, eastern, and Lake States forests.

In the great Douglas-fir, spruce, and pine forests of the West, crawler tractors are used for skidding in many situations, particularly on the steep slopes above the logging roads. Tractors can work downhill with the huge logs but not up. They cause a good deal of disturbance to young trees and to watershed soil mantle. However, the *skyline crane* and *high-lead* methods are preferable because damage to residual stands and the soil is reduced. Skyline crane yarding of logs was introduced in North America as a method of harvesting timber from steep, rugged topography where road construction was impractical or where soil disturbance would lead to excessive erosion and sedimentation. A skyline is normally suspended along the slope, with intermediate supports where needed to maintain adequate height above the ground. Logs are yarded laterally to the skyline, lifted free of the ground by the crane or carriage, and transported down the skyline to a landing that is usually in the canyon bottom. Distance to the landing may be as much as one mile.

With conventional *high-lead* yarding (Figure 8–1), the main line is fed through a block high on a spar tree or steep crane to provide a lift or *high-lead* to the logs. This helps prevent the logs from gouging out soil as they move along and helps them ride up and over stumps and other obstructions. Logs drag on the ground all the way to the landing, which is usually on a ridgetop. Maximum yarding distance seldom exceeds 1000 ft, and the average is usually under 500 ft. The longer yarding distances possible with skyline yarding permit a road density less than one-third that needed for conventional high-lead yarding, thereby reducing construction costs, soil disturbance, and area taken out of timber production.

Labor Force

The logging camp of yesterday is all but gone with the development of good roads and easy access to the woods by car. Single men made up the logging work force in a logging camp. Today young married

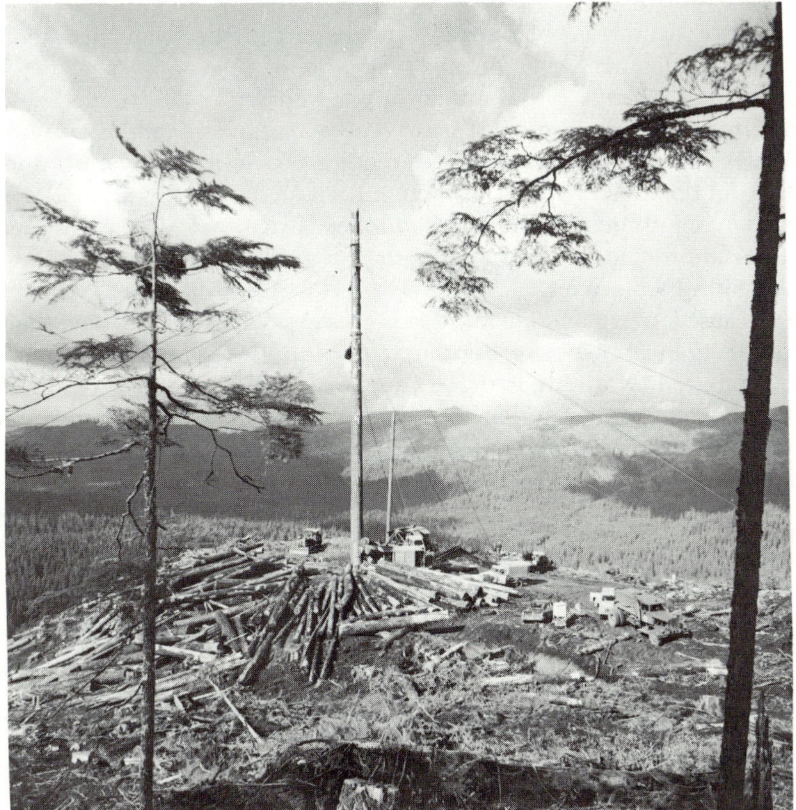

FIGURE 8–1. High-lead logging uses a spar tree to support cables and pulleys for moving logs from stump to a central deck powered by a stationary diesel unit and winches. (American Forest Institute)

people living at home and driving to work have taken their places. The logger must be a skilled worker and machine operator who has had vocational instruction. Woods workers' wages and salaries have risen to levels comparable with other skills, but the forest industries have found they have had to operate training courses in order to attract and keep their labor force abreast of technological changes.

While the logging camp is restricted to only a few remote areas in the West and the Canadian timber country today, temporary housing is sometimes provided in difficult locations elsewhere with auto trailers or logging shacks that can be hauled from place to place.

Logging, Forestry Practices, and Watershed Management

Judicious harvesting of trees is a major part of forest management. Therefore, control over the use and type of machinery is a major element in success or failure in applied forestry. Of course, clear cutting systems require little care except to limit the size of the cuttings. Partial cuttings with marked trees require care in removal of product to avoid damage to residual stand and young trees. Not all modern, efficient equipment is efficient in applied silviculture. Thus, it will be important to choose carefully the machinery to be used as related to silvicultural objectives.

Because logging and logging roads on steep slopes concentrate water runoff, gully and sheet erosion may result unless special precautions are followed. Not only is there a loss of site quality, but siltation of streams can seriously impair fish habitats. Foresters working with soil conservationists in the redwood region of California have recommended a series of practices that are designed to minimize the damage.

1. Leave buffer strips of timber along stream bottoms and small waterways to prevent slash and logging residue from entering streams. This practice has high aesthetic value and provides a seed tree source for nearby logged-over lands.
2. Construct roads on lowest grades possible and prevent water concentration both by use of frequent water bars and dumping water into brushy areas not likely to gully.
3. Avoid logging all areas over 50 percent slope—especially those likely to slide because of skidding disturbance.

4. If clear cutting is followed on steep slopes, it should be in small patches of 20 acres or less and immediately replanted to assure an early ground cover.

Preliminary Planning and Construction

Logging on large tracts of timber takes a great deal more advance planning and construction than in smaller woodland ownerships. Except where logs are taken out by water, there must be available both *feeder* logging roads and high standard trunk roads. Main trunk lines of railroads are still used extensively but logging spur lines are disappearing fast. Logging *drives* on Canadian rivers are still used for pulpwood in a few places, but elsewhere they have disappeared into the romantic past of this colorful industry.

Road building, then, must be the first step preceding actual logging of large forest tracts. Today most lumber companies use large trucks for the initial haul of logs from the woods. These require good roads, frequently graveled, and wide enough for two-way traffic. Construction of the truck road must be started well in advance of actual logging operations. It involves careful planning and execution. Roads in hilly country must follow gradual grades, and in laying them out, a topographic map with contours is extremely useful. Hand levels are used to determine the exact location on the ground. Grades should generally not exceed 7 percent (vertical rise of 7 ft per 100 ft of distance) except for very short distances where 10 or 12 percent may be permissible. Anything steeper is dangerous and causes hard wear on trucks as well as greater erosion. Locating the road is an engineering job and requires considerable training, but the principles are fairly simple. A base map must be available, preferably topographic, on which the road may be plotted. Where the road travels along hillsides, it is cut on one side and filled over on the other (Figure 8–2). Where roads cross hills and low spots, the hills are cut through and the lows are filled in with the material removed. Where sufficient *fill* material is not available from the cuts, a *borrow pit* is required.

Curves must be planned for safe travel of trucks, and cannot be too sharp. Road surfaces in most cases must be graveled so that they will stand up under the extremely heavy wear and tear from logging and weather, and if heaving and chuck holes are to be avoided. Proper drainage is necessary to carry off excess water during rainy weather. In order to cross large streams and rivers, bridges must be constructed. Ordinarily, with plenty of timber available for construction

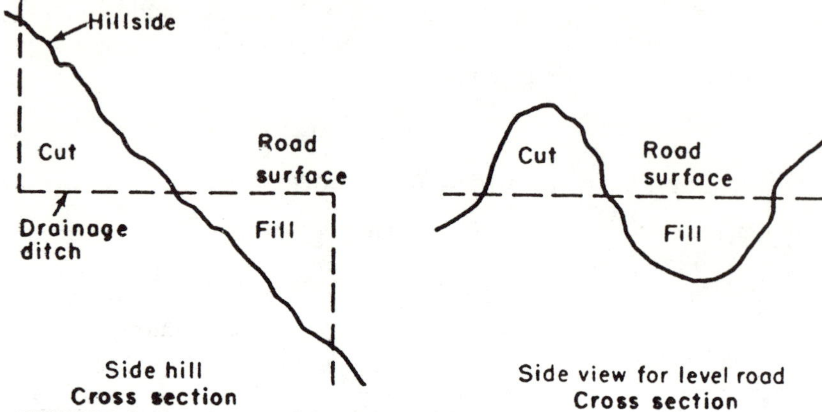

FIGURE 8–2. Cuts and fills in road building.

material, this can be done at relatively low cost, but the principles of good bridge construction engineering must be strictly adhered to if loads are to be carried safely across. Since these are engineering problems, the details will not be developed here. However, where small streams are to be crossed, wooden or steel culverts are often adequate and cheaper than bridge building, especially where length of service is a consideration. It is important that the culverts over streams be amply large to take care of flood waters.

PLANNING THE LOGGING JOB

Forest technicians should understand some of the important principles of getting logs out of the woods. Before considering them, it will be wise to establish the essential steps to be used in setting up a logging plan.

1. Prepare a good and accurate forest cover type map showing both variations in stand density and in the topography.
2. Lay out a permanent road system designed for frequent future use. Include log landings, main skidding trails, and turnarounds, correcting the existing road system where necessary. Put roads on gradual slopes and avoid locations that will result in excessive runoff and erosion.
3. Relate the entire road system for accessibility to the nearest public road.
4. Make plans to ensure that the trees will be cut up into the highest grade forest products possible so as to utilize the

entire commercial length of the tree. This means that the log sizes and specifications for the whole tree length should be clearly set forth to the labor force in advance of bucking, to obtain maximum quality.

5. Instruct log skidders to avoid breakage of young trees and to avoid gouging out skidding trails, which will cause erosion. Where such gouging is unavoidable, heal the scars immediately after logging by piling brush in the trail, or seeding with grass seed. Put in simple devices to carry off excess water on steep skid trails.
6. Check loggers as they cut to see that they log only marked trees. Absence of paint marks or blazes on the stumps means that unmarked timber has been cut.

PROCEDURES FOLLOWED IN LOGGING

Essentially, the logging operation involves cutting down the tree (*felling*), sawing it up into proper lengths (*bucking*), dragging it over the ground (*skidding*) to a road where it is piled (*decked*) for loading onto a truck. Frequently, when small or moderatesized timber is being cut, the full tree length is dragged to the landing by the road or water side, and bucking is done there. This makes possible more economical skidding with present-day equipment, and not only more economical but also more intelligent bucking. When bucking is concentrated at the landing, the crew can be trained better and supervised to obtain the maximum quality and quantity of the products desired. The processes by which these operations are accomplished vary widely, depending on the size of the timber, the silvicultural system, the topography, the machinery and equipment used, and the products produced.

Since World War II, woods operations have been affected by a technological explosion. Chain saws, clam hoists, combines and harvesters, crawler tractors, and trucks with self loading jammers have replaced crosscut saws, gin pole jammers, logging sleighs, and railroads and teams of horses. Production per worker day has been vastly increased, primarily in clearcutting operations. There are disadvantages to the new equipment, which is also destructive to the forest understory, encourages erosion, and is entirely dependent on petroleum energy sources. The crawler tractor, however, with a winch, is very useful in selective cutting because individual trees or logs can be pulled out with a cable and tongs to a skid road without damaging the residual stand. Even more ecologically adaptable is the horse, which can wind its way through the woods around small trees and burns only hay and oats!

Pulpwood logging is the simplest. In pine and aspen woods the small trees are cut into 4- to 8-ft lengths, depending on the specifications, and are carried out to a woods road where they are often loaded directly onto trucks by hand or with self-loaders mounted on trucks. Pine pulp sticks are often piled in *pens* in the South or decked in the North for partial drying and measurement. This is probably the simplest of all logging because pine forests are usually open and level. In heavy hardwoods or in conifer swamps in the North, teams or tractors generally skid out the pulpwood to a landing where it is piled and loaded. On some operations where bucking is done in the woods the cut sticks are brought out on *scoots* or drays to a landing where they are decked, or loaded directly onto trucks. Haul roads must be built in advance and, where winters involve a lot of snow, provision must be made for snow plowing.

In bigger timber, where sawlogs are the primary product, cutting and transportation are more complex and require heavier equipment for handling. As recently as World War II, much timber in the eastern United States was cut and skidded by men and teams of horses. Tractors and trucks had made some headway, but mechanical self-loaders and chain saws were still largely experimental. These new developments have taken much of the sweat and back-breaking labor out of logging, but it still is a hard and hazardous business. In the Douglas-fir and redwood regions, heavy wire cables powered with diesel-driven winches have been used for many years to skid logs over the ground or through the air (on skyline *high-lead* systems). In either case, the logs are brought out to roads and decked, ready to be loaded onto trucks or railroad cars.

Each of the major steps in logging is carried out in the following order, with the equipment described.

1. The logging area is laid out with main haul roads and smaller skid roads, which are usually built in advance of cutting. In order to assign a specific parcel of timber to each logger, a cutting area with sufficient timber to last several weeks is laid out. The boundaries of these areas are marked either with paint or blazes.
2. *Felling, limbing,* and *bucking* are all part of the process of preparing logs. As a first step the tree is usually notched with a chain saw on the side toward is to be dropped (Figure 8–

3). The logger then takes the chain saw and saws into the tree at a point on the opposite side of the stem from the undercut notch, so as to come out just above the bottom of the notch. Wedges are frequently used to keep the saw from pinching and to start the tree tipping in the direction desired. Careful loggers usually fell the tree into openings to avoid *hanging up* and to reduce damage to young trees as much as possible. Before it falls, they yell "T-I-M-B-E-R" to warn others out of the way.

Limbing the fallen tree is the next step. This may either be done with the axe or saw, depending on the size of the limbs. In either case, they are cut off flush with the surface of the tree bole so that there will be no projections to retard skidding or cause accidents.

Bucking the fallen tree into logs may either be done in the woods or at the landing. In either case, decisions must be made by the logger in such a way as to make the best use of the full tree trunk. If the tree is perfectly straight, the logger can cut it up into uniform 16-ft logs or into whatever other lengths the specifications may indicate. However, any small

FIGURE 8–3. Undercutting with a power saw. The sawyer is notching the big ponderosa pine on the side where he wants it to fall. (American Forest Institute)

crooks, a defect, or a fork will dictate where the log should be cut, and lengths of 8, 10, 12, or 16 ft may result. In big West Coast timber 32-ft logs are commonly cut. To allow for trimming boards squarely after they are sawn, loggers leave an additional 2 to 6 in. beyond these specified lengths. In sawing through the downed tree to make logs, the cut is usually made from the top side down through most of the trunk. At this point the tree may begin to pinch the saw, and either a wedge is driven in or the saw is removed so that the cut may be finished from underneath. Sometimes upside down bucking or *plunge cutting* (with a chain saw) from the middle down, and then up, is required in the interest of safety or conservation of material. Bucking should always be carried out from the uphill side of the log for operator safety.

3. The operation of skidding the logs or tree lengths may be accomplished by a number of different methods. In the northern snow country where swamps are common, teams of horses are still used after the ice has formed in the winter, but rubber-tired diesel equipment that can load and haul logs has all but replaced horse power even on small farmer-logger operations (Figure 8–4). In the South, larger softwood operators cut and skid tree lengths to a temporary deck, buck into lengths, debark, saw into lumber and chip slabs, edging, and tops for shipment to pulp mills. In the West, logging arches pulled by larger crawler tractors are used in ponderosa pine, whereas in the mountains *high-lead* cable systems are still common. The tractor has become a very popular skidding device all over the country because it is so adaptable, has tremendous power, and is highly maneuverable (Figure 8–5). Power is hooked onto logs in a number of ways, but a chain or cable used as a choker loop or tongs that grip the log or tree length are most common. Skidding pans are sometimes used to lift the front ends of the logs off the ground and keep them from grinding in grit and gravel (which damage the saw). Logging arches or sulkies are even more common. Pulpwood is seldom skidded but is piled alongside narrow trails by the cutter. If the ground is suitable for trucking, it is loaded directly onto trucks. If not, it is loaded onto scoots with runners and pulled by tractors to decks.

4. Some pulpwood is peeled in the woods in the spring, when the sap is running. The use of a *barking spud* for peeling removes both outer and inner bark. Sodium arsenite has re-

FIGURE 8–4. Mechanized, rubber-tired equipment with a self-loading clam hoist that can be maneuvered into nearly every kind of terrain is not only putting the last of the logging horses out of work but is making it possible to harvest timber in summer from wet swamps. (Norfilm Service)

cently been successfully employed to prolong the peeling season. The chemical is applied to girdles around the trees some months in advance of logging, and the bark loosens so as to permit peeling at any time.

However, here again mechanical equipment has taken over from manual techniques. Mechanical log barkers are now used extensively at pulpwood landings and concentration points. These strip off the bark (and some wood) with rapidly rotating knives in a drum (Figure 8–6). The advantages of this step are rapid drying out of moisture and, hence, lower freight costs; closer piling in shipment; and wood easily stored, free from bark borers at the mill yard. Debarking of sawlogs is usually done at the sawmill. Slabs, formerly wasted or burned, are now converted into pulp chips.

5. Tree length logging is also becoming more and more common. Instead of cutting logs into proper lengths in the woods,

FIGURE 8–5. Skidding pine timber to log deck with crawler tractor and rubber-tired log lift. (American Forest Institute)

FIGURE 8–6. Machine peeling pulpwood in the woods. (U. S. Forest Service)

the full merchantable length is hauled to a log landing (thus requiring fewer units to be handled individually). The tree is then often sawed on a moving chain into sawlogs, pulpwood sticks, or other rough products. Debarking in a tree length often precedes this process.

6. Loading trucks with logs is the next step, and a variety of equipment and methods is used. The most common of these in the past has been the *gin pole* or *jammer*. This is essentially moveable powered cranes that have cables for lifting the logs from the log deck onto the body of the truck. More recently, revolving boom power loaders on wheels or crawler tracks for big sawlogs, or tractors with fork lifts on the front, have been commonly used in smaller timber. Several types of *chain* loaders have been developed that are directly installed on the hauling trucks. Loaders vary greatly in size and design; they range from the truck-mounted log *jammer* used by the small part-time logger to the tractor-mounted crane used at mill sites or sidings. The small to medium hydraulic loader has proved the most economical for most eastern U.S. forest operations. The hydraulic boom, clam-grapple type can be mounted on the hauling device or on the rear of a crawler tractor. The front-end, fork-grapple type can be mounted on a tracked or rubber-tired tractor. The type of loader to be used in any particular situation, of course, will depend on its planned use in the overall harvesting operation.

7. To transport the logs, there are many different types of primary and secondary equipment. These include the extremes of 2- to 3-cord capacity, small, stake-body trucks and 12-cord semitrailers and the 35-cord gondolas used in rail transportation. Unit production costs vary with volume, weight, and size of the material, size of the truck trailer or railcar, road conditions, distance from market, delays, and stand-by time. Small volumes cannot be hauled economically for long distances. The secret to economic hauling for any distance is to minimize delay, loading, and stand-by time.

8. Some of the newly developing equipment for harvesting and transporting can be grouped into two general classifications, each descriptive of the work it does in the total job: combines or harvesters and whole tree shearers.

Combines or Harvesters

Combines are relatively new in the logging industry. They can be used to very good advantage under moderate slope (5 to 10 percent) conditions when clear-cutting timber. Each machine that performs more than one of the harvesting operations cuts, limbs, and skids tree lengths in consecutive steps (Figure 8–7). This is especially adapted to forest plantations where trees grow in rows like corn. Mowing down a group of rows, this forest combine piles tree-length logs on top of its steel cab and hauls them back to a log deck on a main road. Ground skidding is eliminated as well as costly handling of each piece of timber. At the log decks in the woods or at the mill, the tree length is bucked into appropriate products and then sorted out.

Whole Tree Shearers

Shearers to process whole trees have been designed to perform two or more parts of the harvesting operation. One type of processor barks, chips, and loads, whereas others perform such operations as barking and slashing. Auxiliary logging equipment must be available to complement the operation. For example, some of the shearers accomplish the loading operation while others do not. Many units are still in the experimental stage.

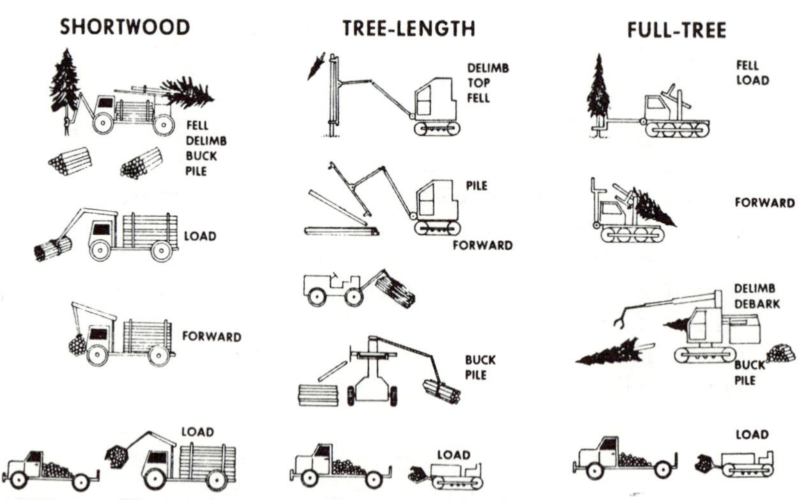

FIGURE 8–7. Processing steps of three fully mechanized harvesting systems.

Logging in the Future

While the new kinds of equipment have wrought great changes in timber harvesting during the past decade, even more amazing machinery is now being tested. To get into some of the more remote mountain forests, both helicopters and balloons are being used in place of high-lead spar logging. One revolutionary new method of logging utilizes a giant helium-filled balloon that acts as a *sky hook* to pull logs out of mountainous terrain. The U. S. Forest Service estimates that 26 million acres of inaccessible forest in the Pacific Northwest and Alaska would be opened to harvest by this method. These have the added advantages of reducing destruction of adjacent timber and eliminating all feeder roads. Watershed soils are left intact because ground skidding is all but eliminated. If these new developments can be perfected to commercial use, nearly a billion more board feet of timber could be harvested at a saving of 20 percent in the logging cost because road building would be greatly reduced.

The day of the new mechanical logging marvels with their heavy dependence on petroleum fuels may soon be moving in new directions. No other industry is so uniquely capable of energy self-sufficiency in that it can utilize its own wastes to generate power. Retooling known systems such as *gasogenes* to manufacture motor fuel as well as the development of completely new processes may become commonplace during the next several decades as we seek substitutes for costly fossil fuels. And don't be surprised to find draft horses (*hay burners*) returning to the woods in ever greater numbers especially for winter logging in rough terrain and coniferous swamps.

Logging Equipment Operation and Maintenance

Logging operations, as well as nearly every other phase of forestry, require the use of many types of machinery, hand tools, and other equipment. One of the first jobs of the forest manager is to keep an accurate account of all machinery and tools, keep them in repair, and maintain them properly. A burned-out tractor or a fire because of an oil leak can mean the loss of lives and valuable timber. On a logging job, breakdowns due to worn-out and unrepaired parts can result in higher costs, lower production, and the loss of jobs. Such minor matters as cleaning out paint guns after marking timber, sharpening axes in spare time, checking the sprayers on back pumps for clogging and rust, and other minor but essential jobs of this sort should be no problem to a person with a sense of responsibility. Keeping up on these matters means observing how the equipment is working and when it needs attention. And it is wise to remember that tools are lost much more easily than they are found. A good record system will prevent such losses.

Safety Precautions in the Woods

Woods work is one of the most hazardous of occupations primarily because too many people forget elementary precautions and become careless. Trees dropped without warning, logs falling off poorly chained trucks, and logs carelessly skidded around corners are all common causes of accidents. People who do not know how to use an axe or saw frequently end up with serious injuries. Many accidents are prevented by having safety meetings and by placing precaution signs in bunkhouses and other locations to remind constantly the workers against carelessness. One of the primary responsibilities of a forest manager on the job is to keep workers from being hurt. Preventing accidents saves time, pain, trips to a doctor, and also saves money. The most dangerous operations and the safety precautions that should be followed to prevent accidents are

1. *Carrying tools* Carry an axe by grasping the handle near the head; never over the shoulder. When a power saw is carried in the woods, the motor should be turned off. People unaccustomed to working in the woods are not as sure-footed as full-time lumberjacks. For this reason, it pays to give more than normal attention to one's footing and the path one is following (Figure 8–8).
2. *Felling* In felling trees, the most important point is to make the undercut to a depth of at least one-fourth the diameter of the tree. Make felling cuts slightly above the undercut (Figure 8–8). Clear the brush and any debris from the ground several feet in all directions from the tree so that when it falls workers can move to safe positions without danger of tripping or falling over them. When the tree begins to fall, the workers should move off to a safe distance at one side (not in back) of the tree both to avoid any falling debris or *kickback* of the butt (Figure 8–8).
3. *Trimming* It is important that cutters stand on the side of the tree opposite from which they are cutting the limbs. If it becomes necessary to trim up short lengths after they have been bucked, the axe should be grasped close to the end of the handle when trimming short lengths.
4. *Skidding* Skidding logs is dangerous, especially at the time the

FIGURE 8–8. Logging safety precautions. (1) Most satisfactory way of felling a straight tree: (a) *undercut, (b) saw cut, (c) felling wedge. (2) Improper undercuts cause kickbacks. (3) The wrong way of carrying tools is shown at the left. If this man stumbles, he may injure himself with the axe. (4) The right way to carry tools is shown at the right. (U. S. Forest Service) The worker should always wear a hard hat and suitable boots in the woods!*

skidding chain is being fastened. Walk back of the load if possible; if not, watch for obstructions and change sides to avoid being sideswiped.

The Occupational Safety and Health Act enacted in the early 1970s has imposed very strict standards on forest industry operations. All workers, for example, are required to use hard hats on all operations. Machinery must have protective equipment installed at every point of danger. And, of course, airborne wastes are subject to strict pollution controls. Yet despite all of these safeguards, the accident rates in logging and processing forest products remains near the top of the industrial list. Insurance companies shy away from liability insurance for woods operations and charge high rates when they do cover them.

MEASURING FOREST PRODUCTS (SCALING)

One of the most common jobs on the logging operation, for someone with woods experience or training, is measuring cut logs and pulpwood. This is done to keep an accurate record of daily or weekly production, and, if the timber belongs to someone else, to make payments based on volume.

Scaling Sawlogs

There are four steps in scaling sawlogs (Figure 8–9).

1. Measure the diameter in inches and the length in feet. The diameter of the log is measured at the small end, inside the

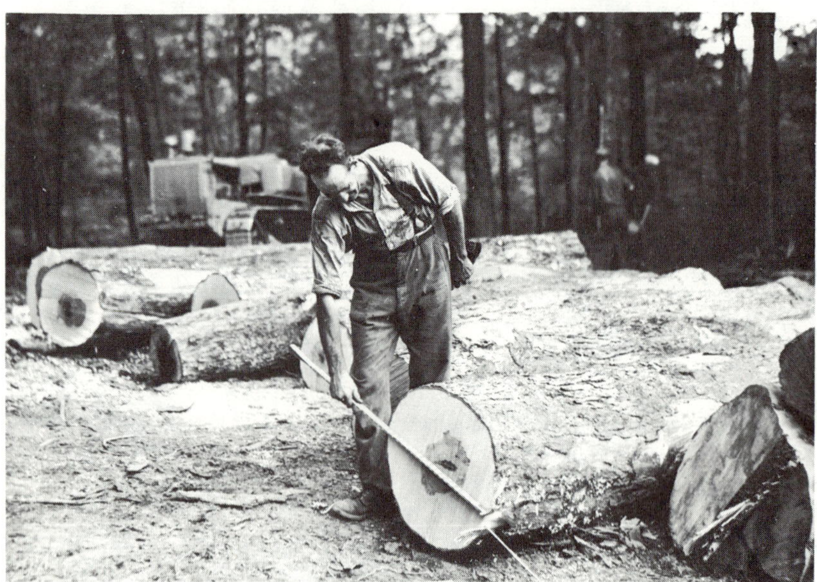

FIGURE 8–9. Scaling decked hardwood logs. As the logs are scaled, the net reading is entered on the log scale tally sheet (Fig. 8–10) and the log marked with a crayon to prevent double counting. (U. S. Forest Service)

bark. Because the end of a log is frequently not a perfect circle, two measurements are usually taken, one across the widest diameter of the circle and one across the narrowest diameter. Then the two measurements are averaged. The length of the log is measured in even feet after allowing about 3 in. at the end for trim. The volumes are entered on a log scale tally sheet (Figure 8–10).

2. Deductions for defects are necessary to give correct net volumes. Logs with a crook or sweep are reduced by sighting a line from center to center of the two ends of the log. Then take the number of inches this line deviates from the center

LOCATION OF LANDING							DATE:		19
LOG NO.	SPECIES								
	SUGAR MAPLE	YELLOW BIRCH	BEECH	HEMLOCK	WHITE PINE	RED OAK	ELM	MISC. CONIFERS	MISC. HARDWOODS
			(Net scale in board feet)						
1									
2									
3									
4									
5									
6									
7									
8									
9									
0									
1									
2									
3									
4									
5									
6									
7									
8									
9									
0									
TOTALS									

FIGURE 8–10. Log scale tally sheet.

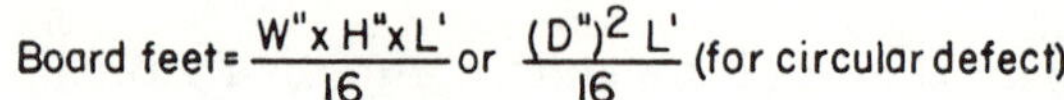

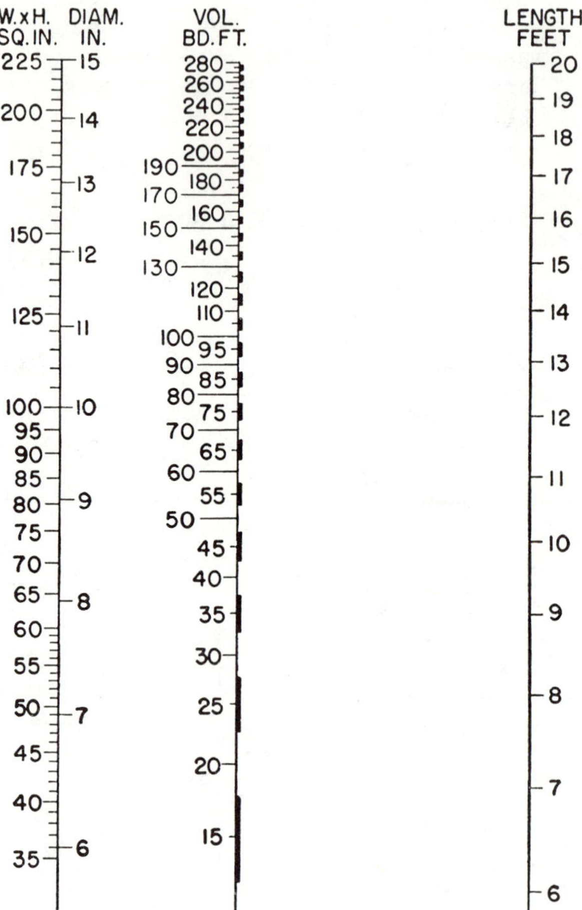

FIGURE 8–11. Chart for determining defect allowance, with the International ¼-in. log rule. Instructions.

1. Measure width and height of defect, in inches. Add 1 in. to each defect to allow for waste.
2. Multiply width by height.
3. Measure or estimate length of defect.
4. Place a straightedge through product of $W \times H$ (left line) and length (right line).
5. Read deduction, to nearest 5 b.f. on center line.

Example: If a defect measured 7 in. × 8 in. × 10 in., the deduction would of the log at the point of maximum sweep, subtract two, and divide the remainder by the diameter of the small end of the log. The result is the sweep deduction, from gross scale, in percent. Interior defects such as rot, and exterior defects such as catfaces, are deducted by figuring the board footage to be lost and deducting this from gross scale. A handy alignment chart for figuring such deductions is given in Figure 8–11. Kinds of defects are shown in Figure 8–12.

Log grading has developed into an important quality measure in recent years. Log grades vary from region by species. The University of Wisconsin Extension Service has described the process of grading and general principles involved* (see Figure 8–13).

3. Record the information called for, for each of the measured logs, on the log tally sheet. The record is made following the procedure for tree scale tally. Logs should be numbered with a crayon on the small end as they are tallied so they will not be counted again, and also so that a check scale can be made of the same logs should disagreement arise. The log volume tables shown in Table 8–1 are the basis for the figures used on a log rule.
4. Total the net scale volume for each species (which may be sold at a different price) and the grand total volume scaled.

**Log Grades*, Extension Service, College of Agriculture, University of Wisconsin, Special Circular 60; revised 1965; with the cooperation of the Northern Hardwood and Pine Manufacturers Association. The Scribner Decimal C Log Rule is used here as the standard log rule.

---

be determined by holding the straightedge through 72 on the left line (7 in. + 1 in.) × (8 in. + 1 in.) and 10 on the right line. The deduction, read from the center line, is 45 b.f.

The board foot deductions thus obtained can be used with the Scribner Scale. For the Doyle Rule, the following factors should be applied to the deductions:

Logs 8 to 11 in.: 0.6

12 to 13 in.: 0.8

14 to 20 in.: 0.9

21 to 31 in.: none

(U. S. Forest Service, *National Forest Scaling Handbook*)

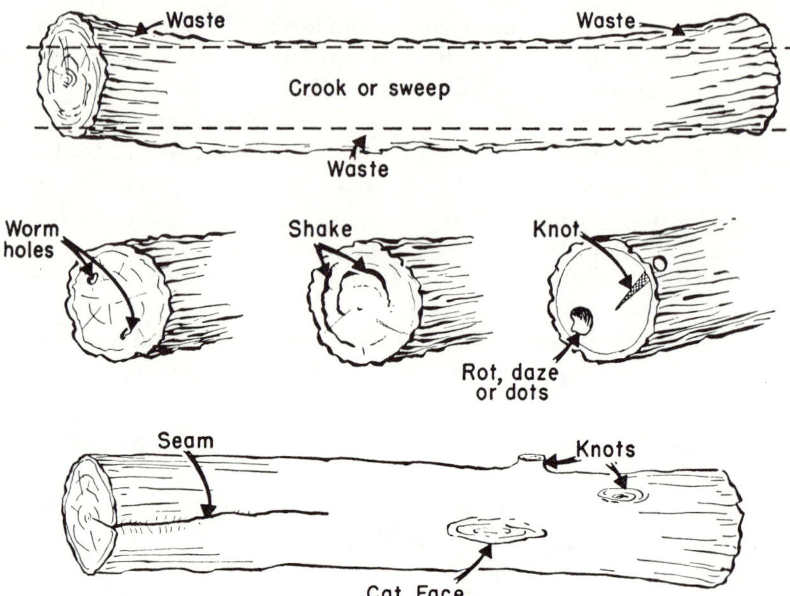

FIGURE 8–12. Kinds of defects in sawlogs. (Redrawn from U. S. Soil Conservation Service)

Scaling Piled Pulpwood

Pulpwood is seldom scaled until it is piled in the woods or loaded on trucks or cars. Many operators and mills now use weight rather than gross stacked volume as a fair unit of measurement. When stacked volume is used, all three dimensions of the pile are measured and then multiplied to obtain the gross cubic foot volume. This is then divided by 128 to give the number of cords. For example, a truck has a load 12 ft long, 8 ft wide, and 4 ft high, a total of 384 cu. ft. Dividing this by 128 shows that the truck has a three-cord load. A shortcut is found in multiplying the length times the height, dividing by 16: $12 \times 4 = 48 \div 16 = 3$ cords.

Deductions are made for rot, undersized wood (usually less than 4 in. at the small end), abnormal voids, and so on, by measuring the squared area and converting this into cubic volume.

In the South, pulpwood is piled in *pens* in the woods. Pens are layers of two sticks each, piled to form a hollow crib 6 ft high. The number of such pens is sometimes used as a basis for paying piece workers. However, many mills are now buying pulpwood by weight; lengths may be odd.

The following tabulations are helpful in determining the number

Hardwoods

Grade No. 1 or Veneer Grade

Diameter: All logs must be 12" or larger in average diameter, as measured from the small end inside the bark.

Length: Standard lengths are 8'6", 10'6", 12'4", 16'4" and 17'. Other lengths may be cut, optional with buyer. Note: 4" to 6" must be added to length for trimming allowance.

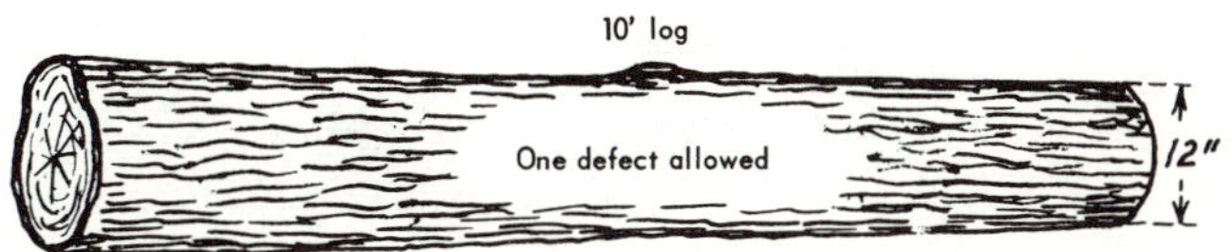

Quality: All logs must be cut from fresh, green timber. Diagrams indicate maximum number of standard defects allowed for various log lengths. Any number of defects located so that they can be cut out in one foot will be considered as only one defect.

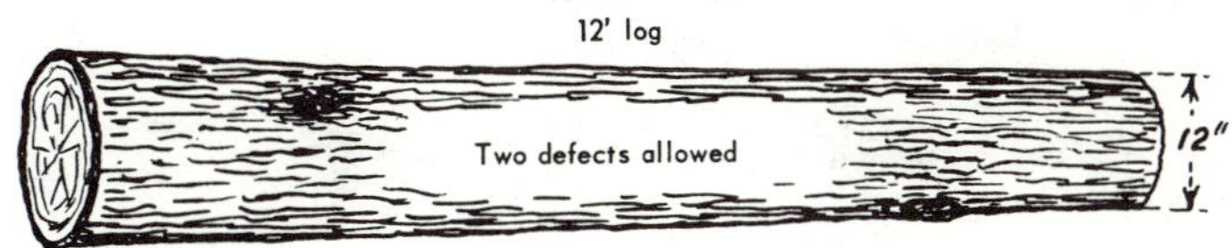

Standard defects: Worm holes, knots, bumps, shake, cat faces, dead and dozy spots, bird pecks, brown spots, pin holes or specified seams are standard defects. Scale off one foot in length for each defect, except for center holes and seams allowed in this grade (see page 2).

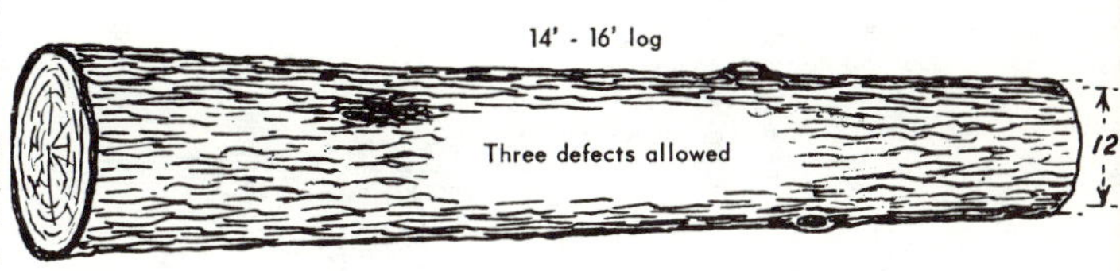

Select Veneer Grade

Diameter: Logs must be 14" or larger in average diameter at small end inside bark.

Length: Standard lengths include 7'6", 8'6", 10'6", 12'4", 16'4", and 17'. All lengths are optional with buyer.

Quality: Select Veneer Grade must be free of all defects, except as provided for center hole defects in Grade No. 1. Logs must be straight. But, logs 14'4" and over may have a slight sweep provided one center cut will make two straight bolts.

FIGURE 8–13. Log grades and specifications. The Scribner Decimal C Log Rule is used here as the standard log rule. (From "Log Grades," Extension Service, College of Agriculture, University of Wisconsin, with the cooperation of the Northern Hardwood and Pine Manufacturers Association).

Defects in Veneer Logs

Center Rot or Hole: Logs 14" in average diameter may have a 3" hole, doze or shake in the heart; 15" in average diameter may have a 5" center defect, and 16" and over in diameter a 6" center defect. There is no deduction in scale for these defects. Logs 16" and over in diameter with center defects greater than allowable size are acceptable if such defects will be reduced to allowable size by deducting 2' from scaling length.

Maple Stain: One half diameter of small end may be black heart or heavy mineral stain, with no deduction in scale.

Seams: No seam is allowed in logs 15" or smaller in diameter. Logs over 15" are allowed one tight, straight seam (such as caused by lightning or frost), not deviating more than 4" from a straight line stretched from end to end of log. An allowable seam counts as one defect with no deduction in scale.

Sweep: All logs must be reasonably straight. Sweep up to 1/6 of diameter of small end is allowed in logs 10'6" and shorter, when measured above the butt swell.

Spiral Grain: Allowed in not more than 1" in 10" of log length. Excessively curly grain will not be accepted in any veneer grades.

Butt Defects: Any defect in butt of log, such as fold, fluted bark, or shallow scar, not extending inside the diameter of the small end, will not be considered a grading defect. No scale deduction will be made. (Applies to all other grades.)

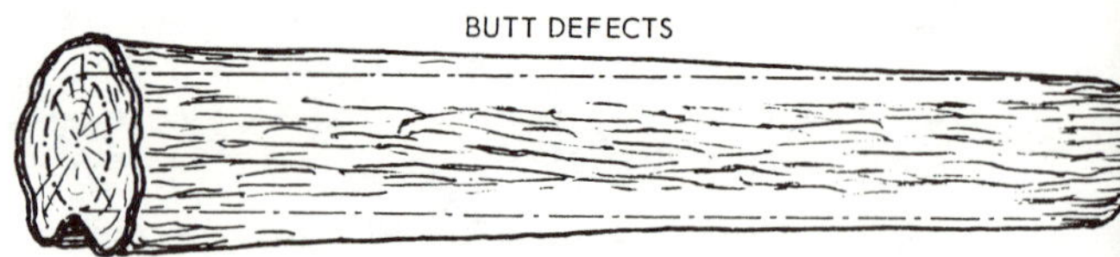

Crotches or Kinks: Crotches, crooks or kinks are to be scaled out when located so that a veneer log can be obtained.

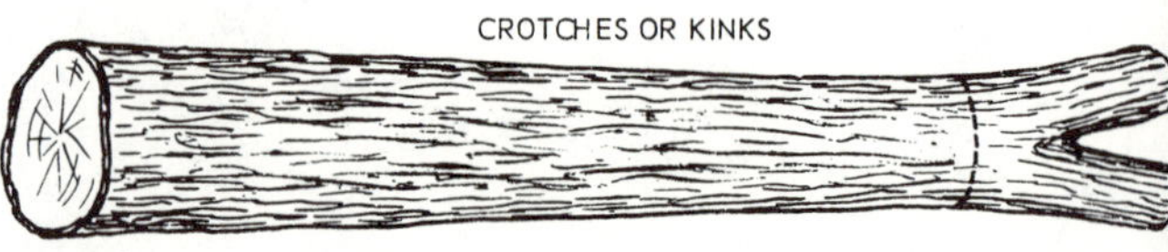

FIGURE 8–13. (Continued)

Grade No. 2

<u>Length</u>: Standard lengths are 8'6", 10'6", and 12'6" or longer. Proportion of 8'6" logs is optional with buyer. A trimming allowance of 6" must be added to standard lengths. No logs are admitted with a net scale of less than 50% of gross scale, with a minimum of 30 board feet for each log.

<u>Diameter:</u> All logs must be 10" or larger in average diameter. Logs 8'6" must be surface clear butt logs (except basswood) with a diameter of 10". Logs 8'6" to 10'6" must have a diameter 11" or larger and 10" basswood or larger. They must have 2/3 or each of 3 faces clear in not more than 2 cuttings per face (cuttings 3' or longer). Logs 12'6" or longer must have a diameter 11" or larger and 10" basswood or larger with 2/3 of each of 3 faces clear in not more than 3 cuttings per face (cuttings 3' or longer). A face is a portion of log extending 1/4 of the circumference of the entire log length.

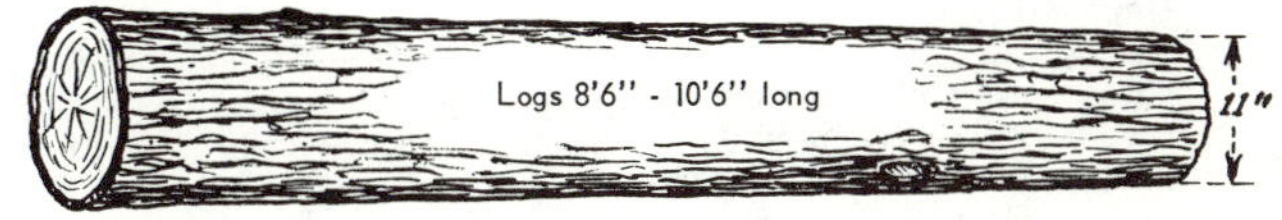

End Defects

<u>Defects:</u> End defects in Grade No. 2 logs may consist of blackheart, mineral stain, heart rot and shake. Defects on small end must amount to less than 1/2 of average diameter for log to be admitted to Grade No. 2.

If defect on small end of log 16" or larger in diameter amounts to less than 60% of average diameter of small end, log is admitted to Grade No. 2.

Any defect in butt logs occurring outside diameter of small end is not a grading defect. These include shallow catfaces, folds, fluted butt bark.

Sweep accompanied by end defects more than 1/4 of diameter at small end, causing a gross scale deduction of 20% or more, is not admitted to Grade No. 2.

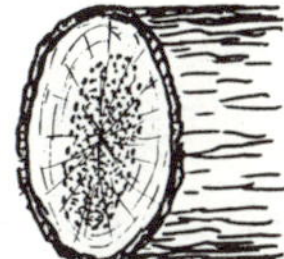

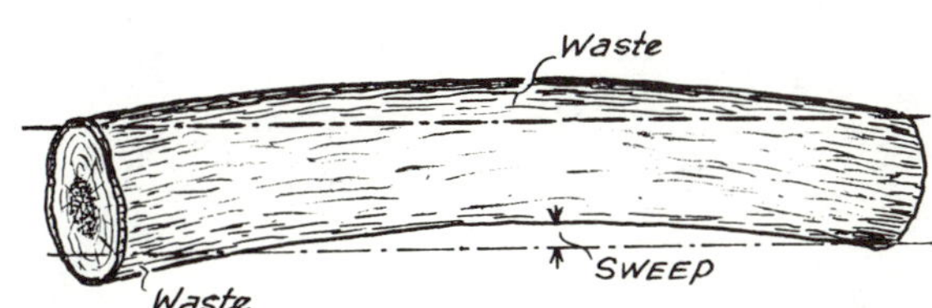

FIGURE 8–13. (Continued)

Grade No. 3

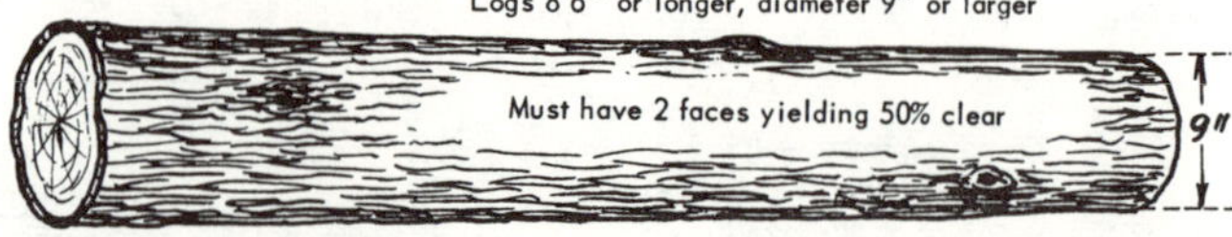

Diameter: All logs which do not qualify for Grade No. 2 must be 9" or larger in diameter to qualify for Grade No. 3. Logs under 14" are allowed with a net scale of less than 50% of gross scale, with a minimum of 30 board feet required in each log. Logs over 14" average diameter are permitted with a net scale of 33-1/3% gross scale.

Length: Logs which do not qualify for Grade No. 2 must be 8'6" or longer to qualify for Grade No. 3. The proportion of 8'6" logs allowed is optional with buyer.

Quality: Must have 2 faces yielding 50% clear.

Tie Cuts

Length: Lengths are 8' or 8'6" as specified. A 2" trimming allowance is required on all cuts.

Diameter: Minimum average diameter is 9" at the small end.

Quality: Tie cuts or bolts must be cut from sound, green timber, free from decay, split, shake, holes, large or numerous knots or other defects impairing strength or durability of railroad ties. If otherwise suitable, dead cedar and tamarack are acceptable.

Softwoods

White Pine

Veneer Grade: Logs must be 16" or larger in diameter and 10' or longer in length. They must be at least 75% clear on each of 3 faces. All knots outside clear cutting must be sound and not over 2-1/2" in diameter.

Grade No. 1. Logs must be 12" or larger and 10' or longer; at least 50% clear on each side of three faces or 75% clear on two faces. Logs must have a net scale after defect deduction of at least 50% gross log volume.

Grade No. 2: Logs must be 12" or over in diameter and 8' or longer in length with a net scale after reduction of at least 50% gross log volume.

Other Softwoods

Norway and jack pine, spruce, white cedar, tamarack, hemlock, balsam fir and aspen logs are included. White pine logs less than 12" in diameter also are included.

Logs must be 9" or over in diameter and 8' or longer in length and have a net scale after deduction for defects of at least 50% gross log volume. Minimum net log scale admitted is 20 board feet.

Ted Peterson
Extension Forester

FIGURE 8–13. (Continued)

TABLE 8–1 LOG RULES FOR SCALING BOARD FOOT CONTENT OF LOGS (SCRIBNER, DOYLE, AND INTERNATIONAL RULES)

Diameter inside bark, small end (in.)	Length of Log (in Feet)														
	Scribner[a]					*Doyle*					*International*[b]				
	8	10	12	14	16	8	10	12	14	16	8	10	12	14	16
6	5	10	12	14	18	–	–	–	–	–	10	10	15	15	20
7	10	10	18	24	28	–	–	–	–	–	10	15	20	25	30
8	10	20	24	28	32	8	10	12	14	16	15	20	25	35	40
9	20	30	30	35	40	13	16	19	22	25	20	30	35	45	50
10	30	30	40	45	50	18	23	27	32	36	30	35	45	55	65
11	30	40	50	55	65	25	31	37	43	49	35	45	55	70	80
12	40	50	59	69	79	32	40	48	56	64	45	55	70	85	95
13	50	60	73	85	97	41	51	61	71	81	55	70	85	100	115
14	60	70	86	100	114	50	63	75	88	100	65	80	100	115	135
15	70	90	107	125	142	61	76	91	106	121	75	95	115	135	160
16	80	100	119	139	159	72	90	108	126	144	85	110	130	155	180
17	90	120	139	162	185	85	106	127	148	169	95	125	150	180	205
18	110	130	160	187	213	98	123	147	172	196	110	140	170	200	230
19	120	150	180	210	240	113	141	169	197	225	125	155	190	225	260
20	140	170	210	245	280	128	160	192	224	256	135	175	210	250	290
21	150	190	228	266	304	145	181	217	253	289	155	195	235	280	320
22	170	210	251	292	334	162	203	243	284	324	170	215	260	305	355
23	190	230	283	330	377	181	226	271	316	361	185	235	285	335	390
24	210	250	303	353	404	200	250	300	350	400	205	255	310	370	425
25	230	290	344	401	459	221	276	331	386	441	220	280	340	400	460

[a]The Scribner Decimal C Rule drops the right-hand digit by rounding off the next digit to the nearest 10 b.f.

[b]Recognized as most accurate.

of sticks of 8-ft pulpwood per cord. They clearly show that small sized wood requires many more trees to make a cord. It is better to let them grow larger before cutting.

Approximate Number of Trees per Cord		*Number of Sticks of 8-ft Pulpwood Required per Cord*	
dbh	*Number of trees*	*Top (in.)*	*Per cord*
5	91	3	217
6	35	4	125
7	21	5	79
8	13	6	54
9	9	7	38
10	7	8	31
11	6	9	24
12	5	10	20
13	4	11	16
14	3	12	14

Measuring Pulpwood by Weight

In recent years many pulp and paper mills have been buying pulpwood from producers on a weight (tonnage) basis. It is believed that this more accurately reflects actual cellulose content and further, that much odd length and crooked material now wasted will be utilized. Production costs are cut both in special efforts to size pulpwood and in scaling both in the woods and at the mill. The following table gives an approximate range of a 128 cu. ft cord of pulpwood by species. The smaller figures are for wood which has been cut for a few months and lost some moisture.

Approximate Weight per Gross Cord of 8-ft Pulpwood

Aspen	
Rough	4300–5000
Peeled	3000–3200
Balsam fir	
Rough	4550–5200
Peeled	3300–3600
Hemlock	
Rough	4550–4900
Peeled	3400–3800

Jack pine	
Rough	4400–4800
Peeled	3100–3400
Spruce	
Rough	4200–4500
Peeled	3100–3400
Southern pine	
Rough only	5300–5800

Because such a variety of units of measure for forest products has developed over time (to which the metric system will soon be added) the conversion Table 8–2 shown below has been designed to aid in the transition from one set of units to another. See also Appendix H for Proposed Metric Equivalents.

Measuring Other Forest Products

Railway ties, poles, posts, and many other products are measured by the piece, according to specifications established by buyers. These specifications are set forth in Table 8–3.

Pocket Slide Calculators

Although log scale sticks from which one can read off the volume of logs directly have been popular, the pocket slide calculator has found

TABLE 8–2 CONVERSION FACTORS FOR CUBIC MEASUREMENT OF WOOD PRODUCTS

Unit of Measure	Board Feet[a]	Cubic Feet[b]	Cords	Cunits[b]	Cubic Meters[b]
One board foot[a]	1	0.1886792	0.0023883	0.0018868	0.0053428
One cubic foot	5.3	1	0.0126582	0.01	0.0283168
One cord (4×4×8)	418.7	79	1	0.79	2.2370309
One cunit	530	100	1.2658228	1	2.8316847
One cubic meter	187.1677335	35.3146667	0.4470211	0.3531467	1

[a]For 14-in. dbh trees. (Scribner Decimal C Log Rule, board foot per cubic foot ratio increases as tree size increases and ranges from 4.4-in. b.f. per cubic foot for 10 in. dbh trees to 6.2 b.f. per cubic foot for 24-in. dbh trees.)

[b]Cubic feet, cunits, and cubic meters are units of measure for solid wood excluding bark and air space.

TABLE 8–3 SPECIFICATIONS OF FOREST PRODUCTS

Kind and measure	Principal species used	Lengths (ft)	Minimum top diameter (in.)	Other specifications
Sawlogs (board ft)	Most hardwoods and softwoods	8, 10, 12 and 16; up to 32 in West	About 8 for softwoods; 10 for hardwoods	Logs may be graded as to size, knots, and defects[a]
Veneer logs (board ft)	Red gum, oak, yellow birch, basswood, walnut, maple, Douglas-fir, white pine, yellow poplar, black cherry, etc.	6–16	12 in East; 24 in West	Same as above
Pulpwood (cords)	Nearly all conifers and aspen, birch, oak, and many other hardwoods	8 ft or 100 in. (Lake States); 4–6 (South); sawlog length in West	4 4	Varying with individual mills

Piling (piece)	All hard pines, spruce, Douglas-fir, oaks, other hardwoods	30–90 and longer	10–6	Gradual taper, minimum sapwood, no rot, trimmed knots, little crook or sweep
Poles (piece)	Pines, cedars	20–75 in 5-ft groups	4–9	Minimum spiral grain, no crook, sweep, or defect
Posts (piece)	Cedars, pines, and other durable species	6–14	3–8	Minimum sweep, defect
Railroad ties (piece by 5 size grades)	Cedars, pines, and most hardwoods	8, 8.5 and 9	6 × 8 7 × 8 7 × 9	Five size grades within specifications of railroad buyers

TABLE 8–3 *(Continued)*

Kind and measure	Principal species used	Lengths (ft)	Minimum top diameter (in.)	Other specifications
Mine timbers	Wide variation in lengths and diameters, depending on type of mining. Contact mine buyer for details before cutting.			
Charcoal wood	Dense hardwoods (birch, beech, maple, oak, hickory) perferred	Variable. Often 52 in. (bolts) or 12–15 in. (blocks)	2 in. minimum. Larger pieces must be split to go thru 10 in. ring. No minimum. Pieces over about 20 in. diam. must be split	Deductions made for rot and excessive crook
Stave bolts (tight cooperage)	White oak	Variable. Usually 39 in. (staves) 24 in. (heading)	Round or split (quartered) from clear sections at least 20 in. in diameter	Soft textured (slow growth) with minimum of sapwood, clear
Furnace poles	All hardwoods	Full tree length	6 minimum; 30 maximum	Green hardwood cull unlimited

[a]Log grading according to size and quality enables the owner to obtain the maximum value present. Log grades form the basis of value scales in many areas. Ungraded logs are usually called *woodsrun*.

ready acceptance. Essentially, this calculator is a light cardboard envelope open at one end with a paper slide with the printed volume table on it that fits inside. Slots near the top of the envelope, one small one which shows diameters at the small end of the log and one longer one providing for log lengths, allow the user to read off the gross volume of the log by picking the proper dimensions in the slot holes. These slide calculators are made for each of the common log rules and are frequently given away by forest products dealers as advertisements.

SPECIFICATIONS OF PRINCIPAL FOREST PRODUCTS

We have already discussed specifications of sawlogs and pulpwood to some extent in connection with measuring and scaling timber and forest products. There are, of course, many kinds of products taken from trees other than these two that form the greatest volume in terms of production. Some of these other products, such as veneer logs, stave bolts, and piling, may have a higher unit value than sawlogs in many localities. Others, like charcoal wood, may furnish markets for sections of trees that would otherwise have to be discarded as waste. Piling is used for docks, building foundations, and other similar construction. Wooden posts separate most of our farm fields and poles hold up our telephone and electric lines. Railroad ties of wood "tie" our railway systems together. Specialized local uses of wood for excelsior, box bolts, stave bolts, and dozens of other products require certain kinds of wood preparation. The more uses important are summarized in Table 8–3, but producers should get more complete and specific information from local wood using industries before cutting. One example is the recent trend to log homes.

METHODS OF SECURING CLOSE UTILIZATION

During the last several decades, American loggers have learned many ways of reducing the large amount of wasted timber that used to be left after average logging jobs. Closer utilization of the whole tree has been made possible by a number of developments, higher values of timber being an important one. In the old days only the best parts of the best trees were taken. Today a large market exists for lower quality material. For example, over wide areas of the East and South, the wide expansion of pulpwood markets has opened up outlets for thinnings and stand improvement cuttings, as well as for some of the larger material left in the tops.

New mechanical equipment, which has replaced much of the old man-and-horse logging, has resulted in lower unit logging costs and closer utilization. Power chain saws, for instance, make cutting lower stumps possible, thus saving a few feet of the best material in the tree, which was formerly left in the woods. People found it difficult to saw a low stump by hand because they had to get down on the ground to do it and thus lost leverage on the saw. The chain saws will cut the tree off right at the ground line. Chain saws have also made it possible economically to cut lower grade trees for the good sections they may contain.

Formerly, material for corduroy roads, skidways, truck and car log stakes was cut from the most available, best, and straightest trees. Now much fine young timber is being saved for future growth by cutting tops, defective, and lower grade species for these purposes.

There have recently been experiments in chipping tops and limbs in the woods with portable wood chippers to prepare wood from waste material for pulp or other uses. This practice is just beginning to develop in a practical way. As this type of equipment is further perfected, the wood cellulose industries will come to depend more heavily upon woods-processed wood chips.

QUESTIONS

1. Before starting to log in any part of the country, what construction must be completed?
2. What are the first three steps in converting a tree into forest products?
3. When are *borrow pits* used?
4. What kinds of mechanized equipment have replaced logging railroads, horses, and river transportation?
5. Describe how to fell a tree in the direction you want it to drop.
6. When trimming branches from a tree with an axe, on which side do you stand?
7. What parts of the tree are measured in scaling cut sawlogs?
8. By each of the three log rules, how many board feet are there in a log that is 12 ft long and has a top diameter of 12 in.?

9. A truck is loaded with pulpwood measuring 10 ft long by 8 ft wide by 5 ft high. How many cords does it contain?
10. A *pen* of pulpwood cut in 4-ft lengths is how many feet high?
11. Why is it necessary to place the scale stick in more than one position across the small end of the log to get a reasonably accurate diameter reading?
12. What are the reasons for knowing the market and products to be cut from a forest before beginning to log?
13. Name several advantages and disadvantages of mechanized logging equipment.
14. Calculate the volume of a defect 5 in. in diameter in a hollow log 15 in. in diameter (at the small end) and 16 ft long. What is the net volume of the log? (Use International ¼-in. log rule.)

EXERCISES

1. Visit a logging operation in your locality and describe methods and equipment used in felling, skidding, loading, and transporting logs.
2. Measure the volumes of 12 sawlogs, using the volume tables shown in the text. Give the proper allowance for log defect.
3. Demonstrate that you know how to carry an axe and a saw properly in the woods.
4. Measure a truckload of pulpwood to determine the number of cords it contains.

NINE

PROTECTING FORESTS FROM FIRE, INSECTS, AND DISEASES

The protection of forests from fire, insects, diseases, and other destructive agents constitutes an important aspect of forestry. No matter how well managed a forest is, it may be destroyed by fire. Insects and diseases, which normally attack the weakest trees, will sometimes destroy an entire stand if not kept under control by forest managers. Wildlife and livestock can create significant problems for the forest by overgrazing, browsing and other destructive activities. And various forms of pollution harmful to trees are now severely affecting forests in various regions around the world.

PROTECTION FROM FIRE

Forest Fire Losses

For about the past 25 years, reported forest fires have numbered from 100,000 to 160,000 per year in the United States—an encouraging reduction from the 500 per day reported in the decade before. Burned acreage varied from 2 to 4 million per year. This was a major drop from the more than 20 million acres burned annually during the prior 15 years. This decrease is attributed to accelerated efforts at prevention and an increasingly intensive fire control program employing modern equipment and techniques.

The great majority of forest fires, especially in the East and South, are *surface fires* that burn mostly in the duff or leaf litter on the forest floor. Promptly attacked with an adequate workforce and equipment, such fires are fairly easy to control. But nearly every small forest fire can become a big one if a combination of dry weather and high winds occurs. A really bad forest fire fanned by high winds will destroy nearly everything in its path. The Peshtigo fire in Wisconsin in 1871 burned more than a million acres, wiped out whole settlements and killed 1500 persons; the great Idaho fires of 1910 wiped out several million acres of virgin timber in a few days. The Tillamook fire in Oregon in 1933 killed as much timber as was cut in the entire United States the preceding year.

A surface fire will damage many of the larger trees and kill seedlings and small trees. Most fires start as surface fires but may develop into other types. Sometimes fires burn deep below the surface in the thick duff of decayed leaves or needles, or in dry peat soils, between surface outbreaks. Such *ground fires*, common in northern bogs, may smolder for days or weeks before being discovered.

The *crown fire*, or a combined surface and crown fire, causes the greatest timber and property damage, and loss of human life. Starting as a surface fire driven by a strong wind, it leaps into the treetops and sweeps through the timber, often jumping by sparks ahead of the main *smoke*. Crown fires occur mostly in coniferous forests, for the green leaves of hardwoods are not easily ignited (Figure 9–1).

Although losses of merchantable timber and property are direct and apparent, forest fires cause damage not so easily recognized. As stated previously, fire may kill the tiny young trees in a forest that would provide future timber crops. Fire in a forest in which valuable pines or spruces predominate may cause that forest to become a mostly scrubby growth of inferior species. Repeated fires have turned many millions of acres of forest land in the United States into unproductive wasteland.

But there are other damages. Surface fires may leave fire scars on the trunks of trees, where wood rots may enter. Fire-weakened trees may be attacked by insects, and are more easily felled by the wind. Storm runoff is greatly accelerated when fires burn the vegetation and surface litter on steep slopes. Fire is responsible for a vast amount of flood damage, for aggravated problems of water supply, and for

FIGURE 9–1. A crown fire. Forest fires destroy timber, wildlife, and watersheds. (U. S. Forest Service)

the silting of reservoirs, stream channels, and harbors with millions of tons of sediment eroded from the land.

Forest fires kill many game animals and birds. Wood ashes washed into streams after a fire sometimes kill large numbers of fish. Destruction of the vegetation along streambanks may cause water temperatures to rise and make the stream unfit for trout. Sedimentation from fire-damaged watersheds has ruined many good fishing streams. Forest fires can also hurt tourist and recreation business. Vacationers are not likely to visit areas where the scenery has been blackened by flames.

Losses such as these, and many other indirect and intangible losses caused by forest fires, are not easily measured in dollars. But in the aggregate they clearly represent a drain on the resources and workforce of the nation.

In few parts of the world is the problem of keeping forests from burning as complex and difficult as it is in the United States. In this country there are many regional variations in terrain, types of vegetation, and seasons of greatest fire danger. The normal fire seasons in the forests of the eastern, northern, and central states are spring and fall. In early spring, soon after the snows have melted and before the deciduous trees have leaved out, a few days of sun and wind can dry out the forest litter and create a high fire hazard. After the leaves fall from the trees in autumn, the forest floor is again exposed to sun and wind, and the dry, new-fallen leaves are added fuel. The fire season may extend through the winter months in the Deep South. The dry summer months are normally the period of greatest forest fire danger. Prolonged droughts may bring periods of danger, and delayed snows may mean that the fire season extends into the winter. Even in normal fire seasons, forest fire danger fluctuates widely. A fire-control organization must be prepared to meet any emergency situation.

The forest fire danger has increased in recent years throughout much of the West because epidemic attacks by insects have killed timber over large areas in Colorado, Montana, Idaho, and Wyoming. This dead timber quickly becomes dry and highly flammable. Increased industrial and recreational use of the forests means greater numbers of people in and near the forests who might start fires.

Causes of Forest Fires

Most forest fires are caused by human carelessness, negligence, or ignorance. Forest fire prevention, therefore, is mainly a problem of changing people's behavior, of creating a better understanding of the importance of forests, an awareness of the danger of fire in the woods, and a sense of personal responsibility to safeguard the forests from damage. That is not an easy job. Urban people accustomed to paved streets, for example, do not remember the flammability of the forest floor when they throw away their cigarettes. A recent percentage allocation of the causes of fires reported on protected forest and watershed lands of the United States is as follows.

Cause	*Percent*
Incendiary	26
Smokers	17
Debris burning	23
Lightning	9
Machinery	7
Railroads	5
Campers and picnickers	3
Miscellaneous or unknown	10

Incendiarism (the willful destruction of property by fire), the leading cause of forest fires, is a problem mainly in the South. Some 90 percent of the forest fires of incendiary origin reported on protected lands are in the southern states. Comparatively, few forest fires caused by humans are set maliciously, but these are often the most serious.

Annual woods-burning has long been a tradition in many rural sections of the South. The woods are fired every spring to "green up the grass," to get rid of underbrush, or because of mistaken notions that ticks or boll weevils can be eliminated by woods-burning. Ideas and customs of long standing will have to be changed by education, coupled with better fire laws and stricter law enforcement.

Careless smokers are responsible for thousands of forest fires each year. They toss cigarette butts or matches while traveling in forested areas. Others are caused by careless hikers, hunters, fishermen, or woods workers. Many states now have laws against throwing burning materials from automobiles.

Debris burning causes many fires in farm woodlands and suburban areas. Too frequently, fires started by landowners to burn trash, eliminate brush, or to clear land, get out of hand and spread to adjacent woods. Although some states require burning permits, a number of states still lack effective laws to foster safe practices in the burning of debris. Burning frequently destroys much organic matter that might have been returned to the soil.

The only important natural and so far unpreventable cause of forest fires is *lightning* (mainly occurring in the West), which accounted for about 9 percent of the reported fires on protected lands.

Machinery caused fires start from sparks emitted with exhaust, engine fires, electrical, and other mechanical problems that result from the use of machinery in forested areas or on roads and trails.

Railroad and logging operations caused many more forest fires in the past than they have in recent years. Improved spark arresters and the conversion to electric and diesel locomotives, have reduced the danger from sparks. The percentage of fires resulting from logging operations is also lower than it was a few decades ago. Many timber owners provide intensive protection on their holdings. Most logging crews observe strict safety precautions, and when bad fires do occur, they are usually among the first reserves to be called.

Campers and picnickers who build campfires in unsafe places or who abandon their still-burning campfires are another cause of forest fires. Educational efforts to induce campers to douse their campfires thoroughly with water before they leave are reducing the number of fires from this cause.

Many *miscellaneous causes* of forest fires have been reported. All told, the great majority of all forest fires are caused by humans and therefore preventable.

Beneficial Uses of Fire

Under certain circumstances—that is, in the proper places, in the right hands, under exacting weather conditions and strict surveillance—fire can be an asset in achieving certain management objectives. Because of their efficiency and the low costs involved, *prescribed fires* (as these controlled burns are also called) have become increasingly popular in forestry as well as in wildlife and range management. This is particularly true for the southern United States, where these fires were first implemented in the 1930s. More than 2 million acres are now being treated with controlled burns annually in that region alone.

Frequently these fires are conducted on rights of way, recent cuts, or even within pine stands, with the objective of eliminating fuel that might otherwise accumulate and support future damaging wildfires on these areas.

As a site preparation measure, controlled fires may improve access for planting crews, enhance seed germination by exposing the mineral soil, or reduce weed competition for future seedlings. Prescribed burns have also become a standard technique in coping with a notorious fungal disease (brown spot) of longleaf pine regeneration.

Although these controlled fires are usually designed to serve one main purpose, they frequently benefit several objectives. A hardwood understory removal burn, for instance, may reduce competition for the pine overstory, result in fuel load reduction, prepare the seedbed for shelterwood cuts, enhance access and aesthetic appeal, and improve the range for both domestic stock and certain wildlife species.

Under no circumstances should these fires be attempted by inexperienced people. It takes considerable judgment of climatic, fire behavior, and fuel components to control fires properly and achieve the objectives. Also, provisions for the possible escape of one of these fires and potential smoke problems are prerequisite.

Under certain conditions in specially designated forests such as some wilderness areas, naturally-caused forest firest are allowed to burn unchecked to maintain the natural ecology of the area. Generally, such "let burn" policies are carefully established and reviewed by forest managers and the fires themselves are closely watched to keep them under control.

Organizing Forest Fire Control

The United States has developed a system of cooperative forest fire control in which the federal government (acting through the Forest Service) cooperates with the states in an organized effort to prevent, detect, and suppress forest fires. In some parts of the West, associations of private forest owners also cooperate in this program, and many industrial forests have their own fire-fighting equipment and crews.

The cooperative fire-control program brings together all of the control facilities of the several private and public agencies. Since the federal government recognizes that it has a responsibility for assisting the states and is responsible to our citizens in assuring future generations of adequate forests, it supplies both a part of the funds (about one quarter) and the technical supervision and coordination of our nationwide forest fire-control system. The following sections describe the operations of this integrated system. Forestry personnel working with one agency often find themselves working with the others in this combined effort.

The protection of the forests from fire involves three general phases of activity. Prevention, preparedness, and suppression.

Prevention

Foresters say that "the best way to stop a fire is never to let it start." Because more than nine-tenths of all forest fires are caused by humans, and are therefore preventable, the U.S. Forest Service, the state forestry departments, the forest industries, and various conservation organizations have for many years conducted educational programs aimed at fire prevention.

During periods of extreme drought and high fire danger, certain areas of state and private lands and national forests are sometimes closed to entry by the public. Hunting and fishing seasons may be suspended and logging operations closed down because of hazardous fire weather. Most states have a system for issuing burning permits and only issue them during safe burning periods such as during and immediately following a rain. This system warns the fire lookout that there will be a *smoke* at a certain location.

Spark arresters on railroad and logging equipment, "no smoking on the job" rules in logging operations, and other safety appliances and rules are prevention measures. Cleanup of logging slash, rubbish, and other flammable debris helps to reduce fire hazards.

Undoubtedly, the Smokey Bear campaign of the Forest Service and the National Advertising Council and the Keep Green campaign of the forest industries were largely responsible for the drastic reduction in the number of forest fires during the postwar period from the years before World War II. The Civilian Conservation Corps also played a major role. This reduction occurred despite substantial increases in public use of forests and outdoor areas in the postwar years.

Preparedness

Preparedness calls for building up, placing, and training an effective fire-control organization. Adequate fire-control plans must cover *detection, communication, transportation,* and provision for the necessary *tools, equipment,* and *workforce.* Weather forecasting service, regular measurement of fire danger, and other technical services must be arranged under the *presuppression* program.

Presuppression Planning

Fire breaks or fire lanes cleared to a width of 30 or more ft along boundaries of large tracts, or cutting brush and trees along existing roads helps to confine fires inside limited areas.

Fire Danger Rating

The National Fire Danger Rating System (NFDRS) integrates fuels, weather, and topography, the principal factors influencing fire po-

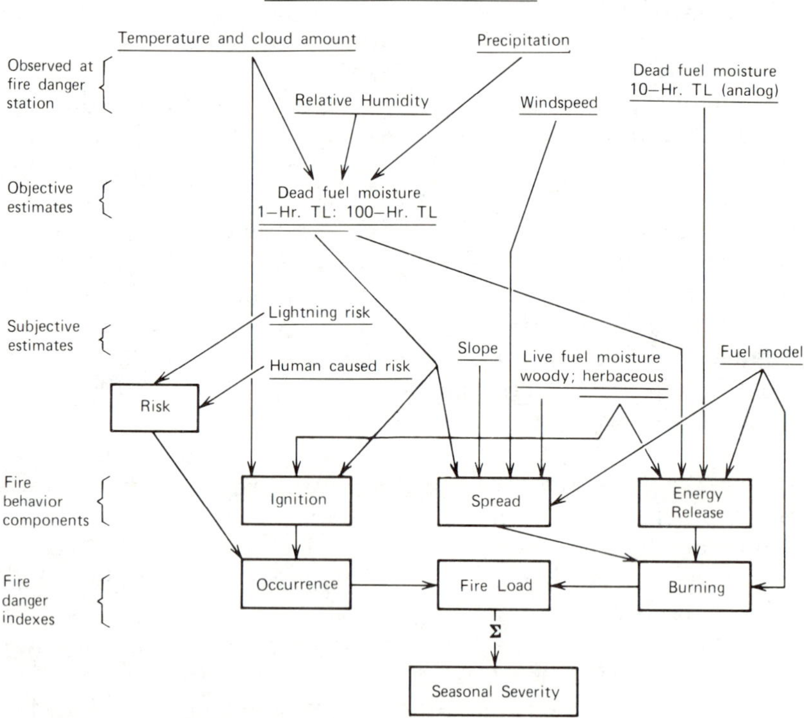

FIGURE 9–2. Structure of the National Fire Danger Rating System.

TABLE 9–1 FIRE DANGER RATING AND BURNING INDEX

Burning Index (percent)	Degree of Danger	Description	Presuppression Planning
50–up	7—Extreme	Explosive conditions. Fires start readily from sparks, burn fiercely, and tend to crown and spot generally.	Man all lookouts on 24-hour basis Extra ground and air patrols Regular and reserve personnel on 24-hour standby
25–49	6—Very high	Fires will start from a glowing cigarette butt or sparks, spread rapidly, and tend to crown generally. Spot fires common.	All equipment ready for immediate action Issue emergency fire warnings: radio, TV, and press
13–24	5—High	Fires start readily from a match or glowing cinders, spread rapidly, and tend to crown in young conifers.	Man all lookouts Full ground and emergency air patrol All personnel at fire duty station, including weekends Have road crews on standby All fire-fighting equipment ready for immediate action Fire danger warnings on radio and TV No burning permits
7–12	4—Moderate	Fires start readily from a match, burn briskly, and tend to spread rapidly as they increase in size.	Man all lookouts Full ground patrol Key personnel within call from headquarters Standby crew ready for immediate call Burning permits early in morning and evening only

TABLE 9–1 *(Continued)*

Burning Index (percent)	Degree of Danger	Description	Presuppression Planning
4–6	3—Low	Fires will start from a lighted match and spread (rapidly in dry grass and leaves) until extinguished.	Air patrol on regular schedule Man primary towers only Personnel same as (1—Safe) below Burning permits
2–3	2—Very low	Fires will start from an open flame but spead slowly and tend to go out.	Air patrol on regular schedule Man primary towers only Personnel same as (1—Safe) below Burning permits
0–1	1—Safe	Fires will not spread beyond the heat of a campfire or burning brush pile.	Air patrol only after lightning storms Personnel used on repair and maintenance work Burning permits

Source: Adapted from Bureau of Land Management, U. S. Department of the Interior.

tential and behavior, in a system that permits the calculation of certain index numbers.

The basic structure of the NFDRS (Figure 9–2) provides three indices designed to aid in planning and supervising fire-control activities on specific fire protection units. These indices are derived from the three fire behavior components: (1) spread component (SC) indicating the rate of spread, (2) energy release component (ERC) indicating the rate of combustion, and (3) ignition component (IC) indicating the ease of ignition. Each is evaluated on a scale of 0 to 100. The indices are defined and applied as follows.

Occurrence Index (OI) A number related to the potential fire incidence within a rating area. A high OI would indicate full readiness for the detection system.

Burning Index (BI) A number related to the contribution that fire behavior makes to the potential amount of effort needed to contain *a* fire of a particular fuel type within a rating area. A high BI would require a large amount of manpower and equipment to combat a single fire.

Fire Load Index (FLI) A number related to the total amount of effort required to contain *all* probable fires occurring within a rating area during a specific period. Readiness plans are keyed to that number.

The seasonal severity index (SSI) serves primarily as an administrative tool and for statistical purposes.

The NFDRS is quite complex and requires instrumental readings and observations with respect to weather, fuel, and topography. These recordings serve as a basis for a series of calculations.

Instruments at each fire weather station record the following factors. Wind velocity is measured by an anemometer, a set of four whirling cups attached to a speedometer. Temperature is measured with wet- and dry-bulb thermometers. Forest fuel moisture content is assessed by comparing the weights of two wooden sticks of exactly the same size and weight located close to the forest floor. One stick is dried in an oven and its weight compared with the undried stick. A delicate scale will show the difference in moisture content.

The NFDRS also incorporates weather information not required by previous fire-danger rating systems. This includes the 24-hour maximum and minimum relative humidities (the amount of moisture in the air) and temperatures, measured by hygrothermograph, rainfall beginning and ending times, the amount of precipitation, measured in a rain gauge.

All readings taken from instruments at fire weather stations are recorded on a standard form, the 10-Day Fire Danger and Weather Record issued by the National Weather Service. The instrument readings and computations are applied to a set of tables contained in the NFDRS booklet in proper sequences and thus determine the fire danger rating values. Different tables are available for each of nine fuel models, another innovation of the NFDRS, designed to account for the various naturally occurring fuel situations throughout the United States.

Detection

Locating a fire in its early stages is of utmost importance to successful fire control. A good detection system usually consists of a network of permanently established fire lookout towers. During normal fire weather only the detection points that give the most complete observation coverage of the surrounding territory are staffed.

Detection of fires from the air by regularly scheduled airplane patrols has been useful in several roadless timberland areas of the Northwest, the Lake States, and elsewhere. It is most successful where fires caused by lightning are the principal problem, and where a few key lookout stations are retained to supplement the air patrol and to act as radio communication hubs. In all forest regions of the country, airplane patrols are often used for supplemental or emergency detection when the danger of fires is unusually high or when haze or a smoke blanket from existing fires in the locality limits the visibility from ground lookouts.

A distinction should be made here between *fire* and *smoke*. The term *smoke* is used until it is certain that a fire is spreading and cannot be controlled by the initial suppression crew. Smoke may originate at an unreported camp site, from rubbish burning, someone burning grass, or similar causes, which may be under control or easily controlled by the initial suppression crew. The term *fire* is used only when it is apparent that the fire is spreading and that greater effort will be needed by the initial suppression crew to control it. Because it is desirable to have everyone alert when a fire does exist, indiscriminate use of the word *fire* could result in a reaction similar to that of the men when the boy cried "wolf!"

Lookout towers or stations are equipped with telephone communication and in some regions with shortwave radio as well. They also contain a *fire finder* for use in accurately locating a fire when smoke is visible. One fire finder, used at many stations, has a front sighting arm containing a cross-hair for accuracy in sighting a smoke column. It is mounted on a map table oriented so that the map directions agree with the compass direction on the ground. The rim of the map table is marked off in *azimuths* or the degrees of a circle, starting with 0 at the north and returning there at 360°.

When the lookout discovers smoke, he or she immediately sights the fire finder at it and records the azimuth and estimated distance from the station, together with other landmarks and location data that can be furnished from a map and the lookout's other knowledge of the country. The lookout telephones all of this information to the district ranger or central dispatcher. Upon receiving a lookout's report on a *smoke*, the dispatcher obtains, if possible, azimuth readings on the fire from other lookout stations and then plots these on a map. The intersection of the plotted lines-of-sight gives the exact location of the fire on the map. This procedure is called *triangulation* (Figure 9–3). The dispatcher, as soon as the necessary information is available from the tower (Figure 9–4) regarding the location, size, and spread of the fire, and the fuel type in which it is burning, dispatches the initial suppression crew with proper instructions.

New Detection Methods

The most highly developed and effective of the new remote sensing detection systems is an infrared system. Infrared is the name assigned

FIGURE 9–3. Locating a forest fire by triangulation. When towermen sight a smoke, *each man calls the fire dispatcher's office, giving the azimuth from his tower. On the dispatcher's map, each tower is located at the center of a 360° circle. Using the pinned threads, the dispatcher lays out the reported azimuths, and the point where two or more threads cross is the location of the fire. (U. S. Forest Service)*

to the lowest wavelength region of the electromagnetic radiation spectrum. Its value is in its ability to detect fires by the energy emitted from the fire by wavelengths rather than by illumination. Thus problems of night detection are eliminated as is the problem of discovering fires that may go unobserved until the heavy smoke of a previous fire has been controlled. The infrared system also provides a method for measuring the size of the fire and for mapping its location to the extent that rivers, roads, and other landscape characteristics are shown. The fire's exact location is then determined and the best approach to the fire is revealed. The intensity and velocity of a fire can be calculated by this system. The infrared system is being used experimentally with aircraft; the system requires an unobstructed view of the sources of the energy or heat to be effective and thus a high observation point is essential.

FIGURE 9–4. Forest fire towers are always located at high points that have a good view of the terrain. (U. S. Forest Service)

Radar and sferics are two types of remote sensing being used and tested for tracking lightning storm situations. Radar is employed by the U.S. Weather Bureau to track cumulonimbus cloud formations, normally associated with thunderstorm activity. Radar operates by transmitting pulses of microwave energy in a narrow beam, then detecting the energy reflected by a target such as a cloud formation.

Radar is quite effective in determining the location of a possible storm but it cannot, as of now, distinguish between an actual storm and one that does not develop. It would thus be used primarily as a planning method in detection and as a study device to learn more about the specific nature of fire-setting lightning storms. From such knowledge, techniques can be developed for early storm warnings and evaluations of wet or dry storms, fast or slow moving storms, and severe or moderate storms. Sferics is a method of tracking lightning by monitoring the discharged electromagnetic energy that is carried in wavelengths of the radio wave spectrum. These waves travel along the curvature of the earth's surface, as well as in a straight line, giving the sferics device the ability to detect lightning from thousands of miles away. This, in addition to a very low cost as compared to radar, makes the sferics equipment quite important. Television and satellites are also being used. Although these have similar limitations as human beings, they have the added advantage of possible use in uninhabitable regions.

Factors Influencing Fire Intensity and Spread

The manner of burning, the shape of the burned area, and the speed and intensity of a fire depend on the kind, quantity, and moisture content of the forest fuels, and upon the wind velocity, topography, air temperature, and relative humidity. The rate of spread and severity of a fire depends on its supply of litter, humus, fallen limbs and trees, underbrush, slash left after logging, and living trees. Except for conifers, green leaves and wood burn with difficulty even in prolonged dry periods, whereas dry fallen leaves, twigs, and punky wood may be easily ignited by a spark or burning object. Coniferous needles are much more flammable than hardwood litter. They produce a hotter fire and burn faster. At certain times of the year, grasses and other herbaceous vegetation become exceedingly dry and are easily ignited.

The moisture content of forest vegetation is directly affected by the atmospheric moisture (or relative humidity) and rainfall. Fuels absorb moisture during periods of high relative humidity or rainfall and lose it during periods of low relative humidity. Where fuels are light and dry readily, it is important to measure and follow the atmospheric moisture and rainfall closely in order to forecast the probable moisture content of the forest fuels.

Before a forest fire will burn, fuel must be heated to a temperature of 600 to 800°F. When the fuel has a high moisture content, more heat is required because water must be evaporated before the fuel is ignited. Once a large volume of heat is created, the fire gains speed and progressively dries the fuel for its own advance. Slash-covered areas with a large accumulation of dry fuel are a menance to adjacent green timber. The severity of a fire is more directly dependent upon the amount of available fuel than on the rate of spread.

The direction and speed of the wind determine the direction and rate in which the head of a forest fire advances. Even a moderate wind increases the rate of speed of the fire and dries the fuel ahead of the fire. Because hot air rises, fires create an upward draft or air current that may pick up and throw sparks forward 600 to 900 ft or as much as half a mile to ignite new fires, called *spot fires*.

The topography—that is, direction of slope, degree of slope, and surface conditions—affects the spread and severity of a fire. In rugged country with varied terrain, the spread of a fire is irregular; rolling topography favors a more uniform development of all sections of the fire. Fires burn rapidly up steep slopes, consuming all before them. Because the heat of the fire itself creates a draft, it intensifies the progress of the fire. Slopes facing south and west burn more severely than other slopes because they are warmer and drier from exposure to the sun.

FIRE-FIGHTING METHODS

Suppression begins only after a fire is discovered and reported. During the lapse of time from the first discovery to the arrival of the first control forces, each of the following steps takes place.

1. *Discovery* Estimated time when fire started to when it is first seen and located.
2. *Report* Time from final discovery to receipt of report of location by control forces at headquarters station.
3. *Getaway* Period required to dispatch forces after report of fire.
4. *Travel* Time required to find and arrive at fire.

In suppressing forest fires, the following are of primary importance: (1) quick arrival at the fire, (2) an adequate force, (3) proper equipment, (4) a thorough organization of the fire crew, (5) skill in attacking and fighting the fire, and (6) mopping up and patrol to prevent new outbreaks. A small fire can usually be put out by a force of one to five people. Large fires may require several hundred to a thousand or more people and take many days to control and mop-up.

The three necessary requirements for a fire—heat, fuel, and oxygen (or air)—can be illustrated by a triangle.

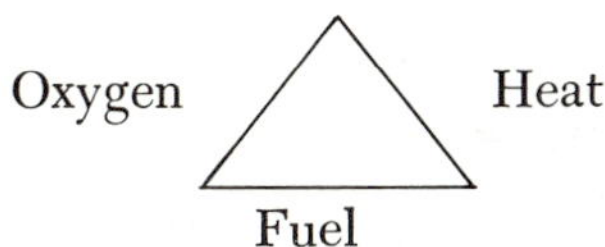

Removal of any one of the three elements will extinguish a fire. Heat can be eliminated by use of water or mineral soil to *knock down* a fire. Fuel can be eliminated, which is essentially what is done when constructing a fire break. Oxygen can be eliminated by dousing with water or burying in mineral soil.

No two forest fires are exactly alike. Fuel types, weather, slope, and exposure of terrain, accessibility, and so forth, vary so much that each fire presents an individual suppression problem. The suppression technique adopted by a fire boss on any fire will be based upon experience and knowledge of fire behavior, but it will usually be an adaptation of one or more of the generally accepted methods of fire fighting. Two general suppression methods are known as *direct* and *indirect* attack on the various parts of a fire (Figure 9–5).

Direct attack, or work directly on the burning edge of the fire, may be used only on fires where the rate of spread is slow and the heat is not too great. Although it is best to build a fire line down to the subsoil, shoveling, raking, or sweeping burning litter back into the fire is also effective. Beating out flames with wet sacks, with specially designed swatters, or even with green branches can retard small fires. Water pumped on the fire is often the most satisfactory if it is available.

Indirect attack involves work at some distance from the burning edge of the fire. It involves either the construction of fire lines or the use of existing barriers as breaks where the spread can be stopped. It is used on hot, fast spreading fires that require attack at a distance to provide the necessary workable conditions and time to get a barrier around the fire.

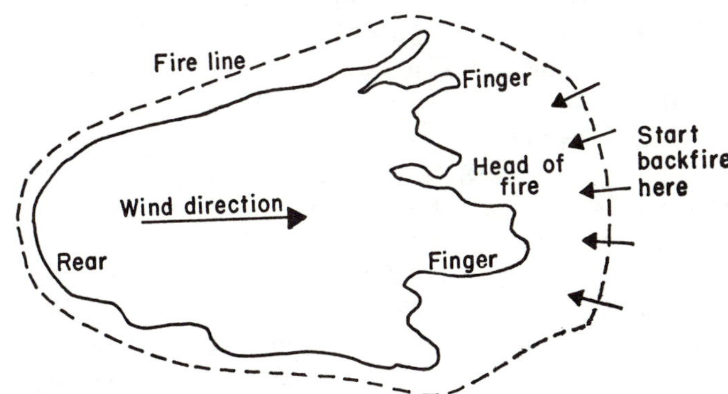

FIGURE 9–5. Parts of a forest fire.

Open land, roads, railroad grades, bare rock ledges, streams, or lakes may provide natural barriers to the spread of a fire, or it may be necessary for the suppression crew, upon arrival at a fire, to construct a special barrier called a fire line or control line around the blaze to confine the fire to the smallest possible area. In constructing a control line, fire fighters cut away the brush, logs, and small trees where the line is to be located. They then dig or scrape the burnable litter to form a strip a foot or more in width to prevent the spread of the fire on the ground. Any snags or dead trees that might throw sparks across the line must be felled. In soils with little rock, fire lines can be plowed with a crawler tractor much faster and wider than people can dig them.

Whenever water is available it can also be used effectively with indirect methods of fire suppression. Fire-control plans, however, can seldom be based entirely on the use of water because in many parts of the country water may be scarce or entirely lacking near a fire. However, in sandy areas with shallow water tables, wells have been driven in a few minutes to furnish water for fire fighting.

Backfiring is an excellent fire control tool when used by a person of experience, but it can easily "backfire" on the inexperienced user, with disastrous results. Trained fire organizations use backfiring effectively, basing their operations on a control line cleared and dug well ahead of the fire (Figure 9–6). A road, trail, stream, or other natural barrier is also often used. With a crew patrolling this line to prevent the fire from jumping it, an experienced forestry supervisor sets a fire along this line, which is allowed to burn back to the main fire. This removes combustible fuels and widens the control line. When the oncoming fire approaches the backfired control line, it will die from lack of fuel. Unburned corners inside the control line may also be burned out during mop-up work to prevent later flareups that might result in the fire getting across the control line.

Organizing fire-fighting crews is similar to organizing soldiers in a battle: the infantry (fire fighters) is deployed to the front lines (fire sectors) in platoons and companies (crews) under the local command of junior officers (sector and crew bosses). The general in charge is the *fire boss* with a *line boss, service chief*, and *plans chief* under immediate command. The service chief has charge of supplies and services to the line bosses' crews. Records, communications, weather, and fire intelligence are the duties of the plans chief. A simplified diagram of a fire organization can be seen on page 220.

Rapid transportation and communication are of the utmost importance in fire suppression. To facilitate quick transportation of personnel and supplies, federal, state, and private fire protection agencies have built roads, trails, and emergency airplane landing fields in many

FIGURE 9–6. Backfiring from a plowed fire line. (Texas Forest Service)

forested areas. But in some sections of the country, there still remain vast roadless areas in which it is necessary for suppression crews to walk long distances to a fire, carrying necessary tools, equipment, and food on their backs. Therefore, forest protection agencies must use aircraft for the delivery of both personnel and equipment by parachute to remote areas.

Mopping-up and Patrolling

Mopping-up after a fire has been controlled must be done or all the effort may be wasted. Without mop-up, fire can break out from smoldering coals the next windy day. Control means stopping the fire from any further spreading of the perimeter. Only when firebrands are no longer present on the edges can it be considered out.

Final mop-up, which is done after the fire is controlled, does not mean extinguishing every bit of burning material. Large fires may have smoldering material far back in the burn, but this is no threat to the flammable materials at the edge of the burned area. Smoldering snags or dead trees near unburned areas should be felled if they are within the maximum spark-throwing range of the fire line. All dead logs, limbs, roots, or anything else that extends into or across the fire

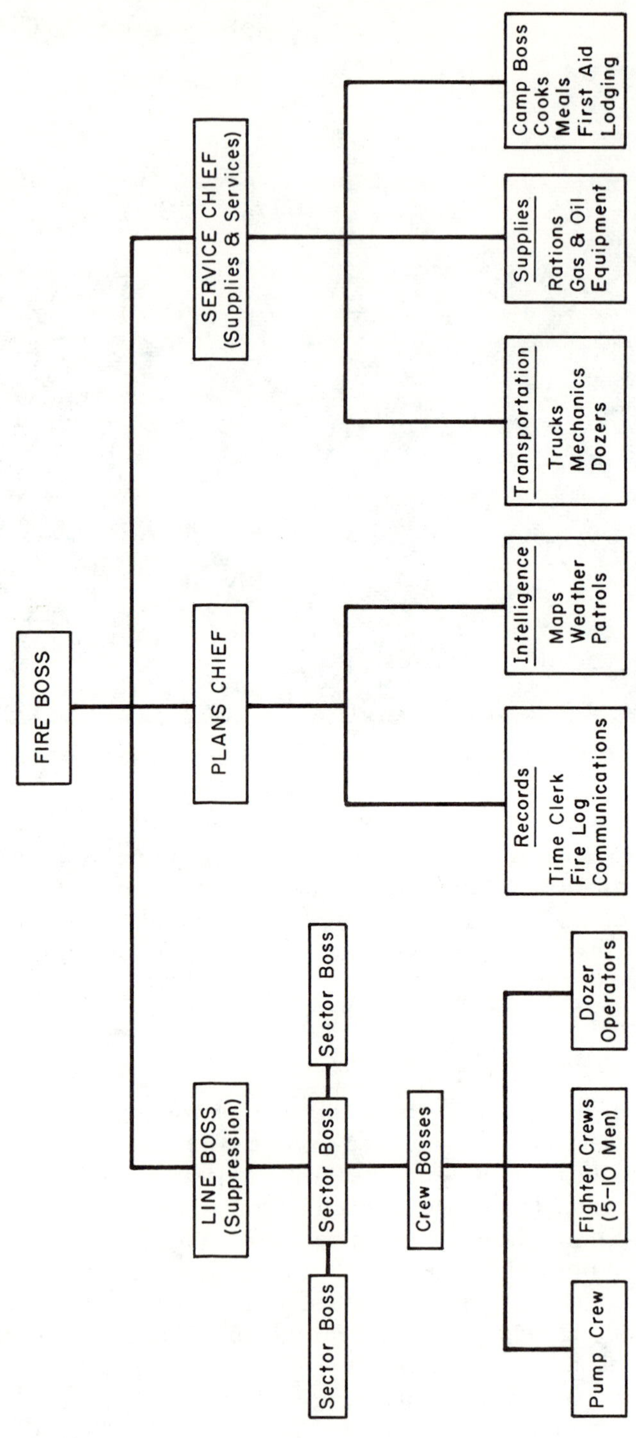

FIRE BOSS
LINE BOSS
(Suppression)
Sector Boss
Sector Boss
Sector Boss
Crew Bosses
Pump Crew
Fighter Crews
(5–10 Men)
Dozer
Operators
PLANS CHIEF
Records
Time Clerk
Fire Log
Communications
Intelligence
Maps
Weather
Patrols
SERVICE CHIEF
(Supplies & Services)
Transportation
Trucks
Mechanics
Dozers
Supplies
Rations
Gas & Oil
Equipment
Camp Boss
Cooks
Meals
First Aid
Lodging

line should be pulled back into the burned out area. Before leaving, the fire boss should go around the entire burned area to make certain no danger spots remain. Then a patrol should be stationed to give continued inspection of a mopped-up fire until it is completely safe.

New Fire-Fighting Techniques

In earlier days, fire fighters relied mainly on axes, shovels, and other hand tools for digging fire lines and throwing dirt on fires. Today gasoline and back pumps are used to bring water to forest fires. Although there is still need for much handwork, fire fighting has become more mechanized with tractors plowing furrows for fire lines. Hand fire tools used by crews on direct attacks are shown in Figure 9–7.

Transportation equipment has been vastly improved. Where once the mule string or pack train was the only means of moving equipment and supplies into remote forest areas, the airplane, helicopters, special trucks, jeeps, and trail scooters now carry a large share of the load.

The use of aircraft has been a big help in implementing a quick-hit policy of forest fire suppression. Their first principal use was for reconnaissance of fires in progress and for detection of fires immediately after lightning storms. In a few instances they have replaced fire towers in otherwise inaccessible country. Now, emergency trans-

FIGURE 9–7. Modern hand fire-fighting equipment. (U. S. Department of the Interior, Bureau of Land Management)

portation of *smokejumper* fire fighters and supplies dropped by parachute have become two of the major roles of aircraft in fire control.

Specially equipped aircraft are used to drop water- or fire-retardant *slurry* to reduce the flammability of wood and wood-fiber materials (Figure 9–8). In many cases, the aerial application of retardant slurry has been the tool that has made the difference between small fires and large fires by holding or retarding the spread until the arrival of suppression crews. Slurry, made up of chemicals (usually phosphates, bentonite clay, or other viscous materials) mixed with water, clings to fuels to reduce inflammability. When dropped at or near the advancing edge of a fire, a fire break is made and the fire is suppressed. Water is often dropped directly on small fires in inaccessible places.

Since 1940, Forest Service smokejumper operations have been conducted every year by people carefully selected and thoroughly trained before the beginning of each fire season. Fires in remote areas can be attacked soon after discovery, whereas ground crews would require many hours to reach them. Hundreds of fires that would have otherwise spread to burn large areas and cause great damage have been quickly controlled by the parachuting fire fighters. In addition, helicopters are often used as a very effective means of transporting fire fighters and supplies into and out of remote areas. Helicopters, unlike

FIGURE 9–8. An air tanker dropping slurry at the head of a California fire. (U. S. Forest Service)

other aircraft, offer the ability to take off and land in rough terrain without a landing strip.

Mechanized Equipment

Groundwork in fire suppression is becoming increasingly mechanized. The Forest Service, state forestry departments, and forest industries are constantly working to improve their equipment and develop new items that will increase the speed and effectiveness of fire control. Water equipment used in fire control now includes efficient backpack pumps, portable gasoline pumps of various sizes and capacities, and large tank trucks capable of good speed on roads. Crawler tractors with specially designed *breaker plows* (which cut deeper and wider than field plows) are able to rip wide, effective breaks in subsoil in minutes.

The Forest Service has special camp equipment for feeding, sheltering, and caring for fire fighters. During a fire emergency, temporary camps must be set up quickly for dozens, and sometimes hundreds or thousands, of fire fighters. Compact camp cooking and other outfits designed for 1 to 25 people, or larger camps, are kept packed ready to go out on a moment's notice.

Communications

Speedy and reliable communications are one of the keys to successful forest fire suppression. Both telephone and radio systems have a part in the communications networks. Primary fire-detection stations are usually connected with headquarters by telephone lines, and many of them also act as radio relay or communication stations for contact with outlying stations and camps. Portable, mobile, and field radios are used by smokechasers and field crews to quickly set up communications when fighting fires. A full line of equipment for use in a higher radio frequency band has been developed. Several state forestry agencies and private concerns have long been active in developing radio communication networks, and during the past few years the use of these mobile and portable radios has rapidly increased. Nearly all states are now using radio in forest protection, as well as for other services such as fish and game work and highway patrol. Special equipment has been installed in several states for tying together state and federal forest radio networks to provide a prompt exchange of fire control information. New scientific research is developing new information on techniques of fire control. For example, *cloud seeding* is developing experimentally in such a way that lightning fires might be prevented, and artificially caused rain made to extinguish fires.

FOREST INSECTS AND THEIR CONTROL

Forest managers are often faced with the threat of insect infestation that may cause serious damage. It is therefore important to be able to identify the more harmful insects and to know what control methods may be applicable. There are literally thousands of kinds of insects in the forest, many of which make their home in trees, but only a relatively few species cause enough damage to require control. Nature in most cases provides for control over outbreaks by insect parasites, insect-eating birds, other natural predators and a variety of climatic factors.

Insects and diseases together have destroyed more timber in recent years than forest fires, but because disease usually affects only a tree here and there, the damage is less dramatic. Occasionally, a very serious insect outbreak will develop—as in the case of the spruce budworm, the Engelmann spruce beetle, or the jack pine sawfly—where whole stands are seriously damaged or killed. Major control measures are needed in these cases to prevent widespread epidemics. From the time the seed is born until the logs are sawed into lumber, trees have a perpetual struggle to survive the attacks of insect enemies—and even the finished wood products are subject to attack. The study of forest insects is called *forest entomology*. It is a complex subject, but for purposes of the working forest manager or forest technician, it can be simplified into a few basic insect groups and control methods. An informed forest manager will be able to detect many of these attacks before they get out of hand and take measures for their control. However, a specialist in forest insects should always be consulted if an outbreak seems to be developing or if the kind of insect attacking is not known. Failure to do so may result in large losses of timber and time.

Control measures used to reduce forest damage from insect infestations are of two kinds: indirect control through properly applied forest management, and direct control, which is a counterattack on the insect itself. Forests subject to insect damage often have numbers of overmature or decadent trees, nearly at the end of their life cycle. They are, therefore, in a weakened condition and more subject to attack by certain diseases and insects. Forest management that removes these trees and maintains healthy, thrifty stands contributes importantly to keeping them free of insects. Strong, fast-growing trees are infrequently damaged, although some insects, especially during outbreaks, will attack all trees in their path, regardless of growth conditions. Where conditions are such that it is impractical to apply indirect control measures, direct control measures may often be required. It is important for the forest manager to be able to recognize the activities of the more damaging forest insects and eventually to learn to identify each kind in the forests of the locality.

Classes of Forest Insects

Because insects attack different parts of the tree and have different habits as well as appearance entomologists have grouped them into various scientific classifications. For forestry purposes, however, seven main classes, based on the way insects attack trees, are recognized.

1. *Inner bark boring insects* Insects that work in the phloem and on the wood surface, causing damage to the cambium layer and death of the tree through girdling or introduction of destructive fungi.
2. *Wood borers* Insects that bore into the sapwood and heartwood, rendering the wood useless for commercial purposes. They also destroy cut logs and wood products.
3. *Leaf eaters (defoliators)* These insects eat the needles or leaves and thus destroy the foliage, slowing down the growth rate or killing the tree by defoliation. (Larvae do the damage in most cases.)
4. *Sap-sucking insects* Insects that feed by sucking the sap from trees (aphids and scales).
5. *Tip feeders* Insects that eat the terminal growth of trees or the tip buds and thus cause deforming damage.
6. *Gall makers* Insects that cause abnormal growths on twigs, limbs, trunks, or leaves of trees, but do not usually kill or damage them.
7. *Seed Feeders* Insects that destroy the fruit, nuts, or seed of trees and thus spoil them as a source of new seedlings.

The first five of the preceding groups are of major concern to foresters and forest managers because they include the principal destructive insects. But before discussing them in detail, it is appropriate to consider insect infestation as it may look in the forest. Much of the damage comes during the growing season, usually early or in the middle of the summer. Most of these groups of insects go through a life cycle beginning with the egg stage. Eggs hatch into larvae ("worms," grubs, nymphs, and caterpillars) that feed on the tree. When full grown, some larvae enter a resting stage where they are transformed into pupae (often in cocoons). After spending some time in the pupal stage, the insects change and emerge as adults. Insects spend the winter either as eggs, larvae, pupae, or adults.

The forest under an insect attack frequently presents a brownish, unnatural appearance at a distance, particularly where defoliators are at work. Sometimes ground droppings in quantity are an indicator. In the case of boring insects, fine wood powder at the base of the tree tells the tale. Sometimes the indicator is drops of pitch on the ground. In tip weevil damage, the new growing leaders may bend and shrivel up or turn red and die. Any of these indications are a cause for alarm.

Control of Forest Insects

The injurious insects are, with few exceptions, native and have been around for many years. It is virtually impossible to completely eradicate either these, or the well-established foreign pests. Under forest conditions, a certain number of insects occur normally and natural control factors maintain the populations at endemic levels. When conditions become especially favorable for a particular insect pest, its numbers rapidly increase and an outbreak occurs, requiring artificial controls.

Natural Control Factors

Insect activity is limited at temperatures above or below an optimum. At temperatures above 120°F, only few insects survive, and this makes possible the control of many species of bark and wood boring insects by exposing infested logs to direct sunlight or kilns. Low winter temperatures, or severe late frosts (occurring after new growth of the trees has begun in the spring) also kills many insects.

Moisture has both a direct effect on the insects and an indirect effect through its influence on the pests' hosts. Inadequate precipitation may lower the trees' resistance to bark beetle attack; flooding or excessive soil moisture also may weaken the trees.

Severe rainstorms have provided excellent control by knocking defoliating larvae from foliage. Windstorms, however, may provide additional breeding sites for bark and wood inhabiting insects that are dependent on the dead wood of broken tops and branches.

Insects, like other living things, have natural enemies that prey upon them and hold them in check. Such birds as nuthatches, chickadees, creepers, warblers, or kinglets consume countless numbers of defoliating and wood-inhabiting insects each year. The meadow mouse, white footed mouse, moles, shrews, voles, chipmunks, and squirrels play important roles in the destruction of forest insects, especially those that spend part of their life in the soil. Although little is known about the real importance of parasitic nematodes, certain species attack bark beetles, wood borers, soil inhabiting grubs, lepidopterous larvae, and grasshoppers.

Many species of insects and mites are distinctly beneficial in that they feed on harmful species. Most native forest insects are attacked by insect parasites. All stages of an insect from egg to adult may be attacked, although as a rule, the larvae and pupae are most heavily parasitized. Unfortunately, many of the beneficial forms are themselves parasitized. This hyperparasitism may be occasionally carried to the second or third degree making the host parasite relationship extremely complex. The effectiveness of parasites, predators, and pathogens is difficult to measure. Their success is influenced by factors such as the character and habits of the host insect, the population density of the host, the presence of alternate hosts, the degree of hyperparasitism, and the conditions affecting hibernation (Figure 9–9).

Silvicultural Control of Forest Pests

Under virgin forest conditions, no checks were placed on the activities of destructive agents other than those imposed by nature. Fires, as well as insect and disease outbreaks, developed, spread, and eventually

FIGURE 9–9. Insects become diseased like other organisms. This pine reproduction weevil (Hylobius pales), *for instance, was killed by a pathogenic fungus, whose spore aggregates show up as prismatic columns arising from the corpse. (H. Schabel, CNR-UWSP)*

ran their course. The whole process, although wasteful, seldom resulted in the permanent destruction of the forests over large areas. Natural checks were imposed and regenerative processes came into play.

With more intensive forest management and the development of control methods, attention was turned to preventive control of forest insects and diseases. In a managed forest, the principal objectives of pest control are to regulate conditions for maintaining natural balance between the destructive insect population and their natural enemies, between the insects and their food supply, and between disease and disease caused tree mortality or degradation. These objectives may be attained more fully in the future through application of silvicultural practices in growing stands where conditions unfavorable for insect development are maintained and greater resistance to insect and disease attacks is achieved. This would involve such measures as (1) the removal of susceptible trees and the regulation of density and composition by means of periodic salvage or improvement cuts and thinnings; (2) the regulation of environmental factors through drainage and density; (3) the selection of insect- or disease-resistant varieties and species of trees; (4) careful seed selection; (5) site selection; (6) adjustment of cutting cycles and methods; and (7) rotation of crops.

Chemical Control

Direct controls with chemicals are employed when other methods of control fail. Forest pest epidemics often appear suddenly in a localized area rendering preventive control measures useless. It then may become necessary to suppress the destructive pest population with a chemical before severe damage results.

Insecticides used against forest insects are of three main types: *contact* poisons, which kill insects upon contact with their skin; *stomach* poisons, which must be ingested before taking effect; and *fumigants*, which enter the target pest through the respiratory system. Stomach poisons are usually applied against defoliators, while fumigants are most useful against insects hidden in wood or soil. Sap-sucking insects are most easily reached with contact poisons or systemic insecticides. The latter are taken up by the host through the root system, by absorption through the cuticle or by injection and are then distributed throughout the host, thereby reaching insects affecting any part of it. They are, therefore, also most useful against insects leading a hidden life within the host's tissues, such as woodborers, leafminers and the like. Many insecticides have several of these properties and may, therefore, be useful against a variety of insects.

As a result of environmental concern, the widespread use of insecticides has recently been curtailed. The Environmental Protection Agency (EPA) is now responsible for administering the two basic federal laws regulating the marketing and use of pesticides in the United States. The Pesticide Amendment of the Federal Food, Drug and Cosmetic Act assures the establishment of tolerances for any detectable pesticide residues on food and feed crops. The Federal Environmental Pesticide Control Act has the following provisions.

All pesticide products must be registered with the EPA.

The use of any registered pesticide in a manner inconsistent with the label instructions is prohibited.

All pesticides are classified as either "General Use Pesticides," which may be handled by the public in conforming with the label information, or "Restricted Use Pesticides," which can be only used by or under supervision of certified personnel.

The EPA sets minimum federal standards for the certification of restricted pesticide applicators. The states carry out certification.

Most important for the potential user of insecticides should be the awareness of and compliance with the label instructions, whose contents frequently reflect the results of years of research.

Biological Control

With the restrictions imposed on many insecticides, alternative control methods, such as biological controls, have recently received new attention. In biological control, efforts are made to augment the impact of predators, parasites, and pathogens by timely introduction of sufficient populations of these agents into the pest population. Although many problems remain to be solved in this area, the massive research efforts of the past decade have already begun to bear fruit. Several bacterial and viral formulations, which are somewhat specific for certain insects, are now registered with the EPA against a variety of forest insects and have been successfully applied under field conditions.

Because many kinds of chemical applications have led to a variety of environmental abuses, including human and animal health problems, the need has grown for a coordinated use of silvicultural, biological, and chemical controls so they will work in concert, not in conflict, with one another. This concept has been evolving and has been titled *integrated pest management* (IPM), an integrated methodology involving several disciplines coordinated with each other. IPM is in its early stages of development, but efforts so far are proving to be a substantial improvement over applications of chemicals with unknown impacts and side effects.

FIGURE 9–10. How bark beetles kill pine trees. (U. S. Forest Service)

Methods of Direct Control

Bark beetles (*Dendroctonus* and *Ips*) are mainly serious in the South and West where they attack pines, fir, and spruce. Large areas of forest have been destroyed by these beetles. They become active in the spring and continue their activity until cold weather, sometimes hatching five or six generations in a season in the South. One beetle can have 100,000 descendants in one summer. As the attack proceeds, the tree's needles change to a reddish-brown color and the bark is loosened as the result of the numerous channels where the insects have been boring (Figure 9–10).

Direct control methods are accomplished by spraying with insecticides or by removal of the *brood trees*. (Brood trees may be identified by the previously mentioned indications.) If the trees are still green, the insect can be prevented from spreading by felling and removing from the stand all infested brood trees from which the young adults will soon emerge. If this is not practical or possible, such trees are treated with insecticides sprayed over the entire length of the trunk, until it drips. A mixture of 2.5 lb of gamma isomer benzene hexachloride with 50 gal of No. 2 diesel oil is recommended. These materials are usually put on with handpumped, pressure-operated sprayers. Where the trees are already dead or dying from a general infestation, rapid logging of the entire infested stand is the only way in which loss can be prevented.

Wood borers usually attack logs and pulpwood decked in the forest or in wood yards and can cause tremendous amounts of direct damage by wormholes in the wood and through introduction of the blue stain fungus. Prevention of this damage can often be accomplished by storing logs in the water, by peeling them before warm weather, or by quick utilization. Large piles of logs are often protected by insecticide sprays. When these wood borers are at work on a pile of logs in hot weather, one can actually hear them grinding their way through the logs!

Leaf eaters or *defoliators* include a large group of insects that attack both conifers and broadleaved trees. Usually they do not kill the trees the first year, but repeated attacks in one or over several years will starve the tree to death by eliminating the foodmaking functions of the leaves and needles. Although there are many different types of defoliators, most of them eat the needles or leaves in the immature stage. Sometimes the only sign of feeding may be a brownish cast at the needle tips. Mature and overmature timber is more subject to serious losses from epidemic infestations. There is great variation in the types and extent of damage from year to year and between different species of insects. The more important defoliators, their victims, and control methods are listed in Table 9–2.

Tip feeders attack the buds and new growing shoots of conifers in the early part of the summer by drilling into the wood tissue and destroying the cambium layer. In effect, the tip is girdled and the shoot dies. Two of the most serious tip feeders are the *white pine weevil*, which attacks eastern white pine, jack pine, and Norway spruce, and the *European pine shoot moth*, which attacks the tips and new leaders of red, Scotch, and Austrian pine. Damage by the white pine weevil can be prevented by spraying the growing tips and buds and previous year's growth with common garden insecticides in mid- to late June before the eggs hatch into the larval stage and begin their work (Figure 9–11). A better way, which assures future straight timber from weeviled trees, is to remove all growth by pruning above the most recent year's whorl (rows of branches from which the tip arises) and all but the best one of the branches in the whorl. This branch will then become the new leader. It is essential that all infested material be carried away and burned or drowned. Smaller stands of young pine may be sprayed with a mixture of insecticide that is directed to the tip and the bud about to start growing. Aerial spraying at low heights, especially with a helicopter, has been found to be an effective and cheap way to control infestations of the weevil in large areas of young pines (Figure 9–11). However, if pines have an overstory of broad-

TABLE 9–2 COMMON FOREST TREE INSECTS—DAMAGE AND CONTROL

Name	Principal Species Affected	Type of Damage	Control Method: Prevention	Control Method: Direct Control	Control Method: Control Season
Gypsy moth	Oaks, birch, aspen	Defoliation		Spraying insecticide	May–June
Bark beetles	Pines	Girdles tree by killing cambium layer under bark	Salvage green, blowndown timber	Fell, peel, and burn bark; salvage infested logs; burn slabs	Spring, summer, fall
Red turpentine beetles	Hard pines—South (especially turnpentined trees)	Bores holes, reduces strength, making subject to blowdown	Remove infested trees	Cut and remove infested and suspected trees	All seasons
Sawflies	Eastern and Southern pines and tamarack	Reduces growth by defoliation; epidemics kill stands	Cut mature and overmature stands	Aerial insecticide spray	Early summer at period of greatest activity
Spruce budworm	True firs, Douglas-fir	Reduces growth by defoliation; kills older trees extensively	Cut mature and overmature stands	Aerial insecticide spray	Early summer as insects emerge
White pine weevil	Eastern white pine, Norway spruce	Kills leaders, causes forked and crooked boles	Maintain shade where possible to 20 ft	Hand spray upper stem and new growth with sodium arsenate or cut and	Early summer as insects emerge

				burn infected tip—leave only best side branch of first lower whorl	
Tent caterpillar	Broadleaved trees (esp. northern hardwoods and aspen)	Defoliates; kills older and weaker trees	Remove tents by hand or burn	Aerial spray of insecticide as insect larvae emerge	Spring
Scales and aphids (also spittle bugs)	All trees	Sap sucking insects reduce growth	—	Insecticide spray or remove infested trees	All seasons
Hemlock looper	Western hemlock	Defoliation; kills oldest trees	—	Aerial insecticide spray	June–July
Tussock moth	True firs, Douglas-fir	Defoliation, all sizes	—	Aerial insecticide spray	June–July
White grubs	Conifer seedlings	Destroys roots and kills trees	—	Force insecticide into soil	Summer
Pales weevil	Pine seedlings and saplings	Girdles bark of seedlings and defoliates saplings	—	Dip seedlings in insecticide	Spring
European pine shoot moth	Pines and spruces (sapling stage)	Deforms trees	Plant only where temperature falls below 10°F	Prune infested shoots and burn them	Fall—late spring

Note: Prescribed control methods include chemicals bacteria, virus, predatory insects, organic and inorganic compounds. Due to their complexity, frequent prescriptive changes, and often unknown environmental side effects, students and landowners should seek out advice from professional forest entomologists.

FIGURE 9–11. Aerial spraying of insecticide by helicopter in conifers. Because helicopters can spray more slowly than planes and blow the chemical directly down to the needles, they are considered more efficient. (American Forest Institute)

leaved trees that keep down the temperature by shading, weevil damage will not be serious. Stand improvement that removes the overstory should be delayed until trees reach a height of 20 ft or more, after which they are fairly resistant to weevil infestation.

Gall makers may damage individual trees, but they usually do not ruin whole stands. Therefore control measures are not usually undertaken. If they should reach epidemic proportions, a forest entomologist should be consulted.

In conclusion, it is important to realize that insect damage can result in great losses to standing timber and that if this is to be prevented, immediate detection is imperative. And new threats constantly show up. For example, three different species of scale insects have been attacking red pine, hemlock, and beech in the Northeast and killing timber stands over a wide area. As yet, no natural controls are evident and no artificial controls have been developed. The potential for epidemic populations is ever present.

FOREST DISEASES AND THEIR CONTROL

Like humankind, trees are subject to many kinds of diseases. Some attack the leaves, others the main trunk, and still others the roots. Although there are hundreds of tree diseases, most of them do not attack healthy forest trees but take advantage of old, weak or injured trees or young seedlings struggling for establishment. Leaf spots, rusts, wilts, blights, cankers, and decays are examples of diseases that either weaken or kill forest trees. Fortunately for the forest manager, relatively few diseases are really serious enough to require direct control. Here again, a healthy forest, well managed and thrifty, is as nearly resistant to disease as nature will allow. The study of tree diseases is called *forest pathology*.

Important Forest Diseases and Methods of Control

Some of the more destructive tree diseases are white pine blister rust, chestnut blight, oak wilt, Dutch elm disease, brown spot needle blight on longleaf pine seedlings, little-leaf disease on shortleaf pine, heart rots, and dwarf mistletoe on western conifers. Most tree diseases are caused by fungi, a form of plant life carried from tree to tree by spores, which are the "seeds" of these parasites. Other diseases are caused by viruses, bacteria, nematodes, and dwarf mistletoes. Most native forest diseases are so well established and so widely distributed that their complete eradication would be impossible. However, the more serious pests can be controlled. It is sometimes possible and feasible to wipe out a newly introduced pest that is still confined to a limited area.

In the long run, good forest management is the best defense against many insects and diseases. Some insect and disease losses can be greatly reduced by harvesting trees before they reach the most susceptible age. Some diseases attack vigorous as well as weakened trees, while some others can be held to a minimum by removing diseased and weakened trees. Although losses from some diseases can be reduced by good forest management, direct control measures are needed for highly contagious diseases, such as white pine blister rust and oak wilt.

Fungi attack the forest in many ways. They kill some trees outright, they reduce the growth rate of many more, and they destroy the heartwood in living trees making it unfit for use. Their total effect on the productivity of the forest exceeds that of all other enemies.

Chestnut blight and *white pine blister rust* are well-known examples of killing diseases. Chestnut blight, which all but eliminated the American chestnut, is caused by a parasitic fungus that was introduced from Asia on nursery plants before this country had enacted quarantine laws to reduce the international spread of diseases. It produces tiny spores, comparable to seed in higher plants, that float through the air, settle on the bark of healthy trees, grow through it, and eventually kill tne tree. As yet, no practical means of controlling chestnut blight has been found, but the search for chestnut trees resistant to the disease is continuing and eventually chestnut may be restored to our forest.

White pine blister rust has unusual life habits. The fungus causing it must live alternately on five-needle pines and on currant or gooseberry plants (genus *Ribes*). It was also introduced from abroad on nursery seedlings. The fungus enters the pines through the needles and grows into the bark, where it causes diseased areas known as *cankers*. About 3 years after a tree becomes infected, orange-yellow blisters form on the cankers. In the spring millions of spores from these blisters are released into the air and scattered by the wind for many miles. These spores can infect only the leaves of currants or gooseberries. There the fungus grows and forms brownish yellow spots, on which a type of spore capable of infecting pines is eventually produced. These are delicate and short-lived and can spread only a few hundred yards. Loss of white pines from blister rust can be prevented by destroying the wild and cultivated *Ribes* bushes growing

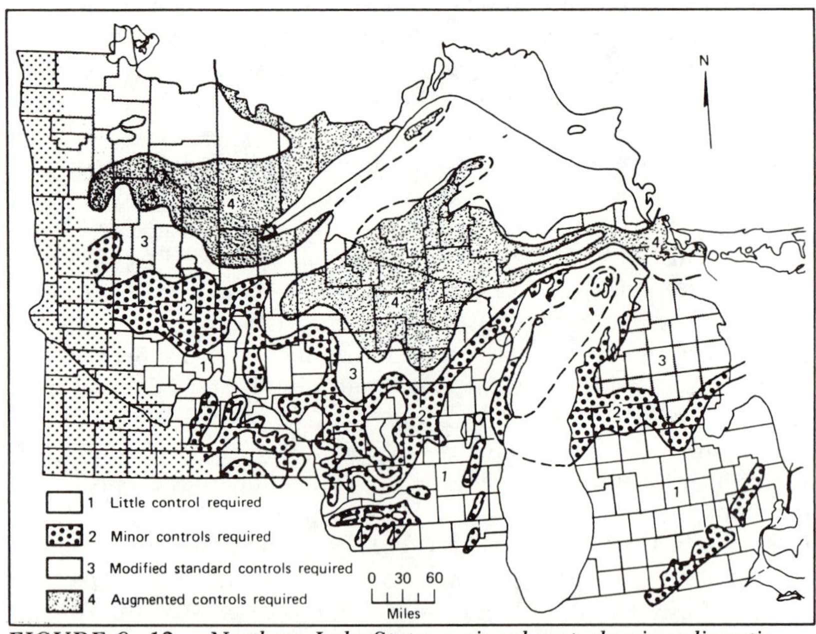

FIGURE 9–12. Northern Lake States regional map showing climactic hazard zones for white pine blister rust infection potential, ranging from Zone 1 with low potential to Zone 4 with a very high potential. (North Central Regional Forest Experiment Station, U. S. Forest Service)

within infecting distance of the trees and by preventing the establishment of new bushes.

For a long time *Ribes* eradication efforts were the basic control program for white pine blister rust. As more information became available about the environmental requirements of the fungus, hazard zones were developed for the Lake States (Figure 9–12). In the high hazard zone, control procedures involving eradication of *Ribes* are too intensive to be economically feasible. In the medium hazard zone, control is justified economically, and in the low and no hazard zones, white pine can be grown with little or no disease control necessary.

Heart rot fungi seldom kill trees, but they change the sound wood of the trunks into a useless, rotten mass. They require a wound to gain entrance to trees. Any broken branch or injury to the bark or

FIGURE 9–13. Conks of decay fungi arising from trunk. At this stage the decay is progressed and removal of these fruiting bodies does not affect anything. (H. Schabel, CNR, UWSP)

roots opens the way. Once the fungus enters the tree, it usually continues to grow until the tree is a hollow shell or is so weakened that it breaks over in the wind. The presence of advanced stages of heart rot becomes evident with the appearance of shelf fruiting bodies or conks that resemble brittle mushrooms (Figure 9–13). Young vigorous trees are generally free of heart rot. Losses may be reduced by protecting trees from injuries and by harvesting them before the fungi can destroy the wood in the trunks.

In recent years, forest managers all over the world have been increasingly concerned by the spread of *Pine root rot,* which can cause extremely high mortality in pine plantations caused by the red heart fungus, *Fomes annosus.* The spores are airborne and infect fresh stumps during thinning operations and pass through the roots to nearby trees. Entire plantations have been threatened.

A crash research program of industry in cooperation with the U.S. Forest Service, forestry schools, and other agencies discovered a definitive answer to *annosus* root rot. They found that application of borax, a harmless household chemical, to a stump immediately after a tree is felled prevents the spread of the fungus. The treatment is simple to apply in the field, inexpensive, and effective.

But there was a second problem. Evidence indicated that the soil, once infested with root rot, retained the infection potential for several years. This could mean further loss of revenue for idle land. Further research on the problem discovered that several common plants, including the familiar marigold, can help to check the disease organism.

Oak wilt has spread rapidly in the midwestern states during the past few years and has been found recently in states in the East and Southeast also. It attacks all native oaks in states where it has been found, but develops most rapidly on red and black oaks, which quickly die.

Present control methods include sanitation cuts in diseased stands and the creation of mechanical or chemical root barriers between neighboring trees.

Dutch elm disease attacks shade and forest elms, killing about 400,000 trees every year in the United States. The most effective means of control is by cutting and burning the diseased trees and pruning dead and dying branches of newly infected trees. It is an impractical method in forest stands, however, because of the expense involved. Elms in the forest that are diseased should be salvaged as soon as possible to prevent local spread of the disease.

In 1976 the EPA approved a new pesticide, Lignasan BLP, for use against Dutch elm disease. Because certain precautions and special pressurized injection equipment are required, this systemic pesticide can only be applied by trained aborists. Lignasan is not a cure-all. The product is, however, effective in preventing the disease in trees not already infected. It will also usually cure the problem in trees with less than 5 percent damage.

An overall Dutch elm disease program should, however, continue to include sanitation practices and the chemical control of the elm bark beetles that spread the disease.

In the South, *brown spot needle blight* attacks longleaf pine seedlings and retards their growth by killing the needles. Continued attacks may kill many of the little trees. Carefully planned burning of infected plantations or areas of natural reproduction helps control the disease in young seedlings. This is an example of how fire can be used to good advantage in forestry. Longleaf pine, which produces both lumber and naval stores (e.g., rosin and turpentine), is one of the most important forest trees in the South.

An enemy of the shortleaf pine, another of the South's important forest trees, is the *little-leaf disease*. Trees with this disease show shortened, yellowish foliage and slow growth. Infected trees die after a few years. The disease is caused by a fungus that kills the fine roots of trees growing in poorly drained soils. Shortleaf pines highly resistant to little-leaf disease have been developed.

Dwarf mistletoes are serious pests of western coniferous forests. They are flowering plant parasites that grow on the branches and stems of trees. The dwarf mistletoes are related to the Christmas mistletoe, but should not be confused with it. They slow the growth of infected trees and kill many of them, stunting and deforming those not killed.

When dwarf mistletoe seeds ripen, they are shot out of the casings with explosive force as far as 60 ft. The seeds are sticky and if they strike branches of the same or other susceptible trees, they may cling to them and start new plants. Dwarf mistletoes tend to spread steadily to other trees in the forest and can only be controlled by removing infected trees or branches in harvest or stand improvement operations. In heavily infested stands, clearcutting may be the only feasible solution. Other means of control are being investigated.

A strong step forward in providing better control of forest pests was taken in 1947 when Congress passed the Forest Pest Control Act. This act recognizes federal responsibility for controlling diseases and insects on federal lands, extends federal aid to control projects on nonfederal lands in cooperation with states and private owners, provides for systematic detection to locate and evaluate pest outbreaks on all forest lands, and offers leadership and funds for planning and carrying out control operations.

The more important tree diseases and their control methods are set forth in Table 9–3.

TABLE 9–3 PRINCIPAL FOREST TREE DISEASES—DAMAGE AND CONTROL

Common Name	Host	Symptoms	Cause	Control
Eutypella canker	Sugar maple, red maple	Lesions on trunk around branch stubs with concentric callus rings	*Eutypella parasitica*	Remove cankered trees in improvement cuttings
Hypoxylon canker	Aspen	Yellowish to reddish-brown sunken areas centered around a wound, developing into elongated cankers delimited by vertical cracks in the bark; trees commonly break at cankers	*Hypoxylon pruinatum*	Remove infected trees in thinnings
Fusiform rust	Slash pine, loblolly pine, occasionally longleaf pine	Spindle-shaped swellings on stem and branches often causing distortion and breakage; orange spores produced in spring on swellings in blister-like pustules	*Cronartium fusiforme*	Encourage early natural pruning by maintaining high density in stands; prune infected branches, particularly after occasional year of heavy infection

White pine blister rust	Five-needle pines of eastern and western U.S.	Yellow to orange lesions develop on bark at base of needle about 2 years after infection; in the third or fourth year these become girdling bark cankers that in spring and summer bear blisters containing orange spores; these infect leaves of currants and gooseberries; cankers grow down branch to stem and kill by girdling	*Cronartium ribicola*	Eradication of all currants and gooseberries (*Ribes*) within the stand and in a protective border of variable width up to 900 ft around the stand; European black currants should be eradicated for a distance of 1 mile
Root rot	Conifers	Death of affected trees; soft, stringy rot in roots and butt. In ponderosa pine, light-brown striations under bark at root collar; decay confined to single root	*Fomes annosus*	Put borax or creosote on freshly cut stumps to prevent spreading; benomyl root dip of transplant conifers
Root and butt rot	Species of pine, mature stands, also plantations 15–25 years old	Decline in vigor, needles short, becoming yellow then dying; cones appear prematurely; fruiting bodies at base of tree or on ground surface arising from roots	*Polyporus schweinitzii*	Avoid planting white or red pine on poorly drained or high pH soils

TABLE 9–3 *(Continued)*

Common Name	Host	Symptoms	Cause	Control
Little-leaf	Shortleaf pine, loblolly pine	Progressive decrease in terminal growth accompanied by yellowing and reduction in needle length; root systems defective, with many roots dead; affected trees die in 3–10 years	Soil fungus *Phytophthora cinnamomi* associated with diseased roots on soils with poor internal drainage	Salvage cuttings in infected stands
Leaf and twig blight; also anthracnose	Hardwoods	Leaves and tips of twigs turn brown and die in the spring, resembling late frost injury	*Gnomonia veneta*	No control for forest trees; for shade trees spray with 4
Rot or decay	Mature trees of all species	Presence of conks of wood-rotting fungi; large open wounds with softened wood; large branch wounds and top injuries; swellings and cankers on trunk	Various fungi, especially species of *Fomes* and *Polyporus*	Prevent wounds, such as those caused by fires and logging; avoid pruning wounds over 3 in. in diameter
Butt rot	Young sprout stands of oak species	Large, unhealed stump wounds or dead companion stems	Species of heart-rotting fungi	Remove unwanted companion sprouts before they reach 3 in. in diameter at base and before stands are 20 years of age; in older stands remove companion stems only if they form a low union and leave a wound over 3 in. in diameter

Western red rot	Ponderosa pine	None, except presence of decay and red discoloration in heartwood	*Polyporus anceps*	Periodic pruning of dead branches on crop trees
Dutch elm disease, associated with attacks by Scolytid beetles	American elm	Progressive dwarfing and yellowing of leaves, accompanied by various degrees of defoliation; followed by death of branches or entire tree	*Ceratostomella ulmi* carried by *Scolytus multistriatus* and *Hylurgopinus rufipes*	Mainly through destruction of infected trees and protection against bark beetles by insecticidal sprays and maintenance of tree vigor by appropriate pruning and feeding practices; lignasan injection
Oak wilt	Oak species, particularly those of the black oak group	Leaves crinkle and become pale green, later turning brown or bronze; mature leaves shed at any symptom stage; lower branches affected last; trees usually die after the summer symptoms appear	*Chalara quercina*	Some promise of control has been obtained by cutting or poisoning healthy oaks for 50–100 ft around spot infections; mechanical or chemical root barriers
Maple wilt	Maple	Sudden dying of single branch, followed by others; eventual death of tree	*Verticillium* spp.	None
Brown spot	Longleaf pine	Small spots on needles causing needle dieback; retards growth of seedlings	*Scirrhia aricola*	Controlled burning in third year of seedling's life or spray with prescribed chemicals

OTHER DAMAGE TO THE FOREST

Hail, windstorms, and glaze ice all cause serious local damage that can result in large losses. In one instance a June hailstorm in northern Wisconsin completely stripped young hardwoods of their leaves and so damaged the cambium layer under the bark as to kill a majority of the trees over an area of 10 miles long and 2 miles wide. Ice damage in the wintertime, especially in the central states, often causes a great deal of limb breakage and exposes trees to diseases. During the winter of 1967, one glaze ice storm cut a swath through 15 Piedmont counties of Virginia 10 to 20 miles wide and 200 miles long. Salvage operations continued for more than a year. But wind is probably the most obstructive natural force; it can blow down huge areas of timberland. Hardwoods resist wind damage when their leaves are off, but conifers are vulnerable at all times. Although the downed timber can usually be salvaged, it is more costly for loggers to get around broken and half-down trees. If the trees are not salvaged, they frequently favor the build-up of many kinds of damaging insects, which can spread to standing timber.

Wildlife and Livestock Damage

Overgrazing by cattle, sheep, and browsing game animals can also be damaging to the forest. Where elk are over-stocked in the West, serious loss of young trees takes place. In the northern Lake States, young white-cedar has become almost extinct in some localities due to overbrowsing by deer. Cattle and sheep grazing in farm areas has eliminated young hardwood reproduction and in some southern and western forests, trampling by livestock has taken out whole generations of seedling reproduction.

Girdling of small trees by rabbits and other rodents takes a heavy toll when these species become too numerous (Figure 9–14). Bears have caused great damage to Douglas-fir by scratching off bark.

Whether it be domestic livestock or wild animals, overpopulation can cause abnormal damage. Livestock numbers can be controlled and must be kept in line with carrying capacity of the forage resource so they are not forced into forest browsing. Wild game numbers can be controlled by harvesting during hunting seasons if bag limits are related to animal numbers.

Pollution Damage

The detrimental effects of air pollution on trees have been known for many years by scientists. Until recently, however, these problems have been mainly associated with urban environments. But during

FIGURE 9–14. Aspen clearcut by beavers. (H. Schabel, CNR, UWSP)

the last decade there has been an alarming increase in the effects of air pollution on forests in rural areas.

Acid rain (and other precipitation) and ozone are the most widely dispersed and damaging types of pollution affecting forest lands. Acid rain results largely from sulfur and nitrogen oxides, given off by fossil fuel combustion, that react chemically in the atmosphere to form sulfuric and nitric acid. It has been estimated that about half the trees in Germany's forests are now dead or dying, and German scientists attribute the cause to acid rain and other air pollutants. The forests of the United States have not yet been as severely affected as those of Europe. However, acid rain and ozone have been blamed for killing trees and aquatic life, and for slowing tree growth in some parts of the country. Ironically, some scientists believe that there may be a fertilization effect on plants resulting from additional nitrogen, but most agree that any fertilization effect is more than offset by acid damage.

Other pollution problems that may affect forests in some circumstances include groundwater contamination from toxic wastes such as leachate from landfills, mine wastes, and salt used along roads for melting ice and snow. Salt, however, is generally more of a problem when it dissolves in water along roads and is sprayed directly onto nearby foliage by passing vehicles.

Protecting forests from pollution can only be achieved by stemming the causes of pollution. Unlike many diseases and insects, there are no agents that can be applied directly to trees or forests to cure pollution damage. Though some tree species are more susceptible to pollution effects than others, all species have a chronic level at which pollutants will overstress them and cause death. Reducing and controlling the use of fossil fuels is believed to be the best way to decrease the damage done by many pollutants.

QUESTIONS

1. Name five common causes of forest fires.
2. Describe the three main types of activity in forest fire protection.
3. The process of locating a forest fire on the map in a dispatcher's office is accomplished when towermen call in two bearings or azimuths. What is it called?
4. Name the three factors that cause a forest fire to spread.
5. Give the two general methods used in fighting forest fires.
6. Name two parts of a forest fire.
7. Describe some of the recently developed mechanized fire fighting equipment.
8. Is it true that insects and diseases usually attack old and overmature trees before they attack healthy trees?
9. Name three important insects that seriously damage forest trees and give the kinds of trees each attacks.
10. Name two important tree diseases and the trees attacked by each.
11. Describe one control method used for a tree disease affecting southern pine forests.
12. Describe how acid rain is formed and what its effects on forest resources are.

EXERCISES

1. Visit a forest fire tower and discuss with the towerman how a *smoke* is sighted and reported.
2. Go to a central forest fire control headquarters and study the system used to report and locate fires and dispatch fire-fighting crews.
3. Examine different kinds of hand and mechanical fire-fighting equipment.
4. Write your state forester for information on any outbreaks of forest insects or diseases in your area and go into the field to identify these at the proper season.

T E N

Processing and Marketing Forest Products

Forest managers, who are primarily interested in producing as much raw material as the forest can be made to yield economically, must have a general knowledge of the processing of rough forest products and the ultimate manufactured products. American forest industries include large and small sawmills that produce lumber and pulp, paper mills that manufacture a wide variety of paper products, veneer mills that supply plywoods and veneers, and dozens of other smaller specialized industries that produce everything from toothpicks to laminated timbers (Figure 10–1). Most of these manufacturing plants, which use rough wood in the form of small and larger logs, are located in communities near the forest. This is because it costs more to transport raw material than it does to transport the finished products. Many smaller communities could not exist were it not for the paper mill or sawmill that is their principal industry.

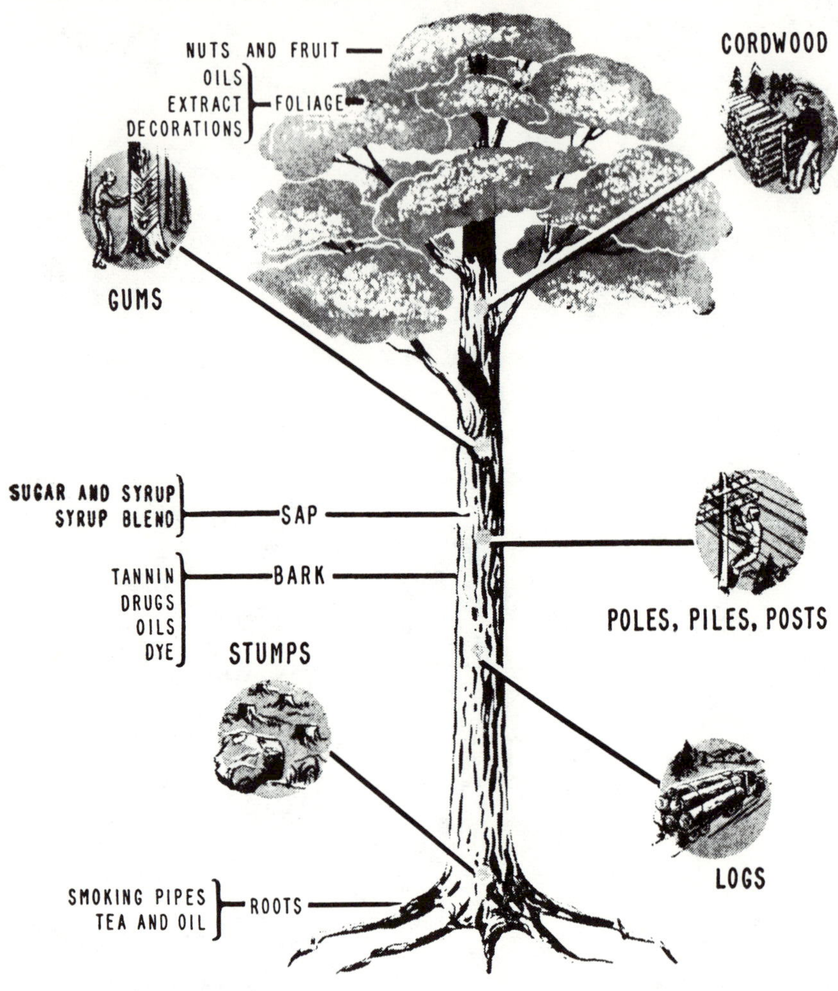
NUTS AND FRUIT
OILS
EXTRACT
DECORATIONS
FOLIAGE
CORDWOOD
GUMS
SUGAR AND SYRUP
SYRUP BLEND
SAP
TANNIN
DRUGS
OILS
DYE
BARK
POLES, PILES, POSTS
STUMPS
LOGS
SMOKING PIPES
TEA AND OIL
ROOTS

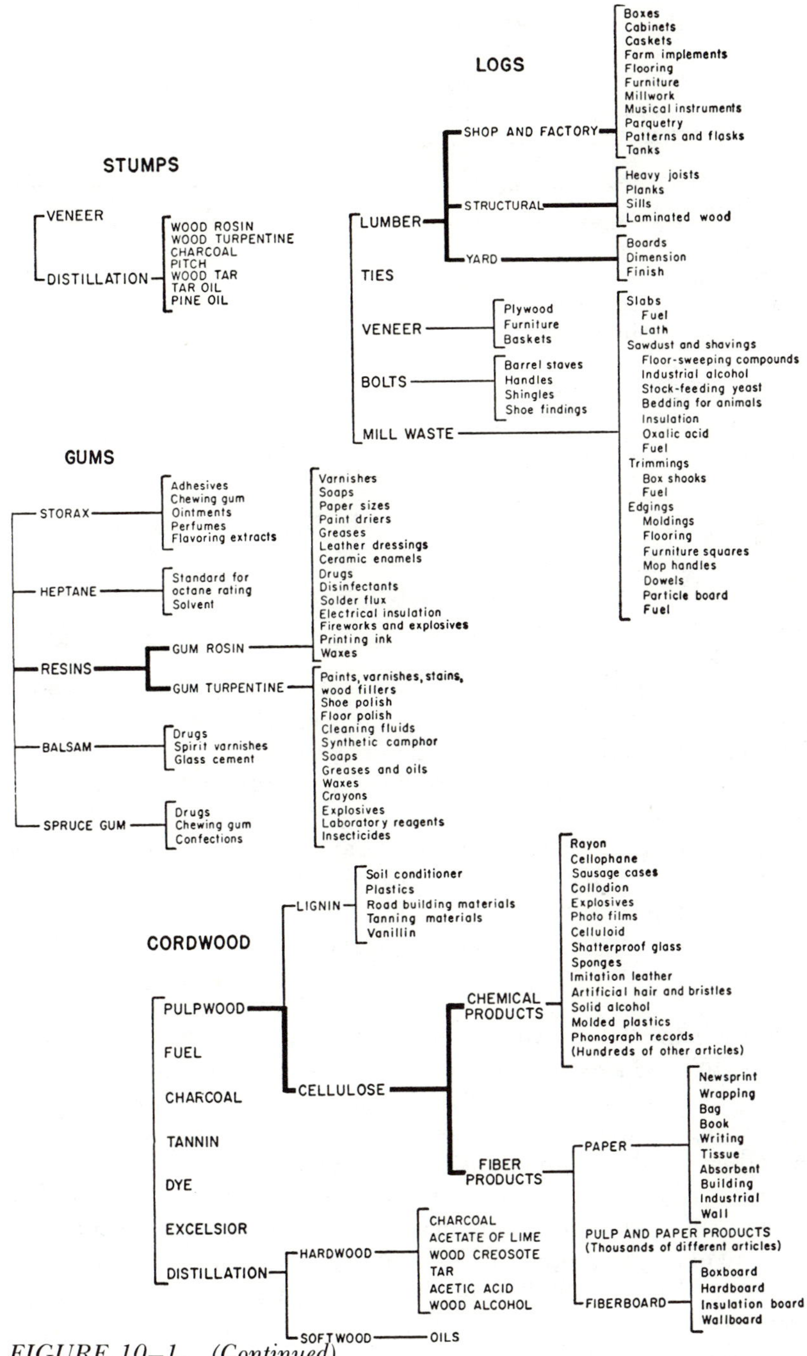

FIGURE 10–1. (Continued)

TABLE 10–1 EMPLOYMENT ATTRIBUTED TO TIMBER IN THE UNITED STATES

Kinds of Timber-Based Economic Activity	*Employment* 1000 Employees	Percent
Forest management	117	4
Harvesting	190	6
Primary manufacturing	427	13
Secondary manufacturing	900	27
Construction	795	24
Transportation and marketing	835	26
Total	3264	100

Source: U.S. Forest Service.

ECONOMIC IMPORTANCE TO THE NATION

Added together, employment in the woods on logging jobs, in wood-processing plants, and in timber-based activities provides jobs for about 3.3 million people, or about 4 percent of the nation's total labor force. In terms of value of product, the forest industry annually contributes about 4 percent of our gross national product. Thus the forest products industries are a very important part of our national economy and are particularly strategic in that they are decentralized and are the principal industry in hundreds of our smaller communities. The economic importance of each major group of forest industries on the basis of the number of people employed is shown in Table 10–1.

More than 30,000 sawmills, pulp mills, and other processing plants in the United States depend on wood for raw material. In recent years nearly 13 billion cu. ft of timber, including nearly 7 billion cubic feet of sawtimber, was cut to supply the wood used by these plants and by other wood consumers. About 51 percent of the timber cut for commercial use went into sawlogs, which were used chiefly in building construction, shipping, and manufactured products. Twenty-nine percent of the cut pulpwood is used for various forms of paper, board, rayon, and other cellulose products. Eleven percent of the timber harvested went into veneer and plywood for furniture, containers, and similar laminated products. And nearly 8 percent was utilized for a variety of miscellaneous wood products such as poles, piling, mine timbers, barrel staves, posts, and fuel wood.

THE LUMBER INDUSTRY

As an industry, sawmilling had its beginning in Colonial times. White pine and oak lumber were produced by the colonists for export to England and other countries in order to buy manufactured goods. Good white pine boards sawed from New England forests were welcomed in the Old World, which was finding it increasingly difficult to feed a growing population without clearing more and more forest land. Until about 1900 the United States produced more and more lumber from its forests each year until the record cut of more than 46 billion b.f. in 1906 was reached.

Although lumbering first began in New England, it moved on to New York and Pennsylvania, then to the Lake States pineries, to the South, and finally to the Pacific Northwest, where it is still the most important industry (Table 10–2). Following logging, millions of acres

TABLE 10–2 OUTPUT OF TIMBER PRODUCTS IN THE UNITED STATES, BY SECTION, SOFTWOODS AND HARDWOODS, AND PRODUCT (MILLION CUBIC FEET/YR)

Species Group and Product	Total	North	South	Rocky Mountain	Pacific Coast
Softwoods					
Saw logs	5,210	267	1,599	641	2,703
Veneer logs	1,330	3	498	65	764
Pulpwood	2,608	335	1,938	25	310
Miscellaneous industrial	238	27	122	18	71
Fuelwood	132	4	77	24	27
Total	9,518	636	4,234	773	3,876
Hardwoods					
Saw logs	1,432	700	667	1	64
Veneer logs	100	34	63	([1])	3
Pulpwood	1,155	454	677	([1])	24
Miscellaneous industrial	139	100	38	2	([1])
Fuelwood	470	214	246	1	9
Total	3,297	1,502	1,692	3	100
All species					
Saw logs	6,642	967	2,266	642	2,768
Veneer logs	1,431	37	561	65	767
Pulpwood	3,763	789	2,615	25	334
Miscellaneous industrial	378	127	160	20	71
Fuelwood	602	218	323	25	36
Total	12,815	2,138	5,925	777	3,976

Source: Analysis of Timber Trends in the United States, U.S. Forest Service, 1984.

[a]Less than 0.5 million cu. ft.

were burned over in huge forest fires that destroyed or set back new forests for many generations. The development of fire control and other forestry programs during the past quarter of a century has made possible a regrowth that is forming a solid raw-material base for an expanded forest industry. Meanwhile, the still extensive forests of Douglas-fir and other West Coast species produce the most important source of lumber today. Oregon has led all other states in production since 1938. The sawmills of the Pacific Northwest are still large and medium-sized mills that produce millions of board feet per year, whereas in the other parts of the country most of the mills are small. They saw smaller logs and produce considerably less per year. Some of these small mills are portable and are moved from location to location (*setting*) where sufficient logs are accumulated for the duration of the sawing job (Figure 10–2). In recent years, the approximately 9,000 sawmills located in the principal lumber-producing states sawed out 7 billion cu. ft.

Milling Logs into Lumber

The logging process, described in Chapter 8, prepares logs for delivery to the mill by rail or truck from the woods. In the past, log driving down the river systems was the principal form of transportation, but with the removal of timber close to the rivers and the development of modern logging equipment and truck hauling, log drives have passed into a colorful episode of our history. At larger mills, logs are still dumped into log ponds for storage before they are moved up the *jack ladder* (an endless chain conveyor) into the mill (Figure 10–3). At smaller mills, logs are decked on rollways where they are rolled by people with cant hooks up to the sawmill carriage.

Unloading of logs and pulpwood from rail cars on trucks onto decks or into log ponds requires men with skill in handling timber. Logging experience is a valuable preliminary training. Sorting, grading, and measuring the logs as they are received requires a knowledge of log grades and scaling methods, an ability to identify different species, and facility in the use of equipment such as scale rules, cant hooks, and peavies. Because timber is measured as it is received, log scalers must be able to make entries on tally forms, to add up volumes, and be conversant with volume calculations as set forth in Chapter 8. A knowledge of forestry is becoming increasingly important in wood yard operation.

Larger sawmills operate with several types of saws: *circular* and *band* saws are the most common, although *gang saws* and *resaws* are used to increase production. Logs are rolled by hand or tossed by steam

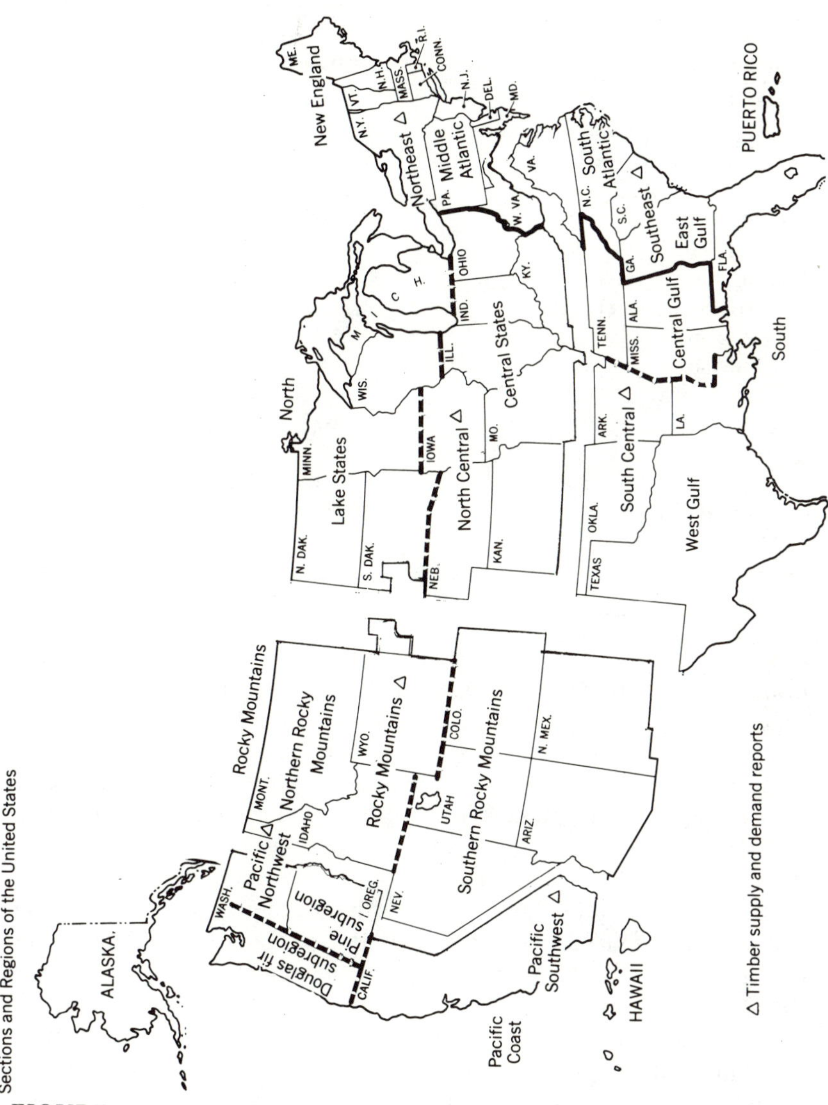

FIGURE 10–2. Sections and regions of the United States used by the Forest Service for timber supply and demand analyses. (U. S. Forest Service)

TABLE 10–3 ESTABLISHMENTS AND EMPLOYEE NUMBERS IN PRIMARY TIMBER PROCESSING INDUSTRIES IN THE UNITED STATES

Industry	Establishments	Employees (thousands)
Lumber		
Logging camps and contractors	15,469	83.3
Sawmills and planing mills	9,000	211.3
Total	24,469	294.6
Plywood and veneer		
Hardwood veneer and plywood	321	22.3
Softwood veneer and plywood	256	46.2
Total	577	68.5
Woodpulp		
Pulpmills	45	16.2
Integrated mills	238	145.2
Total	283	161.4
Other primary timber	5,519	121.2
Total	30,848	645.7

Source: U. S. Forest Service.

piston onto the moving carriage which holds them in place with steel *dogs*. Sawyers are the key people in this operation and it is their judgment that determines how the log shall be cut up (Figure 10–4). They regulate the width of the board to be cut by moving the log on the carriage toward the saw. Then they speed the log on the carriage into the saw and the boards drop off onto a *roller conveyor* that carries them to the edger or trimmer, or to the resaw for further sawing.

Until quite recently a substantial portion of the round log was wasted when it was squared into lumber. If this waste—slabs, edgings, and trimmings plus bark—was not burned to make steam for power, it was conveyed into a *slab burner* (a round silo-like steel structure). In many mills today, bark is removed by jet streams of water or by mechanical means and the slabs and other wood waste ground into chips for conversion to paper pulp, particle board, and even plastics.

In larger mills the boards that still have the bark and irregular edges left move to an *edger*, which squares them on the two sides. From the edger they move along to a *trimmer*, where odd lengths are cut off and the ends are squared. After this, the boards are conveyed out on the *green chain* where graders pick off boards of different

FIGURE 10–3. Sawmill in Maine showing jack ladder with eastern white pine logs on the way to the band saw. (American Forest Institute)

quality and grade and place them onto piles that are moved off on fork lift trucks. They are then piled in the yards for several months of air drying or into *dry kilns* where they can be dried to specification in a few days. Hardwoods, which are difficult to dry evenly in air, are most commonly put through the dry kiln. Following drying, the boards are put through a planing mill to surface them before shipment.

Measuring the lumber as it is cut is frequently a job that forestry-trained personnel learn at sawmills. This is done with a tally sheet on which each board is shown by length, width, thickness, and grade. Each board has a definite number of board feet, as shown in the board volume table (Table 10–4). The boards are tallied by size class on a tally sheet (Figure 10–5), totaled at the end of the shift, multiplied by the number of board feet for each class, and a total added up. With a little practice, the lumber scaler soon learns to distinguish an

FIGURE 10–4. Squaring a log prior to further processing. The sawyer regulates the width of the debarking cut by the bandsaw. (American Forest Institute)

8-ft from a 10-ft 2 by 4 in., and a 1 in. by 6 in. by 8 ft board from 1 in. by 5 in. by 10 ft (Table 10–4).

A handy formula can be employed for determining the number of board feet of wood in any piece of lumber. A board foot is 1 ft long, 1 ft wide, and 1 in. thick. If two dimensions of any board are expressed in feet and one dimension in inches, the board foot content becomes the product of the three numbers. For example, a 2 by 4-in. board 12 ft long contains 2 in. by 4 in./12 in. by 12 ft or 8 b.f.

Lumber is also graded according to quality. The number and size of knots, defects, and other imperfections are the determining factors in lumber grades. Considerable skill, acquired through study and practice, is needed to become a proficient lumber grader.

Although sawmills have not changed radically in layout, design, and processing flow for many years, the movement of logs to the mill and products from it have been greatly affected by fork lift and other mechanical handling equipment. Automated and computer operated sawmill operations have been built and give promise for rapid development in the years ahead.

The timber industry has organized itself into trade associations for

TABLE 10–4 BOARD FOOT CONTENTS OF SAWN LUMBER (COMMONLY USED DIMENSIONS)

Size (in.)	*Length (ft)* 8	10	12	14	16
1 × 4	2⅔	3⅓	4	4⅔	5⅓
1 × 6	4	5	6	7	8
1 × 8	5⅓	6⅔	8	9⅓	10⅔
1 × 10	6⅔	8⅓	10	11⅔	13⅓
1 × 12	8	10	12	14	16
2 × 4	5⅓	6⅔	8	9	11
2 × 6	8	10	12	14	16
2 × 8	10⅔	13⅓	16	19	21
2 × 10	13⅓	16⅔	20	23	27
2 × 12	16	20	24	28	32
4 × 4	10⅔	13⅓	16	19	21
4 × 6	16	20	24	28	32
6 × 6	24	30	36	42	48

each major forest region and has established a national association called the National Forest Products Association. These organizations supply the individual companies with technical information, report on market developments, promote lumber uses, and represent the industry on legislative matters.

THE PULP AND PAPER INDUSTRY

From the forest also comes the raw material—pulpwood—used in the manufacture of paper and numerous other wood pulp products. The basis of paper is pulp made from fibers of wood or other kinds of cellulose, that remarkable material that forms the cell walls of plants. Wood is the most abundant source of commercially used cellulose from the plant world. More than one half of its substance is cellulose fiber.

The United States uses more paper than the rest of the world combined. Soaring demand has increased the use of paper in the United States from about 300 lb per person in 1946 to more than 600 lb in recent years. Our annual production of pulpwood has climbed from 2 million cords in 1900 to over 83 million in a recent peak year. And production is projected to continue to increase in the future. In addition, this country imports large quantities of paper from Canada in the form of newsprint.

DATE 3/4 85	CAR NO. Soo 47823	NO. SHEETS 18
FROM Chittamo Landing		CAP. —
TO Libertyville, Ill.		TARE —
INSPECTED AT SHIPPING PT. ✓ DESTINATION	STARTED 3/3 FINISHED 3/4	INSPECTOR P.C.S.
KIND & GRADE - Norway Pine, No. 2 Com. S/4/S		ORDER NO. 482-A

SIZE	LGTH.	1	2	3	4	5	6	7	8	9	10	11	12	PCS.	FEET
1X6	12	𝍸	𝍸	𝍸										15	90
1X8	12	𝍸	𝍸	𝍸	𝍸									20	160
1X10	12	𝍸	𝍸	𝍸	𝍸	𝍸	|||							28	280
1X6	16	𝍸	𝍸	||										12	96
1X8	16	𝍸	𝍸	𝍸										15	160
1X10	16	𝍸	𝍸	𝍸	||									17	227
2X4	8	𝍸	𝍸											10	53
2X4	16	𝍸	𝍸	||										12	132

FIGURE 10–5. Lumber scale tally sheet. One sheet is used for each grade in each species. "S/4/S" means "surfaced (planed) on four sides." (Redrawn from National Agricultural Supply Co.)

While most of the pulpwood cut is from conifers, new processes are making possible the utilization of larger proportions of hardwoods. However, conifers still account for a majority of the wood used by pulp mills. Pines make up half of this total with spruce, balsam fir, and hemlock contributing most of the balance. Aspen, birch, oak, and gum are the major hardwood species used in making pulp. Great quantities of pulpwood are still stored at mill yards (Figure 10–6), but many mills are either moving logs directly into the mill without yard storage to save handling and losses or shipping them in as chips.

The paper industry includes about 800 paper mills and 283 pulp mills located in 37 states (Table 10–3). Pulp mills convert wood into pulp that the paper mills process into finished paper. The industry was first established in the Northeast and is still an important industry in that region. From there, however, the industry has spread to the

Lake States, the central states, the Pacific Coast, and since 1925 throughout the South, from Virginia to Texas. Cutting pulpwood has become an important source of rural income in most forest areas. Over a million people are employed in the manufacture of paper and paper products. It is the fifth ranking industry in the United States in value of products. The American Paper and Pulp Association and the American Pulpwood Association, as well as several technical organizations, keep the individual company members informed of developments affecting the industry in much the same manner as the lumber trade associations.

Pulp and Paper Manufacturing

Wood is reduced to a fibrous form suitable for paper making by five commercial chemical and mechanical pulping processes. In the mechanical or *groundwood* process, fibers are produced by pressing bolts of wood against the rough surface of a rotating grindstone made of sandstone or synthetic abrasive material. A shower of water cools the stone and conveys the pulp away. In the chemical pulping processes, the wood fibers are separated by dissolving the lignin and other binding material from wood chips. Dissolution of the lignin cementing material is accomplished by heating the chips in cooking *liquor* at high temperature and pressure in large pressure vessels called *digesters.*

FIGURE 10–6. Unloading pulpwood at a paper mill storage yard. The pulpmill is seen in the background. (American Forest Institute)

The three chemical processes commonly used for pulping are the *sulfate* or *kraft*, the *soda*, and the *sulfite*. The sulfate and soda processes employ alkaline liquors and the sulfite process uses an acid liquor. A newer process is making possible the use of short-fibered hardwoods for newsprint and related products.

The semichemical process employs both chemical and mechanical actions. Discovered by a team of scientists at the U.S. Forest Products Laboratory who were seeking a method of pulping short-fibered hardwoods, this process has been adopted quite widely in the eastern United States where there is an abundance of small hardwood trees. In this process, the chips are just given a mild softening treatment with steam or a chemical cooking liquor in a digester, after which they are reduced to fibrous pulp by mechanical treatment in an attrition mill or a *beater*.

After the soft pulp is thoroughly washed, it looks quite similar to wet cotton fibers and may have dye for coloring, fine clay, rosin, and other matter added in the beater. The purpose of these additives is to give the finished paper color a shiny finish, or other surface qualities. The pulp is then flowed out onto a vibrating screen over which it spreads evenly to drain off some of the water and forms a wet sheet. The first wet sheet leaves the screen to go around a series of high-speed heated press rollers (the *Fourdrinier* machine). These rollers dry the sheet, which finally comes out at the end as a huge roll of paper (Figure 10–7). The paper is then either shipped in this form for direct use or remanufactured into hundreds of other paper items for consumer use.

Another product of wood pulp is rayon, a soft, silky fiber that is widely used for clothing and automobile tire-cord material. It is made from some form of plant cellulose, preferably cotton or wood, and at present more than 80 percent of the rayon produced comes from wood cellulose. In the manufacture of rayon, the cellulose is dissolved by various chemicals (which differ with the process employed), and the thick, syrupy solution is forced through minute apertures corresponding to the spinnerets of the silkworm. The fine threads, or filaments, coming through these openings are coagulated either in a fixing bath or by a process of evaporation and several of them formed simultaneously are then twisted into a strand for spinning.

Wood Fiber Board

Production of wall boards by the use of wood fiber in rougher form than needed for paper has become an increasingly important building industry material. Under most processes, unrefined wood fibers are

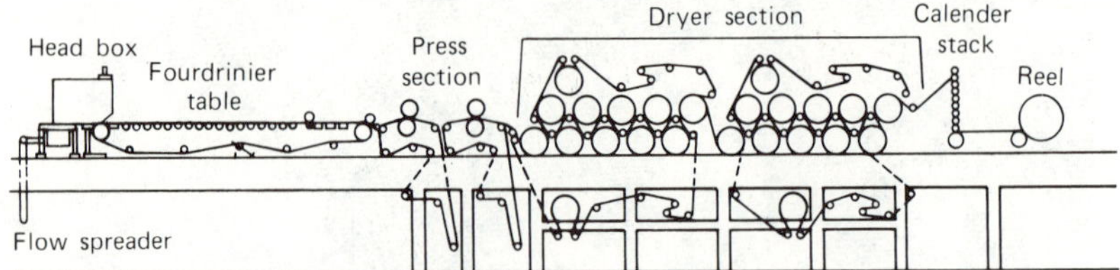

FIGURE 10–7. A Fourdrinier machine. The many steps of paper production are combined in this machine from the introduction of pulp into the head box at the left to the rolling up of the finished product on the reel at the right. (Beloit Corporation)

formed with a binder into thick sheets and pressed into soft wall board. Hard board variations of this product are made either by compressing wood chips with a resin binder or by exploding chips into fibers (after cooking under steam pressure and releasing) that are then passed through steel presses. These processes form a hard board that can be substituted for lumber in roof sheathing and for plywood in home building. Some predictions have been made that reformed wood fiber products will soon be the principal forest product.

OTHER PRODUCTS FROM THE FOREST

Vast quantities of logs are consumed in the veneer industry to produce thin sheets of wood used in the making of plywood and baskets, berry boxes, and other containers. Douglas fir plywood and southern pine, which constitute by far the largest proportion of plywood, are largely used in building and other construction. High-grade hardwood veneers are used extensively in the manufacture of furniture. Maple, oak, gum, and birch veneers are highly prized for furniture.

The Douglas-fir plywood and veneer industry is located in the Pacific Northwest where large-diameter *peeler logs* are still available in quantity. Hardwood veneers are manufactured in the South where red gum and oak grow, and in the northern hardwood areas of the Lake States and the Northeast where maple, yellow birch, basswood, and other hardwoods are found. The large-sized quality material demanded by the veneer industry is becoming increasingly scarce and has forced log buyers to search over wide areas for suitable raw material. The high value of veneer logs permits long-distance freight hauling.

The cooperage industry annually consumes large quantities of logs and bolts in the manufacture of staves and headings for barrels, kegs, and buckets. White oak is prized for "tight" cooperage because of its ability to prevent passage of liquids. Vast quantities of wood are also used for fuel, piling, poles, posts, railroad ties, mine timbers, and for other miscellaneous products. Although the use of wood as a fuel declined rapidly in importance since World War II, it is again becoming one of the major uses in terms of volume. Most of the other products are treated with wood preservatives in order to extend their usable life.

After wood, the most important forest products are perhaps turpentine and rosin. They are obtained by the distillation of the gum that exudes from the longleaf and slash pines of the South. The gum is bled from the trees into small cups. Later it is carried to a still where it is cooked in closed iron retorts. Another source of resin is obtained from the distillation of chipped wood from old stumps. The turpentine is given off in the form of a vapor, which is collected in a condensing coil. The rosin is the part of the gum left after the turpentine has been distilled. The name *naval stores* was originally given to these products because for many years they were mostly used in shipbuilding. Naval stores are now used in the manufacture of paints and varnishes.

By-Products from Waste Recovery

Gone are the slab and sawdust burners of the lumber industry, and going rapidly are the water and airborne wastes of the paper mills that have caused much contention over pollution. Some wood waste such as bark, knots, and branches are going into producing precious energy—to replace gas and oil to makes steam for boilers and electric generators. One Canadian newsprint mill produces 5 million lb of synthetic vanilla from formerly wasted lignin. Resin from southern pine pulp chips is converted to turpentine.

The term *silvichemicals* has been coined to cover the broad group of chemicals derived from woods and mill wastes now being converted into wood alcohol, ammonia, formaldehyde, and even petroleum. Silvichemicals and their derivatives include such products as solvents, soil conditioners, adhesives, and tall oil (used in fungicides, printing ink, and carbon paper).

Equally important is the recovery of the chemicals used in processing of wood. Sulfates, calcium, and other spent materials that were formerly dumped into rivers or burned may now be converted into other useful products. Even hot stack gases are being cooled as a source of energy. Much more research is needed if more of these by products will become economical to process and market. The result will be prevention of pollution by closer utilization of wasted materials, which is the best solution because we can create new and useful materials and prevent pollution at its source.

Maple Syrup and Sugar

From New England to Minnesota and down the Appalachians to West Virginia, maple sap is collected in the early spring when days warm up and nights are cold. On the old-time farm, the maples in the "sugar bush" were tapped with bored holes, spouts, and hung buckets. Full sap buckets were emptied into a horse drawn tank sleigh that transported the sap to the sugar house where it was evaporated in pans heated by firewood (Figure 10–8).

Today modern techniques—such as power drills for tapping, plastic tubing to transport the sap, and oil- or gas-heated evaporators—have taken over for the larger production units. The discovery that bacteria can cut the flow of sap even at low temperatures has led to more sanitary processing at each stage.

In addition to developing new production techniques, research in tree selection is increasing the sugar content of maple trees by selecting stock for planting from trees with higher than average sugar yields. Although standards of quality vary from state to state, maple products enjoy a wide market and the demand, even at high prices, exceeds the supply. As a steady source of income to owners of northern hardwoods, maple syrup has no equal.

There are also many specialized forest products of importance in

FIGURE 10–8. This traditional method of tapping maple trees and collecting sap is giving way to the use of plastic tubes leading directly to the boiling pans in the sugar house. (U. S. Forest Service)

certain localities. The bark blisters of balsam fir produce a resin that, when refined, has a limited market. Despite all the work and skill of chemists, wood and bark remain the chief sources of tannins; and dyes from various trees, such as black oak and Osage orange, are still to be found in trade channels. Many kinds of edible nuts, fruits, and crude drugs are important sources of income to some rural communities.

Christmas Trees

Christmas trees and greens for wreaths and roping have been important sources of seasonal income to residents of coniferous forested areas for many years. Until quite recently, however, wild trees from young natural forests have been the source of most of the material harvested and marketed. But with the development of new forest plantations into Christmas-tree size, forest landowners are finding this market an important outlet for thinnings and prunings. Northern and mountain-grown balsam fir, Douglas-fir, and spruce are finding increasing competition from white, red, and Scotch pine produced from plantations of private landowners and public forests. Consumers in many cities are showing a liking for these species, which hold their needles well and are sheared every year to assure that they are well rounded and symmetrical. Over 40 million trees are cut annually for Christmas trees (Figure 10–9).

Another development has been the small table spruce treated with a solution for holding needles, sprayed with paint, and mounted on a stand. These little trees—produced entirely from northern Minnesota stunted black spruce—are particularly popular with apartment dwellers.

Christmas-tree growers have been organizing into associations in recent years in an effort to keep better informed on market conditions and prices, and to reduce marketing waste. Much information has been developed by foresters on the special techniques needed for shaping trees in order to obtain the best prices. Because closely planted stands are just right for thinning when they reach Christmas-tree size, this market is a highly beneficial one for intensive forestry. However, competition from artificial trees made from nonrenewable natural resources are having a serious impact in many urban markets.

MARKETING FOREST PRODUCTS

Individual owners of forest lands who have no direct connection with the forest industry face marketing problems very similar to those of farmers with crops to sell. Some landowners prefer to sell timber

FIGURE 10–9. Harvesting Christmas trees in Minnesota. (American Forest Institute)

standing; others do the logging, or hire contractors, and offer cut products for sale to industry buyers. Larger lots of timber or forest products are usually contracted for in advance and bring better prices than smaller quantities.

The forest products industries obtain much of their raw material through direct purchases from forest owners and logging operators. Some pulpwood, for example, is produced on company lands, but more comes from company operations on stumpage purchased from federal, state, or individual private owners. A location close to a paper mill, sawmill, or other timber industry is a distinct advantage to the owner (because of lower hauling costs), although good quality and sizes of timber can be sold in almost every section of the United States. Material that is of lower quality or small size is frequently difficult to sell at any price.

Marketing Methods

The buying and selling of forest products is accomplished through individual transactions rather than through central marketing exchanges, as is the case with many other important farm commodities. Most larger wood-processing industries have log buyers whose business it is to know the timber and the timber producers in their territory. Local loggers and sawmill operators can usually direct forest owners to these buyers. Market and price information, including lists of wood-buying industries, are being compiled and published by some state foresters. Most foresters are familiar with prices and market conditions in their locality and are able to furnish this information if published material is unavailable.

Prior to cutting any timber, the forest owner should have a written contract with a buyer at a firm price. Otherwise, it is possible that a slow market could force the owner to leave a considerable amount of cut timber on hand, which could be ruined by wood borers and rot.

Before selling merchantable standing timber, the forest manager must decide whether to sell standing trees or to conduct the logging operation independently. The first system relieves the owner of detailed supervision, financing, and other tasks connected with logging; but in selling stumpage, the owner loses the opportunity to make an operating profit. In either case the owner should definitely make a volume estimate of the timber and make sure that proper silviculture methods are followed by marking only those trees that are to be cut.

One recent study showed that owners who sold their timber on volume scaled or estimated received nearly double returns as compared with those who sold without any measurement of volume, either standing or cut! Most sellers took the offered price of the buyer, but they would have found that it pays to shop around for the best price.*

In preparing to sell standing timber that has been estimated and marked for cutting, an advertisement stating the amount, minimum acceptable price and the location is placed in local papers and regional trade journals. Bidders are asked to visit the tract, cruise it if they wish, and submit their bids. The successful bidder is asked to sign a timber sale agreement that establishes certain conditions, including proper cutting of marked trees. (See Appendix D.) The advice of an experienced forester is suggested in assisting the owner with the first sale or two until the process becomes thoroughly familiar.

Where the seller decides to conduct the logging operation and to offer cut products for sale on the market, a considerably different procedure is required. After the timber has been estimated and the merchantable volume marked, a written contract with a buyer should be obtained to record the details of the agreement. This contract states the total volume, the specifications of each product by species, the point of delivery, unit of measure and method of scaling, price per unit, and the period during which delivery can be made. With the contract in hand, the forest manager makes plans for logging either by hiring and operating a private crew and equipment or by contracting with a logging operator who agrees to deliver the cut products at a cost per mbf or cord. (See Appendix D for logging contract form.) Chapter 12 supplies several important kinds of information to forest owners wishing to obtain the assistance of forestry agencies and industry groups in working out problems connected with each of the previously mentioned steps.

The federal government in cooperation with the states funds the cost of placing state employed foresters in most forested counties in the United States. These foresters are available, often free of charge, to provide forestry assistance to small forest landowners. Most large forest products manufacturing companies also provide forestry advice to Tree Farm cooperators. Consulting foresters are available to work with forest landowners where more time is demanded, specialized skills are required, or the task of management requires geographic mobility.

In every case, it is to the advantage of the timber owner to employ a professional forester's assistance in preparing a timber sale and seeing it to its satisfactory completion.

WOOD AS FUEL—A RENEWABLE SOURCE OF ENERGY

As our nation and the rest of the world move into a deepening energy crisis resulting from wasteful overuse of our limited fossil fuels, wood (as a fixed form of solar energy) is coming back into popularity—particularly for home heating. The steadily increasing cost of natural gas, petroleum, and even coal has reestablished the importance of wood for fuel, particularly for farms and those communities located in or near forested areas. During World War II, people in several European countries developed *gasogenes*—a compact form of retort that fit in the trunk of an automobile and produced wood gas to fuel the motor.

Although wood supplied less than 1 percent of our total energy consumption in the mid-1980s (largely for fireplaces), this neglected form of fuel can be expected to fill an important gap in the future. There has been a trend for some time to replace fuel oil and gas furnaces with wood-burning equipment. And if we harvest our fuelwood resource using sound forestry practices, it can last forever. But if we don't, we can exhaust our forests as we have our oil and gas wells. There is a definite need for a fuelwood forest policy to remove low-quality timber for fuel and improve the growth of better trees.

Fuelwood can be produced from three primary sources: logging waste (tops and limbs), mill residues (bark, slabs, and chips), and noncommercially useful cull and other trees removable in timber stand improvement (TSI) operations. At least one-third of the wood volume in the standing tree is now left as logging waste after pulpwood and logs are removed. In Chapter 2 it was noted that 90 percent of the hardwood forests (preferred for fuelwood) will require TSI work to reach full productivity. If only 10 cords of this nonmerchantable fuelwood is available per acre during a 70-year rotation from 90 percent of our 250 million acres of eastern hardwoods, 32 million cords could be safely harvested every year for fuelwood in addition to logs and pulpwood—enough to heat 3.2 million homes. Such prudent utilization would benefit the forests and reduce the demand for diminishing fossil fuels.

There is much work to be done to bring back wood as a commonly accepted fuel. Logging operators will need to be trained to select poor trees and to utilize material now left in the woods. Transportation by rail needs to be encouraged through lower rates and marketing programs should be arranged. Fortunately, American ingenuity is developing much more efficient wood-burning stoves and furnaces that yield adequate heat with less fuel.

Although there are wide variations in the heating value of individual species, the British thermal unit (Btu) equivalent of 1 cord (128 cu. ft) of hardwood is about 1 ton of coal or 150 gal of fuel oil. See Table 10–5 for heat values by species.

The opportunity in the newly opened markets for fuelwood will certainly mean an increase in forestry activity—more jobs for foresters, more income for forest owners, and beneficial to the forest if done properly. Most of all, it will contribute to the solution of our national energy dilemma.

How Fuel Wood is Measured and Sold

Firewood is normally measured by the 128 cu. ft cord (4 ft by 4 ft by 8 ft). Before purchasing wood, one should be sure of the wood species that will be included in the purchase because one could afford to pay nearly twice as much for a cord of beech firewood as one could pay for a cord of poplar or white pine because of their heating values. Other terms such as a face cord or a fitted cord are used to indicate that the wood has been cut into pieces shorter than 4 ft. For example, a pile of 2-ft sticks 4 ft high and 8 ft long would amount to only one-half a regular cord. If the sticks are large it will also be important to know in advance whether the wood will be split before purchase.

Splitting the wood helps to maintain regular burning conditions and speeds up the drying of the wood.

How Wood Burns

There are four steps in burning wood: (1) The water must be removed from the wood by vaporization requiring heat; (2) the wood must be broken down chemically into charcoal, gas, and other volatiles; (3) these gases must be burned off; (4) the charcoal must be burned. When these four processes take place under proper conditions in a good stove, the maximum heating value is recovered, creosote problems are minimized, and ash production is minimum. This is complete and efficient combustion.

TABLE 10–5 ENERGY VALUES AND EQUIVALENTS OF WOOD AS A FUEL

Approximate Fuel Values for 28 Eastern Trees

Species	Air Dry Heat Values[a] (Btu's)	Species	Air Dry Heat Values[a] (Btu's)
Black locust	26,500,000	Black cherry	18,500,000
Shagbark hickory	25,400,000	White or paper birch	18,200,000
Hophornbeam	24,700,000	White elm	17,700,000
Beech	21,800,000	Birch	17,500,000
Sugar maple	21,800,000	Hemlock	15,000,000
Red oak	21,700,000	Spruce	15,000,000
Yellow birch	21,300,000	Aspen	14,100,000
White ash	20,000,000	Balsam fir	13,500,000
Tamarack	19,100,000	White pine	13,300,000
Red maple	19,100,000	Basswood	12,600,000

Characteristics of 12 Common Woods for Home Heating

Species	Ease of Starting	Coaling Qualities	Sparks
Apple	Poor	Excellent	Few
Ash	Fair	Good	Few
Beech	Poor	Good	Few
White birch	Good	Good	Moderate
Cherry	Poor	Excellent	Few
Cedar	Excellent	Poor	Many
Elm	Fair	Good	Very few
Hemlock	Good	Low	Many

TABLE 10–5 *(CONTINUED)*

Species	Ease of Starting	Coaling Qualities	Sparks
Hickory	Fair	Excellent	Moderate
Black locust	Poor	Excellent	Very few
Sugar maple	Poor	Excellent	Few
Red oak	Poor	Excellent	Few
White pine	Excellent	Poor	Moderate

Comparison of Other Fuels to 1 Cord of Seasoned Wood

Species of Tree	Equivalent Coal (tons)	Equivalent Fuel Oil (gal)
Beech	1.20	169
Sugar maple	1.18	166
Red oak	1.18	166
White ash	1.10	154
American elm	0.93	130
Aspen (poplar)	0.69	97
White pine	0.67	94

Note: It should be remembered, however, that these statistics are true only if the wood is burned in a reasonably efficient stove or furnace to meet the particular needs of the combustion of wood. A fireplace is quite inefficient and causes considerable loss of heat directly up the chimney. A heatilator fireplace does help to retain heat in the room by circulating room air inside the steel shell.

[a]Btu values/standard cord (4 × 4 × 8 ft).

Previously we noted the need for a national forestry fuelwood policy that would establish procedures for harvesting fuelwood of low quality (i.e., crooked and diseased trees) that would benefit the residual timber stand both in rate of growth and resistance to insects and disease. Unless this is done, haphazard tree cutting of the kind currently practiced will skim the cream of the timber crop in the long run.

QUESTIONS

1. More than half of all cut timber goes into the manufacture of lumber. What is the next largest use for timber?
2. Name the two most important lumber-producing regions in the United States today.

3. The largest volume of lumber is sawed from Douglas-fir trees. What group of species makes up the second largest volume and in which region does the production take place?
4. Name three important methods for converting pulpwood into pulp and paper.
5. Give four other important products from trees besides lumber and paper.
6. How important are the forest products industries to our national economy?
7. Why is it important to provide for the sale of forest products before they are cut rather than after?
8. Before selling standing timber (stumpage), what should an owner know about timber?
9. What are the advantages of a written agreement or contact to the forest owner?
10. How many board feet are in an 8-ft 2 × 4? In a 12-ft. 2 × 6? In a 16-ft. 2 × 8?

EXERCISES

1. Visit the nearest sawmill operation in your area.
2. Locate any other wood-using industry and find out required specifications for rough forest products.
3. Find out how forest products are marketed in your locality.
4. Visit local Christmas tree, naval stores, or maple syrup operation in your area.

*To work successfully, a market economy depends on the buyer's and seller's knowledge of the product or service to be sold. Because no forest products commodity exchanges exist for raw timber products, woodland owners and timber producers rely on reports of sales prices gleaned from rumors, neighborhood reports, or from regular price reporting services, which are only available in 14 states. By writing to a forester in a state agricultural college, it is possible to learn whether a price report on forest products is published regularly.

ELEVEN

Managing Forest Lands for Other Purposes

Although forest products are the most tangible commodities derived for human consumption from forest lands, many other "products" are important in their own way. Most of these cannot be measured concretely nor can we put an exact dollar value on them, but they might be considered forest by-products and services. Included in this broad group are wildlife, watershed protection, recreational uses (such as hunting, fishing, camping), and forage for grazing livestock—mainly cattle and sheep.

Many of these forest by-products will develop whether we consciously plan for them or not—if we manage the forest well for timber alone. But by including certain additional practices for improving the environment for game and fish, for providing recreational facilities, for preventing erosion on logging sites, and other practices described in the following pages, the forests can be made to serve us far better. This chapter describes some of the more important methods by which these additional forest values can be obtained.

Forests exert a number of influences on the land. The leaves and needles of the tree crowns break up and lessen the impact of raindrops; as a result rain falls more gently to the ground so that more rain soaks into the soil and less of it runs off quickly. Forest soils are a deep accumulation of dead leaves and decayed wood that filters moisture into the soil much more rapidly and in larger amounts than is possible under other types of cover. The temperature of the air in a forest is usually relatively cool in the summer, due to the shade transpiration; and the air contains a high relative humidity. Wind velocities are usually much lower in the forest than out in the open (in either summer or winter), due to the protective influence of the trees. These are some of the attributes of the forest that are important to the public, even though the owner does not actually obtain any income from them. Let us see how they affect forest management practices.

THE MEANING OF MULTIPLE USE

As complex ecological mechanisms, forests can produce a combination of benefits if they are managed accordingly. A pure pine plantation set out in rows without an understory, or any large broadleaved trees is as monotonous a sight as a cornfield and no more inviting to recreational visitors than to wildlife. However, it does afford protection of watersheds. By contrast, a forest made up of a variety of species and size classes produces multiple values. Thus the objectives of the owner will determine whether a forest is managed for multiple-use benefits or primarily for cellulose production.

Most corporate forests emphasize the latter goal, whereas public forests must satisfy a number of demands. This point was well made by the chief of the U. S. Forest Service, Richard E. McArdle, shortly after the passage of the Multiple Use Act in 1960 when he said:

> *An essential of multiple use is positive, affirmative management of the several uses involved. Haphazard occurrence of these uses on some particular tract does not constitute multiple-use management. Multiple use is not a passive practice. On the contrary, it is the deliberate and carefully planned integration of various uses so as to interfere with each other as little as possible and to supplement each other as much as possible. Multiple use is by no means an assemblage of single uses. It requires conscious, coordinated management of the various renewable natural resources, each with the other, without impairment of the productivity of the land. . . . [As foresters] we must be forest land managers instead of primarily timber growers.*

To be forest managers in command of all aspects of multiple use means that foresters will need to be specialists as well as generalists.

It means that foresters must have a working knowledge of hydrology and soils; recreational planning and administration; economics and business administration; wildlife management and range conservation; and must understand social concerns and be adept at public relations; for there are many kinds of people and groups interested in and using our forests. It will be possible to give only a brief summation of each of these other aspects of forestry in the balance of this chapter. But it will be evident that—although timber is often the primary *economic* benefit—the other uses of the forest are vital to our well-being and will demand knowledgeable command of related disciplines.

WATERSHED PROTECTION AND MANAGEMENT

In addition to providing areas for timber production, land for wildlife, and forage for grazing animals, forest lands have important influences on surface water runoff and groundwater flow. Well-managed forested watersheds have less erosion of the soil and, hence, contribute very little sediment to streams, resevoirs, and harbors. Many communities protect and manage the watersheds around their water supplies from fire, grazing, and logging to protect their sources of water—a resource more valuable than any other forest product. Good management of the forest, however, can produce both timber and water, as well as wildlife.

Here is how the forest acts to protect watersheds. As we have said, the tree crowns of different heights, together with the mass of shrubs below them, intercept the rainfall on its way to the ground. By breaking up large drops into smaller ones, the vegetation feeds water to the porous forest soil that is covered by the loose litter and duff of decomposing leaves and twigs. Fallen leaves on the ground act further to break up large raindrops. The action of bacteria, earthworms, fungi, insect larvae, and other minute forms of plant and animal life keeps the soil porous and spongy—ideal for holding, storing, and filtering large quantities of water. Tiny drops of rain are thus fed into this spongy mass instead of running off the surface, as on a plowed field, for example.

Below the organic surface soil is the subsoil layer with its greater mineral content. It is not as porous as the surface soil, but has many openings and channels made by roots and burrowing animals that allow water to penetrate to greater depths. Later on, some of the water returns to the surface in the form of springs. Thus the speed and volume of water movement into the soil depend on the structure and number of pore spaces formed by plant and animal activity. When rain falls on a forest, a part of it clings to the leaves and needles of trees and other plants, from where it gradually evaporates. Some trickles down the trunks and plant stems into the soil. During long, hard rainfalls, the spongy forest floor will become soaked to the point where surface runoff will begin to take place. Thus it is possible for floods to develop in forested areas, but they usually occur more slowly and the water contains much less silt than the runoff from agriculture or burned-over areas (Figure 11–1).

Part of the rainfall that soaks into the ground is used by trees and other plants for their growth. Some evaporates from the plants, some is soaked up by the spongy forest soil, and, as we have seen, some goes deep down into the groundwater. After all these things have reached their capacity, surface runoff will begin. But that requires long, hard rains. Some forest soils in good condition can absorb 50 percent of their total volume in water before this happens.

Forest cover has a strong influence on snowfall. It protects snow from the sun and wind, enabling it to remain on the forest floor weeks after it has melted off open ground. Frequently, the forest will prevent the soil from freezing and thus keep it receptive for infiltration when the snow melts in the spring.

Overgrazing, careless logging that tears up the forest soil through skidding, and forest fires are the sources of greatest damage to watersheds. Overgrazing destroys much ground cover, compacts the soil, and causes water to run off rather than soak into the ground. Skidding and road construction disturbs the soil and can start eroding gullies that may carry off water and silt.

A well-managed watershed shows up sharply in contrast to a poor one. The plant cover is thick—both the understory of small trees and plants as well as the overstory of trees—and the soil is porous and spongy. Clear streams and flowing springs—even in dry seasons—are another sign of a good watershed. Streambanks are well covered with vegetation—not caving in or cluttered with logging debris—and the cool, clear streams may have a good fish fish population.

Watershed Conservation Practices

Forest management plans that take into consideration watershed values (and in all cases they should) include special provisions for grazing, logging, and road building. Grazing animals are limited in numbers

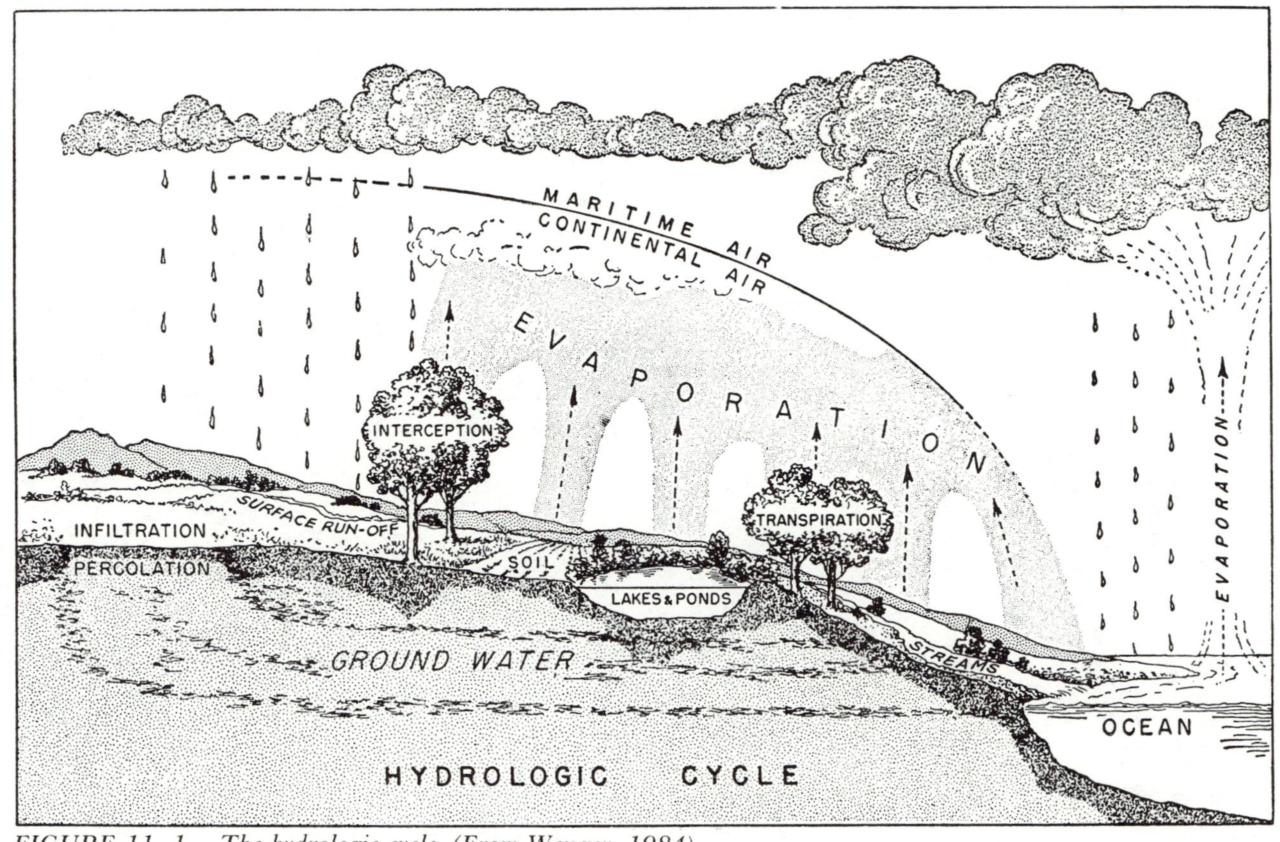

FIGURE 11–1. The hydrologic cycle. (From Wenger, 1984)

and are moved from place to place so that they will not overgraze plant cover nor compact the soil. Recreational uses are located so that fire danger will be kept to a minimum and pollution of streams will be prevented by the proper design and maintenance of sanitation facilities.

Well-designed management plans will locate roads so as to cross streams and rivers infrequently, thus keeping sediment from entering the streams. Instead, roads will parallel waterways some distance back from them so that sediment will be filtered out through the forest before reaching the streams. Raw roadbanks and any raw streambanks will be sloped and planted to stabilize the soil that has been disturbed in construction.

Where feasible, *high lead* cable systems can be substituted for ground skidding in steep areas to avoid disturbing the soil. Where ground skidding is unavoidable, skidways should be planted with grass, and water diversion bars should be constructed immediately upon completion of use. Logging debris and other slash should be kept out of stream channels by felling the trees away from streams. Reserving a strip of untouched timber along waterways will not only prevent damage to the stream, it will preserve esthetic and fishery values as well.

And finally, any open lands with insufficient ground cover should either be reseeded with grass (if in western grazing country) or planted with trees as soon as funds become available. If these measures are followed—and in most cases they simply require some foresight and direction—adequate protection of the watershed will result.

Some of the soil erosion control techniques for range conservation are applicable in watershed protection. Where problems exist, one of the most effective ways to reduce sedimentation and slow runoff is the fencing of forest land to exclude livestock. Allowing undergrowth and tree reproduction to develop, and preventing compaction of the soil by animal hoofs will markedly improve the infiltration capacity of forest soils.

A series of new techniques, still in the experimental stage, is being developed to increase water yields from mountain areas with a water deficiency. It has been found that snow intercepted and held on the crowns of conifers is lost in direct evaporation and sublimation into the atmosphere. By partial cuttings and other techniques that reduce crown densities, and by replacing conifers with hardwoods, increased water can be made available to water-shortage areas without damaging the watershed. Figure 11–2 shows a station for measuring stream flow.

FIGURE 11–2. A stream gauging station on a North Carolina watershed. This weir makes it possible to maintain a continuous record of the stream flow, using an automatic recorder located in the small building. (U. S. Forest Service)

Some Watershed Conservation Practices Common in Logging

1. Leave buffer strips of uncut timber at least 100 ft on each side of streams and seasonal waterways to prevent damage to streambanks, siltation, and slash-clogged drainage channels.
2. Fell trees away from streams.
3. Locate roads on favorable grades (maximum 8 percent) well above stream bottoms.
4. Provide for water bars to slow runoff to prevent water from concentrating and eroding roads and skid trails.
5. Seed and mulch raw banks on road cuts and fills.
6. Remove temporary bridges at stream crossings after logging; do not fill in drainages.
7. Skid logs on the contour so far as possible; do not concentrate skid trails.

WILDLIFE MANAGEMENT IN FORESTRY

Previously, the relationship of plants and animals to each other and their environment was discussed as the study of ecology. Wildlife is the product of the land. Forests provide a home, or habitat, for many kinds of wildlife—such as game animals, songbirds, and many forms of tiny insects and animal life. Hundreds of kinds of plants make their home under the forest canopy and could not exist without it. The important elements of wildlife habitat are food, cover, and water, and the combination and balance of these factors determines the kinds of wildlife to be found in any forest area. Most game fish, for instance, prefer clear, cool streams in forested watersheds.

Some of the well-known game animals and birds found mainly in forested areas are deer, elk, bear, moose, squirrel, turkey, ruffed grouse, wood duck, woodcock, and raccoon. There are also many songbirds and other small mammals that are essential to a well-balanced forest community. The shade of dense old-growth forests is often too great to provide the shrubs and herbs needed for food by birds and animals, but a well-managed forest with openings can produce abundant supplies. Weeds and shrubs that produce edible seeds spring up along with grasses and tree seedlings when the sun's rays can reach the ground. Well-planned forest management will create small openings such as these and leave a few hollow old wolf trees for animal dens, bird nests, and for the nuts or acorns they may produce. Wildlife tends to prefer the edges, between the woods and the openings, because food lies on one side and escape cover on the other.

Forest managers can do much to improve the area under their control for wildlife habitat. In addition to creating openings and leaving den trees, they can assist nature by supplemental plantings. For example, plantings of pines or spruces in or near hardwood forests make good winter escape cover from both enemies and snowstorms. Many shrubs that bear persistent seeds make good food and cover when planted along the edge of plantations or openings in the forest. These measures will tend to increase the numbers of wildlife present in the area, and this will usually be beneficial. More songbirds and game birds mean better protection against insect outbreaks.

Water is essential to all forms of wildlife, and its scarcity or abundance influences their numbers and distribution. Beaver, ducks, and fish require it for their homes. As a protector of watershed, the forest yields steady supplies of water for these species from springs and slows runoff into lakes, streams, and swamps.

Destructive cutting over wide areas, like a forest fire, greatly alters the habitat for wildlife and it may be years before balanced conditions are restored. Sometimes wildlife–forest relationships are out of balance due to man's interference. Cutover areas spring up with millions of hardwood seedlings that provide excellent deer food. The deer population increases greatly, but the trees soon grow out of their reach, thus forcing them to eat any form of vegetation (Figure 11–3). Sometimes this results in great damage to young conifers such as hemlock and white-cedar. Unfortunately, humans have largely eliminated wolves, which are predators of deer. And in many areas, the number of human hunters is not large enough to keep the deer population in balance.

National and state forests are usually open to hunting and fishing, subject in both cases to state laws. The forest manager must be acquainted with the laws and with the habits of the hunter and fisher, both for purposes of wildlife management and to protect the forest against carelessness with fire. On private forests more control over hunters and fishers is exercised, but recently many landowners have found that it is not only good public relations but also good management to allow hunters and fishers to use their lands. Proper sites for camping sportsmen are often provided in forests in order to encourage the concentration of use in designated areas.

FIGURE 11–3. Deer reaching for forage in overbrowsed habitat. (U. S. Forest Service)

By using care in constructing roads, in preserving trees along streams, and in keeping logging slash out of streams, the forest manager can maintain healthy water for fish.

Some Forest—Wildlife Management Practices

With little additional work, but with intelligent advance planning, many practices to improve the forest for wildlife can be developed. Sometimes it is merely a matter of timing; in other cases simply preserving a few den trees from logging will bring results. Although wildlife management is a field that requires special training, just as forestry does, the forest manager can master a few techniques that will improve the wildlife habitat in the forest. A few important ones are listed, but it is suggested that students do additional reading on the subject, particularly if their work requires them to do extensive wildlife work. (See Appendix F.) Keeping in mind that birds and animals all need food, water, nesting sites, and escape cover, the following practices have been found to harmonize with forestry programs (Table 11–1).

1. In the heavy deer country of the North, winter logging, stand improvement, or thinning—if done in mid- or late winter—will make browse available from tops and limbs just at the time the deer need food to survive.
2. In mountainous, hilly, or dry country with long distances between water courses, it has been found beneficial to build small ponds to hold back seepage or runoff water on the slopes. This has the effect of distributing wildlife over the forest and may reduce damage to young trees from deer browsing. Larger ponds may be used by waterfowl, including the beautiful wood ducks if houses are provided. (See Figure 11–4.)
3. To improve ruffed grouse habitat, it has been found that the planting of clover along logging roads will increase the food supply. In acid soils, this planting of clover must be accompanied with lime.
4. In badly burned northern forest areas, where young forests have few fallen logs, distribution of a few old hollow logs near low spots is a useful means of encouraging ruffed grouse to spread out during the "drumming" period at mating time.

TABLE 11–1 SEASONAL REQUIREMENTS OF SOME SELECTED WILDLIFE SPECIES

Species	Spring	Summer	Fall	Winter
Deer	Browse Grasses Forbs[a] Escape cover	Browse Grasses Forbs Escape cover	Browse Acorns Escape cover Wintering cover	Browse Acorns Escape cover Wintering cover
Turkey	Insects Nesting cover Escape cover Grasses and forbs	Insects Soft mast and berries Brooding cover Escape cover Grasses and forbs	Acorns Rootsing cover Soft mast Escape cover Grass and weed seeds	Acorns Roosting cover Soft mast Escape cover Wintering cover
Quail	Insects Nesting cover Escape cover Grass and weed seeds	Insects Brooding cover Grass and weed seeds Escape cover	Escape cover Roosting cover Wintering cover Seeds from trees, shrubs, vines, and herbaceous plants	Escape cover Roosting cover Wintering cover Seeds from trees, shrubs, vines, and herbaceous plants
Grouse	Insects Nesting cover Fruits and drupes Buds and flowers	Brooding cover Escape cover Insects Fruits and drupes	Escape cover Wintering cover Grass and weed seeds Buds, grapes	Escape cover Wintering cover Grass and weed seeds Soft mast, evergreen forbs—buds
Squirrel	Den sites Buds and flowers Hard mast[b]	Leaf nest sites Buds and flowers Berries Fruit	Den sites Hard mast Soft mast	Den sites Hard mast Soft mast

Source: The American Tree Farmer.

[a]Forbs: herbaceous plants and other grasses.

[b]Hard mast: nuts, acorns, beechnuts, etc. Soft mast: softer tree seeds.

FIGURE 11–4. This pond supplies water, slows runoff, attracts waterfowl, and provides fishing. (U. S. Forest Service)

5. Creating small openings in the forest during logging and planting them with berry bearing shrubs (if none are present) will increase the food supply of many birds and small animals.
6. Planting of coniferous stands in hardwood forest areas or in open farming country will provide the best kind of protection for wildlife from winter snowstorms and high winds.
7. Placing rock or log deflectors in small streams permits the current to cut out deeper pools than the normal streambed and thus makes better fish habitat. The proper handling of forests to assure steady streamflow, however, is the most important contribution that can be made for fish habitat. Whereas special practices may be carried out, they usually require considerable advance planning by fisheries' biologists.
8. Quail habitat in the South can be greatly improved along the edges of the forest and in small openings by planting lespedeza, leaving brushy edges between the forest and adjoining fields, and excluding grazing animals where grazing is too intensive.
9. Fencing farm woodlots to exclude livestock will encourage brush and young trees for wildlife food and cover.

Field observation and the study of wildlife management methods will suggest other practices when one is actually practicing forestry. The assistance of a wildlife specialist is suggested in planning the details of technical applications.

SPECIAL WILDLIFE MEASURES FOR ENDANGERED OR THREATENED SPECIES

Many threatened and endangered species of wildlife (e.g., bald eagle, osprey, and red cockaded woodpecker), as well as others that are rare and uncommon (e.g., moose, pine marten, fisher, lynx, wild turkey, pileated woodpecker, and many more) require large acreages of forest land with big trees to survive. Eagles and ospreys need tall trees near water that are free from human disturbance; woodpeckers require decadent trees for food and nesting cavities. Many other species must simply have one or more of the special kinds of ecological *niches* found mainly in natural—as opposed to managed—forests. Although preserved wilderness and natural areas in the public forests, parks, and wildlife refuges supply some of this habitat, additional areas must be managed for the critical needs of such species. Because each species has different requirements, it is suggested that the forest manager consult a wildlife specialist to evaluate any particularly unique tract so that proper safeguards will be prescribed for preserving the habitat situations needed.

MANAGING FOREST LANDS FOR GRAZING

Grazing on forest lands, if not controlled, can do more harm to the basic resource than the income that it may yield. This has been especially true of the hardwood forest areas in the central states and in the East, where dairy cattle and hogs have done extensive overgrazing. (See Figure 11–5.) Elimination of plant and tree reproduction and compaction of forest soils are all too common results from overgrazing on farm woodlands. Studies by forest experiment stations have clearly demonstrated that forage yields in farm woodlands are very low and water runoff is greatly accelerated where soil has been compacted from overgrazing. On the other hand, light grazing for very short periods may occasionally be beneficial. During drought emergencies, when pastures dry up, farm woodlands can be a useful source of forage. Generally, however, farmers must make a choice between pasture and timber. Steeper slopes should be retained in trees, whereas on level lands economic needs will probably dictate that grazing should prevail.

FIGURE 11–5. Without frequent herding, livestock quickly overgraze forest areas, causing damage to the watershed by compacting the soil and reducing vegetative cover. (U. S. Soil Conservation Service)

Both in the southern states and in the West, cattle grazing is an important auxiliary forest use. Handled properly, the forest can produce a moderate amount of forage, but the number of grazing animals must be kept in line with the volume of forage. This is essentially sustained-yield management of the forage.

Range management is the science and art of planning and directing the use of the range to obtain the maximum production of forage for livestock and wildlife without damaging the forest and watershed. Here again is a specialized field of work that requires additional study. The forest manager should be familiar with some of the essentials of range management because grazing can be a source of additional income to the forest owner.

In the South there are many fields and openings in the pine forests and some in the hardwoods, both of which produce varying amounts of forage. For many generations, people believed that burning accumulated dead grass and shrubs would improve spring grazing. It did, in certain situations, but sometimes it was done too often and too indiscriminately. Thus many valuable plant nutrients, such as nitrates and phosphates, were lost into the air. Damage to timber and destruction of seedlings are of course serious at best and completely destructive at worst.

In managing the southern forested areas, it is vitally important both to the trees and to the cattle that only such grazing be permitted as will support an optimum number of cattle adequately without damage to plant and tree reproduction. As in the West, the number of livestock permitted to graze should depend upon the kind and abundance of forage available—that is the *carrying capacity*. This is determined by range surveys made by range experts familiar with the species of grass and other palatable forage plants. There are, however, several rules-of-thumb that an observant forest manager can follow in detecting overgrazing. For example, if grasses are closely cropped, unpalatable weeds are abundant, brush and small trees are nipped and the lower leaves cropped off of larger shrubs and trees, erosion is found near cattle trails or streambanks, it is time to suspect overgrazing. The carrying capacity of a forest range depends largely upon the number of openings in which grasses can become established. Most well-managed forests in the South do not have much open land, but if a combination of livestock and timber production is desired, management plans can provide for open fields. Intensive livestock production will require that these fields be planted with good perennial pasture grasses for management of forage. Over large areas of open land in the South, 5 acres with good soil will supply forage for one cow or "head" for a year. Mixed forest and open land will require anywhere from 10 to 40 acres per head.

Although western forest ranges are usually in the mountains, whereas those in the South vary all the way from coastal plains to Appalachian highlands, most of the principles are very similar. Western forest ranges do not ordinarily support as many head of livestock for a given area because the forage production is lower as a result of low rainfall. Greater care must be taken against overgrazing in the West because regrowth of damaged range grasses takes a long time.

Fortunately, most of the forest range land in the West is under public control—national forests and federal grazing districts—and grazing is more closely regulated than on the private lands of the South. Range management specialists try to keep a close check on the progress of grazing and to limit livestock when overgrazing seems imminent. In some cases this has led to political pressure from livestock owners to open up the lands to more intensive grazing. Only when the public agencies have been able to resist this pressure have improved range conditions resulted.

Range Conservation Practices

A number of successful measures have increased the amount of forage on range lands and reduced possible damage from livestock. Prior to undertaking them, the range manager generally makes an estimate of the carrying capacity of the area based on an inventory and classification of the grasses according to palatability. The most important and generally used range conservation practices are as follows.

1. Fencing the tract into several *pastures* allows for rotating grazing from area to area and thus permits development of grasses until an area is ready for grazing.
2. Water impoundments, windmill pumps, stock tanks, and other sources of water can be developed at scattered points to provide adequate water in many places for small groups of animals.
3. Salt licks are placed away from water holes to keep the animals from concentrating their grazing and to distribute them.
4. Killing brush and weeds that occupy good grazing land may be accomplished by spraying chemicals and following up with a seeding of grass.
5. Large areas are also disked and reseeded to palatable grasses after the poorer grasses and brush are removed, especially areas where sagebrush, cheat grass, or other poor forage plants have moved in and replaced better grasses following overgrazing.
6. Firebreaks that are kept open by occasional disking (especially in the South) can be seeded to forage grasses and made to yield livestock feed. Grazing keeps these breaks clear so that they still serve their primary purpose.
7. Small gullies that have cut through the soil because of rapid runoff of water resulting from overgrazing can often be controlled with brush and log dams if the watersheds above them have been reseeded. Larger gullies may often require substantial engineering and earth moving; building dams to make water impoundments at the upper ends of gullies is usually quite successful.
8. Water-spreading devices of several types can be constructed to make the maximum use of flash floodwaters and thus increase forage production in the areas immediately below the water spreaders. These include diversion terraces, check dams, and contour furrows.
9. In the South, some prescribed (controlled) burning has been beneficial in eliminating certain types of unpalatable, en-

croaching vegetation. This must be executed by people completely familiar with the forest and range conditions. Burning should never be done in hardwoods and only under expert planning in pine woods.

10. Complete exclusion of livestock from overgrazed rangeland should be maintained until recovery of native grasses restores watershed porosity.

RECREATIONAL USES OF THE FOREST

Since World War II there has been an explosion in the demand for outdoor recreational facilities of all kinds. For such activities as camping, hiking, fishing, sight-seeing, skiing, canoeing, boating, and summer cabins, forest areas near lakes and rivers have widespread attraction. While the natural features attract recreational visitors, facilities for their accommodation must be provided—campgrounds, trails, access roads, parking lots, overlooks, boat landings, docks, and beach facilities for swimmers as well as administrative quarters. All of these are best located away from or outside the natural attractions.

This great increase in demand for outdoor recreation is shown in some recent figures developed by the U.S. Department of Interior.

The impact of this continuing increase in the use of outdoor recreation areas is being particularly felt in community forests and parks located near metropolitan regions. Hence the demand for facilities such as golf courses, swimming pools, playgrounds, picnic areas, and tennis courts is particularly heavy.

National and state forests and parks offer a wide variety of natural attractions to large numbers of recreational visitors both from within

	Millions of Occasions		
Activity	1972[a]	1978[a]	2000[b]
Picnicking	405	449	1022
Walking and hiking	541	624	1210
Canoeing and boating	144	170	210
Camping	211	240	328
Fishing	278	307	574
Hunting	17	20	25
Off-the-road vehicles	26	30	2

[a]Actual.

[b]Projected.

and beyond urban areas. Each site is unique, differing in topography, forest and vegetative cover, streams, rivers and lakes, and so forth, and this presents different combinations of outdoor recreational opportunities where facilities play a less important role. Here hiking trails, campgrounds, scenic overlooks, and sometimes motel accommodations to serve the public are needed.

In order to classify the kinds of outdoor recreational land uses, the Outdoor Recreational Resources Review Commission proposed the following groupings.

1. High-density recreation areas, intensively developed for mass use, such as for swimming, playing outdoor games, winter sports, and docking and servicing boats.
2. General outdoor recreation areas, substantially developed for a wide range of activities such as picnicking, boating, nature walks, trailer parks, and camping at well-developed campgrounds.
3. Natural environment areas, suitable for such traditional outdoor activities as hiking, camping, with simple facilities, hunting and fishing—all in a natural, "as is," environment and usually in combination with other resource uses.
4. Unique natural areas, of outstanding scenic splendor, natural wonder, or scientific importance, managed to permit visitors to enjoy or study the central features preserved in their natural condition.
5. Wilderness and primitive areas, with natural wild conditions undisturbed by roads and managed solely to preserve their primitive characteristics.
6. Historic and cultural sites, of local, regional, or national significance.

Such a classification system provides guidance for recreation zoning based on available resources and terrain, and on judgments as to which uses and developments are compatible and which are not. It recognizes that each area has its own individual recreation potential. Any one administrative unit, such as a park or forest, may include areas of more than one classification.

These classifications are useful to the land administrator, usually a park or forest ranger in charge of a specific unit of land, because they indicate the level of management intensity required. Management of recreational areas involves the management of human use so that people obtain the greatest benefit from their visit with the least impact on the natural terrain.

Planning for Recreational Uses

Each of these classes of recreational land uses may be designated on the land use map or indicated on an aerial photo. Symbols depicting details such as campgrounds, picnic areas, hiking trails, or ski runs should be located on the map as the next step for quick location and identification. Within recent years a further refinement in mapping natural and cultural features of the land has taken form in landscape environmental inventory maps. These inventories show interesting features such as virgin timber tracts, waterfowl marshes, abandoned mines, and points of historical value. They are particularly valuable for selecting tracts where public values deserve special efforts to preserve them.

Recreational planning has two important aspects: one is the selection of new areas for public acquisition, such as a national lakeshore, state park, or a wild and scenic river; and the other is the planning for the use of the area, particularly visitor and administrative facilities. Both require expertise of a special sort. Choosing new areas is a lengthy process that usually involves top specialists in federal and state planning agencies who draw from a long background of field experience. But planning and design of visitor facility layouts and the flow of uses are usually accomplished by people trained in landscape architecture who specialize in recreation area planning. It is important for the forest land manager to develop some knowledge and appreciation for this kind of planning in order to be able to administer the uses efficiently and in accordance with the plan.

Providing for people in forest areas requires an advance estimate of the number of people and the type of use to be expected. Because recreational uses are expected to increase in the next few years, plans and developments for facilities must be made. These estimates are usually made by the planning staff of the forestry or park administration that has access to such information as past uses and demands on similar areas, and the amount of space needed for a tent or trailer camp, picnic ground, or group use. Once these decisions are made, a recreational management plan can be developed. Preparations of plans for buildings, outdoor fireplaces, water systems or toilets, and waste disposal areas are usually handled by the staff planners. A map of the area is drawn up with the location of each of the above facilities shown on it. Designs for each type of facility—for example, fireplaces, toilets, or picnic tables—are prepared by engineering staffs. Many designs of recreational improvemnts are set forth in Wenger (1984).

Prior to actual construction of facilities, preparation of the campsites and surrounding areas involves careful work. It is essential that the attractiveness of the forested surroundings be preserved, but it is also essential that fire hazards be reduced to a minimum (a fire lane around the camp is often needed) and that dangerous dead trees be removed. Mosquito control is often needed in areas where these pests persist. The facilities that are provided should be fitted into the natural scene to reduce the need for cutting trees.

The need for campsite and trail conservation cannot be stressed too strongly. Heavy visitor use through trampling usually compacts the soil, not only causing damage to the land through loss of plant cover but encouraging soil erosion as well. Trees often die with heavy soil use above their roots. Campsite and trail rotation is one important way to reduce this kind of pressure so as to allow nature's recuperative powers to heal the damage. Revegetation can begin when a campsite or trail is moved to a new location.

Visitor concentration and overcrowding at the attractive and highly scenic areas, such as Yellowstone Falls and Yosemite Valley, is forcing an adjustment in park planning. Location of visitor facilities away from these scenic attractions will be necessary if the natural values are to be preserved. Visitors can use and view scenic wonders in this natural condition by travelling into parks in buses from overnight accommodations located outside.

Forestry and Natural Scenic Beauty

Since the surge of conservation and environmental activity in the 1960s, public attention and interest has focussed on the appearance of America's countryside. Views of hillsides ruined by billboard advertising, attractive rural roads littered with bottles and cans, and destructive logging have incited public scrutiny and criticism.

People unfamiliar with sound forestry and logging practices have generally been critical of logging. In addition to public education to show that all logging is not bad, it is important for forest managers to give attention to the esthetic aspects of their forestry measures. The desirability and even necessity of leaving timber strips along streambanks has previously been discussed. Roadside strips of uncut timber several hundred feet wide are as important as timber belts around recreational facility areas to preserve forest esthetics. The removal of fallen, defective, and some overmature trees will not harm the scenic effect of these strips if the tops and limbs left from logging slash are cut up and removed for firewood.

The following forestry practices are suggested by the Massachusetts Extension Forester.

1. Utilize all material possible from harvesting operations.
2. Perform light harvest cutting operations that leave the forest intact.
3. Favor trees of special interest as to foliage coloration, form, and branching habit.
4. Enhance esthetic qualities of the landscape by developing vistas and emphasizing desirable topographic features of the area by either creating or utilizing existing openings in the forest.
5. If you must clearcut, do it in small patches separated by standing timber.
6. Protect uncut trees, seedlings, and shrubs by careful felling, skidding, and hauling practices.
7. Replace cut trees, if needed, by (1) planting seedlings, (2) utilizing natural seedings, or (3) releasing desirable understory stems already established.
8. Protect the site against erosion by proper extractive procedures including well-planned skid and haul road layout, and adequate water drainage facilities.
9. Afterward, clean up such unsightly things as refuse, tin cans, discarded equipment, and parts.
10. Cut up logging slash and severely damaged trees to lie close to the ground after a harvesting operation.

Where clearcutting in patches is required by silvicultural prescription, areas of less than 10 acres scattered throughout the forest are the least offensive to the landscape. If edges of corner cuttings are rounded and conform to the contour of the land rather than sharp lines and corners, scenic values may actually be enhanced by variety and contrast. Likewise, forest tree plantings established to fit contours and composed of mixed species are less offensive than straight lines of the same species up and down the hill like rows of corn. Planting trees along the contour also saves moisture and reduces soil erosion.

WILDERNESS AND NATURAL AREAS

Some forest and other wild lands have been determined by the American people through congressional action as most properly suited for permanent wilderness status as part of the National Wilderness Preservation System. The Wilderness Act of 1964 and the Eastern Wilderness Act of 1975, which set up a process for establishing this system, had originally included 11.6 million acres of national forest, and 0.9 million acres of national park and wildlife refuge lands. Through review procedures provided in these acts, proposals for additional acreage have been examined by Congress. In the national forests there were 62 million acres of roadless lands that underwent scrutiny for additions to the Wilderness System through a process known as Roadless Area Review and Evaluation (RARE). A second RARE process (RARE II) was also conducted to further analyze roadless lands. These reviews have resulted in additional lands being set aside for wilderness preservation by Congress. However, there is still much concern over the fate of many acres of roadless land in the national forests.

On a smaller scale, there are now several thousand small tracts of original forest, prairie, wetland, as well as geological and archeological areas that represent unique or remnant vegetation or cultural specimen situations. These areas, seldom larger than a few hundred acres, are not widely known—for if they were, the vegetation being preserved might be trampled by a curious public.

The principal purpose of wilderness and smaller natural areas is to allow the natural interplay of biological processes and the environment with limited influence from humans. Constraints on road, trail, and other facility construction, the restriction of motorized vehicles to limit visitor mobility as well as prohibition of mining, logging, and other exploitive uses are essential safeguards to the protection of the wilderness.

The arguments for preserving some natural and wilderness areas are compelling. The wilderness areas represent the last of the frontiers. These fragments of unconquered land and water are a heritage from a past that had a great influence on our national character and, therefore, contribute greatly to our culture.Their value as habitats for endangered and threatened species of wildlife has been indicated earlier in this chapter. As the sole source of undisturbed *gene pools* of vegetative and animal life in the natural state, wilderness and natural areas fill a critical biological gap. In its recreational value as back country, wilderness offers inspiration and solitude found nowhere else on this crowded planet. But only the hardy need apply!

Concluding Observations on Multiple Use

The task of fitting forestry practices together with wildlife requirements, watershed protection, range livestock, and recreational uses cannot be easily quantified in a formula nor neatly computerized. It is largely a matter of human judgment; judgment based on a solid grasp of each of these separate but equivalent and intermingled uses of the forest. Probably the most effectively presented publication setting forth a system for reconciling the several multiple uses is a Bureau of Land Management bulletin titled, "Making Multiple Use Decisions." To assist in the study of this subject, this bulletin is reproduced in full in Appendix G.

QUESTIONS

1. Name three important uses of the forest other than timber production.
2. How does a forested watershed reduce the runoff of water?
3. How do grazing and improper logging act to increase water runoff?
4. Name four important game animals or birds that are found primarily in forested areas.
5. What are the three important things that make up a wildlife habitat?
6. Why is burning land for grazing a poor practice?
7. What damage does livestock do to a forest?
8. What is the most desirable type of forest recreational area from the user's viewpoint?
9. Why should an expansion in available recreational facilities be provided in the near future?
10. Should any recreational improvements and facilities be provided in wilderness or natural areas?
11. What is a den tree?

EXERCISES

1. Find out whether any soil conservation or watershed projects are being carried out in your area.

2. Visit with a state conservation department or with wildlife management specialists and examine several field projects that may be underway for wildlife habitat improvement.
3. Go to a state or other park area where camping facilities are provided and describe the improvements made available.
4. Determine whether grazing on forest lands in your area is damaging the forest or if it is well managed.

TWELVE

ORGANIZATION AND ADMINISTRATION OF FORESTRY PROGRAMS

All of the various activities connected with managing a forest area must be separated into units for convenient administration. Nearly all of the large forest areas, both public and private, have consistent and continuous management. Some owners of smaller forests manage their lands themselves with the help and advice of a forester, or they leave it to the foresters to manage. But because most of these forest lands are still inadequately managed, they constitute one of forestry's greatest challenges. Because the methods of handling forestry programs differ considerably by kinds of organizations, they will be described separately and in detail.

In addition to the actual management of forest lands, there are many other forestry programs directed toward forestry problems that are not necessarily connected with one or another type of ownership. Such programs as fire prevention and control, insect and disease control, administration of forest tax laws, provision for technical assistance to private owners, and many other programs cross ownership lines. Research in forestry is a major activity of the U.S. Forest Service and is becoming increasingly important in several universities and in private industry.

Forestry programs are included in two departments of the federal government: the Department of Agriculture, which has both the Forest Service and Soil Conservation Service; and the Department of Interior, which has the Bureau of Land Management, the Bureau of Indian Affairs, the Fish and Wildlife Service, and the National Park Service.

The basic laws establishing the programs administered by these agencies were detailed in Chapter 2. Many have been expanded and developed as the forestry needs of the country have increased. The organization charts in this chapter show how these bureaus are organized. On the state level, all 50 states have forestry divisions within their conservation departments or as separate agencies. (See Appendix E.) Large private holdings are usually managed by the lumber or paper company which owns them. Because most state and many large private forestry agencies are organized along lines similar to those of the Forest Service, the operational situations and functions of this large federal agency will be given in detail.

FEDERAL FOREST LANDS AND PROGRAMS

U. S. Department of Agriculture

Forest Service

Forestry programs of the federal government are centered in the Forest Service, a bureau in the Department of Agriculture (Figure 12–1). Its principal activities, which are highly decentralized, include the administration of 155 national forests and the operation of a research program centering around nine regional Forest Experiment Stations and the Forest Products Laboratory at Madison, Wisconsin. In addition, the Forest Service supervises cooperative federal–state programs dealing with forest protection, technical assistance to private owners, and various other cooperative activities with the states, private owners, and the general public. The Smokey Bear program is probably the most familiar to the public. Another important activity is the general dissemination of information on forestry and conservation.

The policy of the Forest Service has been to make the national forests serve the greatest number of people, which is consistent with proper resource management. The principle of multiple use is a primary objective. All the resources of the national forests—timber, forage, minerals, hunting and fishing privileges, recreational facilities, wilderness, and other resources—are available for public use under regulations designed to assure their long-term conservation. Because many of the forests lie in remote areas, it has been necessary to build access roads, telephone lines, radio relays, trails and portages, bridges, and ranger stations in order to make available the greatest possible forest development and utility.

Generally speaking, the objectives of national forest management may be summarized as follows.

1. Sustained production of timber supplies for both local and national uses under scientific principles of applied silviculture, including reforestation, fire protection, and other management measures, and programs to make the forests serve as demonstration areas for applied forest management.
2. Management and protection of watersheds (1) to ensure a stable flow of water for municipal and industrial use, power, and irrigation, (2) to reduce or prevent floods and siltation of rivers, and harbors, and (3) to maintain navigability of streams.
3. Continued production of palatable forage for big game and livestock through managed use of the range.
4. Preservation of the beauty and attractiveness of the forests and development of opportunities and facilities for recreation.
5. Management of wildlife habitats for optimum production of game and fish.

In addition to these objectives for the national forests, the Forest Service carries on an active forest and range research program through the regional Forest and Range Experiment Stations and project research centers.

The headquarters of the Forest Service are maintained in Washington, D. C., under the direction of the chief forester and a staff of associate and deputy chiefs. Their work is divided into five major units: administration, National Forest System programs, legislation, state and private forestry, and research. The organization chart shown in Figure 12–1 outlines the relationship of the Forest Service to the other agencies in the USDA. The most important functions of the Washington office involve direction of policy, handling relations with Congress, supervising the work of the regional offices and the ex-

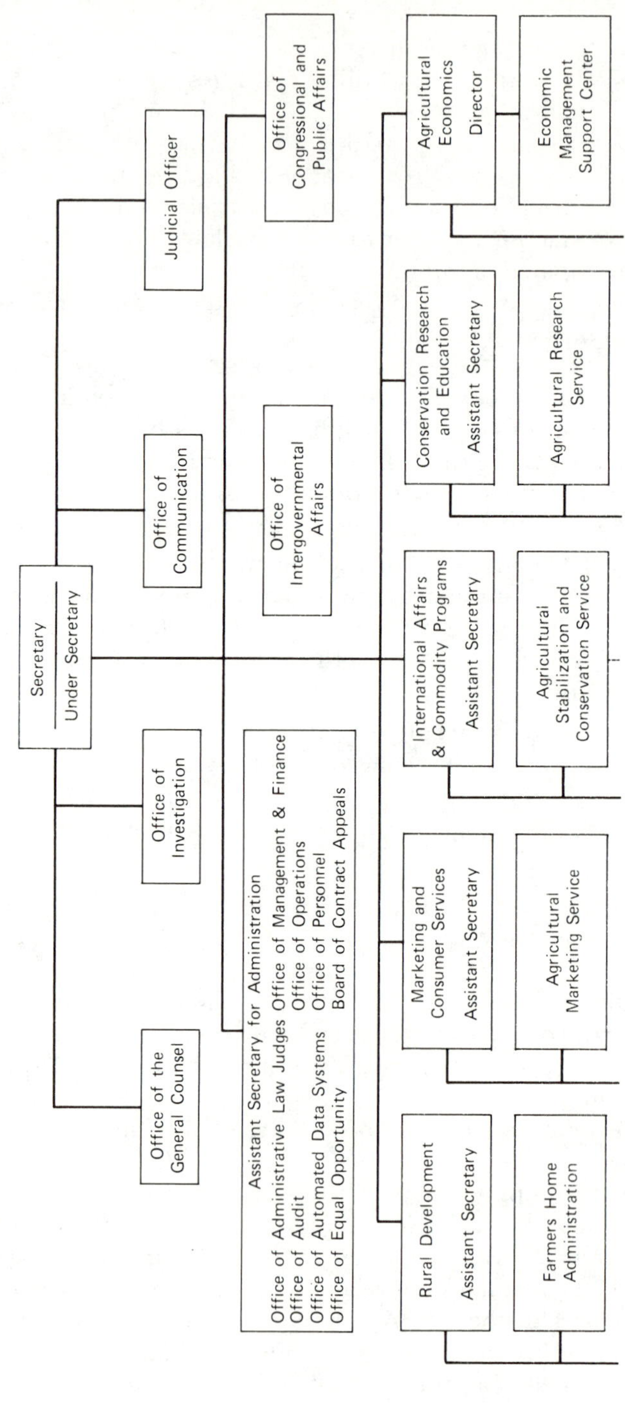
Secretary
Under Secretary
Office of the General Counsel
Office of Investigation
Office of Communication
Judicial Officer
Assistant Secretary for Administration
Office of Administrative Law Judges
Office of Audit
Office of Automated Data Systems
Office of Equal Opportunity
Office of Management & Finance
Office of Operations
Office of Personnel
Board of Contract Appeals
Office of Intergovernmental Affairs
Office of Congressional and Public Affairs
Rural Development
Assistant Secretary
Farmers Home Administration
Marketing and Consumer Services
Assistant Secretary
Agricultural Marketing Service
International Affairs & Commodity Programs
Assistant Secretary
Agricultural Stabilization and Conservation Service
Conservation Research and Education
Assistant Secretary
Agricultural Research Service
Agricultural Economics
Director
Economic Management Support Center

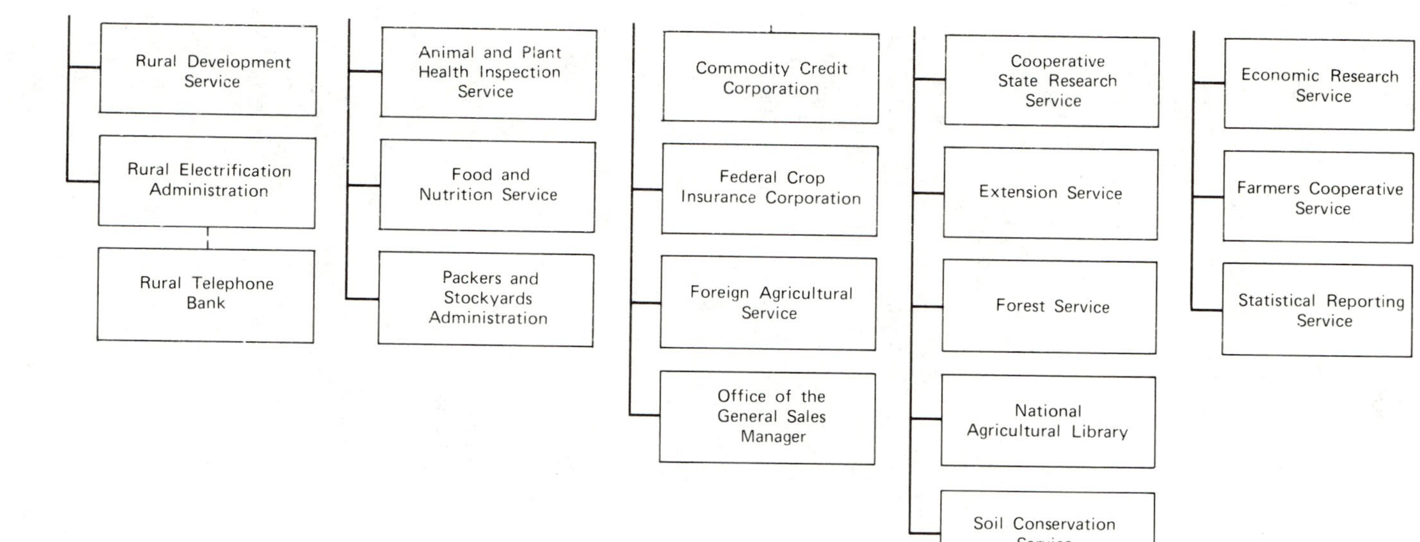

FIGURE 12–1. Organization chart of the U. S. Department of Agriculture.

periment stations, and correlating programs involving state cooperation.

In 1908 it was realized that the work of the national forests required decentralization from Washington and that many of the local problems and much of the work could be better and more efficiently administered from regional offices strategically located in the major forest regions. Since that time, the work has been divided into nine field regions (Figure 12–2).

Each national forest is operated through a forest supervisor's office located in a nearby town and is divided into a number of *ranger districts*, containing up to several hundred thousand acres each. The forest supervisor, who has responsibility for all the forestry activity in the forest, is assisted by district forest rangers with direct on-the-ground responsibility.

The district ranger is the key person in managing and protecting a forest unit. He or she makes important decisions dealing with the sale of timber, layout of roads, management of grazing lands, supervision of the protection program, outdoor recreational uses, wilderness and minerals management, and the one thousand and one other important details that go with forest administration. The district ranger usually has an assistant and a number of other trained people, as well as a seasonal labor force for reforestation after logging, fire fighting, fence repairs, road building, campground maintenance, and so forth. To help in planning and in making decisions, the district ranger relies on the staff specialists in the supervisor's and regional offices where engineering plans are drawn up, timber estimates compiled, timber sales announced, bids received on timber, equipment purchased, and accounts maintained.

The actual work in marking a timber sale, surveying a road, and checking on logging progress, including scaling of timber, is frequently handled under the ranger's supervision by a forestry technician familiar with these activities. Many of these operations are becoming increasingly complex so that training in forestry is essential. Foresters often begin their career in the Forest Service at this level, and their promotions depend to a large extent on their increased knowledge gained through additional training and field experience.

Soil Conservation Service

The Soil Conservation Service (SCS,) established in the Department of Agriculture in 1935, maintains a small forestry program directly connected with its farm planning work on the approximately 2700 Soil Conservation Districts through which it functions. Each district has a district conservationist who is assigned by the SCS to develop farm plans for soil and water conservation. Although the major part of the district conservationist's work is in planning soil conservation measures on crop and pasture land, the district conservationist makes recommendations for improvements in woodland management as well. Although technically trained people have usually been appointed to the district jobs, those with vocational agricultural experience are being increasingly called upon. Opportunities for forestry technicians are greater where forest areas are a dominant part of the district.

U. S. Department of Interior

The Department of Interior was established by Congress in 1849 to administer the territories acquired by the United States through various treaties with other nations (e.g., Louisiana Purchase), and Indian tribes. Through the passage of time, the Department of Interior's role became that of manager and developer of publicly owned natural resources—although its name still implies that it is exclusively concerned with the "interior frontier." Presidents F. D. Roosevelt, Nixon, and Carter have sought to combine natural resource functions from other departments into one politically accountable and responsible department similar to the departments of natural resources in most states, but Congress has resisted such a change. Figure 12–3 shows an organizational chart of the Interior Department as of early 1977. Should reorganization take place, the resource agencies of the USDA and the U. S. Army Corps of Engineers would be consolidated into the new department.

The Bureau of Land Management

This bureau is responsible for administration of the remaining public domain lands in the 12 western states including Alaska—a total of 170 million acres in the former and 300 million acres* in the latter. The BLM is responsible for the rectangular land survey system, original land title transfer records for the public domain, management of grazing, timber, minerals, recreation, and watershed resources on the National Resource Lands (public domain lands classified for federal retention). This agency functions through district offices that supervise use of lands, provide protection from fire, and enforce federal laws respecting them. Because the national forests in the West were created from the public domain, the BLM has only a limited forestry program. But it hires many foresters to carry out its multiple use resource management responsibilities.

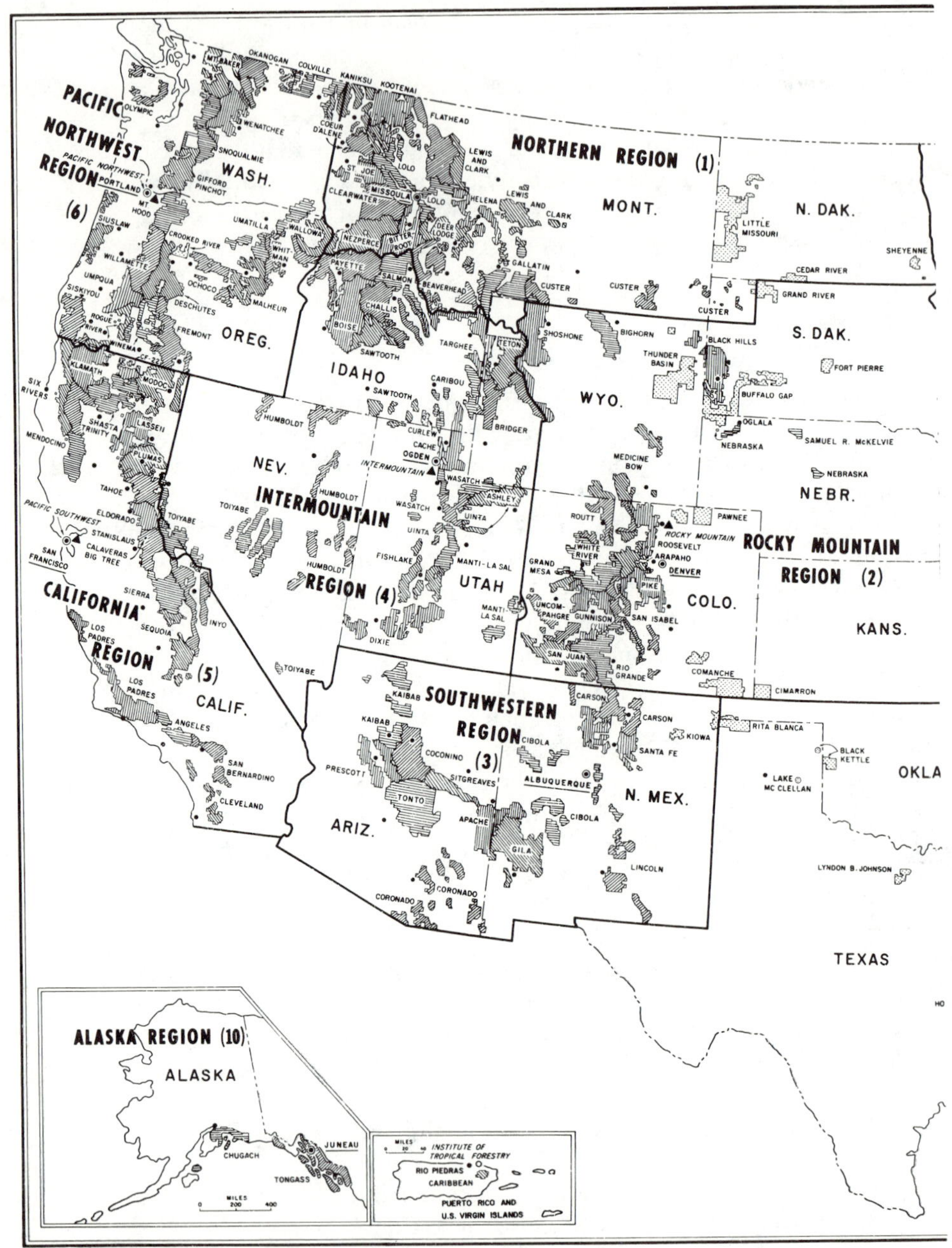

FIGURE 12–2. *Regions of the National Forest System.*

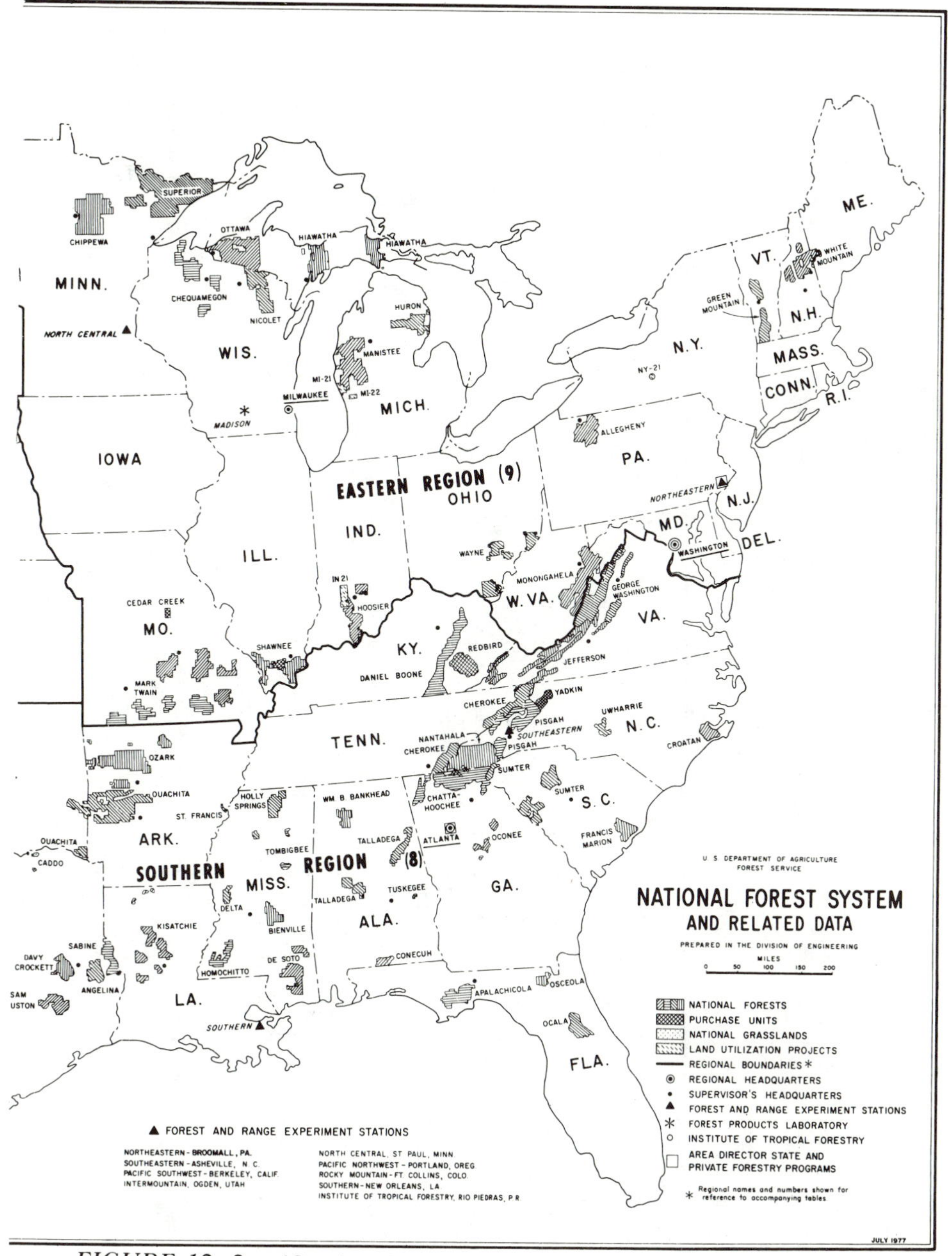

U. S. DEPARTMENT OF AGRICULTURE
FOREST SERVICE
NATIONAL FOREST SYSTEM
AND RELATED DATA
PREPARED IN THE DIVISION OF ENGINEERING
MILES
0 50 100 150 200
NATIONAL FORESTS
PURCHASE UNITS
NATIONAL GRASSLANDS
LAND UTILIZATION PROJECTS
REGIONAL BOUNDARIES *
REGIONAL HEADQUARTERS
SUPERVISOR'S HEADQUARTERS
FOREST AND RANGE EXPERIMENT STATIONS
FOREST PRODUCTS LABORATORY
INSTITUTE OF TROPICAL FORESTRY
AREA DIRECTOR STATE AND
PRIVATE FORESTRY PROGRAMS
* Regional names and numbers shown for reference to accompanying tables
▲ FOREST AND RANGE EXPERIMENT STATIONS
NORTHEASTERN - BROOMALL, PA.
SOUTHEASTERN - ASHEVILLE, N. C.
PACIFIC SOUTHWEST - BERKELEY, CALIF.
INTERMOUNTAIN, OGDEN, UTAH
NORTH CENTRAL, ST PAUL, MINN.
PACIFIC NORTHWEST - PORTLAND, OREG.
ROCKY MOUNTAIN - FT. COLLINS, COLO.
SOUTHERN - NEW ORLEANS, LA.
INSTITUTE OF TROPICAL FORESTRY, RIO PIEDRAS, P.R.
EASTERN REGION (9)
SOUTHERN REGION (8)
MINN.
WIS.
MICH.
IOWA
ILL.
IND.
OHIO
PA.
N.Y.
ME.
VT.
N.H.
MASS.
CONN.
R.I.
N.J.
DEL.
MD.
W. VA.
VA.
KY.
MO.
TENN.
N. C.
S. C.
GA.
ALA.
MISS.
ARK.
LA.
FLA.
SUPERIOR
CHIPPEWA
OTTAWA
HIAWATHA
CHEQUAMEGON
NICOLET
HURON
MANISTEE
MI-21
MI-22
MILWAUKEE
MADISON
NORTH CENTRAL
GREEN MOUNTAIN
WHITE MOUNTAIN
NY-21
ALLEGHENY
NORTHEASTERN
WASHINGTON
WAYNE
MONONGAHELA
GEORGE WASHINGTON
IN 21
HOOSIER
CEDAR CREEK
SHAWNEE
MARK TWAIN
REDBIRD
DANIEL BOONE
JEFFERSON
CHEROKEE
YADKIN
PISGAH
SOUTHEASTERN
UWHARRIE
NANTAHALA
CROATAN
SUMTER
OZARK
OUACHITA
ST. FRANCIS
HOLLY SPRINGS
WM B BANKHEAD
CHATTAHOOCHEE
ATLANTA
OCONEE
FRANCIS MARION
TOMBIGBEE
TALLADEGA
TUSKEGEE
CADDO
DELTA
KISATCHIE
BIENVILLE
SABINE
DAVY CROCKETT
ANGELINA
SAM HOUSTON
DE SOTO
HOMOCHITTO
CONECUH
APALACHICOLA
OSCEOLA
OCALA
SOUTHERN
JULY 1977

FIGURE 12–2. (Continued)

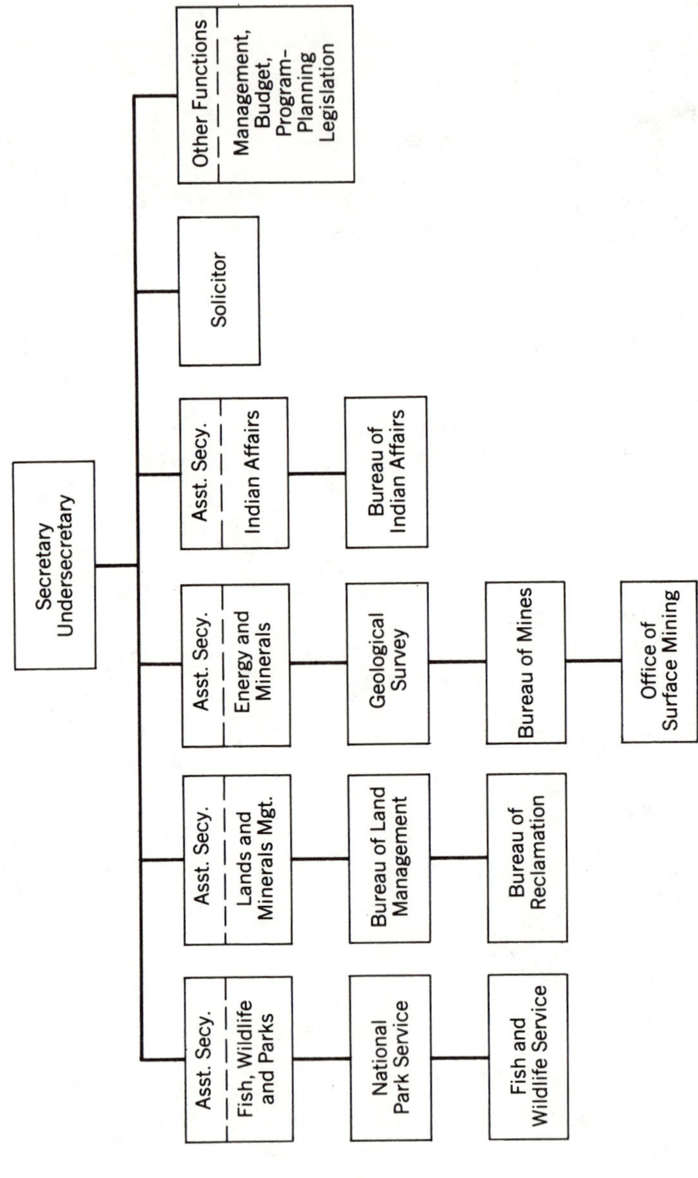

FIGURE 12–3. Organization chart of the U. S. Department of Interior (1985).

The Heritage Conservation and Recreation Service

This bureau was created in 1962 by Secretary of Interior Stewart Udall as a result of studies by the Outdoor Recreation Resources Review Commission (ORRRC). It serves as the federal focal point for coordinating, planning, and financing public recreation. It administered the federal Land and Water Conservation Fund grants to states for planning, acquisition, and development of public outdoor recreation areas and to federal agencies for acquisition of nationally significant recreation lands and waters. In addition, it was responsible for studies to preserve wild and scenic rivers and to implement the National Scenic Trails System. As the principal federal recreational resource planning agency, it is responsible for the coordination of recreational plans and programs of the federal and state land managing agencies into a nationwide outdoor recreation plan.

The Bureau of Indian Affairs (BIA)

Although concerned mainly with administration of social and economic programs of the many Indian tribes, BIA also supervises the management of natural resources on tribal lands. Forests, grazing lands, and minerals of great value are present on many indian reservations and these resources require cooperative administration between the BIA as "trust officer" and the Indian tribes that own them. Many professional and technician foresters are employed by the BIA that gives preference to people of native American ancestry.

The National Park Service

This service has charge of all national parks, monuments, and related historical sites included in the National Park System. The service carries on an active forestry program designed to protect the forests, but not to cut timber or harvest game from them, because undisturbed forests in our national parks are an essential part of these outstanding natural scenic areas. Forestry activity is largely confined to protecting the forests from fires, insects, and diseases, removal of dead and diseased trees, and some planting. Many of the national parks also have specific tracts set aside in their natural state in order that scientists will have an undisturbed outdoor laboratory of plants and animals for research purposes. In these tracts, forest management stops short of any attempt at changing the primitive and undisturbed nature of the forest. Roads are limited to those necessary for proper access to major points of attraction, and campgrounds are placed only in designated places. Management of park areas must include sufficient planning for recreational use as well as wildlife and fisheries habitat management. Basic training in forestry is of value in the handling of protection programs, but special consideration must be given to the recreational and wildlife aspects discussed previously.

The Fish and Wildlife Service

This service carries on some forestry activities on the national wildlife refuges for which it is responsible. Forestry is mostly incidental because most of these federal refuges are devoted primarily to waterfowl or the preservation of endangered and threatened species of wildlife. Forests do occupy considerable land areas in the refuges and require proper management for their best development. Consequently, in making their management plans, the refuge managers include provisions for forest protection, timber sales, reforestation, and improvement cuttings where needed. Timber sales are quite common. Generally, those in charge have sufficient background in forestry to handle such problems whenever they arise. Many forestry-trained people who start out in forestry are employed by the Fish and Wildlife Service working on wildlife management.

Forestry in Other Federal Agencies

In addition to the previously named agencies, several others carry on forestry programs or hire foresters in connection with their activities. The Tennessee Valley Authority has maintained quite an active forestry program throughout its whole area—largely devoted to assisting private owners to attain better management on their lands. The U. S. Army corps of Engineers and defense agencies hire foresters to manage reservoir lands and military reservations. Other agencies employ forestry specialists in tax matters, for forest industry statistical and research studies, and for other similar activities.

STATE FORESTRY PROGRAMS

The states operate and maintain forestry divisions either within their natural resources departments or as separate units. The responsibilities of these divisions are large and encompass a sizable group of programs, many of which were established with the encouragement of the federal government. Although close cooperation with the federal forestry programs continues, the states administer their own with a large degree of flexibility. Most important is their forest fire protection system, but they also operate tree nurseries and distribute seedlings to private owners for forest planting, administer state forests and parks in ways not unlike those of the federal agencies, and provide technical woodland management assistance programs to private owners.

The organization of the state forestry divisions is usually divided along these major lines of responsibility, under the supervision of a state forester (Figure 12–4). The state is divided into forestry districts for administration and protection purposes with a system of forest fire towers and ranger stations equipped with fire fighting tools and machinery. State forest land administration is handled by a forester-in-charge of one or more state forests with duties and assisting personnel comparable to the federal forest rangers. Technical forest management assistance to private owners is carried out, under the Cooperative Private Forestry Assistance program, by service foresters located in smaller towns in the forested areas. Usually the tree nursery program includes one or more state-operated nurseries under the

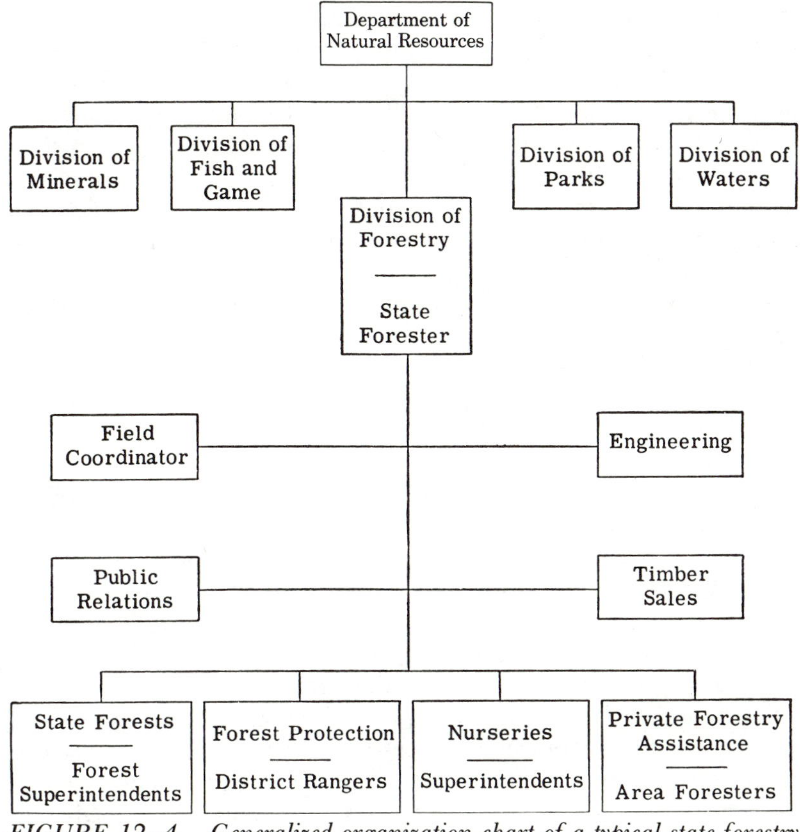

FIGURE 12–4. Generalized organization chart of a typical state forestry division.

Source: The Bureau of Land Management, U. S. Department of Interior.

supervision of technically trained foresters and a tree distribution system handled through the state forester's office.

The agricultural colleges' extension service in most states also employs extension foresters whose job it is to assist private owners through education and field demonstration in carrying out approved forestry techniques. Extension foresters also work through county agricultural agents in order to make their efforts more effective and to cover a larger area. One important job that many extension foresters are doing is to assist owners with marketing and price information; another is to demonstrate new forestry techniques at group meetings.

Employment opportunities with state forest agencies include nearly all of the jobs described in Chapter 1. The entrance requirements are usually less complex than those for entering the federal services and the opportunities for advancement are better for workers with technical training. Most states have civil service or merit systems in their forestry and conservation programs, which reward employees with ability through promotions. Many people who have started at the lower levels and who develop and broaden their knowledge through additional formal courses have reached important positions in state organizations. For example, if those who are employed as fire control assistants take the trouble to learn about other branches of the forestry program and organization and to be able to do such additional work as timber cruising and mapping or other essentials of silviculture, they will find that they can qualify for openings in the other activities of the division beyond fire control.

INDUSTRIAL FORESTRY PROGRAMS

Private companies that need wood as a raw material for their plants conduct large scale forestry programs. On the industrial forests and larger tree farms, forestry organizations with a full-time forestry staff carry out many of the activities of the public agencies heretofore described. Their major forestry work, of course, centers around timber inventories, mapping, stand improvement and planting, and supervising the logging operations on their forests. Road maintenance is important to assure access to all parts of the timberland. Although the state forest fire protection system is usually relied upon to protect private forests from fire, some companies have supplementary facilities to take care of emergency situations. One activity that industrial foresters have found to be of increasing importance has been insect and disease control to suppress outbreaks of forest-destroying infestations. Public agencies usually take the leadership, but close cooperation with private owners is essential to assure prompt action and to coordinate the control effort. In addition, many private companies are furnishing technical forestry advice and assistance to individual forest owners, including farmers, in their wood producing areas.

Employment opportunities on large private forests for trained people have been increasing by leaps and bounds, and salaries compare well or better with those of other forestry organizations. Basic training is essential to those who want to rise above the skilled labor group to a variety of types of jobs within the organization. Most of the private forestry jobs are on industrial forests.

FORESTRY SERVICES AVAILABLE FOR SMALL PRIVATE FOREST LANDS

Because most owners of small tracts of forest land do not have enough timber to warrant hiring full-time foresters, forestry programs have been developed to assist them in undertaking sound management practices. They need forestry advice and service at nearly every stage: planting, stand improvement, marking mature timber for harvesting, marketing standing timber or cut products, and mapping and estimating timber volumes. To take care of this need, both private and public facilities are available.

Private forestry assistance programs include the services available through private consulting foresters and those services that are furnished by the foresters of the larger forest industries and their trade associations in many parts of the country. Consultants are more often employed by owners who have several hundred or more acres of woodland and who are anxious to apply forestry measures that will yield good returns for the cost of the service. Mention has already been made of the services that industrial foresters will give to landowners located within the areas served by the mills. Owners are not ordinarily required to market their products through the company performing the service, but it is usually more convenient to do so. In addition, a number of services are available locally through some of the industry-sponsored or other groups, including Trees for Tomorrow at Eagle River, Wisconsin; the Southern Pulpwood Conservation Association and Forest Farmers Cooperative at Atlanta, Georgia; and the Industrial Forestry Association in Portland, Oregon. The American Forest Institute (AFI), in Washington, D. C., acts informally as a coordinating group and is available to tell forest owners where to look for advice. The AFI is the sponsor of the national Tree Farm movement, which includes more than 35,000 forest properties covering over 70 million acres of private forest land.

A number of publicly sponsored forestry assistance programs have developed through the years. Probably the most widespread is the Private Forest Management Assistance program, a joint federal—state effort. Area cooperative foresters, called *service foresters, farm foresters, county foresters*, or *local foresters*, who work under the state forester and serve a group of counties, are available in most forested states. Although their work is not restricted to small owners, much of their effort is devoted to helping such owners by making preliminary examinations of their lands and by giving advice and assistance in measuring and marketing the tree crop. On larger holdings, this work is frequently followed up by private consulting or industrial foresters. Also available to private owners are the services of the extension forester who, as we have seen, coordinates the forestry advisory work of the county agricultural agents. Extension foresters have taken the lead in bringing new forestry methods to landowners through group meetings and they have provided invaluable market and price information. In order to encourage private owners to carry out sound forestry measures, the Agricultural Conservation Program provides funds for cost sharing in timber stand improvement and tree planting projects. Insect and disease control measures are also available cooperatively to private owners under programs supervised by the state forester's office.

Table 12–1 sets forth in summary form the programs available to assist private forest owners and the means of finding out about them. Vocationally trained forest managers are finding opportunities opening up in both private and public programs as assistants to the technical foresters in charge. Appendix E lists forestry organizations employing technically trained individuals.

RESEARCH—THE SCIENTIFIC RIGHT ARM OF FORESTRY

Americans have become accustomed to the many new products that scientists have developed for our use. In fact, too many people think of science as a field that exists simply to develop new gadgets or chemicals. Actually, scientific effort is a system of disciplined thought that brings together all the knowledge developed on the problem at hand in order to learn more about it. Scientists obtain new knowledge by controlled experiments in which they test new ideas. Sometimes new inventions come from applied science; sometimes new, basic knowledge is gained before any concrete results may be foreseen. Sometimes no answer results from scientific effort, except to learn the possible limitations. But this scientific effort often leads to and underlies the discovery of new scientific truths.

A lot that is new in forestry has developed from scientific effort: new methods for controlling brush and insects, new techniques for estimating and mapping timber, new types of logging machinery, mechanical equipment for fighting forest fires, and many other things. We credit research with much of the knowledge we have for managing each timber type. New methods are continually being developed that are more efficient than the old methods, so we must always keep an open mind—read, study, observe, and learn.

Most of the new developments in timber growing come from the research of forest experiment stations of the U.S. Forest Service and from university and state research. The McIntyre–Stennis Act passed by Congress in 1962 has provided federal assistance to state university research and has proven to be a strong stimulus. Research in the development of new wood products and better methods in processing all products has been widespread. In addition to the Forest Products Laboratory at Madison, Wisconsin, and the Institute of Paper Chemistry, a number of universities and industries are making important contributions in the wood-utilization field. Several universities and many companies support research laboratories or sponsor special research projects done by others.

Research as an Element in Future Forestry Progress

The complex nature of producing, protecting, and utilizing the nation's basic forest resources—timber, soil and water, forage, wildlife and fish habitats, and recreation areas—emphasizes the need for a strong supporting research program. The steady and rapid increase in the need for resources and services from the forests and the growing pressures and conflicts in use cannot be met and solved without reliable information produced by systematic study. The current and anticipated changes in forest resource use are very great, as the following summarization shows.

The estimated 250 million people in the United States in the year 2000 will require substantially more timber than is now being produced.

Forest fires, insects, diseases, and other destructive agents continue to take a heavy toll of forest growth. They constitute a serious drain on timber resources and growth potential. The spread of newly discovered destructive agents are a serious threat to expanding tree planting activities and intensified forest management programs.

Forest recreational use is climbing rapidly. The 200 million annual visitors to national forests represent only part of the current use of

TABLE 12–1 FORESTRY PROGRAMS TO ASSIST PRIVATE OWNERS

	Publicly Sponsored[a]						*Privately Sponsored*	
Program or Facility	Nursery stock for tree planting	State–Federal cooperative management assistance	Soil conservation districts	Agricultural conservation program	Cooperative insect and disease control programs	Extension foresters	Forest industry sponsored programs[b]	Consulting foresters
Type of ownership serviced	Public and private	Farmers and other individual landowners	All landowners in district	Farmers and small forest owners	All landowners	All landowners	Farmers and forest landowners	All landowners
Purpose	Production and distribution of tree planting stock for forests and windbreaks, Christmas tree stock	Provide technical service to smaller landowners and wood processors	Land use planning service to farmers and other landowners	Direct payment to small forest owners for part of cost of tree planting, stand improvement, etc.	Provide for control measures against outbreaks of insects and diseases	Assist county agents and local forestry groups to disseminate latest forestry techniques	Provide technical service to landowners in cruising, marking, planting, marketing, etc.	Provide technical service to landowners on all phases of forestry

Cost of service	Usually at cost	Small per-acre fee or free for service	Service usually available at no cost	Payment rates based on cost of practice	On cost-sharing or other basis	No cost to owners	Usually at no cost	Service charges on fee basis
To obtain further information, write	State forester in your state capital	State forester or U.S. Forest Service, Washington, D.C.	Soil Conservation Service in your county seat	USDA Agricultural Conservation Program Committee in your county seat	State forester in state capital (see Appendix E)	Extension forester at the agricultural college in your state	American Forest Institute, Washington, D.C.	Society of American Foresters, Washington, D.C.

[a]Includes Tree Farm and Tree Farm Family programs, Trees for Tomorrow program in Wisconsin, and programs of local forest industries.

[b]In addition, the Farmers Home Administration and the Federal Land Banks make credit available to forest owners for both long- and short-term loans.

all forest lands, conservatively expected to increase substantially by the year 2000.

The country's 380 million acres of grazed range, more than one-fourth forested and one-half intermingled with forests, support about one-half of our beef cattle and more than three-fourths of our sheep for at least 6 months of the year. Many of these grazing lands are vital watershed areas as well.

Forests and related rangelands provide the main habitat for 10 million big-game animals and countless other forms of wildlife. Thousands of miles of forest streams provide habitat for fish. Hunters and fishers are increasing in numbers and adding to the demands on fish and wildlife resources.

The need for water is projected to increase from the 1980 consumption of 450 billion gallons per day to 600 billion gallons per day by the year 2000. Since more than half of the nation's streamflow originates on forest lands, the future protection and management of these watersheds to maintain and increase good quality water supplies is an absolute necessity.

The expanding needs of the nation's future economy can best be met with a rich and abundant natural resources base. Wood, the most versatile of raw materials, occupies a key place in providing the needed structural materials, fiber, extractives, and chemicals. But improved and more efficient utilization of forest products must be achieved in the face of a general decrease in the quality and size of timber trees and stiffer competition from substitute materials.

Needs for all forest and range resources are growing rapidly. These pressures against the forest resource base give sharp emphasis to conflicts in use that are occurring now and could greatly increase in the future. They stress the need for harmonious management of forest and range lands to reap the maximum benefits under the principles of multiple use.

FOREST AND RANGE MANAGEMENT RESEARCH PROGRAMS

The basic renewable natural resources of the forest and ranges on which the nation will rely to an increasing extent in the years to come are timber, soil and water, forage, wildlife and fish habitats, and recreation areas. Their greatly intensified development is necessary during the next few years to meet both short- and long-term objectives. This will require a substantial increase in research to support and guide the accelerated resource production and management programs.

Timber

The overriding objectives of timber management research will be to provide the improved forest trees and the intensive cultural practices needed to double the nation's production of wood and related tree products by the year 2000. There are more than 130 commercially important forest tree species in the United States, each differing in its quality and product value and each varying in the requirements for crop production. Natural forests, moreover, are usually made up of mixtures of species and have strong responses to and interactions with environmental changes.

The accomplishment of timber management research objectives will require increased emphasis on the fundamentals of genetics, growth, and other vital life processes of the tree itself—areas of study that have heretofore been largely neglected. Also required will be expanded efforts to provide answers to many practical operating problems to increase the efficiency of establishing, growing, and harvesting of timber on a sustained-yield basis under a wide variety of conditions.

The research proposed, emphasizing both basic and applied aspects, will

1. Accelerate, through work in forest genetics, the production of trees superior in growth rate, wood quality, resistance to insects and diseases, and other special qualities; for use in planting programs on public and private forest lands.
2. Develop new cultural practices to increase the production of high-quality seed through establishment and management of seed orchards; better methods of harvesting, storing, and processing seed; and more efficient and faster planting practices, including direct seeding with aircraft. It must intensify plantation management research.
3. Find less costly, environmentally safe, and more effective methods for converting brushfields and other low-value vegetation on potential timber sites to profitable timber stands.
4. Improve the techniques for stand culture, such as weeding to control composition, thinning to regulate spacing and growth rate, pruning to improve quality, and other practices to increase the health, vigor, and quality of the forest. It must especially emphasize methods suitable for use by the owners of small forest properties.
5. Perfect methods for correcting soil deficiencies or improving the productive capacity of forest soils through use of soil fertilizers and other measures—such as silvicultural control

to favor soil-improving tree species that promote the decomposition of forest humus.

6. Find ways to control animal damage to tree crops, including loss of seed and newly planted seedlings to birds and rodents and loss of older trees to porcupines, bears, and browsing animals.
7. Develop better timber harvesting systems to maintain productive amounts of growing timber in logged areas for sustained yield and to ensure natural regeneration of preferred timber species.
8. Improve volume and yield tables, rotation age data, and other information for regulating timber growing-stock densities in managed forests, including methods to estimate growth rate, yield, allowable cut, and quality of forests as affected by environmental and silvicultural treatment.

Forest Soil and Water

The basis for effective and efficient watershed management practices is an understanding of the fundamental relationships involving soil, climate, vegetation, and water. These factors and their interactions are complex and vary over the wide span of forest and related range lands. A more complete understanding of these environmental relationships is required to speed the development of applicable techniques and measures to ensure good protection and management of the vital watersheds of the national forests and grasslands and other forest and range lands.

The research proposed will include

1. Studying soil erosion processes as related to chemical, physical, and biotic characteristics of soils, and developing effective and efficient measures to stabilize eroding slopes.
2. Developing better information and guides for logging and road location, construction, and maintenance under various soil and topographic conditions to prevent accelerated erosion and sedimentation.
3. Studying snow deposition, melt, evaporation, and metamorphism as related to possible alterations of forest types and timber harvest patterns to increase water yields or prolong stream flow into the summer.

4. For wetland forest areas, developing methods for control of water to increase forest regeneration and growth, giving attention to the basic hydrologic relations involved.
5. Improving the use of forest soil surveys in land management planning and action programs.

Wildlife and Fish Habitats

The consumptive and nonconsumptive use of wildlife and fish resources is being continually increased by a growing number of outdoor recreationists. Serious conflicts have developed between wildlife habitat needs and the demands for production of water, timber, and forage for livestock. Continued research will help determine the food and cover requirements of various wildlife species. Hopefully, it will point out the way forest and related range lands could be managed and improved to meet the increased requirements for forest resources while supporting maximum wildlife and fish populations.

Continued research will help to

1. Determine the wildlife populations that can be supported by the various vegetation types; develop practices that improve wildlife distribution and allow more uniform and efficient utilization of available forage and cover.
2. Develop methods for improving depleted and naturally unproductive big-game habitats by seeding and planting browse, controlling undesirable vegetation, manipulating desirable plant cover, or other measures to alter or regulate the environment.
3. Work out ways to improve wildlife habitat through modified timber cutting and stand improvement practices so that wildlife production will be encouraged, while watershed values are maintained or enhanced.
4. Devise techniques of seeding and planting to create improved habitat for small upland game in forest openings and permanently cleared powerline and pipeline rights-of way.
5. Accelerate work on problems of improving fish habitat and food supplies by regulating shade and water temperatures through management of streamside vegetation, by stabilization of channels, and other measures.

Forest Recreation

Research on forest recreation problems is basic to the development of sound administrative policies and the formulation of programs to meet skyrocketing future recreational needs on public forests and private forest lands. The research planned gives emphasis to national forest problems, but the problems of other forest lands will not be neglected. Hence, research results are expected to have broad application to both public and private forest lands.

Examples of the research needs will be in

1. Determining the most efficient physical layouts for forest campgrounds and other recreational installations to provide for optimum use and recreational enjoyment with minimum adverse effects on the forest environment.
2. Determining ways of administering forest recreation business efficiently and at minimum cost. This will include the development, maintenance, and operation of recreation areas and the use of self-help devices and other procedures for reducing litter cleanup and similar maintenance costs on mass recreation areas.
3. Developing guides for measuring recreational carrying capacity of various forest types based on water, soil, and vegetation conditions, and users' sense of satisfaction.
4. Obtaining information needed to plan and administer the special use of wilderness, including data on the use wilderness areas receive—for example, what kind and how much, when it occurs, and how it is distributed. Defining the key features of wilderness environment as a basis of inventory, evaluation, and allocation of resources as wilderness.
5. Determining how timber harvesting can be modified to embrace forest recreation, with particular attention to road, stream, trail, and lakeside zones, and commercial stands of old-growth timber.
6. Developing biologically sound measures to rehabilitate recreational areas depleted by overuse.

FOREST PROTECTION RESEARCH

Some of the possibilities for greatest gains in extending the supply of forest resources and maintaining forests and ranges at highly productive levels lie in the prevention and control of fire, insects, and disease. Acceptable progress will require strong fundamental research programs to establish the basis for new methods of attack. Destructive forces such as fire, insects, and diseases do not halt at property lines and, hence, are of direct concern to all types of forest-land owners.

Forest Fire

Reducing the risk of forest fires to encourage profitable long-term investment in intensive forestry is a major objective for organized research. Over a number of years, 90 percent of the costs and damages suffered from fires has resulted from less than 5 percent of the total number of fires. Yet we lack the knowledge that will enable the fire-control specialist to identify the potential runaway fire early in its course. Because the heaviest losses occur from unpredictable and erratic fire behavior, scientists must look deeply into the fundamentals of the combustion process, as influenced by an ever-changing environment, to understand runaway fires for their prevention and control. Moreover, federal, state, and local fire control agencies have to overcome many problems in preventing and suppressing fires. These deal with improving aerial fire attack, more effective planning for use of forces and facilities, and techniques and programs for reducing the number of fires caused by humans.

The forest fire research proposed will

1. For each important forest region, improve methods of measuring and rating fluctuating forest fire danger through studies of microclimate and the integration of these systems into a national fire danger rating procedure.
2. Improve fire control systems and organization through operations research techniques, leading to more efficient, faster, and safer fire suppression.
3. Develop new and more effective systems of aerial fire control, including the improvement of chemicals to retard and extinguish fires and devise better methods of application.
4. Expand knowledge relating to the prevention of the fires people cause and effective methods of minimizing careless, thoughtless, or malicious fire-starting activities of humans.
5. Intensify basic research on atmospheric factors leading to the formation of fire-starting lightning storms and develop methods for reducing the lightning potential by cloud seeding or other means.
6. Improve the techniques for using fire effectively and safely as a silvicultural or a hazard-reduction device to eliminate unwanted vegetation, litter, or accumulations of logging slash.

Forest Insects

Although provisional measures of direct chemical control are available for suppressing outbreaks of many forest insects, the greatest promise for the future lies in breakthroughs in preventive control through the use of biological control factors or in improved forest management measures. Accelerated research on the use of insect enemies or on the utilization of radiation techniques to control insect reproduction cycles, offers great promise. Many practical questions also need continuing research attention to provide for modern solutions to special insect problems. Of particular concern are problems that arise from sudden increases in endemic populations of pests in areas where forest management is most advanced and where investments are highest. In such instances, strong programs of basic research on insect life histories, their biology and physiology, and relations of insect populations to environments are extremely important to future control.

The balanced program of proposed investigation will include

1. Research on parasites, predators, and diseases of insects that damage forests and ranges to develop techniques to control new epidemics.
2. Intensified research on factors responsible for insect outbreaks and development of silvicultural practices designed to prevent outbreaks.
3. Research to develop safer and more effective and economical chemicals for direct control of Dutch elm disease.
4. Increased understanding of insects that damage wood by boring into the trunks of living trees or attack and destroy wood products used in structures or for other purposes; and development of improved methods for preventing or controlling damage caused by these insects.
5. Accelerated research on the physiology of the most destructive forest insects with emphasis on nutrition, genetics, and the development of sterilization techniques.
6. Expansion of knowledge concerning prevention or control of destructive populations of forest insects through the acceleration of fundamental studies of insect habits and behavior and of environmental factors affecting insect abundance.

Forest Diseases

Before effective measures can be devised to substantially reduce the annual loss of billions of board feet of sawtimber from diseases, the nature and extent of this damage needs much more intensive study. Of special concern are the mounting problems caused by the introduction of new diseases or the sudden flare-up of previously innocuous ones that are favored by more intensive management practices—such as one-species plantation culture, thinning, and pruning. These problems are costly to cope with and they cannot be quickly solved without more basic information on the identity and life processes of pathogens, which can be obtained only through study of their taxonomy, genetics, physiology, and ecology. Similarly, there is need for a great deal more knowledge of the toxic principles associated with the damage caused by noninfectious diseases due, for example, to air pollution, severe weather, or unfavorable soil conditions. Control measures utilizing direct chemical, biological, or indirect silvicultural approaches must be developed. Once control measures are applied, continuing study is needed to evaluate their effectiveness under a variety of conditions and to better adapt and adjust them to meet many different situations. The following are the broad areas of research in forest pathology.

1. Create an understanding of relationships between tree roots and microorganisms in various soils to develop preventive and control methods for *annosus* root rot of southern pines and *poria* root rot of Douglas-fir.
2. Select and breed trees genetically resistant to epidemic diseases such as fusiform rust and little-leaf of southern pines, blister rust of white pines, dwarf mistletoes on western conifers, and heart rots of all important species.
3. Determine the physiological and biochemical action of systemic antibiotic compounds for the direct control of forest diseases such as the rusts and dwarf mistletoes of conifers, stem cankers of hardwood, and oak wilt.
4. Determine the toxic components in noxious industrial fumes and acid rain and how they interfere with normal tree growth and health.

FOREST PRODUCTS AND ENGINEERING RESEARCH

A strong program of basic and applied research on forest products utilization problems is vital to achievement of the nation's future timber production and utilization objectives for three main reasons.

1. Ways must be found to remove and utilize—at reasonable cost—large volumes of poor-quality timber that now occupy extensive and valuable growing space.
2. Logging and mill residues and bark and wood extractives, now wasted or little used, must be used more extensively to increase processing efficiency and the income from forest products.
3. Ways must be found to realize the full potential of wood as a versatile raw material base for industries that will expand markets for timber and create industrial employment opportunities, especially in rural areas.

Much valuable research has been done on forest products to the move toward increased utilization. However, many important problems need more intensive study. Research to utilize wood in unmodified forms through better engineering design and fabrication techniques will contribute to increased utility. Basic studies of how wood substance may be modified and converted into new or improved fiber and chemical products also hold great promise.

The engineering aspects of establishing forests, tending them, and harvesting crops systematically and with the benefits of mechanization have received far too little research effort up to the present. Future forest management efforts must be well engineered and appropriately mechanized to keep costs at acceptably low levels.

FOREST RESOURCE ECONOMICS AND MARKETING RESEARCH

At every step in the complex process of producing, protecting, and utilizing forest resources, the landowner or manager must consider the costs and economic advantages of alternate methods of organizing and operating resource programs. Administrators of public forests must develop economically sound management policies. They must have a sound basis for selecting alternative combinations of resource uses that are necessarily based on sound biological principles, but also on favorable economic returns. Industrial foresters must base their recommendations and practices on cost and return determinations within the framework of company policies and objectives. The 4.5 million farmers, business executives, professional people, and other occupational groups who own in small parcels 53 percent of the nation's commercial forest land make decisions on timber growing that are influenced to a large degree by economic considerations. Thus, a comprehensive program of forest resource data collection and analysis and of research on the economics of production, harvesting, and the processing and marketing of forest products occupies a key place in future forest development.

Forest Economics

Research in forest economics will have as one of its main objectives the determination of the costs and returns that may be expected from timber growing and harvesting activities. Another aim will be to develop concepts and principles for economic evaluation of combinations of forest land uses and guides for decisions on coordinated management of timber production, grazing, recreation, wildlife, and water uses. The problems of the small owner will receive special emphasis.

Projects that illustrate the research needs are

1. Determining the opportunities for profitable timber growing for different combinations of site, forest type, class of ownership, and market location, and the potential returns from investments in planting, thinning, pruning, or other cultural measures.
2. Developing procedures and guides for evaluation of multiple uses of forest lands for timber, water, recreation, forage, and wildlife and fish habitats, to be aimed especially at optimum use and management of the national forests and other public forest lands.
3. Evaluating opportunities and methods for profitable combination of timber growing, recreation, and other uses of small forest ownerships.
4. Providing criteria for evaluating relative benefits from capital investments in forest development and road construction in the national forests and private holdings, and for investments of private capital in industrial facilities for timber production.
5. Evaluating forestry programs for small ownerships aimed at improving forestry practices on the major part of the nation's forest land that is in such holdings, including pilot area studies of owner associations and other devices for stimulating timber production.
6. Developing and evaluating more efficient arrangements for harvesting and marketing timber crops produced by small

ownerships. These embrace various forms of leases, management and marketing cooperatives, price and market reports, and promising modifications of marketing practices, which will be pilot tested.

7. Determining possibilities for increasing efficiency in the processing and marketing of lumber and other wood products, with the aim of reducing costs and improving the competitive position of timber products.
8. Evaluating potential markets for wood products and opportunities for new or expanded forest industries, particularly in areas needing economic development and relief from chronic underemployment.

QUESTIONS

1. What is the largest federal forestry agency and in which department is it located?
2. Give the names of three other federal agencies employing forestry-trained workers.
3. Name at least two important forestry activities of state forestry agencies.
4. Give two important duties of forestry-trained people on private company forestry operations.
5. Name two programs where a private owner of a small tract of forest land can get technical assistance.
6. What does research contribute to the practice of forestry?
7. Give the name and address of the state forestry agency in your state.
8. Name two industry-sponsored forestry associations.
9. Name the principal centers engaged in forestry research.
10. In your own words, describe the purpose of scientific research.
11. Why is forest economics research needed for small private forestry operations?

EXERCISES

1. Obtain the name of your state forester and the nearest local forester employed by the state.

2. List the local conservation agencies operating in your area and the names and titles of the people in charge of each.
3. Find out how many tree farms are in your county.
4. Find out how many private owners are using technical or other assistance programs.
5. Visit the nearest forestry research activity in your area and describe two research projects in process, including the problem to be solved.
6. Describe two proposed research studies and tell how they will contribute to the solution of forestry problems.

APPENDIX A

Forest Terminology

Access road A road built into isolated stands of commercial timber so they can be reached by loggers, fire fighters, and others.

Acid Rain Rain and other precipitation that is abnormally acidic due to atmospheric reactions involving oxides of sulfur and nitrogen produced by the combustion of fossil fuels.

Acre A unit of land measurement, 43,560 sq. ft, 10 square chains, or a square 208.7 ft on each side.

Alidade An instrument used in fire towers to locate forest fires. The alidade is equipped with sights for determining direction of fire.

All-aged Applied to a stand in which, theoretically, trees of all ages up to and including those of the felling age are found. See also *even-aged* and *uneven-aged.*

Allowable cut The volume of timber that may be cut from a forest under optimum sustained-yield management.

Annual ring A ring of wood put on each year by a growing tree; that is, the line indicating the growth for the period of one year. From the annual rings the age of the tree may be determined.

Aphid A plant louse, a very small insect that lives on plants.

Arboriculture The science and art of growing trees, especially as ornamental or shade trees.

Aspect The direction toward which a slope faces; exposure.

Back fire A fire intentionally set along the inner edge of a control line located ahead of an advancing fire. The back fire is set against the fire to be fought to exhaust the fuel, so that when the two fires meet, both go out.

Bacteria Very tiny living plants, some of which cause diseases and others of which are useful.

Barber chair In logger's slang, a stump on which is left standing a slab that splintered off the tree as it fell. Generally it indicates careless felling.

Bearing (of a line) The direction or course of a line in relation to the cardinal points of the compass.

Board foot (b.f.) The volume of wood contained in an area with outside dimensions of 12 × 12 × 1 in.

Blaze A mark made on the trunk of a standing tree by painting or chipping off a spot of bark with an ax. It is used to indicate a trail, boundary, location for a road, trees to be cut, and so on.

Board measure Signifying measurement in board foot or feet.

Bole The stem or trunk of a tree, usually the lower, useable or merchantable portion of the tree trunk.

Bolts Small logs or sections of larger logs that have been split. A bolt is usually less than 4½ ft long.

Broadleaf A tree with two cotyledons, or seed leaves; it usually is deciduous, that is, it sheds all its leaves annually. The broadleaved trees, such as maple and oak, have relatively broad, flat leaves, as contrasted with the conifers, such as pines, which have narrow leaves, or needles.

Buck As used in forestry: to saw felled trees into logs or bolts.

Burl A hard, woody growth on a tree trunk or on roots, more or less rounded in form. It is usually the result of entwined growth of a cluster of buds. In lumber, a burl produces a distorted and unusual (but often attractive) grain.

Burning, prescribed Burning carried out under the direct supervision of crews especially trained in the methods of when, where, and how fire can be used beneficially to improve timber management.

Butt Base of tree or lower end of log.

Caliper (or calipers), tree An instrument used to measure diameters of trees or logs. It consists of a graduated rule with two arms; one fixed at right angles to one end of the rule, the other sliding parallel to the fixed arm.

Cambium A laterally disposed sheath of generative tissues usually found between the xylem and phloem. It gives rise to secondary xylem (wood) and phloem, a part of the inner bark.

Capacity, grazing In range management, the ability of a range unit, exclusive of severe drought years, to give adequate support to a constant number of livestock for a stated period each year without deteriorating the land because of grazing or other proper land use; expressed in number of livestock per acre of given kinds, or in number of acres per specified animals.

Catface A scar on the surface of a log, generally elliptical in shape, resulting from wounds that have not healed over; also a fire scar at the base of a tree.

Cells All plant life is made up of living cells that are microscopic units containing protoplasmic substances and a nucleus and separated by cell walls consisting of cellulose.

Cellulose A fibrous substance made up of carbohydrates (carbon, hydrogen, and oxygen) that forms the cell walls of plants. Common examples of cellulose are cotton fibers and paper made up of tiny matted wood fibers.

Check A lengthwise separation of the wood that usually extends across the rings of annual growth, commonly resulting from stresses set up in wood during seasoning.

Chlorophyll The green coloring matter in plants necessary for photosynthesis.

Class, age One of the intervals into which the range of ages of vegetation is divided for classification and use.

Clear cutting A method of cutting that removes all merchantable trees on the area in one cut.

Climax A plant community that does not change unless there is a change in conditions (e.g., from climate, logging, or fire). It is the culminating stage in natural plant succession. The plants in a climax community are favored by the environment that they themselves create, and so are in balance with it.

Clones A group of living organisms that have identical genetic composition.

Closed crown A full, close, forest canopy that excludes sunlight.

Conifer A tree belonging to the order *Coniferales* usually evergreen, with cones and needle-shaped leaves, and producing wood known commercially as softwood.

Conk A definite, individual, woody, spore-bearing fruiting body of a wood-destroying fungus, which projects beyond the bark.

Contour planting Planting so that the rows run around the hill or slope on the same level, rather than up and down.

Commercial forest land Land producing or capable of producing crops of timber and not withdrawn from use.

Cord A volume measure of stacked wood. A standard cord is 4 × 4 × 8 ft or 128 cu. ft of space. A long cord (unit) contains 160 cu. ft of space and is 4 × 5 × 8 ft. Since round wood cannot be stacked to give solid volume, actual wood volume varies between 70 and 90 cu. ft per cord.

Corduroy road A road built of logs or poles laid side by side across the roadway, usually in low or swampy places.

Core A slender cylinder of wood taken from a tree by an increment borer. Growth rings are counted on such cores to determine rate of tree growth.

Cotyledon The first leaves of the embryo plant in a seed. In corn and bean seeds the cotyledons are thickened with a store of food for the young plant.

Crop trees Trees that are designated to make up the final or rotation timber crop.

Crosshaul A method of loading log-transportation vehicles. One end of a line is passed over the load, around the log to be loaded, and made fast to the load. Power applied to the other end of the line imparts a rolling motion to the log.

Crown The upper part of a tree, including the branches with their foliage.

Crown fire A forest fire that extends to and sweeps along in the tops and branches of trees.

Cruise A survey of forest lands to locate and estimate volumes and grades of standing timber; also, the estimate obtained in such a survey. (*Scaling* is the measurement of the volumes of individual logs after the trees have been felled.)

Cull A tree or log of merchantable size rendered unmerchantable because of poor form, limbyness, rot, or other defects.

Cut The yield, during a specified period, of products that are cut, as of grain, timber, or, in sawmilling lumber.

Cutting, improvement A cutting made in a stand past the sapling stage for the purpose of improving its composition and character by removing trees of less desirable species, form, and condition in the main crown canopy.

Cycle, cutting The planned interval between major felling operation in the same stand.

dbh Diameter (of a tree) at breast height, or 4½ ft above the ground.

Deciduous A term applied to trees that lose their leaves in the fall.

Deck, log A pile of logs or a rollway.

Defect Any irregularity or imperfection in a tree, log, piece product, or lumber that reduces the volume of sound wood or lowers its durability, strength, or utility value.

Defoliation Loss of a tree's leaves by insects, disease, or other causes.

Dendrometer An instrument for measuring tree diameter growth.

Density, crown The compactness of the crown cover of the forest, dependent upon (1) the distance apart and (2) the compactness of the individual crowns. A loose term combining the meanings of crown closure and shade density.

Dibble A tool used in planting tree seedlings.

Dominant trees Those in the forest that are tallest, largest, and generally most valuable.

Drive Logs or timbers that are being floated on a stream from the forest to a mill or shipping point.

Ecology The science that deals with the relation of plants and animals to their environment and to the site factors that operate in controlling their distribution and growth.

Entomology, forest The science that deals with insects and their relation to forests and forest products.

Erosion The mechanical moving of soil by water or wind.

Even-aged A term applied to a stand in which relatively small age differences exist between individual trees. The maximum difference in age permitted in an even-aged stand is usually 10 to 20 years, although where the stand will not be harvested until it is 100 to 200 years old, larger differences, up to 25 percent of the rotation age, may be allowed.

Exotic Not native; foreign. Those trees and plants introduced from other climates or countries.

Fire, surface A fire that runs over the forest floor and burns only the surface litter, loose debris, and smaller vegetation.

Firebreak An existing barrier, or one constructed before a fire occurs, from which all or most of the inflammable materials have been removed; designed to stop or check creeping or running but not spotting fires, or to serve as a line from which to work and facilitate the movement of fire fighters and equipment in fire suppression.

Forest floor The covering of the mineral soil of a forest—humus, duff, and litter under forest growth.

Forestry, multiple-use The practice of forestry that combines two or more objectives, such as production of wood or wood derivative products, forage and browse for domestic livestock, proper environmental conditions for wildlife, landscape effects, protection against floods and erosion, recreation, production and protection of water supplies, and national defense.

Fungus A plant without chlorophyll that derives its nourishment from the organic matter of other plants.

Girdle To encircle the stem of a living tree with cuts that completely sever bark and cambium and are often carried well into the outer sapwood for the purpose of killing the tree by preventing the passage of nutrients or by admitting toxic materials.

Go-devil A small, short sled (scoot) without a tongue, used in skidding logs.

Ground fire A forest fire that consumes humus and duff beneath the surface.

Ground water Water that stands or flows beneath the ground surface in soil or rock material that is thoroughly saturated. The upper surface of this saturated zone is called the water table.

Growing-stock volume Net volume in cubic feet of live sawtimber and poletimber trees from stump to a minimum 4-in. top outside bark or to the point where the central stem breaks into limbs.

Habitat The unit area of environment, practically synonymous with site; the kind of place in which the plant or animal lives.

Hardwood Generally, one of the botanical group of trees that have broad leaves, in contrast to the needle-bearing conifers; also wood produced by broadleaved trees, regardless of texture or density.

Heartwood The inner core of a woody stem, composed completely of nonliving cells and usually differentiated from the outer enveloping layer (sapwood) by its darker color.

Heeled in Trees or plants covered with moist earth in a shallow trench or ditch.

High-grading The removal of only the best trees from the stand.

Hot-logging A logging operation in which logs go from the stump to the mill without pause.

Humidity, relative The ratio of actual mass of water vapor per unit of volume to mass of water vapor that would saturate that volume at the same temperature and pressure, or roughly the percent saturation of the space.

Humus The plant and animal residues of the soil, litter excluded, that are undergoing decomposition.

Hybrid The offspring resulting from mating two plants or animals that differ in one or more hereditary factors. This is the narrowest —the geneticist's—use of the term. A hybrid is more commonly understood to be the plant resulting from crossing two plants that are so distantly related as to belong to different races, varieties, species, or even genera.

Hypsometer An instrument used for measuring tree heights.

Incendiarism Malicious setting of fires.

Increment borer An instrument for measuring the growth of trees.

Indigenous Native to the locality.

Integrated logging A method of logging designed to make the best use of all timber products. In one cutting it removes all timber that should be cut and distributes the various timber products to the industries that can use them to best advantage.

Intolerance The incapacity of a tree to develop and grow in the shade of and in competition with other trees.

Kiln-dry The seasoning of lumber in a kiln.

Litter The uppermost layer of the organic debris composed of freshly, fallen or slightly decomposed organic materials. Commonly designated by the letter L.

Log To cut and remove logs from an area.

Log rule (1) A table indicating the amount of lumber that can be sawed from logs of given sizes. (2) A log-scaling stick.

Log scale A scaling stick for measuring the contents of logs in terms of board feet.

Logger (1) A person who is engaged in logging operations. (2) Locally, a person who hauls logs to landings and skidways.

Lookout A station or post used primarily in the detection of fires. A permanent lookout is generally equipped with a lookout tower or structure.

Lumber jack One who works on logging operations; colloquial for logger.

Marking, timber Selecting and indicating, usually by blaze or paint spot, trees to be cut or retained in a cutting operation; spotting.

Maturity For a given species or stand, the approximate age beyond which growth declines or decay begins to increase at a rate likely to assume economic importance.

mbf Thousand board feet.

mbm Thousand (feet) board measure.

Mensuration, forest A science dealing with the measurement of volume, growth, and development of individual trees and stands, and the determination of various products obtainable from them.

Merchantable Trees or stands of a size and quality suitable for marketing and utilization. They may or may not be so located as to be accessible for logging. Also, a specific grade of southern yellow pine timbers.

Net annual growth The net increase in the volume of trees during a specified year. Components include the increment in net volume at the beginning of the specific year surviving to its end, plus the net volume of trees reaching the minimum size class during the year, minus the volume of trees that died during the year, and minus the volume of trees that became rough or rotten during the year.

Niche Habitat necessary for the existence of a species.

Nitrate A type of compound that contains nitrogen. Nitrates are one kind of mineral found in the soil and required by plants.

Node A place on the stem where a leaf or bud grows; a joint in a stem.

Normal forest One in which growing stock is so distributed by size and age classes as to provide a sustained yield of nearly equal annual volumes through growth.

Normal growing stock The maximum volume that any given site is capable of maintaining in relation to economic conditions and the desires of the operator.

Notch To cut a notch in a tree before sawing to prevent splitting and binding and to control the direction of fall.

Old growth Timber stands in which no cutting has been done. Also known as first growth timber and virgin timber.

Overgrazing Grazing so heavy as to impair future forage production and cause range deterioration through consequential damage to plants or soil or to both.

Overrun The excess of the amount of lumber actually sawed from logs over the estimated volume or log scale, usually expressed in percent of log scale.

Overstory The upper crown canopy of a forest.

Parasite A plant or animal that lives in or on the body of another living thing and takes its food from that living thing.

Pathology, forest The science that deals with diseases of forest trees.

Peavey A stout wooden lever for rolling logs. A curvy metal hook is hinged to the lower part of the handle and the tip is armed with a sharp steel spike.

Peeler (1)Usually one who removes bark from timber cut in the spring months when bark slips. (2) A log used in the manufacture of rotary-cut veneer.

Petiole A leafstalk; the slender stalk by which the blade of a leaf is attached to the stem.

Pistil The female part of the flower that receives the pollen.

Plan, management A written plan for the operation of a forest property, using forestry principles. It usually records data and prescribes measures designed to provide optimum use of all forest resources.

Poletimber trees Live trees of commercial species at least 5 in. in diameter breast height, but smaller than sawtimber size and of good form and vigor.

Pollen The dust-like fertilizing powder produced by stamens; functionally the same as the male sperm in animal reproduction.

Precipitation Deposits of atmospheric moisture in liquid or solid form, including rain, snow, hail, dew, or frost.

Preservative A chemical substance that, when suitably applied to wood, makes it resistant to attack by fungi, insects, or marine borers.

Preserve In wildlife management, a game shooting area on which game species are propagated, released, or otherwise maintained.

Pruning The removal of live or dead branches from standing trees. This may be done artificially or naturally. Natural pruning results from such causes as decay, snow, ice, deficiency of light, and so on.

Public domain Territory over which a commonwealth has dominion or control; used in connection with the land owned by the federal government.

Pulpwood Wood cut or prepared primarily for manufacture into wood pulp for subsequent manufacture into paper, fiber, board, or other products, depending largely on the species cut and the pulping process.

Range Land not under cultivation that produces forage suitable for grazing by livestock; includes forest land producing forage.

Ranger An administrative officer in charge of a unit of forest land, usually a subdivision of a public forest or park. Various classifications are recognized, as forest ranger, district ranger, park ranger, and county ranger.

Reforestation The natural or artificial restocking of an area with forest trees; most commonly used in reference to the latter.

Regeneration See Reproduction, natural.

Release cutting A cutting of larger individual trees that are overtopping young trees, for the purpose of freeing the young trees to permit them to make good growth.

Reproduction The process by which a forest or range is renewed, including (1) artificial renewal by direct seeding or planting (reforestation) and (2) natural renewal by self-sown seeds, sprouts, rhizomes, and so on (regeneration). Also seedlings or saplings of any origin (young growth), the result of reproduction.

Reseeding, range Sowing of seed on range lands to restore or increase forage production.

Resistance The ability of a plant to develop and function normally despite adverse environmental conditions or the attacks of disease or insects.

Restocking Applied to an area on which the forest is being reestablished by natural means.

Ring, annual The growth layer of one year, as viewed on the cross section of a stem, branch, or root.

Root hairs Tiny feed roots that absorb water and nutrients.

Rotation The age at which the stand is considered ready for harvesting under the adopted plan of management.

Rosin A hard, brittle, natural resin obtained from the oleoresin exudate of certain trees. Rosin is a particular kind of resin. Rosin is obtained either from gum that exudes from the living pine tree or from wood by extraction. Wood rosin and gum rosin are kinds of resin.

Rot, heart A decay characteristically confined to the heartwood; it usually originates in the living tree.

Rotation Planned period of years between tree or stand establishment and final harvest.

Roundwood Rough logs, bolts, or other round sections cut from trees.

Runoff, surface The rate at which water is discharged from a drainage area, usually expressed in cubic feet per square mile of drainage area.

Sapling A young tree less than 4 in. dbh. The minimum size of saplings is usually, though not invariably, placed at 2 in. dbh.

Saprophyte A plant that gets its food from plants or animals that have died.

Sapwood The light-colored wood that appears on a cross section of wood. The sapwood is composed of living cells and serves to conduct water and minerals to the crown.

Saw timber Timber stands in which trees of sawlog size make up most of the volume.

Sawtimber Trees Live trees of commercial species containing at least one 12-ft sawlog or two noncontiguous 8-ft logs, and relatively free from defect. Softwoods must be at least 9 in. in diameter and hardwoods must be at least 11 in. in diamter at breast height.

Scale The estimated sound contents in terms of a given log rule or a log or group of logs; to estimate the sound contents of a log or group of logs.

Scarify To tear up earth by disking or dragging to prepare for seeding.

Schoolmarm A term used by loggers to describe a tree forked above the first log.

Season, fire The period or periods of the year during which fires are likely to occur, spread, and to do sufficient damage or otherwise warrant organized fire control.

Second growth Timber growth that comes up after removal of the old stand by cutting, fire, or other cause. Typical second-growth conditions may come about in a forest that is untouched so far as lumbering is concerned.

Section A unit of land measurement, 640 acres or 6400 square chains, 1 mile or 80 chains square; 1/36 of a township.

Seedling A tree grown from seed. The term is restricted to trees smaller than saplings.

Seed tree A tree that produces seed; usually trees reserved in a cutting operation to supply seed.

Selective logging or cutting The removal of selected mature, large, or diseased trees as single, scattered trees or in small groups of trees. Young trees start in the openings thus made; the result of this type of cutting is an uneven-aged forest.

Shake A lengthwise separation of wood that usually occurs between and parallel to the growth layers.

Shelterbelt A wind barrier of living trees and shrubs maintained for the purpose of protecting farm fields. As applied to individual farmsteads, it is termed a windbreak; also called a belt.

Silvics The life history and general characteristics of forest trees and stands, with particular reference to environmental factors.

Silviculture The science and art of producing and tending a forest; the application of the knowledge of silvics in the treatment of a forest; the theory and practice of controlling forest establishment, composition, and growth.

Site An area, considered as to its ecological factors with reference to capacity to produce forests or other vegetation: the combination of biotic, climatic, and soil condition of an area.

Site index A measure of site quality; expressed as height in feet of dominant trees at least 50 years of age.

Skid To pull logs from the stump to the skidway, landing, or mill.

Skidway Two skids laid parallel at right angles to a road, usually raised above the ground at the end nearest the road. As they are brought from the stump, logs are usually piled upon a skidway for loading upon sleds, wagons, or cars.

Slash Branches, bark, tops, chunks, cull logs, uprooted stumps, and broken or uprooted trees left on the ground after logging; also, large accumulation of debris after wind or fire.

Smokechaser A member of a fire fighting crew.

Snag A standing, dead tree from which the leaves and most of the branches have fallen, or a standing section of the stem of a tree broken off at a height of 20 ft or more. If less than 20 ft high, it is properly termed a stub.

Softwood One of the botanical group of trees that generally have needle or scalelike leaves such as the conifers; also, the wood produced by such trees, regardless of texture or density.

Species (of trees) Subordinate to a genus; trees having common characteristics. In common language, a kind of variety such as sugar maple, white pine.

Springwood The less dense, larger-celled, first-formed part of a growth layer.

Spud A hand tool used in stripping bark from felled trees.

Stand An aggregation of trees or other growth occupying a specific area and sufficiently uniform in composition (species), age, arrangement, and conditions as to be distinguishable from the forest or other growth on adjoining areas.

Stand, mixed A stand in which less than 75 percent of the trees in the main crown canopy are of a single species.

Stand, pure A stand in which at least 75 percent of the trees in the main crown canopy are of a single species.

Stock, growing The sum (in number and volume) of all the trees in a forest.

Strip survey Estimating timber by strips running through the stand.

Stumpage Uncut standing timber that has commercial value.

Succession The progressive development of the vegetation toward its highest ecological expression, the climax. The replacement of one plant community by another.

Summerwood The denser, smaller celled, later-formed part of a growth layer.

Survey, forest An inventory of forest land to determine area, condition, timber volume, and species for specific purposes such as timber purchase, forest management, or as a basis for forest policies and programs.

Sustained yield As applied to a policy, method, or plan of forest management, the term implies continuous production, with the aim of achieving, at the earliest practicable time, an approximate balance between net growth and harvest, either by annual or somewhat longer periods.

Table, volume A table showing the average contents of trees by diameter and merchantable length in a specified unit of volume.

Technician, forestry One who is familiar with the principal field activities connected with the practice of forestry. Usually trained in vocational, technical, or ranger school as distinguished from a professional forestry course.

Thinning Cutting in an immature stand to increase its rate of growth, to foster quality growth, to improve composition, to promote sanitation, to aid in litter decomposition, to obtain greater total yield, and to recover and use material that would be otherwise lost.

Tolerant Ability of a tree to grow in the shade of other trees.

Tote road A term used for smaller logging roads in some parts of the country.

Towerperson A lookout stationed at a tower.

Trainer A tree intermediate in size that shades lower branches of adjacent larger trees.

Transpiration The process by which water moves up through the living plant and vapor leaves the plant and enters the atmosphere.

Transplant To replant a nursery seedling in another part of the nursery for further development.

Tree, den A dead or deteriorating tree containing cavities resulting from decay or holes created by birds or other animals.

Tree, weed A tree of a species with relatively little or no value.

Tree, wolf A tree occupying more space than its silvicultural value warrants, curtailing better neighbors. A term usually applied to broad-crowned, short-stemmed trees.

TSI Timber stand improvement; usually applied to intermediate cutting.

Type, forest A descriptive term used to group stands of similar character as regards composition and development due to certain ecological factors, by which they may be differentiated from other groups of stands.

Understory That portion of the trees in a forest stand below the overstory.

Uneven-aged A term applied to a stand in which there are considerable differences in age of trees and in which three or more age classes are represented. See also *all aged.*

Utilization, forest That branch of forestry concerned with the operation of harvesting and marketing the forest crop and other resources of the forest.

Watershed The total area above a given point on a waterway that contributes water to the flow at that point.

Wedge In logging, to drive a wedge into the saw cut to prevent the saw from binding and to direct the fall of the tree.

Widowmaker Logger's term to describe a tree cut off at the stump but hung up in tops of adjacent trees that keep it from falling.

Windbreak A wind barrier of living trees and shrubs maintained for the purpose of protecting the farm home, other buildings, garden, orchard, or feedlots.

Wind firm Able to withstand heavy wind.

Woodsrun Cut logs delivered to a mill at a set price without prior sorting for quality logs.

Year, seed A year in which a given species produces (over a considerable area) a seed crop greatly in excess of the normal. Applied usually to trees of irregular or infrequent seed production.

APPENDIX B

CHARACTERISTICS OF IMPORTANT COMMERCIAL TIMBER SPECIES

The purpose of this appendix is not to supply detailed tree identification information concerning all commercial species for use in the field. Instead, its purpose is to acquaint the student with the scientific names and a few essential characteristics of important forest trees, and their principal uses. Tree identification manuals, which are available at low cost, do not usually give all of this information. However, the student is urged to obtain one for field use. Previously, the forest regions in which these species are naturally found have been described and the species listed.

None of the exotic (or nonnative) tree species that have been planted in the United States are listed here. Only a very few have developed to the extent that they may be a factor in the production of forest crops; the principal species are Norway spruce (*Picea excelsa*), Scotch pine (*Pinus sylvestris*), and European larch (*Larix europa*), all from northern Europe and planted in our northern states. Most other exotics are ornamentals only.

The descriptive information is set forth in the following order: common name, scientific name (genus and species), size of tree, principal uses and products, and description of needles, leaves, fruit, and other pertinent information.

IMPORTANT EASTERN FOREST TREES[a]

Common and Scientific Name	Size[b]	Uses[c]	Characteristics[d]
Eastern Conifers			
Eastern white pine (*Pinus strobus*)	L	1, 2	Fine timber tree; leaves in clusters of 5, 3 to 5 in. long
Jack pine (*Pinus banksiana*)	S	1, 2, 3	Common on sandy soil; leaves in clusters of 2, ¾ to 1¼ in. long
Red pine (*Pinus resinosa*)	M–L	1, 2, 3, 4, 8	Leaves in cluster of 2, 5 to 6 in. long
Loblolly pine (*Pinus taeda*)	L	1, 2, 3, 4	Leaves in clusters of 3, 6 to 9 in. long; cone 3 to 6 in. long diameter
Shortleaf pine (*Pinus echinata*)	L	1, 2, 3, 4	Leaves in clusters of 2 and sometimes 3, 3 to 5 in. long; cone small, 1 to 2 in. in diameter
Virginia pine (Scrub pine) (*Pinus virginiana*)	S		Leaves in clusters of 2, 1½ to 3 in. long
Slash pine (*Pinus elliottii*)	L	1, 2, 3, 4	Leaves in clusters of 2, sometimes 3, 7 to 10 in. long; important turpentine tree
Longleaf pine (*Pinus palustris*)	L	1, 2, 3, 4	Leaves in clusters of 3, 8 to 18 in. long; important turpentine tree
Tamarack or Eastern larch (*Larix laricina*)	S–M	1, 2, 3, 4	Leaves nėedle-shaped, ¾ to 1¼ in. long, in dense, brushlike clusters; falling off in winter; a swamp tree
White spruce (*Picea glauca*)	M–L	1, 2, 8	Leaves ⅓ to ¾ in. long, arranged singly around the smooth twigs; whitish
Black spruce (*Picea mariana*)	S	2, 8	Similar to white spruce, but twigs are minutely hairy; cones strongly attached; a swamp tree

IMPORTANT EASTERN FOREST TREES[a]

Common and Scientific Name	Size[b]	Uses[c]	Characteristics[d]
Red spruce (*Picea rubra*)	M–L	1, 2, 8	Similar to black spruce, but cones begin to fall when ripe
Eastern hemlock (*Tsuga canadensis*)	L	1, 2	Leaves ⅓ to ⅔ in. long, attached by tiny leafstalks; cones ½ to ¾ in long
Bald cypress (*Taxodium distichum*)	L	1, 3	Leaves ½ to ¾ in. long, falling off in winter; cones ball-like; a swamp tree
Balsam fir (*Abies balsamea*)	S	2, 8	Leaves ½ to 1¼ in. long; cones upright, falling to pieces when ripe
Northern-white cedar (*Thuja occidentalis*)	M	3	Leaves scalelike; cones ⅓ to ½ in. long, upright
Atlantic white-cedar (*Chamaecyparis thyoides*)	M	3	Cones ball-like; leaves somewhat resembling arborvitae
Eastern red-cedar (*Juniperus virginiana*)	M	1, 3	Leaves scalelike, those on young shoots and seedlings awl-shaped and spreading; fruit is a firm berry
Broadleaved Hardwoods			
Sweet gum (*Liquidambar styraciflya*)	L	1, 5, 9	Leaves star-shaped; fruit a bur-like ball suspended by a long stalk
American sycamore; plane (*Platanus occidentalis*)	L	1, 5	Leaves broad and coarsely toothed; base of leafstalk inclosing a winter bud in peculiar manner; fruit a hard-surfaced, long-stalked ball
White oak (*Quercus alba*)	L	1, 5, 7, 9	Leaves deeply lobed, not bristle-tipped; acorns ripening in one season
Bur oak (*Quercus macrocarpa*)	L	1, 5, 7, 9	A white oak with fringe-edged acorn and larger leaves more deeply lobed
Chestnut oak (*Quercus prinus*\	L	1, 5, 9	A white oak with leaves resembling those of the chestnut, and with long, large, shallow-cupped acorns

IMPORTANT EASTERN FOREST TREES[a]

Common and Scientific Name	Size[b]	Uses[c]	Characteristics[d]
Northern red oak (*Quercus rubra*)	L	1, 5, 9	Leaves deeply cut, with bristle-tipped points; the acorns, ripening in 2 seasons, are large, with very shallow cups
Black oak (*Quercus velutina*)	L	1, 5	An oak with thick, large glossy leaves that are more or less minutely woolly beneath; acorns with small caps, as deep or deeper than wide
Southern pin oak (*Quercus palustris*)	L	1, 5	A red oak with smaller leaves and smaller and shallower cupped striped acorns
Northern pin oak (*Quercus ellipsoidalis*)	M	1, 5	A red oak very similar to Southern pin oak except for the elliptical acorn
Southern red oak (*Quercus falcata*)	L	1, 5, 9	A red oak with leaves very deeply cut, the upper central portion being very narrow and sometimes slightly curved, and with dense, tawny-yellow wool beneath
Live oak (*Quercus virginiana*)	M–L	1	An evergreen oak with narrow, smooth-bordered leaves which are turned under on the edge, pale woolly beneath and glossy above; small, pointed acorns with long stalks
American basswood; American linden (*Tilia americana*)	L	1, 9	Leaves smooth, broadly heart-shaped with finely toothed edge; fruit a cluster of little woody balls suspended from the middle of a long narrow leaflike bract
American (white) elm (*Ulmus americana*)	L	1, 5	Leaves sharply toothed; fruit flat, papery, about ½ in. long, fringed with tiny hairs

IMPORTANT EASTERN FOREST TREES[a]

Common and Scientific Name	Size[b]	Uses[c]	Characteristics[d]
Slippery (red) elm (*Ulmus rubra*)	M–L	1, 5	Long leaves, very rough on the upper side; inner bark is slippery when chewed, and the flat fruits have a smooth edge
Rock elm (*Ulmus thomasii*)	M	1, 5	Differing from other elms in having fruit minutely hairy all over, and twigs with conspicuous, corky ridges
American beech (*Fagus grandifolia*)	L	1, 5	Leaves with saw-toothed edge; fruit a light brown spine-covered bur containing a 3-cornered brown nutlet
Eastern cottonwood (*Populus deltoides*)	L	1, 2	Leaves triangular, long-pointed, toothed, smooth, with flattened leafstalk
Quaking aspen (*Populus tremuloides*)	S	1, 2	Leaves broad, finely toothed, leafstalks flat, longer than blades
Bigtooth aspen (*Populus grandidentata*)	S	1, 2	Leaves broad, coarsely toothed, with flattened leafstalks
Paper birch (*Betula papyrifera*)	M	1, 2, 5, 9	Leaves broad at base, finely toothed, fruit a papery cone which falls apart when ripe; white bark peeling off in thin sheets
Yellow birch (*Betula alleghaniensis*)	L	1, 5, 9	Bark yellow-gray; tiny scales of the cones minutely hairy along edges
Black cherry (*Prunus serotina*)	M	1, 5, 9	Fruit resembles common chokecherry, but smaller and thin-fleshed.
Yellow poplar; tulip tree (*Liriodendron tulipifera*)	L	1, 2, 9	Leaves large, blunt or with deep notch at end; flowers large yellow, tulip-like; cone-like woody fruit, upright

IMPORTANT EASTERN FOREST TREES[a]

Common and Scientific Name	Size[b]	Uses[c]	Characteristics[d]
Black tupelo (or gum) (*Nyssa sylvatica*)	M	1, 5	Medium tree; leaves oval with smooth edge; fruit an elongated black berry with seed but little flattened and scarcely ridged
Sugar maple (*Acer saccharum*)	M–L	1, 5, 9	Leaves 5-lobed; with large paired winged fruit ripening in early autumn, yields maple sugar
Red maple (*Acer rubrum*)	M–L	1, 5, 9	Leaves 5-lobed, finely toothed; reddish fruit ripening in spring or early summer
Boxelder (*Acer negundo*, including 6 varietal forms)	M	1, 5	Leaves compound, the leaflets toothed; fruit ripening in early summer and remaining on trees during winter
Black locust (*Robinia pseudoacacia*)	S	3	Leaves compound, leaflets with smooth margins; fruit a pod 3 to 4 in. long; trees with pairs of short thorns at base of leaves and twigs
Bitternut hickory (*Carya cordiformis*)	M	1, 5, 6	Nut broader than long, without angles, very thin-shelled; bitter kernel, thin husk
Shagbark hickory (*Carya ovata*)	M	1, 5, 6	Buds with many scales (all of the preceding hickories have buds with few scales); bark loosening from trees in shaggy strips
Mockernut hickory, known also as bigbud or white hickory (*Carya tomentosa*)	M	1, 5, 6	Leaves large, hairy; buds large, budscales many; bark closely furrowed, not separating from the trunk; nut with thick husk, large, angled, thick-shelled
Black walnut (*Juglans nigra*)	M	1, 9	Leaves compound with toothed edges; spherical fruit growing singly or in pairs; bark brown, furrowed

IMPORTANT EASTERN FOREST TREES[a]

Common and Scientific Name	Size[b]	Uses[c]	Characteristics[d]
Butternut (*Juglans cinerea*)	M	1, 9	Leaves compound, with toothed edges; fruit in clusters of 3 to 5, pointed and elongated, with viscid hairs when young; velvety cushion just above leaf-scar; bark gray and smooth on young trees
White ash (*Fraxinus americana*)	M–L	1, 5, 6, 9	Smooth twigs, opposite; leaves compound, leaflets toothed or wavy on the margins and paler beneath; seed with a plump, well-rounded body and a wing extending almost entirely from the end and borne in dense clusters; high-ground tree
Green ash (*Fraxinus pennsylvanica*)	M	1, 5, 6	Like the preceding, except twigs are smooth, leaflets sharply toothed; body of seed and pointed wing very narrow; bottomland tree
Black ash (*Fraxinus nigra*)	M	1, 5	Leaflets stemless, finely toothed, 7 to 11; seeds with a flat, wide wing, that entends conspicuously down the sides of the seed body and is blunt; bottomland species

[a]Mainly eastern half of the United States, east of the Great Plains.

[b]Size: L, large; M, medium; S, small.

[c]Uses: 1, lumber; 2, pulpwood; 3, poles and posts; 4, piling; 5, railroad ties; 6, tool handles; 7, specialty; 8, Christmas trees; 9, veneer.

[d]Characteristics. Most fruits ripen in fall unless otherwise noted.

IMPORTANT WESTERN FOREST TREES[a]

Common and Scientific Name	Size[b]	Uses[c]	Characteristics[d]
Conifers			
Western white pine (*Pinus monticola*)	L	1	Needles 5 in a cluster, blue green, 2 to 4 in. long; cone slender, 7 to 8 in. long
Sugar pine (*Pinus lambertiana*)	L	1	Needles 5 in a cluster, 3 to 4 in. long; important timber tree; largest of the pines
Ponderosa pine (*Pinus ponderosa*)	L	1	Needles 3 or 2 in a cluster, stout, 4 to 7 in. long; cones short-stalked, 3 to 6 in. long, with prickles
Lodgepole pine (*Pinus contorta*)	L	1, 2, 5	Needles 2 in a cluster, stout, yellow green, 1 to 3 in. long, cones up to 2 in. long, staying closed on tree many years
Western larch (*Larix occidentalis*)	L	1	Needles many in a cluster, about 1 in. long, shedding in fall; cones upright, 1 to 1½ in. long
Western hemlock (*Tsuga heterophylla*)	L	1, 2	Needles ¼ to ¾ in. long, flat, shiny; cone 1 in. long. Important timber tree
Englemann spruce (*Picea engelmannii*)	L	1, 2, 9	Needles 4-angled, ⅝ to 1⅛ in. long; cones 1½ to 2½ in. long
Colorado Blue spruce (*Picea pungens*)	S–M	2, 8	Needles 4-angled, ¾ to 1⅛ in. long, blue green cones 2½ to 4 in. long
Sitka spruce (*Picea sitchensis*)	L	1, 2, 9	Needles flat, ⅝ to 1 in. long, dark green; cones 2 to 3½ in. long, with long, stiff scales, rounded and irregularly toothed; used as lumber for many purposes, and as pulpwood
Douglas-fir (*Pseudotsuga menziesii*)	L	1, 2, 8, 9	Needles flat, ¾ to 1¼ in. long, dark green; cones 2 to 4 in. long, with long, 3-toothed bracts extending between scales; pointed buds

IMPORTANT WESTERN FOREST TREES[a]

Common and Scientific Name	Size[b]	Uses[c]	Characteristics[d]
Grand fir (*Abies grandis*)	M–L	1, 2, 8	Needles flat, 1 to 2 in. long, dark green above, silvery white beneath; cones upright, 2 to 4 in. long, green
Noble fir (*Abies procera*)	M	1, 2, 8	Needles of lower branches flat, and of top branches 4-angled, 1 to 1½ in. long, blue green; cones upright, 4 to 6 in. long, with long bracts covering the scales
Redwood (*Sequoia sempervirens*)	L	1, 3, 5, 7	Leaves lanceolate, unequal in length, ¼ to ¾ in. long, spreading in 2 rows; cones ¾ to 1 in. long; tree up to 370 ft tall and 25 ft in diameter; used for heavy construction, planing-mill products, tanks
Giant sequoia (*Sequoia gigantea*)	L	1, 3	Leaves scalelike, ⅛ to ¼ in. long; cones 1¾ to 2¾ in. long; tree up to 320 ft tall and 35 ft in diameter at swollen base; largest trees preserved in national parks and national forests
Western red-cedar (*Thuja plicata*)	L	1, 3, 7	Leaves scalelike, 1/16 to ⅛ in. long, dark green; cones ½ in. long
Port-Orford-cedar (*Chamaecyparis lawsoniana*)	L	1, 3, 7	Leaves 1/16 to ¼ in. long; cones about ⅜ in. in diameter; thick bark

[a]Mainly Rocky Mountains, Black Hills, and Pacific Coast states, west of the Great Plains.

[b]Size: L, large; M, medium; S, small.

[c]Uses: 1, lumber; 2, pulpwood; 3, poles and posts; 4, pilings; 5, railroad ties; 6, tool handles; 7, specialty; 8, Christmas trees; 9, veneer.

[d]Characteristics. Most fruits ripen in fall unless otherwise noted.

APPENDIX C

EXAMPLE OF MULTIPLE USE FOREST MANAGEMENT PLAN

FOR PROPERTY THAT HAS BEEN MANAGED FOR MORE THAN FOUR DECADES

(Period Covered 1875–1985)
Wolf Springs Forest
Minong, Wisconsin

Location and Area

300 acres, comprising seven and one-half 40-acre tracts in Section 9, T 42N R 11W, located in the northeastern part of Washburn County, Wisconsin. (See forest type, Fig. 6–5, and aerial photo maps, also Figs. 6–6 and 7–3, which apply to this property.)

Land and Timber	
Total land area	300 acres
Forest land	210 acres
Brushy and open wetland	38 acres
Water area (3 ponds, 2 lakes, springs, and stream)	40 acres
Open upland (fenced fields and pastures)	12 acres

Distribution of Forest Cover Types	
Norway (red) and white pine type (upland)	76 acres
Balsam fir, spruce, tamarack, and cedar (swamp)	35 acres
Pine and spruce plantations (upland)	32 acres
Mixed pine and balsam fir reproduction under aspen (upland)	40 acres
Aspen	27 acres

History of the Tract

The property was originally acquired by James Wolfe, who settled on it in 1889 and worked with the logging crew that cut off the pine timber the same winter. By protecting the area from fire, a dense volunteer stand of pine developed, which was allowed to grow untouched until the present owner acquired the property in 1936. In the spring of 1931, a light ground fire passed through the area. The fire scarred larger trees and killed seedlings and saplings in the open areas. The tract has been managed since 1936. Wolfe developed a small trout hatchery and sold trout in the market.

Physical Features

12 flowing cold water springs near headwaters
3 trout ponds (stocked with brook and rainbow trout)
2 artificial lakes (constructed in 1955 and 1959), waterfowl nesting area in upper ends; muskrat, mink, otter, and beaver use whole area; bait minnow production under lease
⅓ mile of trout stream (stocked with brook andd rainbow trout)

Wildlife Habitat

Excellent waterfowl nesting and resting habitat at upper end of new lake and on islands; ruffed grouse on logging roads; sharptail grouse use open fields and food patches; deet "yard up" in cedar swamps; woodcock along swamp borders; brook and rainbow trout stocked in ponds and stream; game food shrubs have been established near wildlife nesting and concentration areas.

Buildings and Equipment

Main lodge
1 guest cabin
1 machine shed and tool shop
1 main hall and 2 bunkhouses for youth camp
1 logging truck with clam hoist
1 crawler tractor with blade and winch
1 Farmall A tractor with attachments

Forest Management Record

Forest growing stock has been inventoried at regular intervals; sample plots for growth studies established; thinnings, release cuttings, pruning of crop trees, and application of shelterwood and selection methods in timber harvesting (a total volume of 106 mbf and 545 cords plus 1500 cedar posts and 300 cedar poles have been removed during the 40-year management period); 32 acres of forest plantation established; 40 acres in natural pine reproduction.

MULTIPLE-USE MANAGEMENT OBJECTIVES

The objective in the management of Wolf Springs Forest shall be for an optimum combination of uses including: (1) timber production; (2) wetland, watershed and spring source protection; (3) management of vegetation to produce diversified habitats for all native wildlife and wild animal communities; (4) protection of shorelands and preservation of special natural areas; and (5) provide maximum human recreational opportunity within the carrying capacity of the area. This multiple-use management objective will be carried out through the coordination of timber harvesting with wildlife, watershed, soil conservation and scenic quality protection. A diversity of tree species, edges, and age classes shall be achieved through application of the following silvicultural practices to each forest type.

GENERAL FOREST MANAGEMENT GUIDELINES

Silvicultural Guidelines

White–Red Pine, and White Spruce–Balsam Fir.
The two-cut shelterwood system shall be prescribed for these forest types in which an initial or preparatory cut opens up the site for natural reseeding and protection of new growth prior to removal of the residual stand. Red pine and white spruce will be planted to assure full stocking.

Additional guidlines to reconcile timber production with other multiple uses include the following.

1. Special management practices will be designated for eagle and osprey netting sites, deer yards, lake and stream shoreline zones, sensitive soil types, springs and important watersheds, selected aesthetically managed roadsides, and for land use zones under restrictive management.
2. Where streams, lakes, springs, and seasonal waterways occur in logging areas, 100-ft strips of timber will be left uncut as a management zone to protect stream bank integrity and water quality except that individual trees may be marked for cutting within 100 ft if skidding is done away from the streamside zone.

3. Plantations of conifers and natural second growth northern hardwood (hemlock) will be managed to attain natural succession toward maturity as nearly as possible. Openings to produce wildlife habitat should be planned as appropriate.
4. Where *vegetation manipulation* is carried out for improving wildlife habitat, especially deer and ruffed grouse, the same guidelines will apply with respect to clearcutting in aspen and jack pine—except where extensive openings are necessary for sharptail grouse and waterfowl.

Northern Hardwoods (and Hemlock).
The selection system will be followed to perpetuate and improve the natural all-aged condition of the forest. Small openings (group selection) may be used to encourage yellow birch, red oak, and other shade-intolerant species. Occasional den trees (culls) will be left for nesting birds and animals. And emphasis will be given to growing large size hardwoods for veneer and saw timber as well as for their value.

Aspen, White Birch, and Jack Pine.
Where clearcutting is prescribed for these shade-intolerant forest types, timber sale areas of several years duration will be planned so that cutting layouts (1) take advantage of the site protection afforded by the seed sources of surrounding stands, (2) provide maximum irregular *edge effects* for wildlife, and (3) are so patterned and spaced as to produce a variety of size classes in the succeeding forest. Clearcut patches shall average about 5 to 10 acres, except where salvage of timber lost to insects, diseases, windthrow or fire makes larger cutting areas necessary. Where artificial reforestation is necessary, plantings will include species diversity so far as possible.

Financial Projection

An estimated annual cut of 150 cords of pulpwood and 20 mbf of sawlogs harvested on a sustained-yield basis to produce a stumpage income of $3000, labor returns of $5000, and operating profit of $1200 per year at 1978 timber prices.

Rental and operation of recreational camp for summer season—$2800 net after overhead costs.

Revenue potentials also exist in fur bearers, fishing privileges, sale of watercress, other food products, and Christmas greens—not estimated.

Forest Management Records and Plans by Compartments

Compartment I: NE Pine Block, 10 acres. This standard is composed of well-stocked white and Norway pine about 80 years of age and averaging 8 to 14 in. dbh. The site index varies from medium to good.

Management History. Thinned in 1938, 1941, 1952, and 1956; volume removed 59.3 cords of pine pulpwood. Crop trees pruned in 1939–41 and 1946–47. Regular salvage of white pine infected with blister rust. Five sample plots for growth measurements established.

Future Plans. Harvest cuttings following two-cut shelterwood system with very light first cut to reduce invasion by hazel brush to start in 1980s.

Present Volume:	220 mbf plus 153 cords pulpwood
Growth rate:	1.1 cords per acre per year

Compartment II: South side Pine Block, 15.5 acres. Medium to well-stocked second-growth red and white pine ranging in age from- 10 to 80 years, with aspen and balsam fir (removed in 1946–48); average of main stand 10 to 16 in. in diameter, variably composed of pulpwood and sawtimber. Reproduction in understory largely balsam fir and white pine supplemented with planted Norway (red) pine and white spruce in 1941 and 1947. Site index varies from medium to good.

Management History. Release cutting of mature aspen over pine and balsam fir in 1940 removed 28.4 cords of excelsior bolts; light harvest cutting and thinning in 1946 and 1947 removed remaining aspen, all poorly formed sawtimber, and pulpwood-sized trees; salvage cutting of windthrown trees in 1949. Pruning of selected crop trees in 1941 and 1947. Total cut between 1946 and 1950, 42.2 mbf pine and 47.4 cords of pine, 67.6 cords of aspen, and 33.5 cords of white birch. During the first half of the 1970s, 40 cords of pine and balsam pulp and 16 mbf of blister rust infected sawlogs were removed.

Future Plans. Harvest cuttings to follow shelterwood system along with inter and underplanting of white spruce, red pine and hemlock.

Present Volume:	196 mbf and 81 cords of pine, 42 cords of balsam fir
Growth Rate:	210 b.f. per acre per year plus 0.2 cord

Compartment III: SW line fence—Pine Block, 3.8 acres. Medium stocked Norway pine sawtimber 80 years old averaging 14 to 18 in. dbh and three 16-ft logs per tree. Understory of white pine and underplanted (1940) Norway and Scotch pine in heavy brush. Good site.

Management History. Salvage of windthrow in 1949 removed 3 mbf pine in 1962 removed 8 mbf of white pine sawtimber.

Future Plans. Further underplanting after harvest cutting began 1962 under three-cut shelterwood system.

Present Volume:	17.2 mbf plus 3 cords
Estimated Allowable Cut:	Harvest of entire merchantable volume during 1980s

Compartment IV: North side, Aspen-Pine Understory Block, 48 acres. Scattered aspen that sprouted after 1931 ground fire, badly damaged by June, 1946, hailstorms, serves as overstory for white pine reproduction up to 12 ft in height. Two hay field totaling 7 acres (bordered with wildlife shrubs) and about 8 acres of nonproductive swamp.

Management History. Five plantations established in following years (1) 1946, (2) 1951, (3) 1952, (4) 1957, (5) 1962; thinning or stand improvement to date. White pine weevil control (intensive) 1960, annual maintenance thereafter.

Future Plans. Thinnings will be needed in plantation during next decade; release of white pine saplings under aspen during same period, after trees reach 15 or more ft and danger of weevil damage to tips has largely passed. Continue plantings and underplantings in open areas.

Compartment V: West Swamp Conifer Block, 36.2 acres. Mixture of balsam fir, black spruce, tamarack, white-cedar, and some white spruce (edges), with scattered black ash and yellow birch. All age and size well-stocked stand until cutting 1945–47 and windstorm of 1949. Sizes ranged from 2 to 8 in. dbh, with merchantable pulpwood, cedar pole, and post material predominating. Fairly well drained and good site.

Management History. Undisturbed until partial logging in 1946–47, which was followed by a good stocking of seedling conifers and a heavier salvage cutting of windthrown timber in 1949. Heavy timber removal 1946–49:

30 cords spruce
85 cords balsam
15 cords tamarack
230 cedar poles
1200 posts

No cutting since. No additional cultural or other work performed. Reproduction of spruce, balsam, and black ash developing well, but cedar and yellow birch being overbrowsed by deer. Some spots have too much alder or raspberry for satisfactory tree growth.

Future Plans. No silvicultural work planned except harvest of merchantable material in remaining balsam thickets, about 1970.

Present Volume:	200.4 cords balsam fir
	50.3 cords tamarack
	407.0 cords cedar
	39.1 cords black ash
	17.1 cords white birch
Growth Rate:	Estimated at 0.3 cord per acre per year

Compartment V-A: Pond Swamp Conifer Block, 6.1 acres. Balsam, fir, cedar, with some spruce, white birch, and aspen lying along and around upper trout pond and spring and within Compartment I. All ages and sizes up to 12 in.

Management History. Logging in upper ends of swamp in 1946–47 removed 28 cords (balsam, spruce), scattered posts, and a few poles. Salvage cutting in beaver flowage area in 1948. Black spruce planted in a few open spots, 1954. Preserve uncut as natural area group of large cedar.

Future Plans. No cultural work except salvage of such windthrow as may develop from time to time. Harvest cuttings on south and west edges planned in near future will require cable skidding because of springy ground.

Present Volume: Included in V

Compartment VI: West side, upland, 47.7 acres. Located on west side of Sprague Lake, and Wolf Creek. Contains two plantations (1) white spruce, and (2) Norway pine. Balance of areas understocked, with poor aspen, scattered pine, and balsam fir reproduction.

Management History. Plantations (1) established in 1939, (2) in 1940, and (3) in 1961. Access road built in 1955 and 1957.

Future Plans. Continue planting pine and spruce in open spots. Prune plantations; harvest Christmas trees. No merchantable volumes for growth estimate.

Utilization and Marketing

Timber stand improvement cuttings and thinnings for pulpwood to coincide with fall demand for pine, balsam, and cedar boughs. Cut pulpwood from tops of sawlog trees when making harvest cuttings. Hire logging done by contract or piece cutters and sell cut products in order to make operating profit (rather than sell timber as stumpage). Keep list of buyers in files, and limit cutting to periods of best prices.

Fire Protection

Located 6½ miles from the state ranger station at Minong and on an accessible road. Fire on the property can be easily detected by state tower and controlled by state equipment. Road on east side, access roads to all parts of interior, and streams, ponds, lake, and swamps lend property facilities for fire protection not common to most areas. Essential fire equipment maintained on premises: back and power pumps, hand tools, tractor, and plow.

Insects and Disease

White pine blister rust control has been undertaken by *Ribes* elimination in 1935, 1943, 1954, and in 1966; but abandoned as too costly. Control white pine weevil by pruning tips of white pine reprodocution until 15 ft in height. Observe for other insects, especially spruce budworm. Report to state forester and obtain control information if needed.

Agriculture

Twelve acres of open lands to be maintained for pasture or hay for beef cattle and saddle horses. Estimate carrying capacity of range, 10 head (if supplementary winter hay is purchased) without damage to forest reproduction. Watercress beds established and planted at springs. Small acreage of blueberry land burned over at intervals to maintain new canes.

Wildlife
The following measures have been undertaken to improve wildlife habitat: seeding of woods roads with white clover for ruffed grouse feed; establishment of variety of berry-bearing shrubs for wildlife food to persist above snow height; placing of houses for wood ducks along lake shore. Other measures include maintenance of small openings and edges and the application of new techniques as they develop. Harvest fur bearers. Protect eagle nest near river by preserving large trees and avoiding disturbance during nesting season.

Fisheries
Spring at upper end of first pond has been dammed with rock masonry to aerate water; trout-rearing pens established below springs for raising fingerling rainbow and brook trout to release at catchable size in three trout ponds; bundles of brush, log rafts, log and rock deflectors established at effective spots in three trout ponds and in stream. Large lakes planted with large-mouth bass and bait minnows. Dredging of trout ponds to increase depth and capacity for trout completed in 1967.

Recreational Development
Rental of camp constructed in 1959 for youth and conservation groups.

Amendments
The basic plan can be revised as needs develop. Revisions and new technical developments should be incorporated on Compartment Operations Record Map (see Fig. 7–3), as should a running record of variations technical applications, management, and operating results.

Property Taxes
A total of 210 acres are registered under the Wisconsin Forest Crop and Woodland Tax Laws (both at a fixed rate per acre and the former requiring a 10 percent yield tax on cut products).

Records
Current cash records will be kept in the Timbermen's Operating Account Book and job records (as suggested in Chapter 7).

Wolf Springs Forest has been licensed by the state of Wisconsin as a private fish hatchery, and certified as a tree farm. If game birds or fur bearers are to be raised and sold as a crop, it will be necessary to obtain a Game and Fur Farm license from the state. The property is also cooperating with the Washburn County Soil Conservation District and with the Agricultural Conservation Program of the U.S. Department of Agriculture.

APPENDIX D

TIMBER SALES AND OPERATING AGREEMENT FORMS

Three suggested forms for use by forest owners are presented to help illustrate the processes of marketing and operating arrangements. Modifications may be necessary to fit the requirements of individual situations and if they are of significant proportion, the assistance of a lawyer is suggested. These forms include a: (1) *Timber Sale Contract* (for selling standing trees of determined volume at stated price per unit of stumpage), (2) *Forest Landowner–Logging Operator Contract* (for hiring of logging contractor), and (3) *Forest Products Sale Agreement* (for selling cut forest products to a wood-using industry or buyer).

SAMPLE TIMBER SALE CONTRACT

CONTRACT entered into this _____ day of ____________ 19 ___, by and between ________________________________ of __________ __________ (state), hereinafter called the Seller, and __________ __________ of ______________________, hereinafter called the Purchaser.

WITNESSETH:

I. The Seller agrees to sell and the Purchaser agrees to buy for the total sum of ____________________________ dollars ($____________) under the conditions set forth in this contract all of the live standing timber marked or designated upon an area of approximately ______ acres, situated in the ______________ of Section ______________, Twp. __________________, R. ______________, ____________________________ County, (state) on land owned and recorded in the name of ____.

The purchaser further agrees to pay to the Seller as an initial payment under this contract the sum of ____________________________________ dollars ($__________), receipt of which is hereby acknowledged, and a final payment in the sum of ______________________________________ dollars ($__________), prior to any cutting or removal of timber under this contract.

II. The Seller further agrees to mark and dispose of the timber conveyed in this contract in strict accordance with the following-conditions:

(a) All trees to be included in this sale will be marked with a distinctive mark on the bole and stump of each tree.

(b) No trees under _____ inches in diameter at a point 4½ ft from the ground will be marked for cutting.

(c) No concurrent contract or subcontract involving the area or period covered in this contract has been or will be entered into by the Seller without the written consent of the Purchaser.

(d) The Purchaser and his employees shall have access to the area at all reasonable times and seasons for the purpose of carrying out the terms of this contract, and he shall maintain roads in a serviceable condition during the contract period and restore them for use at end of contract.

(e) Unless otherwise specified, all material contained in the marked or designated trees is included in this sale.

III. The Purchaser further agrees to cut and remove all of the timber conveyed in this contract in strict accordance witht the following conditions:

(a) Unless an extension of time is agreed upon in writing between the Seller and Purchaser, all timber shall be paid for, cut, and removed on or before and none after the __ day of ________________, 19____, and any material not so removed shall revert to the Seller.

(b) Timber shall be scaled by the ____________________ rule and measured at ____________________ by the ____________________.

(c) To furnish the Seller a statement of actual scaled volume removed, each ________________ such statement to be furnished on or before ____________________ in which such removal takes place and if requested, duplicate copies of scaling records.

(d) Unmarked trees and young timber shall be protected against unnecessary injury from felling and logging operations. If, however, unmarked trees are cut, damages shall be paid the Seller at the rate of $________ per tree plus $______ per mbf for ________________ and $________ per mbf for all other species, and in the event that any such trees are cut, said trees shall remain upon the premises and shall be the property of the Seller.

(e) Necessary logging roads shall be cleared by the Purchaser only after their locations have been definitely agreed upon with the Seller or his representative and any trees to be removed in the clearing operations shall first be marked by the Seller. The Purchaser and his employees have right of ingress and egress during the life of this agreement.

(f) During the life of this contract and on the area covered, care shall be exercised by the Purchaser and his employees against the starting and spread of fire, and they shall do all in their power to prevent and control fires.

(g) Any liability for damage, destruction, or restoration of private or public improvements of personal damages occasioned by or in the exercise of this contract shall be the sole responsibility of the Purchaser, and the Purchaser shall save harmless the Seller on account of such damages.

IV. The Seller and Purchaser mutually agree as follows:

(a) All modifications of the contract will be reduced to writing, dated, signed, and witnessed and attached to this contract.

(b) The total volume conveyed is ____________, composed of the following species:

____________________, ____________________,
________________, ________________, ____________.

(c) In case of dispute over the terms of this contract, final decision shall rest with a reputable person to be mutually agreed upon by the parties to this contract. If the parties hereto do not agree upon a third party within 10 days following the initiation of the dispute, or in the case of further disagreement, then within 15 days from the initiation of the dispute, it shall be submitted to a Board of Arbitration of three persons, one to be selected by each party to this contract and the third to be selected by the other two. The Board shall decide the dispute within 5 days after the matter has been referred to it.
In the event that damages are awarded to the Seller by the Board of Arbitration and are not paid on the date that the award is made, then all operations of the Purchaser shall immediately cease, and if the award is not paid or satisfied within 30 days after the date of award, the Seller may take immediate possession of the premises upon which the timber is located, shall retain as liquidated damages all money paid by the Purchaser, and the title to all timber shall revert to and become the property of the Seller.

In Witness Whereof, the parties hereto have set their hands and seals this ________ day of ____________________, 19_____.

WINTESSES: SIGNED:

____________________ ____________________, Purchaser
(For the Purchaser)

____________________ ____________________, Seller
(For the Seller)

FOREST LANDOWNER–LOGGING OPERATOR CONTRACT

This CONTRACT made and entered into this ________ day of _____, 19 _____, by and between ______________________________ of ______________________ (state), owner of timber to be cut hereinafter referred to as the Owner, and ____________________ of ______________________________, hereinafter referred to as the Operator.

WITNESSETH:

Whereas, the Owner owns standing timber located in ____________
____

and whereas, the Operator desires to contract with the Owner to __ ____________________________________ and ____________ __________ for the requirements of the Owner, now, therefore, it is agreed between the parties,

I. The Operator agrees that he will ____________________ ________________ and ____________________ all the marked or designated timber, standing and being on the ________ owned by the Owner, situated in ____________________.

II. The Owner agrees to pay for the ____________________ ____________ and ________________ of said timber the sum of ________ per ________________ as measured by the ____ rule by ______________ at the ____________________. Payment for these services shall be made to the Operator on ______ ____.

III. The Operator agrees to use proper precautions to avoid damage to fences and other property of the Owner; and agrees to indemnify the Owner against any and all damage and injury to any person or persons, including employees of the Operator caused or arising out of said operation.

IV. The Operator further agrees that the work will be done in a workmanlike manner and completed on or before ____________ ____.

V. The Operator agrees to comply with all federal and state laws or regulations controlling his operations, including state forest practice laws governing leaving of seed trees. The Operator agrees to indemnify and hold harmless the Owner from any and all claims or demands that may be made against him by reason of the Operator's operation or violation by the Operator of any laws or regulations governing said operation.

VI. It is mutually understood by the parties hereto that the Operator is not an employee of the Owner, but that he is an independent contractor; also, that if the Operator subcontracts any portion of the operation, the Operator as primary contractor shall be responsible for all acts by subcontractor.

VII. It is agreed between the Owner and Operator that the payment of ____________________ per ________________ of timber cut as hereinbefore specified shall include full payment for the use of any and all equipment used in connection with the operation.

VIII. It is agreed that the Owner may terminate the cutting at any time by providing the Operator with written notice of date of termination at least ____________________ in advance of date of termination and by paying in full as above specified for all material ________________________ and ___________________________ by the Operator.

In Witness Whereof, the parties have hereunto set their hands the day and the year first above written.

WITNESSES: SIGNED:

___________________________ ________________________, Operator

____

(For the Operator)

___________________________ ________________________, Owner

(For the Owner)

FOREST PRODUCTS SALE AGREEMENT

[For selling forest products cut by owner to industry or other buyer] This contact made and entered into this ____ day of ______________, 19____, by and between ____ of ____________________________ (state),hereinaftercalledtheseller,and

of ____________________, hereinafter called the Purchaser.

WITNESSETH:

The Seller agrees to deliver to the Purchaser at ____________________ ____________________________ the products listed below, estimated to be about ____ ____________________________ more or less on or before ________________ ____.

The Purchaser agrees to purchase said products at the prices listed below as measured by ____________________________ at ________________ ________________________ by ____________________________, products subject to specifications of the Purchaser.

Product				
____________	@	____________	per	____________
____________	@	____________	per	____________
____________	@	____________	per	____________
____________	@	____________	per	____________

It is mutually agreed that payment for said products will be made ____.

In Witness Whereof, the parties have hereunto set their hands on the day and year first above written.

WITNESSES:	SIGNED:
____________________ (For the Purchaser)	____________________, Purchaser
____________________ (For the Seller)	____________________, Seller

---

Note: There are several points forest owners should include in their contracts: (1) A time limit, the purpose of which is to assume that the logger will finish the job and not take off everytime a better woodlot beckons. Set the time according to the volume to be cut and the logger's estimate of how long the job will take plus a margin for bad weather and accidents. (2) Price. Put in writing the amount per cord and thousand board feet to be paid for each type of wood to be cut. (3) Forest practices and repair work. Spell out what the logger is expected to follow (marked trees, slash away from roads, repair of damaged roads, etc.) during the course of the job. (4) Option of dismissal of logger in case of poor and shoddy work.

APPENDIX E

PRINCIPAL FEDERAL, STATE, AND PRIVATE FORESTRY ORGANIZATIONS

FEDERAL

Bureau of Indian Affairs, U. S. Department of the Interior, Washington, D. C. 20245

Bureau of Land Management, U. S. Department of the Interior, Washington, D. C. 20240

Farmers Home Administration, U. S. Department of Agriculture, Washington, D. C. 20250

Forest Service, U. S. Department of Agriculture, P.O. Box 2417, Washington, D. C. 20013

National Park Service, U. S. Department of the Interior, Washington, D. C. 20240

Soil Conservation Service, U. S. Department of Agriculture, P.O. Box 2890, Washington, D. C. 20013

STATE AGENCIES

Alabama: Forestry Commission, 513 Madison Ave., Montgomery 36130

Alaska: State Forester, Department of Natural Resources, Pouch 7--005, Anchorage 99510

Arizona: Forestry Division, Land Department, 1624 W. Adams, Phoenix 85007

Arkansas: Forestry Commission, P.O. Box 4523, Asher Station, Little Rock 72214

California: Department of Forestry, The Resources Agency, 1416 Ninth St., Sacramento 95814

Colorado: Colorado State Forest Service, Colorado State University, Fort Collins 80523

Connecticut: State Forester, Department of Environmental Protection, State Office Bldg., Hartford 06106

Delaware: State Forester, Department of Agriculture, Drawer D, Dover 19901

Florida: Division of Forestry, Department of Agriculture and Consumer Services, State Capitol, Tallahassee 32301

Georgia: Georgia Forestry Commission, P.O. Box 819, Macon 31298

Hawaii: Division of Forestry, Department of Land and Natural Resources, 1151 Punchbowl St., Honolulu 96813

Idaho: State Forestry Department, State Capitol Bldg., Boise 83701

Illinois: Forestry Division, Department of Conservation, Lincoln Tower Plaza, Springfield 62706

Indiana: Division of Forestry, Department of Natural Resources, State Office Bldg., Indianapolis 46204

Iowa: State Forester, State Conservation Commission, State Office Bldg., Des Moines 50319

Kansas: Department of Forestry, State and Extension Forestry, 2610 Claflin Rd., Manhattan 66502

Kentucky: Division of Forestry, Department of Natural Resources, Capital Plaza Tower, Frankfort 40601

Louisiana: Office of Forestry, Department of Natural Resources, Baton Rouge 70821

Maine: Forest Service, State House, State 28, Augusta 04333

Maryland: Forest Service, Department of Natural Resources, Tawes State Office Bldg., Annapolis 21401

Massachusetts: Division of Forest and Parks, Department of Environmental Management, 100 Cambridge St., Boston 02202

Michigan: Forest Management Division, Department of Natural Resources, P.O. Box 30028, Lansing 48909

Minnesota: Division of Forestry, Department of Natural Resources, 300 Centennial Bldg., St. Paul 55155

Mississippi: Forestry Commission, 908 Robert E. Lee Bldg. Jackson 39201

Missouri: Forestry Division, Department of Conservation, P.O. Box 180, Jefferson City 65102

Montana: Forestry Division, Department of Natural Resources and Conservation, 32 South Ewing, Helena 59601

Nebraska: State Forester, State Extension Service, University of Nebraska, Lincoln 68583

Nevada: Division of Forestry, Department of Conservation and Natural Resources, Capitol Complex, Nye Bldg., Carson City 89710

New Hampshire: Division of Forests and Lands, Department of Resources and Economic Development, P.O. Box 856, Concord 03301

New Jersey: State Forester, Division of Parks and Forestry, Department of Environmental Protection, Labor and Industry Bldg., Trenton 08625

New Mexico: Forestry Division, Natural Resources Department, P.O. Box 2167, Santa Fe 87503

New York: Division Lands and Forests, Department of Environmental Conservation, 50 Wolf Rd., Albany 12233

North Carolina: Forest Resources, Department of Natural and Community Development, P.O. Box 27687, Raleigh 27611

North Dakota: State Forest Service, First and Brander, Bottineau 58318

Ohio: Division of Forestry, Department of Natural Resources, Fountain Square, Columbus 43224

Oklahoma: Forestry Division, State Board of Agriculture, 2800 N. Lincoln Blvd., Capitol, Oklahoma City 73105

Oregon: State Department of Forestry, 2600 State St., Salem 97310

Pennsylvania: Bureau of Forestry, Department of Environmental Resources, P.O. Box 2063, Harrisburg 17120

Rhode Island: Division of Forest Environment, Department of Natural Resources, 83 Park St., Providence 02903

South Carolina: Forestry Commission, P.O. Box 21707, Columbia 29221

South Dakota: Forestry Division, Department of Game, Fish and Parks, Sigurd Anderson Bldg., Pierre 57501

Tennessee: Division of Forestry, Department of Conservation, 701 Broadway, Custom House, Nashville 37203

Texas: Forest Service, College Station 77843

Utah: Division of State Lands and Forestry, 3100 State Office Bldg., Salt Lake City 84114

Vermont: Director of Forests, Agency of Environmental Conservation, Montpelier 05602

Virginia: Division of Forestry, Department of Conservation and Historic Resources, P.O. Box 3758, Charlottesville 22903

Washington: Department of Natural Resources, Public Lands Bldg., Olympia 98504

West Virginia: State Forester, Department of Natural Resources, 1800 Washington St., East, Charleston 25305

Wisconsin: Bureau of Forestry, Department of Natural Resources, P.O. Box 7921, Madison 53707

Wyoming: State Forester, State Forestry Division, 1100 W. 22nd St., Cheyenne 82002

PRIVATE ORGANIZATIONS

The following associations are principal private forestry and conservation organizations

American Forest Institute, 1619 Massachusetts Ave., NW, Washington, D. C. 20036

American Forestry Association, 1319 18th St. NW, Washington, D. C. 20006

American Pulpwood Association, 1025 Vermont Ave, NW, Suite 1020, Washington, D. C. 20005

Forest Farmers Association, P. O. Box 95385, Atlanta, 30329

National Forest Production Association, 1619 Massachusetts Ave, NW, Washington, D. C. 20036

Society of American Foresters, 5400 Grosvenor Lane, Bethesda, M.D., 20814

NATIONAL CITIZENS CONSERVATION AND ENVIRONMENTAL ORGANIZATIONS

Conservation Foundation, The, 1717 Massachusetts Ave., NW, Washington, D. C. 20036

Environmental Action, Inc., Rm. 731, 1346 Connecticut Ave., NW, Washington, D. C. 20036

Environmental Defense Fund, Inc., 1525 18th St., NW, Washington, D.C. 20036

Environmental Policy Center, 218 D St., SE, Washington, D. C. 20003

Izaak Walton League of America, Inc., The, 1701 N. Fort Meyer Dr., Suite 1100, Arlington, Va. 22209

National Audubon Society, 950 Third Ave., New York, N.Y. 10022

National Wildlife Federation, 1412 16th St., NW, Washington, D. C. 20036

Natural Resources Council of America, 1412 16th St., NW, Washington, D. C. 20036

Natural Resources Defense Council, Inc., 15 W. 44th St., New York, N. Y. 10036

Nature Conservancy, The, Suite 800, 1800 N. Kent St., Arlington, Va. 22209

Sierra Club, 530 Bush St., San Francisco, Calif. 94108

Wilderness Society, 1400 I St., NW, Washington, D.C. 20005

Wildlife Management Institute, Suite 725, 1101 14th St., NW, 709 Wire Bldg., Washington, D. C. 20005

APPENDIX F

Bibliography

The following is not meant to be an inclusive bibliography, although it includes most of the books and publications that have been reviewed in preparing the manuscript. Many of these are suggested for additional reading by the student.

GENERAL REFERENCES

Callison, C. H. (ed.). *America's Natural Resources*. New York: The Ronald Press Co., 1967.

Clepper, H. *Careers in Conservation*. New York: The Ronald Press Co., 1965.

Clepper, H., and Arthur B. Meyer. *American Forestry: Six Decades of Growth*. Washington, D. C. Society of American Foresters, 1960.

Clepper, H., and Arthur B. Meyer. *The World of the Forest*. Boston: D. C. Heath and Co., 1966.

Forbes, Reginald D., and Arthur B. Meyer (eds.). *Forestry Handbook*. New York: The Ronald Press Co., 1955.

Forest Farmers Association. *Forest Farmers Manual*. Atlanta, Ga. (published annually).

Mobley, M. D., and R. N. Hoskins. *Forestry in the South*. Atlanta, Ga.: Turner E. Smith & Co., 1956.

Moon, Franklin, and Nelson C. Brown. *Elements of Forestry*, 3rd ed. New York: John Wiley & Sons, 1937.

National Wildlife Federation. *Conservation Directory*, 30th ed., Washington, D.C., 1985.

Society of American Foresters. *Forestry Terminology*. Washington, D. C., 1958.

U.S. Department of Agriculture. *Trees* (Yearbook, 1949), Separate No. 2156. Washington, D. C.: U. S. Government Printing Office, 1949.

Weaver, H. E. and David A. Anderson. *Manual of Southern Forestry*. Danville, Ill.: Interstate Printers, 1954.

Wenger, K.F. (ed.). *Forestry Handbook*, 2nd ed. New York: John Wiley & Sons, 1984.

CHAPTER 1

Allen, S. W., and G. W. Sharp. *An Introduction to Forestry*. 3rd ed. New York: McGraw-Hill Book Co., Inc., 1976.

Clepper, H. E. *Origins of American Conservation*. New York: The Ronald Press Co., 1966.

Forest Service, USDA. *Careers in Forestry*, Miscellaneous Publication 249 revised. Washington, D. C.: U. S. Government Printing Office, 1965.

Forest Service, USDA. *In Your Service—The Work of Uncle Sam's Forest Rangers*, Agriculture Information Bulletin No. 136. Washington, D.C.: U. S. Government Printing Office, 1955.

Greely, W. B. *Forests and Men*. New York: Doubleday & Co., 1951.

McCulloch, Walter F. *The Foresters on the Job*. Corvallis, Orego: Oregon State College Cooperative Association, 1950.

Meyer, Arthur B. *Forestry as a Profession*. Washington, D. C.: Society of American Foresters, 1956.

Shirley, Hardy S. *Forestry and Its Career Opportunities*, 3rd ed. New York: McGraw-Hill Book Co., 1973.

CHAPTER 2

Dana, Samuel T. *Forest and Range Policy*. New York: McGraw Hill Book Co., 1979.

Forest Service, USDA. *An Analysis of the Timber Situation in the United States 1952–2030*, Forest Resource Report No. 23. Washington D.C.: U. S. Government Printing Office, 1982.

Forest Service, USDA. *Highlights in the History of Forest Conservation*, Agriculture Information Bulletin No. 83. Washington, D. C.: U. S. Government Printing Office, 1952.

Forest Service, USDA. *Timber Resources for America's Future*. Washington, D. C.: U. S. Government Printing Office, 1958.

Forest Service, USDA. *Timber Trends in the United States*, Forest Resource Report No. 17. Washington, D. C.: U.S. Government Printing Office, 1965.

Forest Service, USDA. *The Outlook for Timber in the United States*, F. R. Report No. 20. Washington, D. C.: U. S. Government Printing Office, 1973.

Forest Service, USDA. *A Recommended Renewable Resource Program*, 1977–2000. Washington, D. C.: U. S. Government Printing Office, 1976.

Ise, John. *United States Forest Policy*. New Haven: Yale University Press, 1920.

Public Land Law Review Commission. *One Third of The Nation's Land*. Washington, D. C.: U. S. Government Printing Office, 1970.

Worrell, Albert C. *Principles of Forest Policy*. New York: McGraw-Hill Book Co., 1970.

CHAPTER 3

Collingwood, Harris, and Warren D. Brush. *Knowing Your Trees*, rev. ed. Washington, D. C.: The American Forestry Association, 1955.

Fowells, H. A. (ed.) *Silvics of Forest Trees*. Agricultural Handbook No. 271. Washington, D. C.: U. S. Government Printing Office, 1965.

Fuller, H. J., and O. Tippo. *College Botany*. New York: Henry Holt & Co., 1950.

Harlow, W. M., and E. S. Harrar. *Textbook of Dendrology*. 4th ed. New York: McGraw-Hill Book Co., 1958.

Little, Elbert L., Jr. To know the Trees. In *Trees* (USDA. Yearbook, 1949), Separate No. 2156. Washington, D. C.: U. S. Government Printing Office, 1949.

Spurr, S. H. *Forest Ecology*. New York: The Ronald Press Co., 1964.

Wilson, B.F. *The Growing Tree*. Amherst: University of Massachusetts Press, 1985.

CHAPTER 4

Graham, E. H. Natural *Principles of Land Use*. New York: Oxford University Press, 1944.

Lutz, H. J., and R. F. Chandler, Jr. *Forest Soils*. New York: John Wiley & Sons, 1946.

McCormick, Jack. *The Life of a Forest*. New York: McGraw-Hill Book Co. 1966.

Society of American Foresters. *Forest Cover Types of North America*. Washington, D. C., 1954.

Toumey, J. W., and C. F. Korstian. *Foundations of Silviculture upon an Ecological Basis*, 2nd ed. New York: John Wiley & Sons, 1947.

U. S. Department of Agriculture. *Forest Trees and Forest Regions of the United States*, USDA Miscellaneous Publication No. 217. Washington, D. C.: U. S. Government Printing Office, 1939.

Wilde, S. A. *Forest Soils*. New York: The Ronald Press Co., 1958.

CHAPTER 5

Baker, F. S. *Principles of Silviculture*. New York: McGraw-Hill Book Co., 1950.

Barney, Daniel R. *The Last Stand* (with introduction by Ralph Nader). New York: Grossman, 1974.

Barrett, John W. *Regional Silviculture of the United States*. New York: The Ronald Press Co., 1962.

Bruckhart, John R. Taming a wild forest. In *Trees* (USDA Yearbook, 1949), Separate No. 2156. Washington, D. C.: U. S. Government Printing Office, 1949.

Burk, Dale A. *The Clearcut Crisis*. Great Falls, Mont.: Jursnick Printing, 1970.

Forest Service, USDA. *Managing the Small Forest*, Farmers Bulletin No. 1989. Washington, D. C.: U. S. Government Printing Office, 1962.

Koroleff, A., and J. P. Fitzwater. *Managing Small Woodlands*. Washington, D. C.: The American Forestry Association, 1947.

Minckler, Leon S. *Woodland Ecology: Environmental Forestry for Small N.Y.: Owners*. Syracuse, Syracuse University Press, 1974.

Smith, D. M. *The Practice of Silviculture*, 7th ed. New York: John Wiley & Sons, 1962.

Twight, Peter A., and Leon S. Minckler. *Ecological Forestry for the Central U.S. National Parks and Conservation Association* Hardwood Forest. Washington, D. C. 1972. (Also included in this series of bulletins are the *Lake States, Redwoods, Douglas-fir* and *Southern Pine Forests.*)

CHAPTER 6

Breed, C. B., and G. L. Hosmer. *Principles and Practices of Surveying,* 8th ed. New York: John Wiley & Sons, 1945.

Bruce and Schumacher. *Forest Mensuration,* 3rd ed. New York: McGraw-Hill Book Co., D. C., 1950.

Bureau of Land Management, USDI. *Surveying Our Public Lands.* Washington, D. C., 1960.

Chapman, H. H., and W. H. Meyer. *Forest Mensuration.* New York: McGraw-Hill Book Co., 1949.

Demoisy, Ralph G. *Forest Surveying.* Corvallis, Oreg.: Oregon State College Cooperative Association, 1949.

Forest Service, USDA. *Elementary Forest Sampling,* Ag. Handbook No. 232. Washington, D. C.: U. S. Government Printing Office, 1962.

Forest Service, USDA. *The Service Forester's Tool Kit,* Region 9, Milwaukee, Wisc., 1957.

Husch, Bertram. *Forest Mensuration and Statistics.* New York: The Ronald Press Co., 1963.

Küchler, A. W. *Vegetation Mapping.* New York: The Ronald Press Co., 1967.

Kulow, D. L. *Elementary Point Sampling,* Circular 116. W. Va. Agricultural Experiment Station, Morgantown, W. Va.

Soil Conservation Service, USDA. *Forestry Handbook,* 5th ed., Agriculture Handbook No. 13. Washington, D. C.: U. S. Government Printing Office, 1950.

Spurr, Stephen H. *Forest Inventory.* New York: The Ronald Press Co., 1952.

Spurr, Stephen H. *Photogrammetry and Photo-Interpretation,* 2nd ed. New York: The Ronald Press Co., 1960.

CHAPTER 7

Davis, Kenneth P. *Forest Management Regulation and Valuation.* New York: McGraw-Hill Book Co., 1966.

Duerr, William A. *Fundamentals of Forestry Economics*. New York: McGraw-Hill Book Co., 1966.

Gregory, G. Robinson. *Forest Resource Economics*. New York: John Wiley & Sons, 1972.

Matthews, Donald M. *Management of American Forests*. New York: McGraw-Hill Book Co., 1935.

Meyer, H. A., A. B. Recknagel, D. D. Stevenson, and Ronald A. Bartoo. *Forest Management*, 2nd ed. New York: The Ronald Press Co., 1961.

Vardaman, James M. *Tree Farm Business Management*. New York: The Ronald Press Co., 1965.

CHAPTER 8

Brown, Nelson C. *Logging*. New York: John Wiley & Sons, 1949.

Forbes, Reginald D., and Arthur B. Meyer (eds.). *Forestry Handbook*. New York: The Ronald Press Co., 1956.

Forest Service, USDA. *Logging Farm Wood Crops*, Farmers Bulletin No. 2090. Washington, D. C.: U. S. Government Printing Office, 1955.

Forest Service, USDA. *Measuring and Marketing Farm Timber*, Farm Bulletin No. 1210. Washington, D. C.: U. S. Government Printing Office (out of print).

Myers, J. Walter, Jr. (ed.). *Forest Farmers Manual*. Atlanta, Ga.: Forest Farmers Association Cooperative (annual issue).

Pearce, J. Kenneth, and George Stenzel. *Logging and Pulpwood Production*. New York, John Wiley & Sons, 1972.

Wackerman, A. E. *Harvesting Timber Crops*. New York: McGraw-Hill Book Co., 1949.

CHAPTER 9

Anderson, R. F. *Forest and Shade Tree Entomology*. New York: John Wiley & Sons, 1966.

Baker, W. L. *Eastern Forest Insects*, Forest Service, Misc. Publ. No. 1175. Washington, D. C.: U. S. Government Printing Office, 1972.

Boyce, J. S. *Forest Pathology*. New York: McGraw-Hill Book Co., 1961.

Brown, A. A., and K. P. Davis. *Forest Fire—Control and Use*. New York: McGraw-Hill Book Co., 1973.

Deeming, J. E., J. W. Lancaster, M. A. Fosberg, R. W. Furman, and M. J. Schroeder. *National Fire—Danger Rating System,* USDA, Forest Service, Res. Paper RM-84. Washington, D. C.: U. S. Government Printing Office, 1974.

Gaylor, H. P. *Wildfires—Prevention and Control.* Bowie, Md.: Robert J. Brady Co., 1974.

Graham, K. *Concepts of Forest Entomology.* New York: Reinhold Publishing Corp., 1963.

Graham, S. A., and F. B. Knight. *Principles of Forest Entomology,* New York: McGraw-Hill Book Co., 1967.

Hepting, G. H. *Diseases of Forest and Shade Trees of the United States,* USDA, Forest Service, Agriculture Handbook No. 386. Washington, D. C.: U. S. Government Printing Office, 1971.

National Academy Press. *A Century of Acid Rain.* Washington, D. C., 1986.

Johnson, W. T. and H. H. Lyon. *Insects that Feed on Trees and Shrubs.* Ithaca, N. Y.: Cornell University Press, 1976.

Hinrichsen, Don. Forest death syndrome. *The Americus Journal,* 1986.

National Research Council. *Pest Control: An Assessment of Present and Alternative Technologies.* Volume IV. Forest Pest Control. Washington, D. C.: National Academy of Sciences, 1975.

Smith, W. H. *Tree Pathology.* New York: Academic Press, 1970.

CHAPTER 10

American Forest Institute. *The Story of Pulp and Paper.* Washington, D. C.

American Forest Products Industries. *The Story of Lumber and Allied Products.* Washington, D. C.

Brown, Nelson C. *Forest Products.* New York: John Wiley & Sons, 1950.

Forest Service, USDA. *Making Paper from Trees.* Washington, D. C.: U. S. Government Printing Office, 1955.

National Lumber Manufacturers Association. *Lumber from Forest to You.* Washington, D. C., 1957.

Panshin, Harrar, Bethel, and Baker. *Forest Products.* New York: McGraw-Hill Book Co., 1950.

Rosen, Barry N. *Price reporting of forest products. Journal of Forestry,* August 1984.

CHAPTER 11

Clawson, Marion. *The Western Livestock Industry*. New York: McGraw-Hill Book Co., 1950.

Colman, E. A. *Vegetation and Watershed Management. New York: The Ronald Press Co., 1953.*

Forest Service, USDA. *Know Your Watersheds.* Washington, D. C.: U. S. Government Printing Office.

Gabrielson, Ira N. *Wildlife Management.* New York: The Macmillian Co., 1951.

Humphrey, R. R. *Range Ecology*. New York: The Ronald Press Co., 1962.

Kittridge, Joseph. *Forest Influences.* New York: McGraw-Hill Book Co., 1943.

Outdoor Recreation Resources Review Commission. *Outdoor Recreation for America* (Summary Report and 28 special studies). Washington, D. C.: U. S. Government Printing Office, 1962.

Stoddart, L. A., and A. D. Smith. *Range Management.* New York: McGraw-Hill Book Co., 1943.

Trippensee, R.E. *Wildlife Management.* New York: McGraw-Hill Book Co., 1948.

Young, Raymond A. (ed.) *Introduction to Forest Science.* New York: John Wiley & Sons, 1982.

CHAPTER 12

Clawson, Marion, and Held Burnell. *The Federal Lands, Their Use and Management.* Baltimore, Md.: Johns Hopkins Press, 1957.

Shanks, Bernard. *This Land Is Your Land.* San Francisco: Sierra Club Books, 1984.

APPENDIX G

MAKING MULTIPLE USE DECISIONS

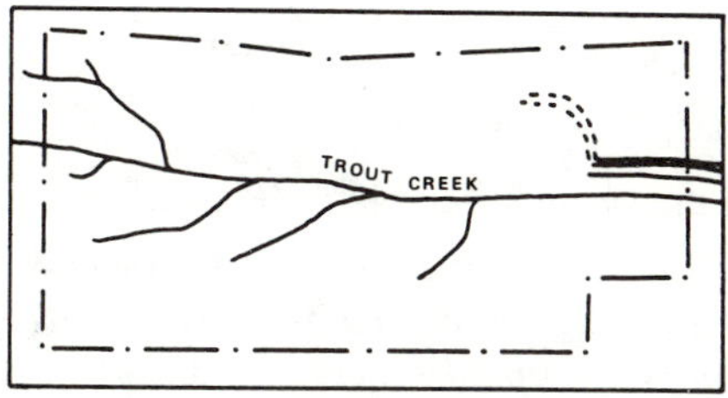

THIS IS A PORTION OF THE BEARPASTURE PLANNING UNIT, SOME 10,000 ACRES CLASSIFIED FOR MULTIPLE-USE MANAGEMENT.

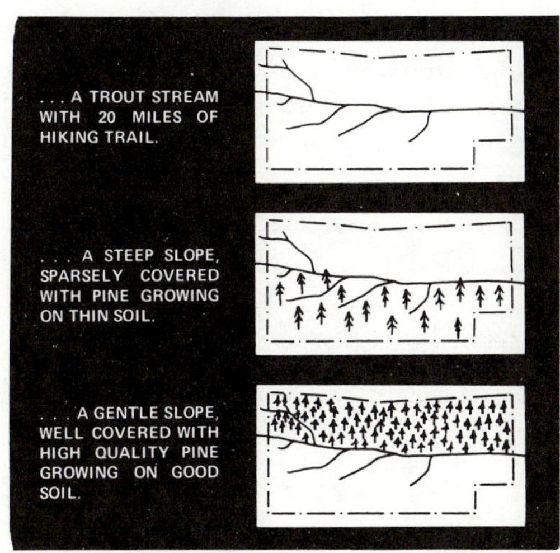

. . . A TROUT STREAM WITH 20 MILES OF HIKING TRAIL.
. . . A STEEP SLOPE, SPARSELY COVERED WITH PINE GROWING ON THIN SOIL.
. . . A GENTLE SLOPE, WELL COVERED WITH HIGH QUALITY PINE GROWING ON GOOD SOIL.

The following pages set forth the steps involved in the process of preparing a multiple use management plan for a tract of public land. To bring a level of practicality into the procedure we are using a Resource Unit—the Bearpasture Unit—of 10,000 acres as an example. Its principal features are set forth in the above sketches.

Also contained in the Unit Resource Analysis is specific information about the establishment of wildlife, quality and quantity of timber, and watershed conditions influencing erosion and downstream sedimentation.

Once the production of natural resources is known, the Manager then examines each resource individually, such as evaluating the benefits of recreation in the fishing stream, trails and buffer zone, production of timber and control of erosion.

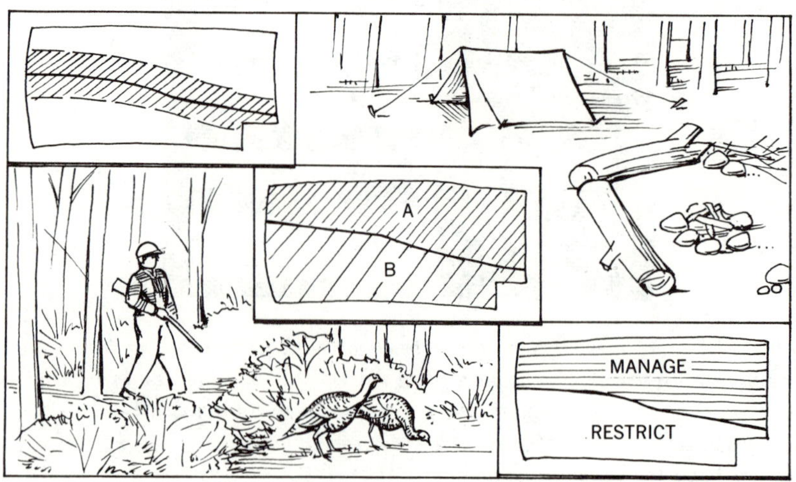

MULTIPLE USE GOALS

There may be up to five distinct multiple uses or outputs for federal public lands, including: (1) Recreation; (2) Timber; (3) Watershed; (4) Grazing; and (5) Wildlife. Fewer than five uses, however, may apply on individual resource units in certain regions. Nevertheless, effective multiple use resource management must attempt to strike a balance between competing public and private interests in the public lands, in a manner that is based on the capabilities of the resource base. To achieve an optimal mix of multiple uses established for a resource unit, clear goals must be stated. For example:

USE OR OUTPUT	*GOAL STATEMENT*
Recreation	*To provide for a variety and supply of quality outdoor recreation uses on the public lands commensurate with public needs and resource potentials*
Timber	*To the extent that benefits exceed costs, increase timber production on a sustained yield basis to help meet increasing demand.*
Watershed	*Appropriate conservation measures.*
Grazing	" " "
Wildlife	" " "

RESOURCE OUTPUT ANALYSIS

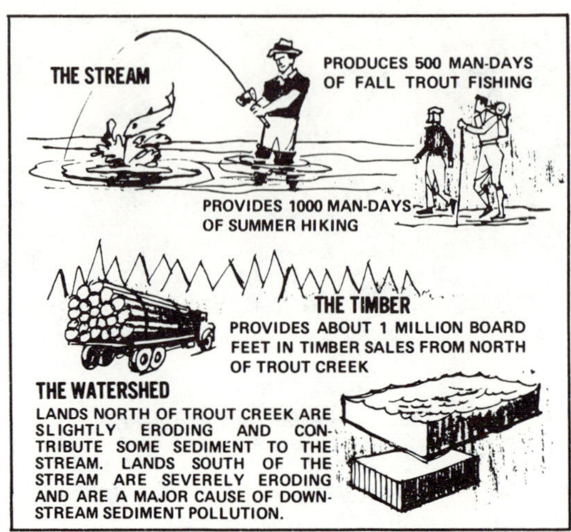

These goals are set forth in the Unit Resource Analysis through the following inventory information: the stream produces 500 man-days of fall trout fishing and 1000 man-days of summer hiking; the timber provides 1 million board feet in timber sales from north of Trout Creek. The watershed lands north of the creek are slightly eroding and contribute some sediment to the stream; lands south of the stream are severely eroding and are a major cause of downstream pollution.

ALTERNATIVE PROGRAM OPTIONS

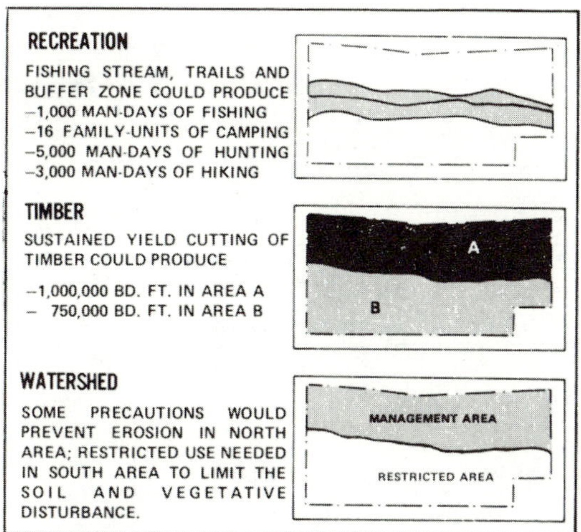

RECREATION
FISHING STREAM, TRAILS AND BUFFER ZONE COULD PRODUCE
–1,000 MAN-DAYS OF FISHING
–16 FAMILY-UNITS OF CAMPING
–5,000 MAN-DAYS OF HUNTING
–3,000 MAN-DAYS OF HIKING
TIMBER
SUSTAINED YIELD CUTTING OF TIMBER COULD PRODUCE
–1,000,000 BD. FT. IN AREA A
– 750,000 BD. FT. IN AREA B
A
B
WATERSHED
SOME PRECAUTIONS WOULD PREVENT EROSION IN NORTH AREA; RESTRICTED USE NEEDED IN SOUTH AREA TO LIMIT THE SOIL AND VEGETATIVE DISTURBANCE.
MANAGEMENT AREA
RESTRICTED AREA

Having identified what the area is now producing, the Resource Manager's next step is to look at program options, examining each resource independently as if others did not exist: fishing stream, trails and buffer zone could produce 1000 man-days of fishing, 16 family units of camping, 5000 man-days of hunting, 3000 man-days of hiking; cutting of timber could produce 1,000,000 board feet in area A, 750,000 board feet in area B. The Manager must make choices on how to manage the land based on community needs now and for the future. The economic profile reveals that the community's needs for jobs in logging and forestry, tourism and water will increase as more private land is shifted to residential use.

CONFLICTS IN DEVELOPMENT PROGRAMS

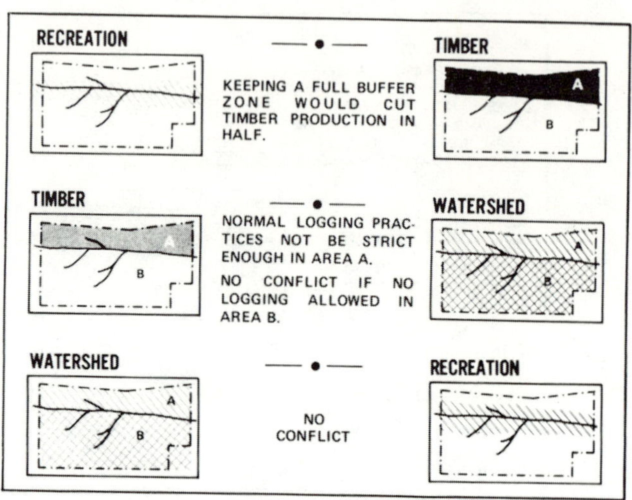
RECREATION
TIMBER
KEEPING A FULL BUFFER ZONE WOULD CUT TIMBER PRODUCTION IN HALF.
A
B
TIMBER
WATERSHED
NORMAL LOGGING PRACTICES NOT BE STRICT ENOUGH IN AREA A.
NO CONFLICT IF NO LOGGING ALLOWED IN AREA B.
A
B
A
B
WATERSHED
RECREATION
NO CONFLICT
A
B

The Manager sees conflicts with the full development of each resource. For example, keeping a full buffer zone would reduce timber production. On the other hand intensive recreation use of trails and campsites could "wear out" these resource facilities.

CHOOSING THE BEST PLAN

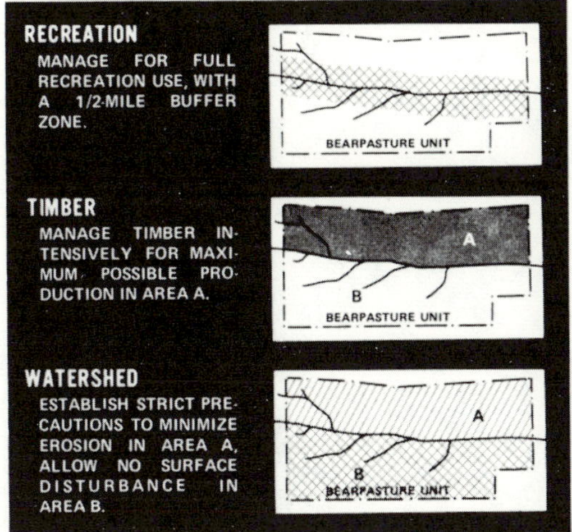

RECREATION
MANAGE FOR FULL RECREATION USE, WITH A 1/2-MILE BUFFER ZONE.
BEARPASTURE UNIT
TIMBER
MANAGE TIMBER INTENSIVELY FOR MAXIMUM POSSIBLE PRODUCTION IN AREA A.
A
B
BEARPASTURE UNIT
WATERSHED
ESTABLISH STRICT PRECAUTIONS TO MINIMIZE EROSION IN AREA A, ALLOW NO SURFACE DISTURBANCE IN AREA B.
A
B
BEARPASTURE UNIT

The Manager reviews again the best plan for each resource considered independently of the others, now including guidance statements, program standards, and supervisory suggestions. Conclusions are to manage for full recreation use with a 200 yard buffer zone, manage timber for maximum possible production, and establish strict precautions to minimize erosion in the north area and restricted use in the south area would limit soil disturbance.

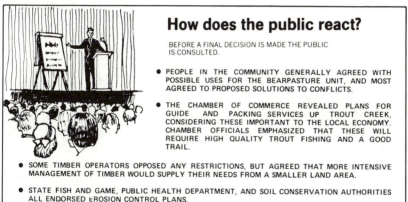

How does the public react?

BEFORE A FINAL DECISION IS MADE THE PUBLIC IS CONSULTED.

- PEOPLE IN THE COMMUNITY GENERALLY AGREED WITH POSSIBLE USES FOR THE BEARPASTURE UNIT, AND MOST AGREED TO PROPOSED SOLUTIONS TO CONFLICTS.
- THE CHAMBER OF COMMERCE REVEALED PLANS FOR GUIDE AND PACKING SERVICES UP TROUT CREEK, CONSIDERING THESE IMPORTANT TO THE LOCAL ECONOMY. CHAMBER OFFICIALS EMPHASIZED THAT THESE WILL REQUIRE HIGH QUALITY TROUT FISHING AND A GOOD TRAIL.
- SOME TIMBER OPERATORS OPPOSED ANY RESTRICTIONS, BUT AGREED THAT MORE INTENSIVE MANAGEMENT OF TIMBER WOULD SUPPLY THEIR NEEDS FROM A SMALLER LAND AREA.
- STATE FISH AND GAME, PUBLIC HEALTH DEPARTMENT, AND SOIL CONSERVATION AUTHORITIES ALL ENDORSED EROSION CONTROL PLANS.
- OTHER FEDERAL, STATE AND LOCAL OFFICIALS SAW NO CONFLICTS WITH THEIR PLANS. THE COUNTY'S DEVELOPMENT PLAN ALREADY ASSUMES TROUT CREEK WILL BE MANAGED FOR RECREATION.

As a final step in the decision-making process the Resource Manager presents the tentative plan to the local people at a hearing. The public responds to the Manager's decision to compromise all resource developments with the application of appropriate forest, soil, wildlife and fisheries and recreation conservation measures. From this point on the Manager's task will be to take the plan from theory into action.

APPENDIX H

PROPOSED METRIC EQUIVALENTS FOR FORESTRY

TABLE H-1 SELECTED METRIC UNITS AND RATIOS AND THEIR SYMBOLS AND USES FOR CANADIAN FORESTRY

Unit or ratio	Symbol	Measurement Use
centimeter	cm	Diameter of single trees Average diameter of trees in stands Diameter of logs, bolts and poles
cubic meter	m^3	Volume of single trees, stands of trees, logs, wood products and liquids
cubic meter per hectare[a]	m^3/ha[b]	Volume of stands of trees per unit area
cubic meter per hectare per year	$m^3/(ha \cdot a)$[c]	Current, mean, and periodic annual increments (cia, mai, and pai) of stands of trees per unit area
gram	g	Mass weight of trees, branches, fertilizers, etc.

TABLE H-1 *(Continued)*

Unit or ratio	Symbol	Measurement Use
hectare	ha	Area of land (instead of the acre)
kilogram	kg	Mass (weight) of trees, branches, fertilizers, etc.
kilometer	km	Distance (instead of the mile)
liter[d]	l or *l*	Volume of liquids
meter	m	Height of single trees Distance (instead of the foot or chain) Average height of stands of trees Length of logs, bolts, poles and lumber
millimeter	mm	Length of panels Width and thickness of lumber and panels
square centimeter	cm^2	Area (instead of the square inch)
square kilometer	km^2	Area (instead of the the square mile)
square meter	m^2	Area (instead of square foot) Basal area of single trees and stands of trees Quadrats (area of reproduction and other vegetation)
square meter per hectare	m^3/ha	Basal area of stands of trees per unit area of land
stacked cubic meter	m^3 (stacked)	Volume of stacked wood (instead of the cord)
stacked cubic meter per hectare	m^3 (stacked)/ha	Stacked volume of wood per unit area
tonne[e]	t	Mass (weight) of wood, etc.
tonne per hectare	t/ha	Mass (weight) of wood, etc. per unit area

[a]Although the hectare (ha) is not an SI unit, it is to be used with the International System of Units for a limited time. One hectare = 10,000 square meters (m^2).

[b]Ratios of this type may also be expressed as $m^3 \cdot ha^{-1}$.

[c]This ratio may also be expressed as $m^3 \cdot ha^{-1}/a$ or $m^3 \cdot ha^{-1} \cdot a^{-1}$ but not as $m^3/ha/a$.

[d]Although the liter is not an SI unit and is not recommended for high-precision measurements, it is used with the International System as a special name for the cubic decimeter (dm^3). Its symbol is *l* or l. The script "l" or the word "liter" written out in full is also recommended when confusion might result from the use of the lower case l (ell) for the numeral 1 in typewritten documents. One liter = 0.001 cubic meter (m^3) = 1 cubic decimeter (dm^3).

[e]Although the tonne (t) is not an SI unit, it is used with the International System of Units. It is not to be taken as the French interpretation of the short ton of 2000 lb. One tonne = 1000 kilograms.

TABLE H-2 CANADIAN YARD/POUND UNITS AND THEIR METRIC EQUIVALENTS

Yard/Pound Units		SI Equivalents
	Length	
1 chain (22 yd)	=	20.116 8 m (exactly)
1 foot	=	0.304 8 m (exactly)
1 inch	=	2.54 cm (exactly)
1 mile	=	1.609 34 km
1 yard	=	0.914 4m (exactly)
	Area	
1 acre	=	0.404 686 ha
1 mil-acre	=	4.046 86 m^2
1 square foot	=	0.092 903 0 m^2
1 square inch	=	6.451 6 cm^2 (exactly)
1 square mile	=	2.589 99 km^2
1 square yard	=	0.836 56 m^3 (stacked)
	Volume or Capacity	
1 cord (128 stacked cu. ft)	=	3.624 56 m^3 (stacked)
1 cubic foot	=	0.028 316 8 m^3
1 cubic yard	=	0.764 555 ms
1 cunit (100 cu. ft of solid wood)	=	2.831 68 m^3
1 gallon	=	4.546 09 *l* (exactly)
	Mass or Weight	
1 ounce (avoirdupois)	=	28.349 5 g
1 pound (avoirdupois)	=	0.453 592 kg
1 ton (2000 lb)	=	0.907 185 t
	Ratios	
1 cord per acre	=	8.956 47 m^3(stacked)/ha
1 cubic foot per acre	=	0.069 972 5 m^3/ha
1 mile per gallon	=	0.354 006 km/*l*
1 pound per cubic foot	=	16.018 5 kg/m^3
1 square foot per acre	=	0.229 568 m^2/ha
1 ton (2000 lb) per acre	=	2.241 70 t/ha

TABLE H-3 METRIC UNITS AND THEIR CANADIAN YARD/POUND EQUIVALENTS

SI Units		Yard/Pound Equivalents
	Length	
1 cm (centimeter)	=	0.393 701 in.
1 km (kilometer)	=	0.621 371 mile
1 m (meter)	=	0.049 709 7 chain (of 22 yd)
1 m (meter)	=	3.280 84 ft
1 m (meter)	=	1.093 61 yds
	Area	
1 cm (square centimeter)	=	0.155 000 sq. in
1 ha (hectare)	=	2.471 05 acres
1 km^2 (square kilometer)	=	0.386 102 sq. mile
1 m^2 (square meter)	=	0.247 105 mil-acre
1 m^2 (square meter)	=	10.763 9 sq. ft
1 m^2 (square meter)	=	1.195 99 sq. yds
	Volume or capacity	
1 *l* (liter)	=	0.219 969 gal
1 m^3 (cubic meter)	=	35.314 7 cu. ft
1 m^3 (cubic meter)	=	1.307 95 cu. yds
1 m^3 (cubic meter)	=	0.353 147 cunit (of 100 cu. ft of solid wood)
1 m^3 (stacked) (stacked cubic meter)	=	0.275 896 cord (of 128 stacked cu. ft)
	Mass or weight	
1 g (gram)	=	0.035 274 0 oz (avoirdupois)
1 kg (kilogram)	=	2.204 62 lb (avoirdupois)
1 t (tonne)	=	1.102 31 tons (of 2000 lb)
	Ratios	
1 kg/m^3 (kilogram per cubic meter)	=	0.062 428 0 lb/cu. ft
1 km/*l* (kilometer per liter)	=	2.824 81 miles/gal
1 m^2/ha (square meter per hectare)	=	4.356 00 sq. ft/acre
1 m^3/ha (cubic meter per hectare)	=	14.291 3 cu. ft/acre
1 m^3 (stacked)/ha, (stacked cubic meter per hectare)	=	0.111 651 cord/acre
1 t/ha tonne (per hectare)	=	0.446 090 ton (of 2000 lb)/acre

CANADIAN METRIC SOFTWOOD LUMBER SIZES

Metric sizes recommended for dimension and boards listed in Tables 1 and 2 are those recommended by the Canadian Sector Subcommittee 8.2.1, softwood lumber.

TABLE H-4 EXISTING AND PROPOSED DIMENSION LUMBER SIZES[a]

	Dry Sizes			Green Sizes[b]		
Nominal Sizes (in.)	Actual (in.)	Metric Equivalent (mm)	Proposed by Canada (mm)	Actual (in.)	Metric Equivalent (mm)	Proposed by Canada (mm)
2 × 2	1 9/16 × 1 9/16	39.7 × 39.7	40 × 40	1½ × 1½	38.1 × 38.1	38 × 38
2 × 3	2 9/16	65.1	67	2½	63.5	65
2 × 4	3 9/16	90.5	93	3½	88.9	90
5	4⅝	117.5	118	4½	114.3	115
6	5⅝	142.9	144	5½	139.7	140
7	6⅝	168.3	170	6½	165.1	165
8	7½	190.5	195	7¼	184.15	190
9	8½	215.9	221	8¼	209.55	215
10	9½	241.3	247	9¼	234.55	240
11	10½	266.7	272	10¼	260.35	265
12	11½	292.1	298	11¼	285.75	290
14	13½	342.9	350	13¼	336.35	240
16	15½	393.7	401	15¼	387.35	390
3 × 4	2 9/16 × 3 9/16	65.1 × 90.5	67 × 93	2½ × 3½	63.5 × 88.9	65 × 90
4 × 4	3 9/16 × 3 9/16	90.5 × 90.5	93 × 93	3½ × 3½	88.9 × 88.9	90 × 90

[a]Sizes apply to boards surfaced one or two sides (thickness) and surfaced one or two edges (width).

[b]green surfaced sizes were developed by increasing the dry surfaced thickness by 2.35 percent and dry surfaced widths by 2.8 percent, then rounding the sizes using a minimum increase of 2 mm between green and dry surfaced sizes.

TABLE H-5 EXISTING AND PROPOSED BOARD SIZES[a]

Nominal Sizes (in.)	*Green Sizes*			*Dry Sizes*[b]		
	Actual (in.)	Metric Equivalent (mm)	Proposed by Canada (mm)	Actual (in.)	Metric Equivalent (mm)	Proposed by Canada (mm)
1 × 2	3/4 × 1 9/16	19 × 39.7	19 × 40	11/16 × 1 1/2	17.5 × 38.1	17 × 38
1 × 2	13/16 × 1 9/16	20.6 × 39.7	21 × 40	3/4 × 1 1/2	19 × 38.1	19 × 38
3	2 9/16	65.1	67	2 1/2	63.5	65
4	3 9/16	90.5	93	3 1/2	88.9	90
5	4 5/8	117.5	118	4 1/2	114.3	115
6	5 5/8	142.9	144	5 1/2	139.7	140
7	6 5/8	168.3	170	6 1/2	139.7	165
8	7 1/2	190.5	195	7 1/4	184.2	190
9	8 1/2	215.9	221	8 1/4	209.6	215
10	9 1/2	241.3	247	9 1/4	235.0	240
11	10 1/2	266.7	272	10 1/4	260.4	265
12	11 1/2	292.1	298	11 1/4	285.8	290
14	13 1/2	342.9	350	13 1/4	336.0	340
16	15 1/2	393.7	401	15 1/4	387.4	390
1 1/4 × 2 etc.	1 1/32 × 1 9/16	26.2 × 39.7	27 × 40	1 × 1 1/2	25.4 × 38.1	25 × 38
1 1/2 × 2 etc.	1 9/32 × 1 9/16	32.5 × 39.7	33 × 40	1 1/4 × 1 1/2	31.8 × 38.1	32 × 38

[a]Sizes apply to boards surfaced one or two sides (thickness) and surfaced one or two edges (width).

[b]Green surfaced sizes were developed by increasing the dry surfaced thickness by 2.35 percent and dry surfaced widths by 2.8 percent, then rounding the sizes using a minimum increase of 2 mm between green and dry surfaced sizes.

U. S. METRIC SIZES FOR SOFTWOOD LUMBER

Butt thicknesses are shown. Tip thickness for all thicknesses and widths of Bevel and Bungalow Siding. Net 3/16 in., Metric 5 mm.

TABLE H-6 DRY SIZES AT 19 PERCENT MAXIMUM–MOISTURE CONTENT

	Thicknesses			*Face Widths*		
Item	Nominal (in.)	Net (in.)	Metric (mm)	Nominal (in.)	Net (in.)	Metric (mm)
Finish	3/8	5/16	8	2	1½	38
	½	7/16	11	3	2½	64
	5/8	9/16	14	4	3½	89
	¾	5/8	16	5	4½	114
	1	¾	19	6	5½	139
	1¼	1	25	7	6½	165
	1½	1¼	32	8	7¼	185
	1¾	1⅜	35	9	8¼	210
	2	1½	38	10	9¼	235
	2½	2	51	11	10¼	260
	3	2½	64	12	11¼	285
	3½	3	76	14	13¼	335
	4	3½	89	16	15¼	385
Flooring	3/8	5/16	8	2	1⅛	28
	½	7/16	11	3	2⅛	54
	5/8	9/16	14	4	3⅛	79
	1	¾	19	5	4⅛	104
	1¼	1	25	6	5⅛	129
	1½	1¼	32			
Ceiling	3/8	5/16	8	3	2⅛	54
	½	7/16	11	4	3⅛	79
	5/8	9/16	14	5	4⅛	104
	¾	11/16	17	6	5⅛	129
Partition	1	23/32	18	3	2⅛	54
				4	3⅛	79
				5	4⅛	104
				6	5⅛	129
Stepping	1	¾	19	8	7¼	185
	1¼	1	25	10	9¼	235
	1½	1¼	32	12	11¼	285
	2	1½	38			

TABLE H-7 DRY SIZES OF SIDING AT 19 PERCENT MAXIMUM–MOISTURE CONTENT

	Thicknesses			*Face Widths*		
Item	Nominal (in.)	Net (in.)	Metric (mm)	Nominal (in.)	Net (in.)	Metric (mm)
Bevel	½	7/16*	11	4	3½	89
	9/16	15/32	12	5	4½	114
	⅝	9/16	14	6	5½	139
	¾	11/16	17	8	7¼	185
	1	¾	1	10	9¼	235
				12	11¼	285
Bungalow siding	¾	11/16*	17	8	7¼	185
				10	9¼	235
				12	11¼	285
Rustic and drop siding ⅜ in. lap	⅝	9/16	14	4	3	76
	1	23/32	18	5	4	101
				6	5	126
Rustic and drop siding ½ in. lap	⅝	9/16	14	4	2⅞	73
	1	23/32	18	5	3⅞	98
				6	4⅞	123
				8	6⅝	169
				10	8⅝	219
				12	10⅝	269
Rustic and drop siding	⅝	9/16	14	4	3⅛	79
	1	23/32	18	5	4⅛	104
Dressed and matched siding				6	5⅛	129
				8	6⅞	175
				10	8⅞	225

TABLE H-8 SIZES OF BOARDS, DIMENSION, AND TIMBERS

	Thicknesses					Face Widths				
	Nominal	Net (in.)		Metric (mm)		Nominal	Net (in.)		Metric (mm)	
Item	(in.)	Dry	Green	Dry	Green	(in.)	Dry	Green	Dry	Green
Boards	3/4	5/8	11/16	16	17	2	1 1/2	1 9/16	38	39
	1	3/4	25/32	19	20	3	2 1/2	2 9/16	64	66
	1 1/4	1	1 1/32	25	26	4	3 1/2	3 9/16	89	91
	1 1/2	1 1/4	1 9/32	32	33	5	4 1/2	4 5/8	114	117
						6	5 1/2	5 5/8	139	143
						7	6 1/2	6 5/8	165	170
						8	7 1/4	7 1/2	185	190
						9	8 1/4	8 1/2	210	216
						10	9 1/4	9 1/2	235	242
						11	10 1/4	10 1/2	260	267
						12	11 1/4	11 1/2	285	293
						14	13 1/4	13 1/2	335	345
						16	15 1/4	15 1/2	385	395

Dimension	2	1½	1⁹⁄₁₆	38	39	2	1½	1⁹⁄₁₆	38	39
	2½	2	2¹⁄₁₆	51	52	3	2½	2⁹⁄₁₆	64	66
	3	2½	2⁹⁄₁₆	64	66	4	3½	3⁹⁄₁₆	89	91
	3½	3	3¹⁄₁₆	76	78	5	4½	4⁵⁄₈	114	117
	4	3½	3⁹⁄₁₆	89	91	6	5½	5⁵⁄₈	139	143
	4½	4	4¹⁄₁₆	102	104	8	7¼	7½	185	190
						10	9¼	9½	235	242
						12	11¼	11½	285	293
						14	13¼	13½	335	345
						16	15¼	15½	385	395
Timbers	5–16	Same as green dimension				5–16	Same as green dimension			
	18		17½		445	18		17½		445
	20		19½		495	20		19½		495
	22		21½		545	22		21½		545
	24		23½		595	24		23½		595

TABLE H-9 SIZES OF 2-IN. AND UNDER SHIPLAP, CENTERMATCH, AND D&M

	Thicknesses					*Face Widths*				
		Net (in.)		*Metric (mm)*			*Net (in.)*		*Metric (mm)*	
Item	Nominal (in.)	Dry	Green	Dry	Green	Nominal (in.)	Dry	Green	Dry	Green
Shiplap	1	3/4	25/32	19	20	4	3 1/8	3 3/16	79	81
3/8 in. lap						6	5 1/8	5 1/4	129	133
						8	6 7/8	7 1/8	175	180
						10	8 7/8	9 1/8	225	232
						12	10 7/8	11 1/8	275	283
						14	12 7/8	13 1/8	325	335
						16	14 7/8	15 1/8	325	385
Shiplap	1	3/4	25/32	19	20	4	3	3 1/16	76	78
1/2 in. lap						6	5	5 1/8	126	130
						8	6 3/4	7	172	177
						10	8 3/4	9	222	229
						12	10 3/4	11	272	280
						14	12 3/4	13	322	332
						16	14 3/4	15	372	382

Center match ½ in. tongue	1	¾	25/32	19	20	4	3⅛	3 3/16	79	81
	1¼	1	1 1/32	25	26	5	4⅛	4¼	104	107
	1½	1¼	1 9/32	32	33	6	5⅛	5¼	129	133
						8	6⅞	7⅛	175	180
						10	8⅞	9⅛	225	232
						12	10⅞	11⅛	275	283
2 in. D&M ⅜ in. tongue	2	1½	1 9/16	38	39	4	3	3 1/16	76	78
						6	5	5⅛	126	130
						8	6¾	7	172	177
						10	8¾	9	222	229
						12	10¾	11	272	280
2 in. shiplap 2 in. lap	2	1½	1 9/16	38	39	4	3	3 1/16	76	78
						6	5	5⅛	126	130
						8	6¾	7	172	177
						10	8¾	9	222	229
						12	10¾	11	272	280

TABLE H-10 SIZES OF WORKED LUMBER SUCH AS FACTORY FLOORING, HEAVY ROOFING, DECKING, AND SHEET PILING

Item	Thicknesses					Face Widths				
	Nominal (in.)	Net (in.)		Metric (mm)		Nominal (in.)	Net (in.)		Metric (mm)	
		Dry	Green	Dry	Green		Dry	Green	Dry	Green
Tongue and grooved	2½	2	2¹⁄₁₆	51	52	4	3	3¹⁄₁₆	76	78
	3	2½	2⁹⁄₁₆	64	66	6	5	5⅛	126	130
	3½	3	3¹⁄₁₆	76	78	8	6¾	7	172	177
	4	3½	3⁹⁄₁₆	89	91	10	8¾	9	222	229
	4½	4	4¹⁄₁₆	102	104	12	10¾	11	272	280
Shiplap	2½	2	2¹⁄₁₆	51	52	4	3	3¹⁄₁₆	76	78
	3	2½	2⁹⁄₁₆	64	66	6	5	5⅛	126	130
	3½	3	3¹⁄₁₆	76	78	8	6¾	7	172	177
	4	3½	3⁹⁄₁₆	89	91	10	8¾	9	222	229
	4½	4	4¹⁄₁₆	102	104	12	10¾	11	272	280
Grooved for splines	2½	2	2¹⁄₁₆	51	52	4	3½	3⁹⁄₁₆	89	91
	3	2½	2⁹⁄₁₆	64	66	6	5½	5⅝	139	143
	3½	3	3¹⁄₁₆	76	78	8	7¼	7½	185	190
	4	3½	3⁹⁄₁₆	89	91	10	9¼	9½	235	242
	4½	4	4¹⁄₁₆	102	104	12	11¼	11½	285	293

INDEX

See also Appendix A (Forest Terminology)